D0371549

Principles of Inventory and Materials Management

Second Edition

Principles of Inventory and Materials Management

Second Edition

Richard J. Tersine
The University of Oklahoma

North-Holland
New York • Amsterdam • Oxford

Elsevier Science Publishing Co., Inc.
52 Vanderbilt Avenue, New York, New York 10017

Sole distributors outside the USA and Canada:

Elsevier Science Publishers B.V.
P.O. Box 211, 1000 AE Amsterdam, The Netherlands

Second Printing, 1983.

Library of Congress Cataloging in Publication Data

Tersine, Richard J.
Principles of inventory and materials management.

Bibliography: p.
Includes index.
1. Inventory control. 2. Materials management.
I. Title.
TS160.T4 1982 658.7′87 81-9813
ISBN 0-444-00641-9 AACR2

Manufactured in the United States of America

Contents

Preface

The allocation of resources is a problem that is common to all organizations. Management must acquire, allocate, and control the factors of production that are necessary for the attainment of organizational objectives. The standard factors of production include labor, capital, equipment, and material. This text is about the factor of production that is called material.

The management of material concerns the regulation of the flow of materials to, within, and from the organization. The efficiency and efficacy of the material flow can substantially influence costs as well as revenue generation capabilities. Thus, materials management has serious implications for marketing, finance, and production. The management of material involves a balance between the shortages of stock and excesses of stock in an uncertain environment. Marketing is influenced through revenue and customer relations, production through efficiency and cost of operations, and finance through liquidity and operating capital.

In the past, the various materials management activities were performed in a routine manner by clerical personnel. These activities have since evolved into sophisticated functions with a pronounced influence on organizational performance. This increased criticality has buoyed inventory and materials management to higher organizational prominence.

The primary emphasis of this book is on inventory systems and their impact on materials management. Although inventory refers specifically to material, it can be considered more broadly as any unutilized asset awaiting sale or use. Its control procedures are also applicable to space (seats) on vehicles, water levels in hydroelectric reservoirs, cash in financial management, manpower levels, and general resource allocations. In a general sense, inventory can include any tangible asset such as equipment, machine parts, tools, personnel, vehicles, cash, or support equipment.

The book is designed for students and operating practitioners. At the college level, it can be used in undergraduate and graduate courses in business administration, materials management, operations management, marketing management, industrial engineering, operations research, financial management, and logistics. For organizational practitioners, it will be useful in operations, physical distribution, production control, accounting, purchasing, inventory control, and physical supply. Theory and practice are combined in the book to provide a complete operating philosophy and conceptual foundation.

I do not attempt to develop all the theoretical models found in the literature. Only those models that are adaptable to practical situations are selected. Simple systems are illustrated initially, and more complex models are introduced as the text progresses. Throughout the book, numerous examples of solved problems are included to extend the reader's understanding.

At the end of each chapter there are questions, problems, and short case studies. The questions at the end of chapters provide a review of topics covered. Solving the problems will improve analytical and quantitative skills. The case studies extend the topical coverage into organizational settings. Some chapters have appendices that provide additional extensions and supporting logic on particular topics.

I acknowledge with thanks the resource support of the University of Oklahoma, and the assistance of numerous people (students, subordinates, peers, and superiors) in this endeavor.

Richard J. Tersine

Principles of Inventory and Materials Management

Second Edition

Overview of the Book

This book is divided into twelve chapters. The logic of the text is illustrated in Figure 1. The *Introduction* (Chapter 1) reveals the significance of materials management to modern organizations. It indicates the dimensions of inventory management and its overall importance. *Forecasting and Market Analysis* (Chapter 2) introduces methodologies for forecasting demand levels. *Fixed Order Size Systems* (Chapters 3 and 4) develops economic order quantities and reorder points under various types of conditions. *Fixed Order Interval Systems* (Chapter 5) derives economic order intervals and maximum inventory levels for time-based systems. *Single Order Quantity Systems* (Chapter 7) outlines procedures for non-repetitive ordering systems. *Material Requirements Planning* (Chapter 8) formulates scheduling and ordering systems for dependent demand items derived from a master schedule. *Inventory Systems and Limitations* (Chapter 6) considers the problems of changes and constraints on inventory structures. *In-Process Inventory Control* (Chapter 9) investigates control procedures for in-process inventory. *Inventory Valuation* (Chapter 10) studies accounting aspects as well as physical control considerations. *Simulation* (Chapter 11) looks at Monte Carlo simulation as an inventory modeling tool. *Aggregate Inventory Control* (Chapter 12) concludes with a macroview of inventory management.

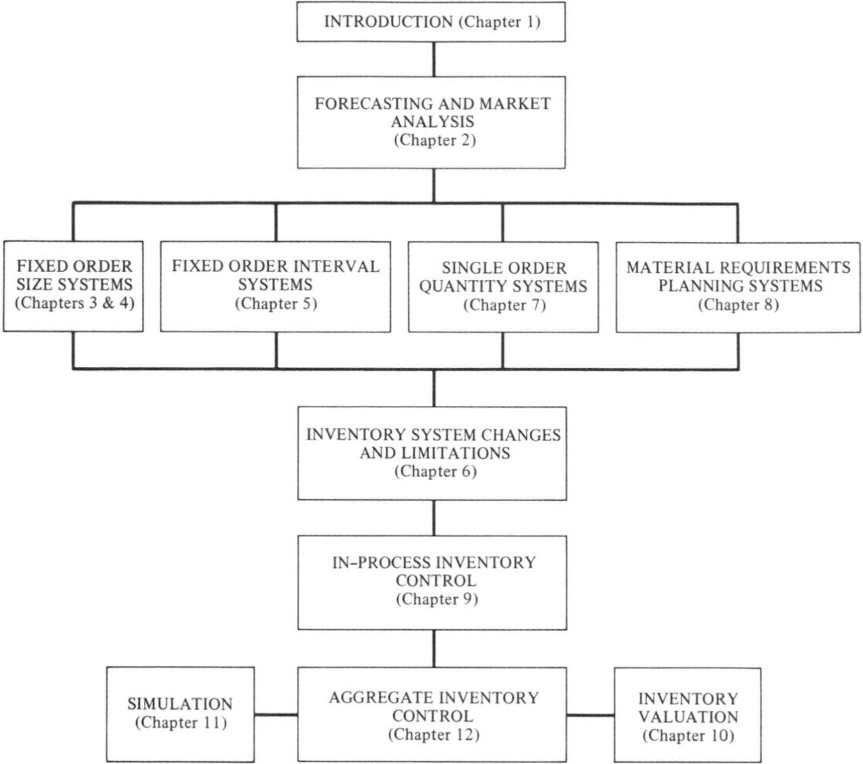

Figure 1. Logic of text.

1 Introduction

INVENTORY

TYPES OF INVENTORY

ORGANIZATIONAL CATEGORIES AND INVENTORY PROBLEMS

FUNCTIONS OF INVENTORY

INVENTORY PROBLEM CLASSIFICATIONS

PROPERTIES OF INVENTORY

INVENTORY COSTS

CONFLICTING GOALS

THE INVENTORY FLOW CYCLE

FINANCIAL CONSIDERATIONS

BUSINESS CYCLE INFLUENCE

CONCLUSION

QUESTIONS

CASES

The past decade has highlighted the significance of materials to the efficient operation of organizations. Shortages of raw materials, components, and products have been experienced on a global scale. A surge in demand from developing countries has challenged the traditional supply–production–distribution systems. With demand exceeding supply, the price of many materials has increased precipitously. Shortages have occurred in such items as foodstuffs, metals, and energy resources. Nations with abundant strategic materials have sometimes used them in the pursuit of their international political objectives. Special interest groups through monopolies and cartels have contrived shortages for their benefit. Both real and contrived shortages have made materials management an important and difficult organizational function.

Materials management is concerned with the flow of materials from suppliers to production and the subsequent flow of products through distribution centers to the customer. It is responsible for the planning, acquisition, storage, movement, and control of materials and final products. It attempts to get the right goods at the right price at the right time to maintain desired service levels at minimum cost.

Designing, financing, manufacturing, and marketing a product have historically been the major organizational functions. Traditionally management devoted more time to the expenditure of moneys for personnel, plant, and equipment than to material. Materials were thought of as cheap, available, and of infinite supply. The realities of the marketplace have changed this myopic view and have added materials management to the list of major organizational functions. For manufacturing organizations today, materials costs usually are the largest single expenditure. Also, with increased specialization, organizations tend to make less and buy more of their inputs. Thus, the number of inputs has multiplied and they are no longer just basic raw materials but also complex components or assemblies. The result is the quantity and complexity of inputs have increased substantially. With more variegated and specialized inputs, the proportion of expenditures on material has increased to a much higher level.

When organizations purchased the same raw materials over and over again, things were much simpler. Basic raw materials have many uses and provide a measure of flexibility. Few purchasing skills were required, and any excesses would eventually be depleted. As organizations became more specialized and produced fewer of the components for their finished products, difficulties began to occur. More purchasing skills were required, since purchases were no longer just basic raw materials, and excesses of inputs were not naturally depleted and might never be needed.

Organizational costs result from both positive and negative quantity errors. Furthermore, organizations usually purchase thousands of items from hundreds of suppliers. To deal with them, the purchasing agent must have technical as well as economic skills.

The average manufacturing firm spends over half of its sales revenue on purchased parts, components, raw materials, and services. A very large portion of the sales dollar of wholesalers, distributors, and retailers is also a materials cost. Wholesalers, distributors, and retailers may own little more than inventory, particularly if they lease their building and facilities. Materials costs vary among organizations, but typically range from 15 to 90% of total product cost. It is typically large enough to deserve serious attention.

INVENTORY

The control and maintenance of inventory is a problem common to all organizations in any sector of the economy. The problems of inventory do not confine themselves to profit-making institutions. The same type of problems are encountered by social and nonprofit institutions. Inventories are common to agriculture, manufacturers, wholesalers, retailers, hospitals, churches, prisons, zoos, universities, and national, state, and local governments. Indeed, inventories are also relevant to the family unit in relation to food, clothing, medicines, toiletries, and so forth. On an aggregate national basis, the total investment in inventory represents a sizable portion of the gross national product.

Inventory problems have been encountered by every society, but it was not until the twentieth century that analytical techniques were developed to study them. The initial impetus for analysis came from manufacturing industries. It was not until after World War II that a concentrated effort on risk and uncertainty aspects of inventory was made. In theory, inventory is an area of organizational operation that is well developed. In practice, it is very backward. This gap will narrow as educational institutions integrate materials management into their course structures.

Historically, inventory management has often meant too much inventory and too little management or too little inventory and too much management. There can be severe penalties for excesses in either direction. Inventory problems have proliferated as technological progress has increased the organization's ability to produce goods in greater quantities, faster, and with multiple design variations. The public has compounded the problem by its receptiveness to variations and frequent design changes.

The term inventory can be used to mean several different things:

1. Stock on hand at a given time (a tangible asset which can be seen, weighed, and counted).
2. Itemized list of goods on property.
3. (As a verb:) act of weighing and counting of items on hand.
4. (For financial and accounting records:) value of the stock of goods owned by an organization at a particular time.

In this text inventory will mean item 1 above unless otherwise specified.

The relative significance of inventory management to an organization can be gaged by the overall investment in inventory and the magnitude of the material costs for all products. The overall investment in inventory can be ascertained by reviewing the balance sheet of an organization. If the investment in inventory is a large percentage of current assets or total assets, major emphasis should be placed on inventory management. Likewise, if material costs are a large percentage of total product costs, inventory management is critical.

Inventory management can save money (reduce cost), generate additional working capital, improve return on investment, and improve customer satisfaction. The inventory of a typical industrial firm usually comprises 10,000 to 50,000 different items. The management of materials can be the most perplexing problem an organization has to face.

Inventories tie up money. For many organizations, the investment in inventories represents a sizable sum. A review of American industry balance sheets reveals that many businesses have 20–40% of their total assets tied up in inventory. Poor control of inventory can create a negative cash flow, tie up large amounts of capital, limit the expansion of an organization due to lack of capital, and reduce the return on investment by broadening the investment base. The pressure for capital and the effective utilization of resources has made decision makers more aware of its significance. Cash invested in inventories could be used somewhere else for profit making, debt servicing, or dividend distribution. Inventory management must determine how much to order and when to order each item purchased or manufactured by the organization. The inventory problem is having enough items available when needed, but not so much that an unnecessarily costly surplus is incurred.

Inventory, plant capacity, and labor are interchangeable factors of production within certain limits. Different mixes of the factors of production make it possible for demand to be independent of procurement, production, and distribution. It permits customers to purchase items freely in an economy with a relatively inflexible production capability. Although inventory represents an idle resource, its cost is justified by the economy of operation it makes possible. Inventory is held because the alternatives are more costly or less profitable. Inventory can stabilize employment levels and permit the efficient utilization of production or distribution capacity.

TYPES OF INVENTORY

Inventory is material held for future use in an idle or unproductive state awaiting its intended purpose. It may consist of supplies, raw materials, in-process goods, and finished goods. *Supplies* are inventory items consumed in the normal functioning of an organization that are not a part of the final product. Typical supplies are pencils, paper, light bulbs, typewriter

Table 1

Input Source	Inventory Type	Output Destination
Suppliers	Supplies	Administration, maintenance, and production
Suppliers	Raw materials	Production
Production stages	In-process goods (unfinished goods)	Next production stage
Suppliers or production	Finished goods	Storage or customer

ribbons, and facility maintenance items. *Raw materials* are the inputs into the production process that will be modified or transformed into finished goods. Typical raw materials for a furniture manufacturer are lumber, stain, glue, screws, varnish, nails, paint, and so forth. *In-process goods* are partially completed final products that are still in the production process. They represent both the accumulation of partially completed work and the queue of material awaiting further work. *Finished goods* are the final product, available for sale, distribution, or storage.

The assignment of inventory to any of these categories is dependent on the entity under study. This is because one entity's finished product may be another entity's raw material. For example, a refrigerator manufacturer considers copper tubing as a raw material, but the firm that produces the tubing considers it as a finished good. The customer for finished goods inventory may be the ultimate consumer, a retail organization, a wholesale distributor, or another manufacturer. Table 1 indicates the types of inventory.

Inventories are a sort of lubrication for the supply-production-distribution system that protects it from excessive friction. Inventories isolate one part of the system from the next to allow each to work independently, absorb the shock of forecast errors, and permit the effective utilization of resources when demand undulations are experienced. It is an objective of inventory management to control the lot sizes so that the overall costs associated with the purchase or the manufacture are at a minimum.

ORGANIZATIONAL CATEGORIES AND INVENTORY PROBLEMS

Different types of organizations have different inventory problems. By classifying organizations as retail, wholesale/distribution, and manufacturing/assembly, the extent of inventory problems can be generally delineated. In traversing from retail systems to wholesale/distribution systems to manufacturing/assembly systems, the problems of inventory increase in magnitude and complexity. Table 2 indicates the organizational category and the types of inventory encountered.

Table 2

Type of Organization	Type of Inventory			
	Supplies	Raw Materials	In-Process Goods	Finished Goods
A. Retail systems				
1. Sale of goods	*			*
2. Sale of services	*			
B. Wholesale/distribution systems	*			*
C. Manufacturing/assembly systems				
1. Continuous production system	*	*	*	*
2. Intermittent production system				
a. Open job shop	*	*	*	
b. Closed job shop	*	*	*	
c. Special project	*	*	*	

Retail systems are organizations that provide the ultimate consumer with goods or services. Retail systems that provide physical goods have inventory problems associated with supplies and finished goods inventory. Typical retail systems that provide goods to consumers are grocery stores, clothing stores, department stores, and hardware stores. Retail systems that provide a physical product to a consumer obtain their goods from a wholesaler or directly from the factory. Retail systems that provide a service to consumers experience only a supplies inventory problem. Typical organizations in this category are hospitals, financial institutions, universities, and penal institutions.

Wholesale/distribution systems comprise organizations that purchase goods from manufacturers in quantity for distribution to retail systems. Organizations in this category do not provide goods to the ultimate consumers. They purchase goods in bulk quantities and dispense them in smaller quantities to retailers. Wholesale/distribution systems have inventory problems associated with supplies and finished goods.

Manufacturing/assembly systems comprise organizations that purchase raw materials and change their form in such a way as to create a unique finished good. These systems have the most difficult and complex inventory problems. Manufacturing/assembly systems can be subdivided into continuous production systems and intermittent production systems. Continuous production systems are typified by mass production assembly lines which require the integration of inventory problems with the scheduling of plant operations. Continuous production is not associated with the production of many different products.

Intermittent production systems can be subdivided into open job shops, closed job shops, and special projects. An open job shop will accept orders from any source that are within its capabilities. A machine shop open to the public is an example of an open job shop.

Closed job shops produce goods for only a limited number of customers in much larger volume than open job shops. Examples of closed job shops are manufacturers that produce items for others under the customer's brand name, such as for Sears (Kenmore) and Montgomery Ward (Signature). Closed job shops may sometimes approach the complexity of continuous production systems.

Special projects are short-lived one-time events such as the Apollo, Polaris, and Gemini projects. Special projects usually have explicit statements of the project's goal or numbers of end items. Only a specified number of end items are produced, and no additional finished goods inventory is maintained. From the number of end items the precise requirement for raw materials is obtained, and the production capability is established according to contract specifications. When the specific project is completed, the project organization is either disbanded or assigned to another special project.

FUNCTIONS OF INVENTORY

Inventory exists because organizations cannot function without it. It exists because supply and demand differ in the rates at which they respectively provide and require stock.

The existence of inventory can be explained by four functional factors—time, discontinuity, uncertainty, and economy. The *time factor* involves the long process of production and distribution required before goods reach the final consumer. Time is required to develop the production schedule, cut raw material requisitions, ship raw materials from suppliers (transit time), inspect raw materials, produce the product, and ship the product to the wholesaler or consumer (transit time). Few consumers would be willing to wait for such an extended period of time on all their purchases. Inventory enables an organization to reduce the lead time in meeting demand.

The *discontinuity factor* allows the treatment of various dependent operations (retailing, distributing, warehousing, manufacturing, and purchasing) in an independent and economical manner.[1] Inventories make it unnecessary to gear production directly to consumption or to force consumption to adapt to the necessities of production. Inventories free one stage in the supply-production-distribution process from the next, permitting each to operate more economically. Raw material inventory isolates the supplier from the user, in-process inventory isolates production departments from each other, and finished goods inventory isolates the customer from the

[1]Some authors call the discontinuity factor the decoupling function of inventory.

producer. The discontinuity factor permits the firm to schedule many operations at a lower cost and a more desirable performance level than if they were integrated dependently.

The *uncertainty factor* concerns unforeseen events that modify the original plans of the organization. It includes errors in demand estimates, variable production yields, equipment breakdowns, strikes, acts of God, shipping delays, and unusual weather conditions. When inventory is available, the organization has some protection from unanticipated or unplanned occurrences.

The *economy factor* permits the organization to take advantage of cost reducing alternatives. It enables an organization to purchase or produce items in economic quantities. Bulk purchases with quantity discounts can reduce cost significantly. Per unit costs can be excessive if items are ordered separately without regard to transportation and lot size economies. Price hedging against impending material cost increases may also favor large quantity purchases. Inventories can be used to smooth production and stabilize manpower levels in undulating and seasonal businesses.

Inventories are usually means to an end. The ends are the objectives established by the organization—its reason for existence. Clearly there are various types of inventory that are intended to serve a variety of purposes. Naturally, not all of them are managed in the same way.

There is an optimum level of investment in any asset, whether it is cash, plant, equipment, or inventory. Having excessive assets can impair income just as much as having too little assets. With inventories, too much can result in unnecessary holding costs, and too little can result in lost sales or disrupted production. An organization must be careful not to overinvest in inventory that ties up capital and may become obsolete, yet it must take care not to run out of materials (thus idling people and equipment) or products (thus losing sales and customers).

INVENTORY PROBLEM CLASSIFICATIONS

Inventory problems can be classified in many ways. They can be classified according to the repetitiveness of the inventory decision, the source of supply, the knowledge about future demand, the knowledge of the lead time, and the type of inventory system. Figure 1 displays the inventory problem classifications with the following subdivisions:

1. Repetitiveness
   a. Single order
   b. Repeat order
2. Supply source
   a. Outside supply
   b. Inside supply

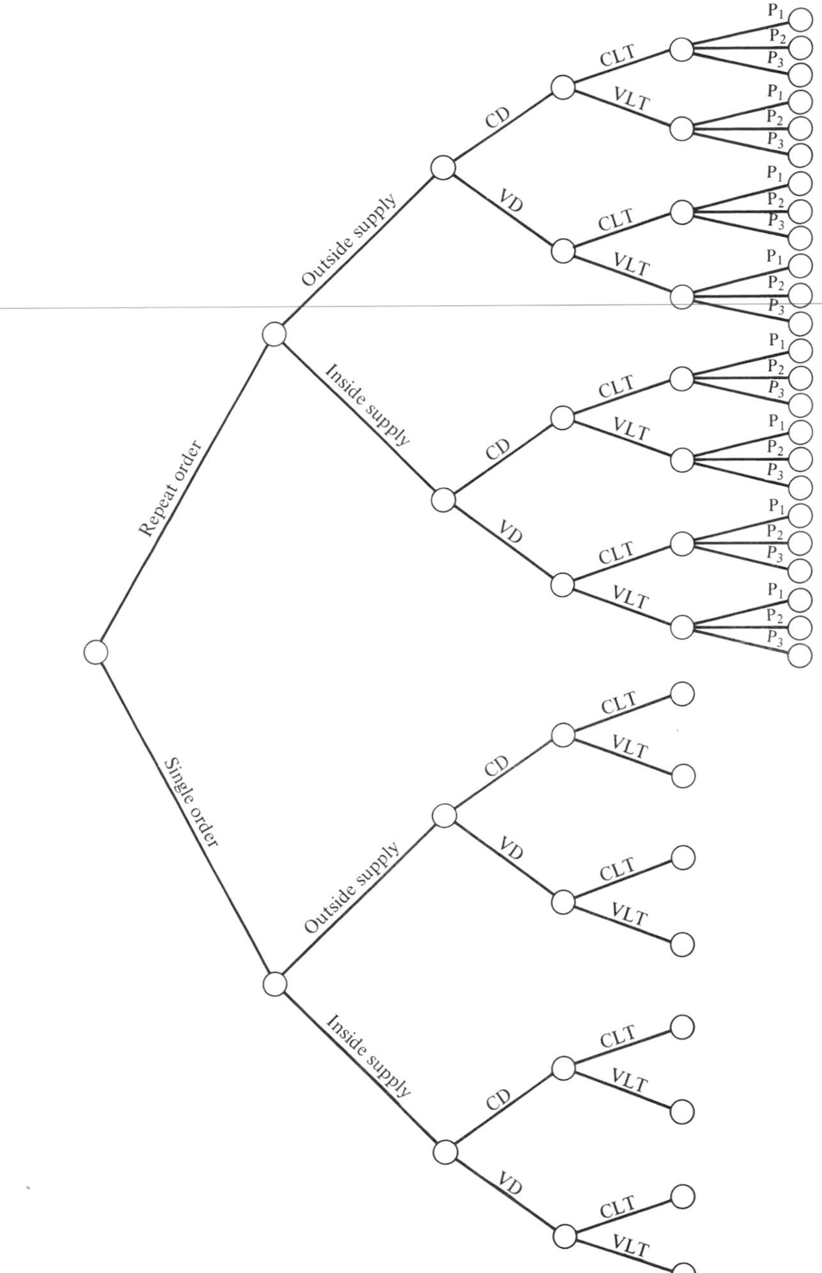

Figure 1. Inventory problem classifications.
Key: CD = constant demand; VD = variable demand; CLT = constant lead time; VLT = variable lead time; P_1 = perpetual inventory system; P_2 = periodic inventory system; P_3 = material requirements planning system.

3. Knowledge of future demand
   a. Constant demand
   b. Variable demand
4. Knowledge of lead time
   a. Constant lead time
   b. Variable lead time
5. Inventory system
   a. Perpetual
   b. Periodic
   c. Material requirements planning

Repetitiveness of the inventory decision refers to order frequency. A single order is placed once and is not repeated in a regular fashion. Examples of a single order are the materials for the construction of an apartment building, a seasonal order for Christmas trees, or some agricultural commodities. A repeat order is for the same item again and again. Stock or units that are consumed are replenished or reordered. Most of the items in supermarkets and department stores are of this variety (though high fashion items in a department store are frequently single order items).

The classification by the *supply source* is twofold, since it may come from an outside supplier or from inside supply. When an item is inside supplied, the company itself produces the item. In essence one part of the company orders from another part of the company that produces the item. The inventory problem in self-supplying companies is compounded by a production scheduling problem. When the supply source is outside (external), items are ordered from another firm. Purchase orders are sent to suppliers to purchase items from an external source. Work orders are utilized to obtain items produced within the organization.

Another inventory classification pertains to the *knowledge of future demand*. The most common assumption about the demand distribution is that the demand is constant over time. The demand can also follow some empirical distribution over time that is not of a standard type, or it can follow some specified distribution such as the normal, Poisson, or beta. Another subdivision of knowledge of future demand includes certainty, risk, and uncertainty.

When future demand is exactly known, we have an inventory problem under certainty. This condition exists on production lines where the exact number of items needed is indicated by the fixed production rate. The same situation occurs in the construction of a building where the blueprints indicate the exact number of steel girders. Some overage in inventory is common even under certainty because of waste, spoilage, pilferage, and scrap.

If the probability distribution of future demand is known, we have an inventory problem under risk. Such information may be available from records of past demand. The demand for many products at the retail level is of a probabilistic nature.

Finally, we may have uncertainty, i.e., no precise notion of the likelihood of future demand. A new product in its early introductory stages might be described as an inventory problem under uncertainty.

Inventory problems can also be subdivided according to *knowledge of lead time*. Lead time is usually considered either constant or variable. If the lead time is variable, its distribution may be determined empirically or specified.

Finally, inventory problems can be classified according to the *type of inventory system*. There are many varieties of inventory systems; the three most common are the perpetual, periodic, and material requirements planning inventory systems. The perpetual inventory system orders stock every time the inventory position reaches a reorder point. Records are maintained of all inventory transactions. The perpetual updating of the records to reveal inventory status and historical performance indicates why the system is termed perpetual. The periodic inventory system orders stock on a time cycle. The state of the system is examined only at discrete (periodic), usually equally spaced, points in time. Decisions on stock replenishment are made only at review times, and usually the decision maker knows nothing about the state of the system at times other than the review period. The material requirements planning (MRP) system orders stock only to meet preplanned production requirements. These systems will be examined in subsequent chapters.

There are other ways of subdividing the inventory problem, but the classifications given above indicate the major dimensions of the problems that can be encountered. To help solve the problems of inventory, it is necessary to build mathematical models which describe the inventory situation. Since it is never possible to represent the real world with total accuracy, approximations and simplifications must be made during the model-building process. These deviations from reality are necessary for the practical reasons that (1) it is impossible to determine what the real world is really like, (2) a very close approximation of reality would be mathematically intractable, and (3) extremely accurate models can be so expensive that their final benefit does not justify their cost. The relevance of a model to a given situation must be based on the reasonableness of its assumptions and limitations. Subsequent chapters will utilize mathematical models for the solution of inventory problems.

PROPERTIES OF INVENTORY

In viewing the properties of inventory systems, several components are common to every system. Demands, replenishments, constraints, and costs are four common components. Demands are units taken from inventory; replenishments are units put into inventory; costs are what is sacrificed in keeping or not keeping inventory; and constraints are limitations imposed on demands, replenishments, and costs by management or physical environmental conditions. Demands, replenishments, and constraints are discussed below; costs are described in the following section.

Demands can be categorized according to their size, rate, and pattern. *Demand size* refers to the magnitude of demand and has the dimension of quantity. When the size is the same from period to period, it is constant; otherwise, it is variable. When the demand size is known, the system is referred to as deterministic. Sometimes, when the demand size is not known, it is possible to ascertain its probability distribution, in which case the system is termed probabilistic. Probability distributions can be discrete or continuous. Discrete distributions can only take on certain values, whereas continuous distributions can take on any value (when purchasing units such as automobiles, it is impossible to obtain fractions of a unit, whereas the purchase of items by volume such as gasoline is not limited to integer values). Standard probability distributions such as the normal, Poisson, and binomial are frequently assumed for demand. The *demand rate* is simply the demand size per unit of time. *Demand patterns* refer to how units are withdrawn from inventory. Units may be withdrawn at the beginning of the period, at the end of the period, uniformly throughout the period, or in some other pattern (seasonality).

Demands can be further categorized as independent or dependent. When the demand rate for an item is determined by some entity outside the organization, it is not known for certain and must be forecasted. When no relationship exists between the demand for an item and any other item, it is called *independent demand*. Finished products, supplies, and maintenance items are usually described by independent demand.

Dependent demand is related to the demand for another item or items. It is the requirement for any components necessary to make some other item. Therefore, instead of requiring forecasts, dependent demand for an item can be derived or calculated from the demand for the parent item of which it becomes a part. Most dependent demand items are used to produce independent demand items. Once an organization determines how many independent demand products it will make, it can calculate fairly accurately the number of dependent items it needs (though allowances must usually be made for scrap and other losses).

Independent demand items are frequently kept on hand almost constantly because demand could occur at any time. Dependent demand items need not be kept on hand constantly, since they are only needed when independent demand items are produced. Many organizations do not produce products continuously even though the demand for the product is continuous. In such intermittent production systems, the demand for dependent items is lumpy and these items need not be available all the time. This lumpy demand for components is much different from the pattern of demand for the product. Thus, the demand for the product may be continuous but the demand for the items composing the product will be discrete unless production is continuous. Independent demand items are usually controlled by a perpetual or periodic inventory system whereas the dependent demand items are more suitably controlled by a material requirements planning system.

Replenishments can be categorized according to size, pattern, and lead time. *Replenishment size* refers to the quantity or size of the order to be received into inventory. The size may be constant or variable, depending on the type of inventory system. When a replenishment order is received, it usually goes into storage and becomes part of the organization's inventory. It is carried on the balance sheet as an asset until is is sold to a customer or consumed by the organization. The *replenishment pattern* refers to how the units are added to inventory. Replenishment patterns are usually instantaneous, uniform, or batch. Instantaneous receipt indicates that the entire lot is received into stock at the same time.

Replenishment lead time is the length of time between the decision to replenish an item and its actual addition to stock. Lead time can be constant or variable. Probability distributions are used in lead time just as they are in describing variable demand. The major components of lead time are as follows:

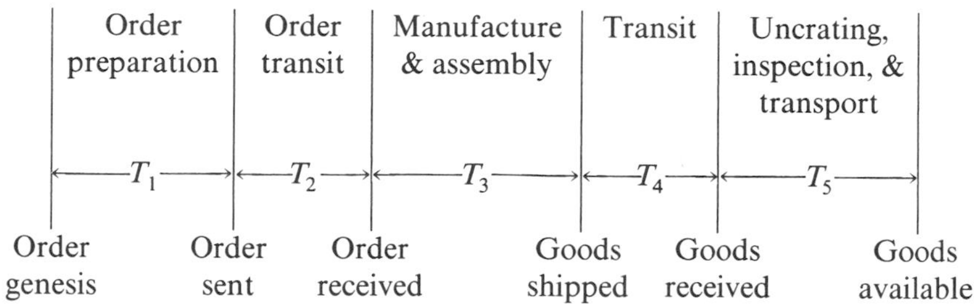

Mathematically, it can be stated as

$$L = T_1 + T_2 + T_3 + T_4 + T_5 = \text{lead time},$$

where

$$T_1 = \text{in-house order preparation time},$$

$$T_2 = \text{order transmittal time to supplier},$$

$$T_3 = \text{manufacture and assembly time},$$

$$T_4 = \text{goods transit time from supplier},$$

$$T_5 = \text{in-house goods preparation time}.$$

Observe that the variables T_2, T_3, and T_4 are largely uncontrollable, whereas T_1 and T_5 correspond to internal activities controllable by the ordering organization.

Constraints are limitations placed on the inventory system. Space constraints may limit the amount of inventory held. Management may impose capital constraints on the amount of money invested in inventories. Management may have policies of never being out of stock on certain items. Administrative decisions can limit and confine the policies of an inventory system in many ways.

INVENTORY COSTS

The objective of inventory management is to have the appropriate amounts of raw materials, supplies, and finished goods in the right place, at the right time, and at low cost. Inventory costs result from action or lack of action of management on establishing the inventory system. The inventory system cost factors include the following:[2]

1. Purchase cost
2. Order/setup cost
3. Holding cost
4. Stockout cost

Inventory costs are costs associated with the operation of an inventory system. They are basic economic parameter inputs to any inventory decision model. The principle costs are purchase, order/setup, holding, and stockout costs. For a particular item, only those cost elements that are incremental (out of pocket) are relevant in an inventory analysis.

The *purchase cost* (P) of an item is the unit purchase price if it is obtained from an external source, or the unit production cost if it is produced internally. The unit cost should always be taken as the cost of the item as it is placed in inventory. For purchased items, it is the purchase price plus any freight cost. For manufactured items, the unit cost includes direct labor, direct material, and factory overhead. The purchase cost is modified for different quantity levels when a supplier offers quantity discounts.

The *order/setup cost* (C) originates from the expense of issuing a purchase order to an outside supplier or from internal production setup costs. This cost is usually assumed to vary directly with the number of orders or setups placed and not at all with the size of the order. The order cost includes such items as making requisitions, analyzing vendors, writing purchase orders, receiving materials, inspecting materials, following up orders, and doing the paperwork necessary to complete the transaction. The setup cost comprises the costs of changing over the production process to produce the ordered item. It usually includes preparing the shop order, scheduling the work, preproduction setup, expediting, and quality acceptance.

[2]Particularly those related to supplies, raw materials, and finished goods. See Arnold Reisman, *Industrial Inventory Control*, New York: Gordon and Breach Science Publishers, 1972, Chapter 5 for procedures for developing relevant cost parameters.

The inventory *holding cost* (H), frequently referred to as the carrying cost, originates from many sources. It includes such items as capital cost, taxes, insurance, handling, storage, shrinkage, obsolescence, and deterioration. Capital cost reflects lost earning power or opportunity cost. If the funds were invested elsewhere, a return on investment would be expected. Capital cost is a charge that accounts for this unreceived return. Many states treat inventories as taxable property; so the more you have, the higher the taxes. Insurance coverage requirements are dependent on the amount to be replaced if the warehouse is destroyed. Insurance premiums vary with the size of the inventory investment. Obsolescence is the risk that an item will lose value because of shifts in styles or consumer preference. Shrinkage is the decrease in inventory quantities over time from loss or theft. Deterioration means a change in properties due to age or environmental degradation. Many items are age-controlled and must be sold or used before an expiration date (food items, photographics, and pharmaceuticals). The usual range of annual holding cost is 20–40% of the inventory investment.

The *stockout cost* (depletion cost) results from external and internal shortages. An external shortage occurs when a customer of the organization does not have his order filled; an internal shortage occurs when a group or department within the organization does not have its order filled. External shortages result in backorder costs, present profit loss (potential sale), and future profit loss (goodwill erosion). Internal shortages can result in lost production (idle men and machines) and a delay in a completion date. The stockout cost depends on the reaction of the customer to the out-of-stock condition. If demand occurs for an item out of stock, the economic loss depends on whether the shortage is backordered, satisfied by substitution of another item, or canceled. In the one situation, the sale is not lost but only delayed a few days in shipment. Typically a company would institute an emergency expediting order to get the item as a backorder. The backorder case results in expediting costs, handling costs, and frequently special shipping and packaging costs. In another situation, the sale is lost. In that case the stockout cost ranges from the profit loss on the sale to some unspecifiable loss of goodwill. A goodwill loss could amount to the customer not returning to purchase other items in the future. The stockout cost can be extremely high if the missing item forces a production line to shut down. It can be seen that the stockout cost can vary considerably from item to item, depending on customer or internal practice.

CONFLICTING GOALS

The goals associated with materials management are not monolithic or even easily delineated. The major goals of materials management are to minimize inventory investment, to maximize customer service, and to assure efficient (low cost) plant operation. Some of the common subgoals are low unit cost, high inventory turnover, consistency of quality, favorable supplier relations, and continuity of supply. It is plain to see that these goals can be inconsistent or even in direct conflict. Goals must be balanced in relation to existing conditions and environmental limitations.

During a war or a period of extreme scarcity, the simple act of locating sources of supply may become the most important objective. This may also be true if a major supplier is closed because of labor difficulties. With unpredicted upsurges in demand, considerable pressure for supply sources can be experienced.

In a young company that is growing rapidly, cash is perpetually in short supply. Most earnings and borrowings are reinvested in plant and equipment. Since material stocks are essential, there is pressure to keep stock levels low to make cash available for other purposes. To buy in small quantities means passing up quantity discounts. Numerous orders and deliveries are necessary to operate on a "hand-to-mouth" basis. These conditions result in high inventory turnover, which can be undesirable if it produces deleterious operational side effects.

Balance is a paramount consideration when goals and objectives are under consideration. Concentration may be on one objective at certain times and on another objective at other times. The tradeoffs must be considered. Concentration on inventory turnover can result in higher unit cost because of smaller, more frequent purchases. Concentration on low unit cost results in large quantity purchases which reduce inventory turnover. A purchasing agent may give undue emphasis to low unit cost while ignoring continuity of supply, quality, and inventory investment. A production manager may overemphasize continuity of supply to the detriment of low unit cost or inventory investment. The objective in too many organizations is to manage materials as cheaply as possible instead of at minimum cost.

Inventories are a source of conflict among different managers in an organization. The conflict arises because different managers have different roles to play which involve the use of inventory. Suboptimization is the term used to describe subsystem optimization at the expense of system goals. Suboptimization results from the conflicting roles that managers play. Tables 3 and 4 depict departmental concerns about inventory.

Table 3. Departmental Orientations Towards Inventory

Functional Area	Functional Responsibility	Inventory Goal	Inventory Inclination
Marketing	Sell the product	Good customer service	High
Production	Make the product	Efficient lot sizes	High
Purchasing	Buy required materials	Low cost per unit	High
Finance	Provide working capital	Efficient use of capital	Low
Engineering	Design the product	Avoiding obsolescence	Low

Table 4. Conflicting Organizational Objectives

Area	Typical Response
Marketing/sales	I can't sell from an empty wagon. I can't keep our customers if we continue to stockout and there is not sufficient product variety.
Production	If I can produce larger lot sizes, I can reduce per unit cost and function efficiently.
Purchasing	I can reduce our per unit cost if I buy large quantities in bulk.
Finance	Where am I going to get the funds to pay for the inventory? The levels should be lower.
Warehousing	I am out of space. I can't fit anything else in the building.

The production manager is concerned about setup costs, scrap, rework, disruptions, and scheduling problems associated with changeovers; he prefers long production runs and lead times, ample raw material inventories, little product variety, and a large work backlog. The purchasing manager is concerned with volume discounts, price fluctuations, vendor performance, and ordering costs; he prefers ordering in large quantities at infrequent intervals, which results in large inventories. The warehouse manager is concerned with stockroom and warehouse space, inventory investment, spoilage, turnover, and obsolescence; he prefers adequate stock levels that are maintained by frequent reorders of small to moderate size. The marketing manager is concerned with prompt customer service, maximum product variety, and frequent production runs so he can offer the customer fresh stock and the latest engineering refinements; he prefers no stockouts, no production backlogs, minimum lead times, and an ample stock of finished goods. The financial officer is concerned with liquidity, cash management, return on investment, minimal stock levels, avoidance of obsolescence, and maximum inventory turnover; he prefers an acceptable level of stockouts and a small investment in inventory.

In reference to supplies and raw materials, it is possible for the financial officer and the purchasing manager to disagree. The purchasing manager usually wishes to purchase items in large quantities so that quantity discounts and transportation economics will result in a low unit cost. The treasurer might favor small purchases which would utilize less resources and release funds for other uses.

In reference to in-process goods, it is possible for the production manager and the controller to disagree. The production manger might desire large inventories which decouple operations and reduce setup costs in high-volume production. The controller might favor small inventories which decrease storage, cost of handling, transfer, and loss.

In reference to finished goods, the sales manager and the warehouse manager might be in conflict. The sales manager wants large inventories which can permit quick delivery and increased sales. The warehouse manager might favor small inventories which require less space and lower holding costs.

The abovementioned situations can result in conflict or at least differences in opinion among managers. Many materials problems result from the different roles that managers play. Many promising materials control systems have been wrecked or subverted by interdepartmental rivalries and cross purposes. Materials policies must be established that result in low cost while balancing the conflicting roles of managers for the benefit of the whole organization.

Inventory management is everybody's concern, but it is not uncommon to find everybody's concern nobody's responsibility. Responsibility for inventory is often divided among departments with particular interests. Purchasing may take charge of raw materials and purchased items, while manufacturing looks after in-process goods, and marketing controls finished goods. The allocations of responsibility appear logical, but it is unlikely that the talent and expertise required for proper control is available in all the departments. It is commonly more desirable to put all inventory responsibility in a single location under a materials manager. Departmental conflicts and suboptimization are less likely to occur when inventories are under a materials manager.

The inventory problem cannot be handled in isolation. It is inextricably woven into the distribution problem, the warehouse problem, the production problem, the materials handling problem, the purchasing problem, the marketing problem, and the finance problem. Inventories are not an island unto themselves. The management of inventory requires a broad viewpoint and should not be treated as a series of independent decisions on individual stock items. Inventory should serve the purposes of the organization as outlined in policy statements. The inventory system is part of a larger operating system, and it should facilitate the goals of the organization.

Inventory must be managed, not delegated to clerical consideration. To overcome its stormy past, inventory management has been broadened into materials management. Materials management is composed of all material-related functions, such as purchasing, transportation, logistics, production control, inventory, and sometimes even quality. The materials manager is made independent and on the same level as the finance, marketing, and production managers. It is the materials manager's job to strive for organizational goals and not to become the stepdaughter of any other functional area.

THE INVENTORY FLOW CYCLE

Inventory management involves controlling the rates of flow of material into and out of a system. In reality, it is a scheduling or timing problem. In the initial phase, materials and supplies are procured from suppliers. This reservoir of items forms the first pool of inventory investment that must be managed. The variety and quantity of items purchased should be timed so they will meet the demand for their utilization by the organization. As these items are released to manufacturing, they join another reservoir of inventory called in-process goods. This second reservoir must also be managed in relation to the capacity of the facility. As items leave the in-process goods category, they enter another inventory reservoir called finished goods. This

Figure 2. Manufacturing inventory flow cycle.

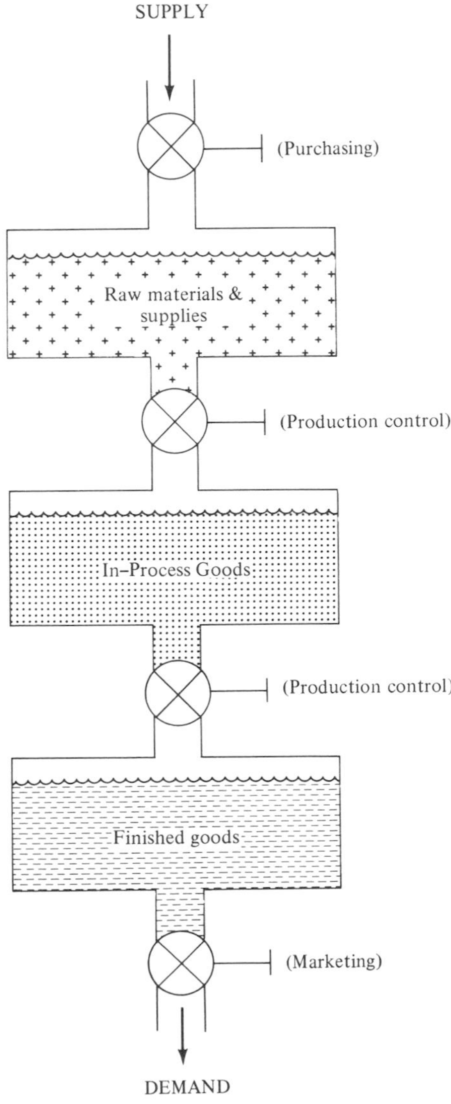

third reservoir must also be regulated with relation to external demand. The cycle can continue into an additional reservoir if the organization maintains warehouses or distribution centers. A typical manufacturing inventory flow cycle is illustrated in Figure 2. It indicates the areas that regulate the flow into and out of the different inventory categories.

All of the inventory categories or reservoirs require a synchronization of the rate of flow into and from it. No particular category can be controlled without respect to the others. When the flow is regulated, an organization can function efficiently. When problems develop in any particular category, it will affect the others and influence organizational effectiveness. It is important that the multistage influence be understood in any inventory flow cycle.

Different organizations may have fewer or more categories to control, but the flow cycle is remarkably similar. For example, retailers and distributors will not have an in-process goods category, since they resell items in the same configuration as they purchased them. However, there are still multistage influences that must be controlled.

The driving force behind the inventory flow cycle is the demand for finished goods. From it, there is a derived demand for all those items that compose it. Whether the demand is forecasted or derived from customers' orders, it starts the operational processes necessary to satisfy it in some fashion. The inventory flow cycle is a vital part of the operational processes that satisfy customer demand.

FINANCIAL CONSIDERATIONS

Organizations are becoming increasingly aware that the overall efficiency and effectiveness of operations are directly related to materials management. The aim of inventory control is to maintain inventories at such a level that the goals and objectives of the organization are achieved. Inventory policies affect cost directly and revenue only indirectly. Inventory does not generate revenue (sales do that), although it makes revenue generation possible. Inventory's contribution to profit comes through cost control. The criterion most frequently applied to inventory control is cost minimization.

The scoreboard for profit making organizations is the income statement and the balance sheet. The income statement shows the performance of the organization in profit or loss terms for a given interval or period of time. The balance sheet reveals the condition of the organization at a given point in time. Inventory influences the income statement and the balance sheet. Inventory is a current asset on the balance sheet. The valuation of inventory for the balance sheet indicates the monetary value of inventory. Inventory is usually valued at cost for the balance sheet. The importance of inventory for the income statement is that the cost of resources consumed by the production process must be allocated before income can be determined.

Inventory is frequently evaluated by *turnover*, which indicates the velocity with which materials move through the organization. Turnover is the ratio of the annual cost of goods sold to the average or current inventory level. This ratio indicates the number of times the inventory has turned over during the year. Generally it is assumed that a large inventory turnover is desirable. The usual approaches to increasing turnover are:

1. Dispose of surplus material.
2. Reduce slow-moving stock.
3. Concentrate control on high annual usage (high cost) items.

Except for broad comparison purposes, inventory turnover is not an effective measure of inventory management efficiency or effectiveness. In some situations, reduced turnover can substantially increase overall operating efficiency. Inventory turnover considers only the financial aspects of inventory and neglects its operating aspects. Overemphasis on inventory turnover can lead to such problems as inadequate raw materials for production operations, lost sales, and higher production costs. The use of inventory turnover as a single inventory control criterion must therefore be viewed with skepticism (another commonly used financial indicator for overall comparison purposes is the ratio of inventory level to total current assets).

For broad comparison purposes, turnover is an adequate measure of performance. Of course, high and low turnover are relative terms, established historically or in relation to a given industry. Some of the disadvantages of high inventory turnover are:

1. Lost sales (stockouts)
2. Lost customers
3. Lost quantity discounts
4. Higher transportation cost per unit
5. Higher purchase cost per unit

The advantages of a high inventory turnover are:

1. Smaller inventory investment
2. Fresher (newer) stock
3. Higher level of liquidity
4. Less deterioration
5. Less risk of obsolescence

Organizations usually have more than one reason for wanting to control their inventories. This is because of the close interrelationships among the activities of smoothing production, maintaining cost control, managing working capital, and obtaining adequate inventory turnover. The application of inventory control often fails because members of an organization do not grasp the economic and mathematical principles on which inventory control rests or they cannot solve the practical problems of data gathering and formula computation. Inventory management must make decisions regarding tangible and intangible values associated with capital investments, operating costs, and customer service.

An inventory manager is interested in the economy, efficiency, and effectiveness of the inventory system. Economy refers to the low-cost operation of the inventory system; efficiency refers to how well the inventory system performs in relation to some standard (such as turnover); and effectiveness refers to how well the inventory system serves the goals of the organization. Thus, overall performance might be measured in terms of cost of operation, historical performance standards, and ability to meet customer demands.

BUSINESS CYCLE INFLUENCE

Business cycles are a characteristic of the national economy. They usually involve successive periods of expansion, contraction, recession, and recovery, with the cycle repeating itself. While not all industries follow the economy's overall movement, few are immune from its influence. Acceptable levels of inventory can vary substantially depending upon the phase of the business cycle.

Inventory accumulation and depletion have long been recognized as contributing factors to fluctuations in the national economy. On an aggregate basis the flow patterns of inventory contribute to the cyclical behavior of business activity. Because of a chain of time delays from the consumer to the factory, information on consumer demand changes is not transmitted directly to the factory.

Inventory accumulation can accelerate business activities dramatically. When business tapers off, inventories continue to rise for some time and stock levels become excessive. Organizations not only stop buying in excess of demand, but they buy substantially less than current consumption. The underbuying causes production to drop precipitously, which helps to accelerate an economic downturn. Finally, an equilibrium point is reached and recovery commences. The recovery catches organizations unprepared, so sales exceed production and inventory levels drop. When production levels eventually exceed sales and inventories start increasing, the cycle begins all over again. The cycle may involve a time horizon of several years, and it is most relevant to durable goods industries that have long production lead times. Economists refer to the above phenomenon as the accelerator effect.

Organizations that are more "distant from the marketplace" tend to be more vulnerable to swings in the business cycle. Such organizations can find changes at the retail level modified by the time their effect on demand is felt.

Time lags in a multistage system can have the effect of amplifying the variations in demand. A relatively small change in demand at the consumer level can generate several times the amount of the demand change at the producer level in multistage systems. Direct feedback from the consumer level to the producer level can reduce the demand delays and stabilize the system against oscillation.

A long distribution chain or network is likely to set up internal oscillations in demand. A small variation in retail sales can cause giant fluctuations in the stock levels of the manufacturer and disrupt the flow of production. This whipsaw effect creates real and artificial cyclical processes in inventories and production levels which can combine, cancel, or dampen themselves. Many manufacturers try to obtain information on demand at the retail level, so some guidance in relation to real or artificial undulations is obtained. Ignorance of the consumer's real behavior can result in very erratic demands being made on the manufacturer. The ideal system is one where the manufacturer knows what is actually happening in the marketplace. Management can dampen oscillations by (1) using a forecasting model that disregards short-term demand changes, (2) adopting a single stage (centralized) system so that two or more stages can be under the control of a single group, and (3) instituting direct communication at the ultimate consumer level to obtain data on the sale.

Basic responsibility for inventory control lies with top management. They should carefully formulate and periodically review the basic policies, plans, and forecasts that constitute the framework for daily inventory control operations. Everyday operational control should be largely a clerical or computerized operation within a carefully defined and controlled structural framework. Routinization must be based on sound top management decisions, which are beyond the scope of clerical personnel.

CONCLUSION

The significance, relevance, and organizational stature of materials management will increase in the future. Numerous forces are dictating changes in this direction. One force is the trend towards increasing the number of highly specialized and complex products. As a result of this development, more organizations in the future will make fewer and buy more of their material requirements. Consequently, materials will represent an increasing percentage of total product costs, and their control will be even more important than it is today. A second major force is the increasing trend toward automation. An uninterrupted flow of materials is required for an automated facility. Failure of supply on a single item can close the facility down. A third major force is the burgeoning cost of materials. An expanding world population with an almost insatiable demand for goods and services is creating shortages in supply which are causing costs to skyrocket. The days of cheap and abundant raw materials appear to be past. These forces and many others indicate that the management of materials is no longer a trivial matter to be delegated to lower managerial levels.

Inventories can be economically puzzling to the casual observer, since they are subject to varied influences. Stock levels may soar if managers expect rising sales or if sales do not measure up to earlier expectations. Inventories may flatten or decline when organizations cannot get all the items they desire, or if decision makers are bearish on future activities. Organizations may hoard inventories when they expect sharply rising prices or materials shortages. In-process inventories can expand rapidly when shortages of key basic materials result in production bottlenecks. It is possible for the same level of inventory to be a blessing and a curse at different points in time. The composition of inventories is frequently just as important as the overall inventory level.

Inventory is a major asset that is usually the most maneuverable asset other than cash itself. Inventories create conflicts because functional segments of the organization tend to view them in the light of their own objectives. When an organization decentralizes into functional areas (finance, production, and marketing), there tends to evolve a peculiar lack of appreciation of overall organizational objectives (suboptimization).

Pressures of the marketplace force organizations into broader product coverage and greater delivery capabilities. As product variety increases, so do the problems of materials management. Greater product variety increases the complexities of forecasting future demand, which escalates the inventory investment needed to maintain customer service levels. Expanded delivery capabilities are established by means of branch warehouses, which also escalate inventory complexity and investment.

All organizations have difficulty managing their inventory. The usual reason is the inability to forecast adequately. When materials are added to inventory, it is in anticipation of demand. If the demand is later than expected or never materializes, the result is excessive stock. If the demand is sooner or stronger than anticipated, the result is inadequate stock. Factors that tend to reduce inventory are better forecasts, improved transportation, improved communications, improved technology, better scheduling, and standardization.

QUESTIONS

1. What is materials management?
2. What is inventory?
3. Name the different types of inventory.
4. What functions does inventory serve?

5. Give three reasons why the existence of inventory can be explained by the *time* factor.

6. What are the four common components of inventory systems? Give a brief description of each.

7. What are the four inventory system costs?

8. What is lead time?

9. Name at least six sources of inventory holding costs.

10. In what type of situation can a stockout cost be extremely high?

11. What is the objective of inventory management?

12. What constitutes the purchase (unit production) cost for an internally manufactured item?

13. In what ways are inventories important for both major types of financial statements (balance sheet and income statement)?

14. What is inventory turnover? What typical problems can develop when inventory turnover is used as a single inventory control criterion?

15. List several examples of materials management problems you personally have experienced.

CASE 1: THREE RING CIRCUS

The general manager was completely frustrated as he walked out of his conference room, where he left a heated argument between some members of his staff—the controller, the marketing manager, and the manufacturing manager. The controller had just presented a financial review of the previous month's performance, and his concluding words were that the inventory was too high and had to be reduced. The marketing manager quickly responded by saying that the finished goods inventory should not be reduced. The customer service performance was bad, and if anything should be changed, it was the finished goods inventory that should be increased. The manufacturing manager turned to the general manager and said, "Don't expect me to reduce the factory inventory if we are to achieve the productivity improvements projected for this year." Then the argument started. When it was evident that no logical conclusion was going to be reached in the present atmosphere, the meeting was adjourned. The general manager went to his office and called the materials manager.

1. Are arguments of this nature inevitable?
2. How should these situations be resolved?
3. Is any party unreasonable or at fault?

CASE 2: ROUGH SEAS

Bay Cove Marine is a distributor that supplies boating paraphernalia to marine companies in the coastal areas of North Carolina and Virginia. Bay Cove distributes several lines of boating equipment plus parts for new and older models of pleasurecraft. The items that Bay Cove distributes to dealers are sold directly to the customer or installed by a service department. The pleasurecraft that the local outlets service include outboards, inboards, outriggers, and small sailing vessels. Bay Cove has always carried complete lines of boating equipment and marine parts. Their excellent reputation has been maintained by a policy of stocking the most complete lines of parts and the widest selection of equipment within the geographical area.

The annual sales profile for Bay Cove has been fairly level over the past two years, with the usual peaks prior to and during vacation periods. The projection for future sales indicates a brief continuation at the present level followed by a gradual and continuing downward trend. Bay Cove has been and expects to be hit doubly hard by major economic problems. The recreational industries are being severely affected by persistent inflation, and the marine industries are having problems related to the high cost of energy.

Bay Cove management recognized the serious position of the industry last year and decided to focus on methods to help them survive the unfortunate economic circumstances. Realizing that the possibility of increasing profits through revenue growth was unlikely, Bay Cove decided to control costs instead. Analysis of the company cost structure revealed that the investment in inventory was the largest percentage of the asset base. Therefore, management concluded that the emphasis in the cost control program should be placed on inventory control.

Knowing that they need more expertise in inventory management, Bay Cove hired a materials/inventory manager over a year ago. When Mr. Barone was hired, management stipulated that he would be evaluated on his contribution to the company's defined goals. Bay Cove was going to stress all actions that could reduce costs, tie up less capital in inventory, and consequently, improve the return on investment. The terms of Mr. Barone's employment specified that his monetary rewards would be based on the effectiveness of inventory control. His performance would be measured strictly on two criteria, a greater inventory turnover and a greater total asset turnover.

Mr. Barone's first year of employment ended, and the upper level managers were reviewing the past year's performance. The scoresheets were the balance sheet and income statement. The managers calculated the relevant financial ratios and discovered that Mr. Barone's performance had fallen short of the anticipated results. Comparison of the turnover ratios with those of the previous year showed no improvement. Management felt that their analysis had detected some weakness in Barone's ability to control inventory costs. Concentrating solely on the outcome of the turnover analysis, one of the managers, Mr. Rigger, castigated Mr. Barone bitterly. He accused him of employing faulty practices and suggested that he be dismissed.

Mr. Drew, another manager, insisted that Mr. Barone be allowed to explain the statistics. Mr. Barone, quite shocked by the ordeal, babbled a series of expletives and made the following statements in his defense: ratio analysis conducted in an unthinking manner is dangerous; the nature and complexity of Bay Cove's inventory items demand mandatory inventory levels; the company has conflicting and interdependent goals; there is a natural sluggishness associated with optimizing methods; there is a need to consider industry averages; there are inherent fallacies and distortions in turnover ratios.

Mr. Rigger stated that Barone's murmurings were incomprehensible and feeble excuses. He believed that the criteria should stand—nothing short of the discovery of an error in the ratio calculation could be a convincing argument.

1. Does Mr. Rigger have a justifiable cause for Mr. Barone's dismissal?
2. Are Barone's retorts feeble and irrelevant?
3. Are there other reasons Mr. Barone could have cited to strengthen his defense?
4. Did Bay Cove use acceptable performance criteria? What else might have been used to judge Mr. Barone's performance?

CASE 3: A NATURAL

New Commonwealth University is an urban university located in a populous city on the Eastern seaboard. The university has always given attention to the urban community it serves in defining its goals and objectives. NCU is committed to meeting the needs of its students and the regional businesses through teaching, research, and advisory/consulting services.

Key administrative positions in the School of Business have just changed hands. The replacements resulted from a dissatisfaction at the university level with the environment that has developed during the last decade and with the lack of direction toward university goals. The new administration is instituting a program of constructive change in an intense effort to rebuild the School of Business. The administration is determined to strengthen the curriculum for the students and to establish a recognizable resource base for the area.

It is the opinion of the administration and prominent faculty members that the majority of the business faculty have not shown any positive updating of business programs for some time. There has been an obvious lack of advisory/consulting relationships with local clients and an absence of faculty research. In response, all departments are being apprised that they are expected to define a departmental mission and to direct teaching, research, and consulting activities toward the fulfillment of adopted goals.

The Operations Management Department is in the process of revising the curriculum and directionalizing its research and consulting projects. Realizing that they have been inactive in any specific area of operations research and have provided only minimal consulting services to this point, its faculty are attempting to identify an area in which they can fulfill their mission. They know that they cannot achieve proficiency in all areas, so they are trying to narrow their scope and focus on a specific portion of their functional area.

Certain criteria become apparent. It is necessary to advise local businesses within the department's chosen area of expertise and to use the results of these advisory projects for publications. They will also have to integrate these faculty efforts with course structures. The courses will have to prepare students for the job market. The department will have to choose an area where the local market will be able to utilize its services. The local market should be large enough to support the program now and in the future.

Niels Holcher, an assistant professor who has just been hired from a large midwestern university, has offered a suggestion. He has told his colleagues that he feels they should emphasize materials management and inventory control in their courses and in their consulting and research efforts. He feels the need exists and is strong enough from local organizations to request professional assistance. He has stated that while inventory systems are very sophisticated theoretically, there is a tremendous opportunity for practical research and application. In terms of quantity and perplexity of local business problems, it is a natural.

1. Does Niels have a worthwhile suggestion? Will his suggestion satisfy the departmental goals?
2. Should the department specialize in the materials management area? What would the future be in this area and why?
3. Would you have suggested an alternative area? If so, what and why?

2 Forecasting and Market Analysis

THE FORECASTING FUNCTION

TIME SERIES ANALYSIS

- **Last Period Demand**
- **Arithmetic Average**
- **Moving Average**
- **Regression Analysis**
- **Exponentially Weighted Moving Average (EWMA)**
- **EWMA with Trend Correction**
- **EWMA with Seasonal Correction**
- **EWMA with Trend and Seasonal Corrections**
- **EWMA Overview**
- **Box-Jenkins Models**

SOLICITING OPINIONS

ECONOMIC INDICATORS

ECONOMETRIC MODELS

CONCLUSION

QUESTIONS

PROBLEMS

CASES

SELECTED BIBLIOGRAPHY

Man has always had a fascination with the future. Astrologers, prophets, wizards, and psychics have been providing insight into the future throughout recorded history. In organizations, forecasting is the window into the future, upon which most major activities are based, in particular, the allocation and use of resources.

Most organizations are not in a position to wait until orders are received before they begin to determine what production facilities, process, equipment, manpower, or materials are required and in what quantities. Few consumers would be willing to wait so long. Most successful organizations anticipate the future demand for their products and translate that information into factor inputs required to satisfy expected demand. Forecasting (predicting the future) provides a basis for managerial planning. For a business to survive, it must meet its customers' needs at least as quickly as its competitors do. The better management is able to estimate the future, the better it should be able to prepare for it.

Forecasting is the estimation of the future based on the past. If the future were certain, forecasting would not be necessary. But the future is rarely certain, and some system of forecasting, implicit or explicit, is necessary.

Many environmental factors influence the demand for an organization's products and services. It is never possible to identify all of the factors or to measure their probable effects. It is necessary in forecasting to identify the broad, major influences and to attempt to predict their direction. Some major environmental factors are:

1. General business conditions and the state of the economy
2. Competitor actions and reactions
3. Governmental legislative actions
4. Marketplace trends
   a. Product life cycle
   b. Style and fashion
   c. Changing consumer demands
5. Technological innovations

A forecast is an estimate of the level of demand expected in the future. Organizations may use many different forecasting bases. Sales revenue, physical units, cost of goods manufactured, direct labor hours, and machine hours are common forecasting bases. The selection of a forecasting base is dependent upon plans for establishing the necessary factor requirements. In many organizations, sales forecasts are used to establish production levels, facilitate scheduling, set inventory levels, determine manpower loading, make purchasing decisions, establish sales conditions (pricing and advertising), and aid financial planning (cash budgeting and capital budgeting).

Top-down forecasting and *bottom-up forecasting* are general forecasting patterns used for predicting product demand. Top-down forecasting begins with a forecast of general economic activity (GNP, national income, etc.) for the geopolitical unit where the organization operates. Industry forecasts are developed from the general economic activity forecast. The organization's share-of-the-market forecast is predicted from the industry forecast, and specific product group forecasts are developed from it.

Bottom-up forecasting begins at the product level. Forecasts are made for each product or product group, and the forecasts are summed to obtain the aggregate organizational forecast. The aggregate forecast can be modified in relation to the general business outlook and the competitive situation. Advertising and promotion may necessitate further forecast revision.

Forecasting, as we are referring to it here, is a short-run tool for establishing input-output levels. In the short run, products, processes, equipment, tooling, layout, and capacity are essentially fixed. All statistical forecasting techniques assume to some extent that forces that existed in the past will persist in the future. A forecast is the link between the external, uncontrollable environment and the internal, controllable affairs of an organization. Adequate forecasting procedures can go a long way toward solving many organizational problems.

THE FORECASTING FUNCTION

Frequently, forecasting is considered as a group of procedures for deriving estimates of future activity, the major emphasis being on the type of forecasting technique. However, it is more desirable to focus on the forecasting function than on the specific forecasting techniques or models. The forecasting function includes techniques and models, but it also highlights the significance of inputs and outputs (see Figure 1).

To develop the forecasting function, it is first necessary to determine the outputs. The outputs (and their format) can be specified by a delineation of the intended uses of the forecasts. This chapter has already mentioned numerous uses for forecasts in organizations. When the users obtain the outputs, specific actions will be taken to assure that future demand will be satisfied. The precision and accuracy of forecasting outputs should be conveyed, along with the intended uses, during the development of the forecasting function.

The initial specification of outputs can simplify the selection of the forecasting model, but the forecasting function is not complete without the input considerations. No matter how long a system is studied, only a few of the many inputs can be isolated. Fortunately, most systems are relatively insensitive to most of their inputs. The size of the problem can be reduced by only including the most significant inputs to the forecasting models. These are the ones that will be closely observed for changes in the future.

By knowing the desired outputs and the significant inputs or variables that affect the demand, a forecasting model may be selected. The selection

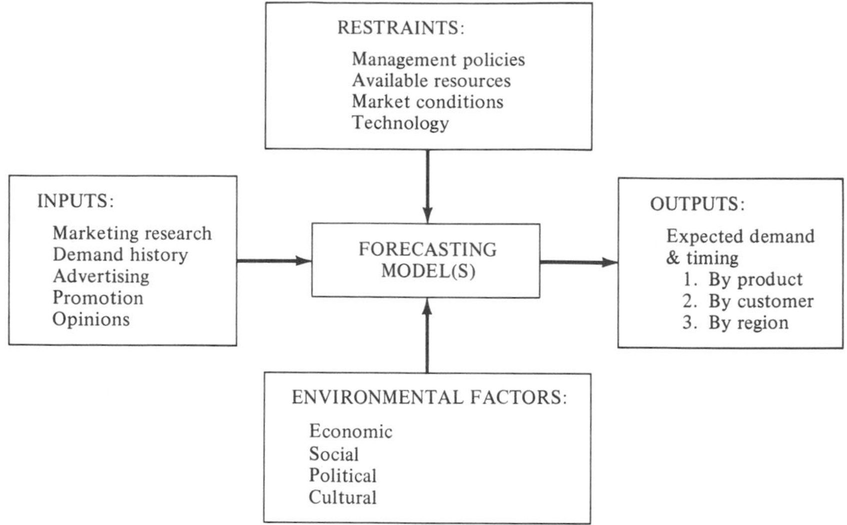

Figure 1. The forecasting function.

of the forecasting model will involve considerations such as cost, accuracy of the model, availability of the input data, and so forth. Sometimes a specific model will be indicated. When a single model is not apparent, several can be tested and the most accurate model adopted.

Forecasting usually involves the following considerations:

1. Items to be forecasted (products, product groups, assemblies, etc.)
2. Top-down or bottom-up forecasting
3. Forecasting techniques (quantitative or qualitative models)
4. Units of measure (dollars, units, weights, etc.)
5. Time interval (weeks, months, quarters, etc.)
6. Forecast horizon (how many time intervals to include)
7. Forecasting components (levels, trends, seasonals, cycles, and random variation)
8. Forecast accuracy (error measurement)
9. Exception reporting and special situations
10. Revision of forecasting model parameters

In most organizations, a small percentage of the material requirement represents a majority of the investment. These high cost or high usage items should receive the greatest degree of forecasting attention. There are also a great many low cost or low usage items that represent a small percentage of the total investment (although a high percentage of the number of items). Very little effort should be devoted to making forecasts for them. For low cost items, crude forecasts supplemented with large safety stocks are sufficient. Forecasting emphasis should be placed on those items that represent a significant investment.

There are four basic demand forecasting techniques—*time series analysis*, *soliciting opinions*, *economic indicators*, and *econometric models*. These techniques are short-range forecasting devices, and their value diminishes as the time horizon increases. Many of the techniques are based on extrapolation into the future of effects that have existed in the past.

The forecasting approaches to new products and established products are dissimilar. For established products, the forecasting techniques of time series analysis, economic indicators, and econometric models may be appropriate. For new products with little or no history of past demand, soliciting opinions is more suitable. There are various places to solicit the opinions. The direct survey approach—asking prospective customers of their buying intentions—is frequently used. An indirect survey approach may also be employed: information is obtained from people (salesmen, wholesalers, jobbers) who know how the customers respond. Also, if a comparable or substitute product exists, comparisons with similar products can be made. Finally a limited market test of the new product can indicate product acceptability to potential customers.

There is no single forecasting technique that is superior in all cases, and the same organization can use different techniques for different products. It is difficult to ascertain the effect of changes in selling price, product quality, marketing methods, promotion, and economic conditions on forecasts. Regardless of the method adopted, the results provide the decision maker with nothing more than a starting point for making the final forecast. The final forecast usually requires an additional input in the form of judgment, intuition, and experience. Nor should any organization make a forecast and adhere to it blindly without periodic review.

TIME SERIES ANALYSIS

Time series analysis predicts the future from past internal data. Past trends may be good indicators of the future, but the forecaster should be alert to factors that may cause severe abruption from the past. External factors frequently have a very pronounced effect on the future, and time series analysis tends to neglect them.

A time series is a set of time ordered observations on a variable during successive and equal time periods. In time series analysis, historical data are analyzed to determine temporal patterns. Usually, the analysis of time series is accomplished by decomposing the data into five components—*levels*, *trends*, *seasonal variations*, *cyclical variations*, and *random variations*.

Levels indicate the scale or magnitude of a time series, while trends identify the rate of growth or decline of a series over time. Seasonal variations consist of similar periodic patterns that occur within each year.

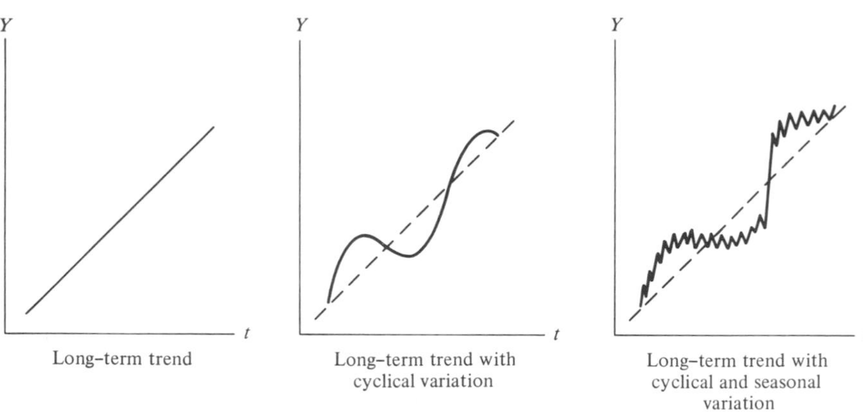

Figure 2. Time series components.

Cyclical variations are the result of business cycles of expansion and contraction of economic activity over a number of years. Random variations are sporadic movements related to chance events that last for only a short time. Figure 2 displays typical trend, seasonal, and cyclical time series components.

Seasonality is present when demand fluctuates in a similar pattern within each year. The twelve month periodicity may be related to weather patterns, tradition, school openings, vacations, taxes, bonuses, model changeovers, or calendar oriented customs (Thanksgiving, Christmas). Examples of products with a seasonal pattern are antifreeze, soft drinks, ice cream, toys, snow tires, grass seed, textbooks, air conditioners, and greeting cards.

Before seasonal corrections are included in a forecast model, some conditions should be met. There should be some known reason for the periodic peaks and valleys in the demand pattern, and they should occur at essentially the same time every year. For the seasonal modification to be worth including, it should be of a larger magnitude than the random variations.

Cyclical variations are long term oscillations or swings about a trend line. The cycles may or may not be periodic. An important example of cyclical movement is the business cycle: prosperity, recession, depression, and recovery. Cyclical fluctuations vary as to the time of occurrence, the lengths of the phases, and the amplitude of the fluctuations. Unfortunately, there are no generally reliable methods for handling cyclical variations that can be applied conveniently. The available methods are involved and beyond the scope of this section.

Random variations represent all the influences not included in level, trend, seasonal, and cyclical variations. They include such things as measurement errors, floods, fires, earthquakes, wars, strikes, and unusual weather conditions. Many times an erratic occurrence may be isolated and removed from the data, but there are no general techniques for doing so. An average process will help eliminate its influence. Random variations are often referred to as noise, residuals, or irregular variations.

There are many techniques for time series analysis. Some of the most common ones are last period demand, arithmetic average, moving average, regression analysis, and the exponentially weighted moving average. All of the techniques assume some perpetuation of historical forces. An objective function frequently employed in determining the best technique is the mean absolute deviation (MAD), which measures the average forecast error. The forecast error is the numerical difference between the forecasted and actual demand. Each technique is tested on the historical data and the one with the smallest MAD is selected as the forecast instrument.

The MAD (*mean* is the statistician's term for average; *absolute* means the plus or minus sign is ignored; and *deviation* means the difference between the forecast and actual demand) is obtained by dividing the number of observations into the sum of absolute deviations.[1] The MAD is calculated from the following formula:

$$\text{MAD} = \frac{\sum_{i=1}^{n} |\hat{Y}_i - Y_i|}{n},$$

where

$$\begin{aligned} \hat{Y}_i &= \text{forecasted demand for period } i, \\ Y_i &= \text{actual demand for period } i, \\ n &= \text{number of time periods}, \\ \hat{Y}_i - Y_i &= \text{algebraic deviation or forecast error}, \\ |\hat{Y}_i - Y_i| &= \text{absolute deviation} \end{aligned}$$

Since forecasts are never exact, it is desirable to have an estimate of the variability of the forecast error. Frequently, a forecast is presented as a specific number together with a confidence limit or margin of error. The specified number is the average or expected value, while the confidence limit is a measure of the variability of the possible outcomes. The measure of variability of a forecast is usually either the mean absolute deviation (MAD) or the standard deviation of the forecast errors. Historical variability is

[1]Sometimes the minimum sum of squared deviations is applied. (This criterion is justified if the cost of making an error is proportional to the square of its size: small errors do not cost much but big errors are expensive.) For a normal distribution, the standard deviation is closely approximated by 1.25 times the MAD. The relationship between the standard deviation and the MAD is important in determining confidence limits for forecasts and in establishing inventory safety stock levels via computer routines.

frequently used as an estimate of future variability. The standard deviation is computed as the square root of the mean squared difference between actual and forecasted demand over time.

While the MAD expresses the extent of the forecast error, it does not indicate the direction. The direction of forecast errors is expressed by the bias, which measures the tendency to consistently overforecast or underforecast. An ideal forecast technique would have zero MAD and bias. The bias is calculated from the following formula:

$$\text{bias} = \frac{\sum_{i=1}^{n} (\hat{Y}_i - Y_i)}{n}.$$

A positive bias indicates a tendency to overforecast, while a negative bias indicates a tendency to underforecast.

Last Period Demand

The last period demand technique simply forecasts for the next period the level of demand that occurred in the previous period. No calculations are required, and forecasted values lag behind actual demand by one period. Mathematically,

$$\hat{Y}_t = Y_{t-1},$$

where

$$\hat{Y}_t = \text{forecasted demand for period } t,$$
$$Y_{t-1} = \text{actual demand in the previous period.}$$

The last period demand technique responds well to trends; it does not compensate very well for seasonals; and it overreacts to random influences.

Arithmetic Average

The arithmetic average simply takes the average of *all* past demand in arriving at a forecast. Mathematically,

$$\hat{Y}_t = \frac{\sum_{i=1}^{n} Y_i}{n} = \frac{Y_1 + Y_2 + \cdots + Y_n}{n},$$

where

$$\hat{Y}_t = \text{forecasted demand for period } t,$$
$$Y_i = \text{actual demand in period } i,$$
$$n = \text{number of time periods.}$$

The arithmetic average technique, unlike the last period demand technique, will smooth out random fluctuations; it will not adequately respond to trends in demand; and it neglects seasonals. Smoothing refers to the dampening or diminishing of random fluctuations and is synonymous with averaging.

The basic objection to the arithmetic average is that it takes too little account of recent data and is not responsive enough to changes in demand pattern. The arithmetic average works well in a stable situation where the level of demand does not change. It is appropriate for data that are stationary (horizontal) and randomly distributed.

Moving Average

The moving average technique generates the next period's forecast by averaging the actual demand for the last n time periods. The choice of the value of n should be determined by experimentation. The objective of the moving average is to include a sufficient number of time periods so random fluctuations are canceled, but few enough periods so irrelevant information from the distant past is discarded. The moving average is computed over time, changing with the addition of new data and the deletion of old data. As data become available for each time period, the latest data are included and the oldest data are excluded from the computation of the mean. Mathematically,

$$\hat{Y}_t = \frac{\sum_{i=1}^{n} Y_{t-i}}{n},$$

where

$\hat{Y}_t$ = forecasted demand for period t,

Y_{t-i} = actual demand in i, the period preceding t,

n = number of time periods included in moving average.

This technique gives more weight to the more current time periods. How many periods to use in the average is difficult to say without examining the particular situation. If too few are used, the forecast fluctuates wildly, influenced by random variations in demand. If too many are used, the average is too stable and current trends are not detected. If there is a trend in demand, the moving average will always lag behind it. If the number of periods in the average is short, the lag will be small, and vice versa.

The moving average technique is a compromise between the last period demand and the arithmetic average technique with the advantages of both and the disadvantages of neither. If the demand rate is steady, the moving average will respond with fairly constant forecasts, as does the arithmetic average method. However, when the average demand does change, the moving average forecast, like the last period demand forecasts, responds fairly quickly to the change, but without the extreme fluctuations that are characteristic of the last period demand forecast. Increasing the number of periods in the moving average will produce forecasts like the arithmetic average forecasts. Decreasing the number of periods will produce forecasts like the last period demand forecast. The moving average dampens random effects, responds to trends with a delay, and does not compensate for seasonals.

EXAMPLE 1

Monthly demand in units for the last two years is listed in Table 1. Evaluate the forecasts with the last period demand, arithmetic average, and two-month moving average techniques. Utilizing the mean absolute deviation (MAD) as a criterion, determine the most desirable of the three forecasting techniques. What is the forecast for the 25th month with each of the three techniques?

Table 2 compares the three forecasting techniques. The two-month moving average has the smallest mean absolute deviation, 7.27 (160/22); the arithmetic average has a MAD of 7.55 (166/22); and the last period demand has the largest MAD, 8.26 (190/23). The two-month moving average technique is the most desirable of the three techniques evaluated, and its forecast for the next month is 59 units.

Regression Analysis

Regression analysis establishes a temporal relationship for the forecast variable. The variable to be predicted (demand) is referred to as the dependent variable, while the variable used in predicting (time) is called the

Table 1

Month	Demand	Month	Demand	Month	Demand
1	34	9	38	17	58
2	44	10	44	18	54
3	42	11	36	19	46
4	30	12	46	20	48
5	46	13	42	21	40
6	44	14	30	22	50
7	56	15	52	23	58
8	50	16	48	24	60
					Total 1096

Table 2

Month	Demand	Last Period Demand		Arithmetic Average		Two-Month Moving Average	
		Forecast Demand	Absolute Deviation	Forecast Demand	Absolute Deviation	Forecast Demand	Absolute Deviation
1	34	—	—	—	—	—	—
2	44	34	10	—	—	—	—
3	42	44	2	39	3	39	3
4	30	42	12	40	10	43	13
5	46	30	16	38	8	36	10
6	44	46	2	39	5	38	6
7	56	44	12	40	16	45	11
8	50	56	6	42	8	50	0
9	38	50	12	43	5	53	15
10	44	38	6	43	1	44	0
11	36	44	8	43	7	41	5
12	46	36	10	42	4	40	6
13	42	46	4	43	1	41	1
14	30	42	12	42	12	44	14
15	52	30	22	42	10	36	16
16	48	52	4	42	6	41	7
17	58	48	10	43	15	50	8
18	54	58	4	44	10	53	1
19	46	54	8	44	2	56	10
20	48	46	2	44	4	50	2
21	40	48	8	44	4	47	7
22	50	40	10	44	6	44	6
23	58	50	8	44	14	45	13
24	60	58	2	45	15	54	6
25		66		46		59	
	1096		190		166		160

independent variable. A cause-effect relationship is implied. The simplest type of relationship is a linear association. Regression analysis by the least squares method will fit a straight line to a plot of data. The line fitted by this method will be such that the sum of squares of the deviations about the line is less than about any other line. The regression line will encompass the trend effect, but not the seasonal effect. The basic equation for a straight line that expresses demand (Y) as a function of time (t) is

$$\hat{Y}_t = \alpha + \beta t,$$

where α is the intersection of the line with the vertical axis when $t=0$, and β is the slope of the line. The parameters α and β are estimated from the following formulas:

$$\beta = \frac{n \sum_{i=1}^{n} t_i Y_i - \left(\sum_{i=1}^{n} t_i \right) \left(\sum_{i=1}^{n} Y_i \right)}{n \sum_{i=1}^{n} t_i^2 - \left[\sum_{i=1}^{n} t_i \right]^2} = \text{slope},$$

$$\alpha = \bar{Y} - \beta \bar{t} = \frac{\sum_{i=1}^{n} Y_i - \left[\beta \sum_{i=1}^{n} t_i \right]}{n} = \text{intercept},$$

where n is the number of periods of demand data included in the calculation.

If the relationship between variables in regression analysis is not perfect, there will be a scatter or variation about the regression line. The greater the scatter about the regression line, the poorer the relationship. A statistic that indicates how well a regression line explains or fits observed data is the correlation coefficient. The degree of linear association of the forecast variable to the time variable is determined by the correlation coefficient. The correlation coefficient ranges between -1 and $+1$. A high absolute value indicates a high degree of association, while a small absolute value indicates little association between variables. When the coefficient is positive, one variable tends to increase as the other increases. When the coefficient is negative, one variable tends to decrease as the other increases. Figure 3 illustrates typical scatter diagram correlations. The following formula is used to compute the correlation coefficient:

$$r^2 = \frac{(\Sigma xy)^2}{(\Sigma x^2)(\Sigma y^2)},$$

Figure 3. Typical scatter diagram correlations.

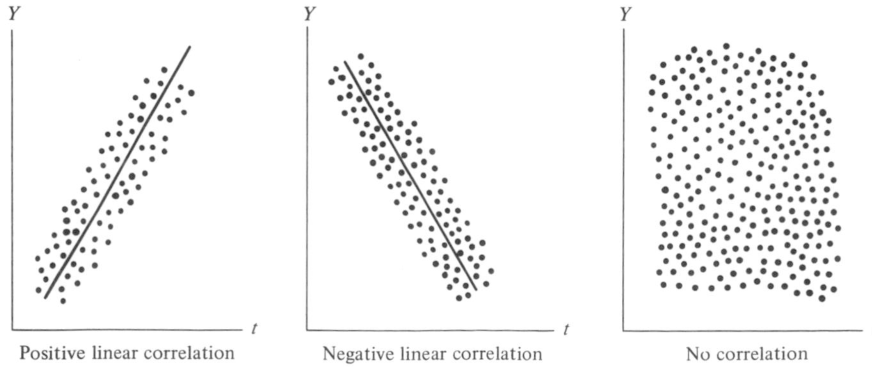

where

$$r = \text{simple correlation coefficient},$$
$$x = t - \bar{t},$$
$$y = Y - \bar{Y}.$$

Table 3 represents a general rule of thumb for interpretation of the coefficient of correlation.

In linear regression analysis, it is assumed that demand is a normally distributed random variable whose mean is the Y coordinate on the regression line at that point in time. By knowing the standard deviation of the distribution, probability statements can be made about the reliability of the forecasts. It is assumed that the standard deviation S_r can be determined from the following formula:

$$S_r^2 = \frac{1}{n-2}\left\{\sum_{i=1}^{n}\left(Y_i - \bar{Y}\right)^2 - \frac{\left[\sum_{i=1}^{n}\left(t_i - \bar{t}\right)\left(Y_i - \bar{Y}\right)\right]^2}{\sum_{i=1}^{n}\left(t_i - \bar{t}\right)^2}\right\}.$$

Once the linear regression line and the standard deviation have been determined, control limits can be established with one, two, or three standard deviations from the mean. When the actual demand occurs, it can be compared with the control limits to determine if the demand is what could be reasonably expected. If the demand falls outside the control limits, there is reason to wonder if the cause system has changed. If it has, a new forecasting model should be developed to replace the inadequate model.

Frequently, time series data are autocorrelated or serially correlated. Autocorrelation occurs where one observation tends to be correlated with the next. Autocorrelation violates the conditions required to produce a valid regression estimate. To be valid, each observation on the data in regression analysis should be totally independent of any other observation. Time series data do not usually meet this condition, since most observations in the series can be forecasted by the last observation plus or minus a small change. This is especially true where a strong trend exists. Regression analysis requires

Table 3

Absolute value of correlation coefficient	Interpretation
0.90–1.00	Very high correlation
0.70–0.89	High correlation
0.40–0.69	Moderate correlation
0.20–0.39	Low correlation
0 –0.19	Very low correlation

that errors about the regression line be small and unrelated to each other and that their expected value be zero.

In some cases a high demand in one period may be an indication of a low demand to follow (the high demand could be due to advance stocking). This condition displays negative autocorrelation. In other cases, a high demand can arise from a cause which will also increase the following period's demand. This condition displays positive autocorrelation.

If autocorrelation exists, regression will underestimate the true variance and result in confidence limits that are too narrow. Many time series with autocorrelation will exhibit no autocorrelation of residuals from a regression in the form of first differences. With first differences, the observed datum Y_t is replaced with its first difference, $Y_t - Y_{t-1}$. Autocorrelation can be determined by the Durbin-Watson statistic or the von Neumann ratio, which can be found in advanced statistics books.

EXAMPLE 2

Annual sales for the last seven years for an organization is given in Table 4. Determine (a) the linear least squares regression line; (b) the standard deviation of the regression; (c) the correlation coefficient; (d) the forecasted demand for next year; and (e) the two standard deviation control limits for next year.

Table 5 develops the pertinent data.

$$\bar{t} = \frac{28}{7} = 4.0, \qquad \bar{Y} = \frac{19.78}{7} = 2.83.$$

(a)

$$\beta = \frac{n \sum_{i=1}^{n} t_i Y_i - \sum_{i=1}^{n} t_i \sum_{i=1}^{n} Y_i}{n \sum_{i=1}^{n} t_i^2 - \left(\sum_{i=1}^{n} t_i \right)^2} = \frac{7(89.35) - (28)(19.78)}{7(140) - 28^2} = 0.365,$$

$$\alpha = \bar{Y} - \beta \bar{t} = 2.83 - (0.365)4.0 = 1.37,$$

$$\hat{Y}_t = \alpha + \beta t = (1.37 + 0.365t) \times 10^6 = 1{,}370{,}000 + 365{,}000t.$$

Table 4

Year	Annual Sales
1	$1,760,000
2	2,120,000
3	2,350,000
4	2,800,000
5	3,200,000
6	3,750,000
7	3,800,000

Table 5

Year t	Demand Y ($\$10^6$)	tY	t^2	x $t-\bar{t}$	x^2 $(t-\bar{t})^2$	y $Y-\bar{Y}$	y^2 $(Y-\bar{Y})^2$	xy $(t-\bar{t})(Y-\bar{Y})$
1	1.76	1.76	1	−3	9	−1.07	1.14	3.21
2	2.12	4.24	4	−2	4	−0.71	0.50	1.42
3	2.35	7.05	9	−1	1	−0.48	0.23	0.48
4	2.80	11.20	16	0	0	−0.03	0.00	0.00
5	3.20	16.00	25	1	1	0.37	0.14	0.37
6	3.75	22.50	36	2	4	0.92	0.85	1.84
7	3.80	26.60	49	3	9	0.97	0.94	2.91
28	19.78	89.35	140		28		3.80	10.23

(b)

$$S_r^2 = \frac{1}{n-2}\left\{ \sum_{i=1}^{n} (Y_i - \bar{Y})^2 - \frac{\left[\sum_{i=1}^{n} (t_i - \bar{t})(Y_i - \bar{Y})\right]^2}{\sum_{i=1}^{n} (t_i - \bar{t})^2} \right\}$$

$$= \frac{1}{5}\left\{3.80 - \frac{(10.23)^2}{28}\right\}$$

$$= 0.0125,$$

$$S_r = 0.112 \times 10^6 = \$112{,}000.$$

(c)

$$r^2 = \frac{\left(\sum xy\right)^2}{\left(\sum x^2\right)\left(\sum y^2\right)} = \frac{10.23^2}{28(3.80)} = \frac{104.65}{106.40} = 0.9836,$$

$$r = 0.992.$$

(d)

$$\hat{Y}_8 = 1{,}370{,}000 + 365{,}000(8) = \$4{,}290{,}000.$$

(e)

$$\hat{Y}_8 \pm 2S_r = 4{,}290{,}000 \pm 2(112{,}000) = \$4{,}290{,}000 \pm 224{,}000.$$

The two standard deviation control limits are $4,066,000 and $4,514,000.

Exponentially Weighted Moving Average (EWMA)

The exponentially weighted moving average is a special kind of moving average that does not require the keeping of a long historical record. The moving average technique assumes that data have no value after n periods. Some value (although possibly very little) remains in any datum, and a model that uses all the data with appropriate weightings should be superior to a model that discards data.

Like most forecasting techniques, EWMA uses historical data as its prediction basis. It is a special type of moving average where past data are not given equal weight. The weight given to past data decreases geometrically with the increasing age of the data. More recent data are weighted more heavily than less recent ones. The major advantage of the EWMA is that the effect of all previous data is included in the previous forecast figure, so only one number needs to be obtained to represent the demand history.

The simplest EWMA model estimates the average forecast demand ($\hat{Y}_t$) by adding to the last average forecast demand ($\hat{Y}_{t-1}$) a fraction of the difference between the actual demand (Y_{t-1}) and the last average forecast demand ($\hat{Y}_{t-1}$):

$$\text{New forecast} = (\text{old forecast}) + a(\text{actual demand} - \text{old forecast})$$
$$= a(\text{actual demand}) + (1-a)(\text{old forecast}),$$
$$\hat{Y}_t = \hat{Y}_{t-1} + a(Y_{t-1} - \hat{Y}_{t-1}) = aY_{t-1} + (1-a)\hat{Y}_{t-1},$$

where

$$Y_{t-1} - \hat{Y}_{t-1} = \text{error in previous forecast},$$
$$a = \text{exponential smoothing constant between 0 and 1}.$$

For example, suppose you are attempting to obtain the forecast of June sales by the EWMA. The relationships would be as follows:

$$\hat{Y}_t = aY_{t-1} + (1-a)\hat{Y}_{t-1},$$
$$\text{June forecast} = a(\text{May actual}) + (1-a)(\text{May forecast}).$$

The smoothing constant a lies between zero (no weight to recent actual data) and 1.0 (all weight to recent actual data). Small values of a put greater weight on historical demand conditions and have a greater smoothing effect (maximum stability with minimum sensitivity). Large values of a put greater weight on current demand conditions (maximum sensitivity with minimum stability). The appropriate value of a for a given set of data is determined by trial on a sample of actual past demand (retrospective testing). It is common to develop forecasting models on the first half of historical data and then test them on the second half.

Guideline values for a range from 0.1 to 0.3. Larger values of a may be used for short time periods when anticipated changes will occur such as a recession, an aggressive but temporary promotional campaign, introduction of a new product, or discontinuation of some products in a line. The value of a should allow the forecast model to track major demand changes while averaging the random fluctuations.

The general formula for the exponentially weighted moving average is as follows:

$$\hat{Y}_t = a\left[Y_{t-1} + Y_{t-2}(1-a) + Y_{t-3}(1-a)^2 + \cdots + Y_1(1-a)^{t-2}\right]$$
$$+ (1-a)^{t-1}\hat{Y}_0,$$

where

$$\hat{Y}_t = \text{forecasted demand for period } t,$$

$$\hat{Y}_0 = \text{forecasted demand for period } 0,$$

$$Y_{t-1} = \text{actual demand for period } t-1.$$

The EWMA attributes part of the difference between actual demand and forecasted demand to a real cause and the remainder to chance causes. The EWMA assigns to the demand values of the previous periods weights that decrease in an exponential manner (exponential decay) as the demand data are removed from the present (thus the name exponentially weighted moving average). The weight of past demands decreases exponentially because the fraction $1-a$ is raised to a power.

A general formula for expressing the weight of an individual demand value in a future forecast is as follows:

$$\text{Weight} = a(1-a)^{n-1},$$

where n is the number of time periods removed from the existing period. For example, if $a=0.2$ and the latest available actual demand is for May, the May demand will have a weight of 0.2 on the June forecast, a weight of 0.16 on the July forecast, a weight of 0.128 on the August forecast, and so forth. The above formula illustrates the lessening importance (exponential decay) of past data as they are farther removed from the forecast period. The weights were obtained as follows:

$$\text{June weight} = 0.2(1-0.2)^{1-1} = 0.2,$$

$$\text{July weight} = 0.2(1-0.2)^{2-1} = 0.16,$$

$$\text{August weight} = 0.2(1-0.2)^{3-1} = 0.128.$$

With the EWMA you can forecast more than one period into the future, but the more distant estimates are the same as the current estimate. The relationship to forecast n periods into the future when you are at the beginning of time t is thus simply

$$\hat{Y}_{t+n} = \hat{Y}_t.$$

Of course this relationship assumes that there are no trend, seasonal, or cyclical effects in the data (only random effects need correction).

The exponential smoothing model without a trend correction reacts slowly to a big change in demand, since the change may be only a random variation. If the change reflects an actual increase or decrease in demand, it will continue in subsequent periods and the exponential smoothing system will track the actual demand and respond to it. The size of the smoothing constant a will determine the sensitivity of the response to changes in demand. Surges in demand can be satisfied by safety stock when a small value of a is used in the forecast system.

There is a simple relationship between the moving average technique and the EWMA without trend or seasonal effects. Just as the sensitivity of a moving average decreases as the number of time periods in the moving average increases, the sensitivity of an EWMA decreases as a decreases. In fact, if n is the number of periods in the moving average, then for the corresponding EWMA we have[2]

$$a=\frac{2}{n+1}, \qquad \text{or} \quad n=\frac{2-a}{a}.$$

Thus, a moving average model with $n=7$ is equivalent to an EWMA model with $a=0.25$ and no trends or seasonal influences.

EXAMPLE 3

From the data in Table 6, determine the best forecasting method by using the smallest mean absolute deviation. Evaluate the last period demand, three-month moving average, and EWMA with $a=0.3$. (Assume $\hat{Y}_0=185$.)

Table 6

	Demand		
Month	1979	1980	1981
1	180	215	225
2	186	208	225
3	179	195	215
4	170	200	225
5	170	194	210
6	165	185	200
7	155	180	204
8	150	180	195
9	170	181	210
10	192	205	220
11	195	225	240
12	205	235	250

Table 7 compares the three forecasting methods with fractions rounded to whole numbers.

The last period demand has the smallest mean absolute deviation, 9.30 (335/36); EWMA has a MAD of 14.05 (506/36); and the three-month moving average has the largest MAD, 14.24 (470/33).

---

[2]See Robert G. Brown, *Statistical Forecasting for Inventory Control*, New York: McGraw-Hill, 1959, pp. 58–62.

Table 7

Month	Actual Demand	Last Period Demand: Forecast Demand	Last Period Demand: Absolute Deviation	Three-month Moving Average: Forecast Demand	Three-month Moving Average: Absolute Deviation	EWMA: Forecast Demand	EWMA: Absolute Deviation
1	180	185	5	—	—	185	5
2	186	180	6	—	—	183	3
3	179	186	7	—	—	184	5
4	170	179	9	182	12	182	12
5	170	170	0	178	8	178	8
6	165	170	5	173	8	176	11
7	155	165	10	168	13	173	18
8	150	155	5	163	13	168	18
9	170	150	20	157	13	163	7
10	192	170	22	158	34	165	27
11	195	192	3	171	24	173	22
12	205	195	10	186	19	180	25
13	215	205	10	197	18	187	28
14	208	215	7	205	3	195	13
15	195	208	13	209	14	199	4
16	200	195	5	206	6	198	2
17	194	200	6	201	7	199	5
18	185	194	9	196	11	197	12
19	180	185	5	193	13	193	13
20	180	180	0	186	6	189	9
21	181	180	1	182	1	186	5
22	205	181	24	180	25	184	21
23	225	205	20	189	36	190	35
24	235	225	10	204	31	200	35
25	225	235	10	222	3	210	15
26	225	225	0	228	3	214	11
27	215	225	10	228	13	217	2
28	225	215	10	222	3	216	9
29	210	225	15	222	12	219	9
30	200	210	10	217	17	216	16
31	204	200	4	212	8	211	7
32	195	204	9	205	10	209	14
33	210	195	15	200	10	205	5
34	220	210	10	203	17	206	14
35	240	220	20	208	32	210	30
36	250	240	10	223	27	219	31
37		250		237		228	
			335		470		506

EWMA With Trend Correction

The exponentially weighted moving average provides an adequate future forecast if no trend, seasonal, or cyclical effects exist. If a trend is present, the EWMA will respond to it with a lag. The apparent trend for each period is the difference between the forecast averages, $\hat{Y}_t - \hat{Y}_{t-1}$. This difference represents another series which can be estimated and smoothed by exponential smoothing. The trend adjustment is as follows:

$$\text{New trend} = b(\text{new forecasted demand} - \text{old forecasted demand}) + (1-b)(\text{old trend}),$$

$$T_t = b(\hat{Y}_t - \hat{Y}_{t-1}) + (1-b)T_{t-1} = \text{trend adjustment for time } t,$$

where

$$b = \text{exponential smoothing constant between 0 and 1.}$$

If there are no seasonal or cyclical effects, the forecasted demand for the upcoming period is given by the following:

$$\text{New forecast} = a(\text{actual demand}) + (1-a)(\text{old forecast} + \text{old trend}),$$

$$\hat{Y}_t = aY_{t-1} + (1-a)(\hat{Y}_{t-1} + T_{t-1}).$$

Frequently a forecast of more than one period into the future is desired. If at the beginning of time t a forecast for the nth period is desired, the forecast is determined as follows:

$$\hat{Y}_{t+n} = \hat{Y}_t + nT_t.$$

EXAMPLE 4

From the one-year record of monthly demand in Table 8, develop a trend adjusted exponentially weighted forecast with $a=0.1$, $b=0.1$, $\hat{Y}_0=40$, and $T_0=0$.

Table 8

Month	Demand
January	47
February	42
March	16
April	47
May	38
June	34
July	45
August	50
September	47
October	54
November	40
December	43

Table 9

Month	Demand Y_t	Trend T_t	Forecast $\hat{Y}_t$	Deviation $\hat{Y}_t - Y_t$
January	47	0	40.00	−7.00
February	42	.070	40.70	−1.30
March	16	.081	40.89	+24.89
April	47	−.167	38.48	−8.52
May	38	−.181	39.18	+1.18
June	34	−.092	38.99	+4.99
July	45	−.141	38.41	−6.59
August	50	−.073	38.94	−11.06
September	47	.038	39.98	−7.02
October	54	.108	40.72	−13.28
November	40	.240	42.14	+2.14
December	43	.216	42.14	−0.86
January		.222	42.42	

The trend adjusted exponentially weighted forecast is derived in Table 9. From this table, the forecast for February is obtained as follows:

$$\hat{Y}_t = aY_{t-1} + (1-a)(\hat{Y}_{t-1} + T_{t-1}) = 0.1(47) + 0.9(40+0) = 40.70.$$

The trend adjustment for February is obtained in the following manner:

$$T_t = b(\hat{Y}_t - \hat{Y}_{t-1}) + (1-b)T_{t-1} = 0.1(40.70 - 40) + 0.9(0) = 0.070.$$

All other values in the above table are determined in a similar fashion for the appropriate period. The process is very simple, although manually it is laborious and time consuming.

EWMA with Seasonal Correction

Seasonal demand patterns are characterized by recurring periods of high and low demand. Exponential smoothing models can be modified to account for seasonal variations. Seasonalization can be achieved by a set of seasonal index numbers which represent the expected ratio of demand for individual periods to an average demand.

Table 10 indicates how indices can be obtained from two years of past monthly data.

$$\text{Average monthly demand} = \frac{1248}{12} = 104.$$

The indices in Table 10 are obtained by dividing the average monthly demand (104) into the respective average for each month. The seasonal index for the month of January is 100/104, or 0.961.

The most common methods of forecasting when there is a seasonal pattern depend on comparing the observed demand with that in a corresponding period in the previous year or with the average of the demand in

Table 10

Month	Demand 19X0	Demand 19X1	Average	Seasonal Index I_t
January	90	110	100	0.961
February	85	95	90	0.865
March	90	100	95	0.913
April	100	120	110	1.058
May	125	141	133	1.279
June	120	130	125	1.202
July	110	120	115	1.105
August	100	120	110	1.058
September	95	105	100	0.961
October	85	95	90	0.865
November	85	95	90	0.865
December	90	90	90	0.865
			1248	

the corresponding periods in several previous years. The standard for comparison is called a base series, and it has a value for each review period. The commonest base series is the actual demand during the corresponding month last year. If the peak demand shifts back and forth by a month or so from year to year, then the average of the demand in the three months surrounding the corresponding month last year may prove to be a more stable base series.

Exponential smoothing can filter out random effects for both deseasonalized demand and seasonal indices. Actual demand data are deseasonalized by dividing by the index numbers, and the resultant demand (with or without trend effects) is forecasted by a smoothing model. The index numbers also are updated by a smoothing routine:

$$I_{t+m}=cI_t\left(\frac{Y_t}{\hat{Y}_t}\right)+(1-c)I_t=\left[\frac{cY_t}{\hat{Y}_t}+(1-c)\right]I_t,$$

where

I_t = seasonal index for the period t,

c = exponential smoothing constant between 0 and 1,

m = number of periods in seasonal pattern ($m=12$ for monthly data and $m=4$ for quarterly data with an annual seasonal pattern).

If no trend exists, the exponential smoothing model with a seasonal adjustment is as follows:

$$\hat{Y}_t=\left[\frac{aY_{t-1}}{I_{t-1}}+\frac{(1-a)\hat{Y}_{t-1}}{I_{t-1}}\right]I_t=\left[a(Y_{t-1})+(1-a)\hat{Y}_{t-1}\right]\frac{I_t}{I_{t-1}}.$$

The approach used to treat seasonal variations consists of the following:

1. Deseasonalize the past data.
2. Apply the forecasting method to the deseasonalized data.
3. Reseasonalize the forecast obtained.

Dividing the actual or forecasted demand by the seasonal index has the effect of deseasonalizing the demand. Multiplying the deseasonalized demand by the seasonal index provides the seasonal correction to the forecasted demand.

For forecasting more than one period into the future the forecast is determined as follows:

$$\hat{Y}_{t+n} = \hat{Y}_t \frac{I_{t+n}}{I_t} \qquad \text{for} \quad n \le m,$$

where n is the future period for which a forecast is desired.

EWMA with Trend and Seasonal Corrections

If both trend and seasonal effects are evident, the exponential smoothing model is as follows:

$$\hat{Y}_t = \left[\frac{aY_{t-1}}{I_{t-1}} + \frac{(1-a)(\hat{Y}_{t-1} + T_{t-1})}{I_{t-1}} \right] I_t$$

$$= \left[aY_{t-1} + (1-a)(\hat{Y}_{t-1} + T_{t-1}) \right] \frac{I_t}{I_{t-1}}.$$

When seasonal effects are evident, the trend must also be modified to a deseasonalized condition. The new formulation is as follows:

$$T_t = b\left[\frac{\hat{Y}_t}{I_t} - \frac{\hat{Y}_{t-1}}{I_{t-1}} \right] + (1-b)T_{t-1}.$$

By dividing the forecasts by their respective seasonal indices, the forecasts are deseasonalized and the trend effect is not confounded with the seasonal effect.

The existence of a trend does not modify the smoothing routine for the seasonal index. The smoothing formula for the index is the same as in the last section:

$$I_{t+m} = \left[\frac{cY_t}{\hat{Y}_t} + (1-c) \right] I_t.$$

For forecasting more than one period into the future the forecast is determined as follows:

$$\hat{Y}_{t+n} = \left(\hat{Y}_t + nT_t\right)\frac{I_{t+n}}{I_t} \qquad \text{for} \quad n \le m,$$

where n is the future period for which a forecast is desired.

EXAMPLE 5

From the data given in Example 3 develop an EWMA model with trend and seasonal corrections for 19X2 from the data for 19X0 and 19X1. Assume $a=0.1$, $b=0.1$, $c=0.3$, $\hat{Y}_0=220$, and $T_0=0$.

The seasonal indices are developed in Table 11. We have

$$\text{Average monthly demand} = \frac{2260}{12} = 188.3.$$

In Table 12 the new seasonal index I_{t+m} for January of the following year is obtained as follows:

$$I_{t+m} = \left[\frac{cY_t}{\hat{Y}_t} + (1-c)\right]I_t = \left[\frac{0.3(225)}{220} + (1-0.3)\right]1.049 = 1.056.$$

The forecasted demand for February is obtained in the following manner:

$$\hat{Y}_t = \left[aY_{t-1} + (1-a)\left(\hat{Y}_{t-1} + T_{t-1}\right)\right]\frac{I_t}{I_{t-1}}$$

$$= [0.1(225) + (1-0.1)(220+0)]\frac{1.046}{1.049} = 219.87$$

Table 11

Month	Demand			Seasonal Index
	19X0	19X1	Average	I_t
January	180	215	197.5	1.049
February	186	208	197.0	1.046
March	179	195	187.0	0.993
April	170	200	185.0	0.982
May	170	194	182.0	0.966
June	165	185	175.0	0.930
July	155	180	167.5	0.889
August	150	180	165.0	0.876
September	170	181	175.5	0.932
October	192	205	198.5	1.054
November	195	225	210.0	1.115
December	205	235	220.0	1.168
Total			2260.0	

Table 12

Month	Demand	Trend	Seasonal Index		Forecast	Deviation
t	Y_t	T_t	I_t	I_{t+m}	$\hat{Y}_t$	$\hat{Y}_t - Y_t$
January	225	0	1.049	1.056	220.00	−5.0
February	225	0.048	1.046	1.053	219.87	−5.13
March	215	0.096	0.993	1.001	209.26	−5.74
April	225	0.153	0.982	1.007	207.59	−17.41
May	210	0.329	0.966	0.972	206.06	−3.94
June	200	0.368	0.930	0.931	199.04	−0.96
July	204	0.377	0.889	0.908	190.68	−13.32
August	195	0.527	0.876	0.884	189.53	−5.47
September	210	0.591	0.932	0.942	202.74	−7.26
October	220	0.667	1.054	1.039	230.70	+10.70
November	240	0.555	1.115	1.110	243.55	+3.55
December	250	0.513	1.168	1.161	255.28	+5.28
January			1.056		229.21	

(Note that all fractions on forecasted demand are rounded to the next whole number.) The trend for February is obtained as follows:

$$\begin{aligned} T_t &= b\left[\frac{\hat{Y}_t}{I_t} - \frac{\hat{Y}_{t-1}}{I_{t-1}}\right] + (1-b)T_{t-1} \\ &= 0.1\left[\frac{219.87}{1.046} - \frac{220}{1.049}\right] + (1-0.1)0 \\ &= 0.048. \end{aligned}$$

All other values in the above table are determined in a similar fashion for the appropriate period. The advantages of using a computer should be apparent from the tedium of the numerous computations.

A summary of the EWMA models outlined in this chapter is contained in Table 13.

EWMA Overview

EWMA facilitates computation and reduces data storage requirements, which are important when many series are being forecasted. Exponential smoothing is computationally simpler and requires much less data retention than other techniques. In numerous instances, the forecast variable is serially correlated.[3] In other words, demand in the present period is closely

[3]Autocorrelation analysis, which is beyond the scope of this chapter, will reveal the existence of trends or seasonality in data.

Table 13. EWMA Models

EWMA Variable	Time Series Components			
	Random	Random/Trend	Random/Seasonal	Random/Trend/Seasonal
Forecast model $\hat{Y}_t$	$aY_{t-1}+(1-a)\hat{Y}_{t-1}$	$aY_{t-1}+(1-a)(\hat{Y}_{t-1}+T_{t-1})$	$[a(Y_{t-1})+(1-a)\hat{Y}_{t-1}]\frac{I_t}{I_{t-1}}$	$[aY_{t-1}+(1-a)(\hat{Y}_{t-1}+T_{t-1})]\frac{I_t}{I_{t-1}}$
Trend adjustment T_t	0	$b(\hat{Y}_t-\hat{Y}_{t-1})+(1-b)T_{t-1}$	0	$b\left[\frac{\hat{Y}_t}{I_t}-\frac{\hat{Y}_{t-1}}{I_{t-1}}\right]+(1-b)T_{t-1}$
Seasonal adjustment I_{t+m}	0	0	$\left[\frac{cY_t}{\hat{Y}_t}+(1-c)\right]I_t$	$\left[\frac{cY_t}{\hat{Y}_t}+(1-c)\right]I_t$
Multiperiod forecast $\hat{Y}_{t+n}$	$\hat{Y}_t$	$\hat{Y}_t+nT_t$	$\hat{Y}_t\frac{I_{t+n}}{I_t}$	$(\hat{Y}_t+nT_t)\frac{I_{t+n}}{I_t}$

and naturally related to demand in the previous period. EWMA is an excellent tool for treating serially correlated data, since it gives the heaviest weight to the most recent historical data.

EWMA is one of the simplest yet most flexible methods of forecasting demand from past observations. It is simple by comparison with the moving average in that it requires only two multiplications and one addition, and only two data in the simplest form. It is flexible in that the weight assigned can be easily changed or revised.

Considerable efforts have been made to obtain the best exponential smoothing constants (a, b, and c). The techniques tend to involve enumerative computer programs that analyze past sales history and determine the best smoothing constants by a trial and error method. For data with no trend or seasonal effects, the only parameter needed is a. Since $0 \leq a \leq 1$, the best parameter value can be approximated by selecting the lowest mean absolute deviation (MAD) from testing a in 0.05 increments. Many analysts recommend that the smoothing factor be in the range from 0.05 to 0.30. When more than one smoothing factor is required, different possible combinations can be tested to obtain the combinations with the least MAD. Manually, the process is very tedious, but with a computer it is not difficult.

In selecting a forecasting technique, it is common to apply numerous techniques to historical data and determine which technique best fits the data. A common criterion is to select the technique with the smallest mean absolute deviation. The errors or deviations for each period are obtained by subtracting the actual demand from the forecasted demand. The *absolute* sum of deviations is used in place of the *algebraic* sum of deviations because it is possible to obtain zero as the sum of algebraic deviations even when the individual deviations are large. This situation is remedied by using the absolute deviation without regard to its sign. Once the specific technique is adopted, the algebraic sum of errors is also used to detect any positive or negative bias in the forecast.

The error in the forecast is defined as the difference between the forecasted demand level and the actual demand level. If the error terms are plotted for a large number of forecasts, a frequency distribution is generated. The distribution of forecast errors should approximate the normal distribution. The dispersion (variability) of the error about the mean error (the mean error should be zero if forecast errors are normally distributed) can be expressed in a common form such as the variance, standard deviation, or mean absolute deviation. The mean absolute deviation is the most readily available measure of dispersion used in EWMA analysis.

The forecasting model having the lowest MAD over a period of time is most desirable. Concurrently, the algebraic sum of errors should cancel out (be at the zero level) over a period of time so no bias remains in the distribution of forecast errors. The algebraic sum of errors helps to indicate how well the forecasting system is estimating demand. When the forecast fails to respond to changes in demand, the sum grows larger and larger in a positive or negative direction. Negative errors indicate that demand is rising faster than the forecast and a larger smoothing constant is indicated. Positive errors indicate a decreasing demand, which may necessitate a smaller smoothing constant.

After a forecasting model has been selected, it is necessary to monitor its performance. A tracking signal can be used to indicate when the forecasting model should be revised. A tracking signal will indicate when a basic change in demand dictates a revision in the forecasting model parameters. It is simply a method of evaluating when a forecast exceeds a tolerable error limit. The tracking signal is calculated by the following formula:

$$\text{Tracking signal} = \frac{\text{algebraic sum of forecast errors}}{\text{MAD}} = \frac{\sum(\text{forecast errors})}{\text{MAD}}.$$

The tracking signal will be used with management established limits, upper and lower. For example, management may determine that a forecast is acceptable as long as the sum of forecast errors does not exceed three MAD (management established tracking signal is three). The tracking signal is automatically reviewed each period and a forecast revision issued if necessary.

Demand patterns for items are subject to change over a product's life cycle. Such changes dictate revisions of the forecasting model. There are many tests that can indicate the need for a permanent change, but usually a plot of the demand will suffice. Also, there are usually external environmental conditions that cause the demand changes, and managers are well aware of their existence and influence.

Sales promotions as well as other factors influence a forecast to such an extent that predictions based on intuitive judgments and experience may override a statistical extrapolation of past data. Forecasts cannot properly estimate future demand when promotional activities are involved. Special promotions and advertisement may produce an "artificial seasonal" effect. They can also borrow sales from the future and cause cycles. When past data contain unusual promotional effects, it is a good idea to "depromotionalize" the data to a normal level.

When the forecast is for many periods ahead, the exponentially weighted moving average can be a perilous technique. The use of a short term forecasting technique for a long time ahead assumes a stability that may not occur. The longer the projection, the less reliable the forecast becomes.

Time series analysis is best suited to items that have a continuous demand. For items with a discrete or lumpy demand, this mode of forecasting is inadequate. Lumpy demand exists when demand is at a low level or quite likely to be zero. For low volume demand items a probabilistic approach based on expected demand or marginal analysis is more appropriate. Christmas trees, seasonal agriculture items, high fashion apparel, and repair maintenance items are examples of lumpy demand items.

In the EWMA only one way of handling trend and seasonality was considered. Trend was considered a linear or additive component, and seasonality was considered as a multiplicative or index component. There are situations where trend might be considered as a constant percentage growth component, and seasonality might be applied as an additive component rather than a function of the level itself. There are other extensions that can be included in EWMA. The particular parameters to apply to the forecasting model are a function of demand behavior, and experimentation with the data is necessary before specific models are adopted. Forecasting model selection is a tailoring process.

Box-Jenkins Models

The most sophisticated time series analysis method is that of Box and Jenkins. The Box-Jenkins procedure is a systematic method that does not assume any specific model, but analyzes historical data in order to determine a suitable model. Their generalized model is called the *autoregressive integrated moving average model* (ARIMA). It consists of several possible separate model combinations. With statistical aids, an analyst rationally eliminates inappropriate model combinations until he is left with an appropriate model. The experience and judgement of the analyst are an important part of the selection process. The ARIMA methodology consists of three steps:

1. Identification of a tentative forecast model.
2. Estimation of parameters for the identified model.
3. Diagnostic checking of the estimated model to determine its appropriateness.

An *autoregressive* model assumes that current data values are dependent on their past values. This means that current performance is a function of past performance. Such a model contains an autoregressive coefficient displaying the portion of the last period's performance affecting or explaining the current period's performance. The autoregressive coefficient is analogous to the slope in traditional regression analysis. A *moving average model* assumes that current data values are dependent on forecast errors of prior periods. The forecast error is the difference between the forecasted value and the actual results. This means that current performance is a function of the difference between the previous period's performance and its forecast. The moving average coefficient represents the proportional effect of deviations from the prior period's forecast on current performance. An *integrated model* is one for which the data have been adjusted for trend and/or seasonality. A given time series may be represented by an autoregressive model, a moving average model, or a mixed autoregressive integrated moving average model. The Box-Jenkins three-step procedure is designed to develop the ARIMA model that best describes the time series to be forecasted.

While the Box-Jenkins procedure can be effective in short-term forecasting, it has not been widely applied to individual item inventory control. The procedure requires large amounts of data for proper use, the tools are difficult to master, and the data must be transformed to achieve stationarity. It is more expensive than exponential smoothing. It is useful where only a few times series need to be forecasted and the extra expense is warranted.

SOLICITING OPINIONS

A subjective approach to forecasting involves the solicitation of opinions concerning future levels of demand from customers, retailers, wholesalers, salesmen, and managers. Through interviews and market research, estimates of future demand can be obtained from customers, wholesalers, and retailers. There are difficulties to this approach, since customers do not always do what they say, and it is not uncommon to obtain a broad spectrum of conflicting opinion.

If a sufficient history of past demand is not available, then forecasts must be based on market potential studies, general surveys, and whatever parallel experiences are available. These factors are then combined with selected experiences, insights, and intuitions. Internal opinions can be secured from salesmen and managers. Each salesman may be asked to estimate future volume in his territory, and the estimates of all salesmen can be added to obtain a forecast for the entire company. This collective opinion approach is frequently used for new products with no sales history, but it becomes ineffective as the length of the forecast horizon is increased.

This less elaborate and less technical approach makes use of the qualitative knowledge of people in the field and the home office. Forecasts of this type tend to be heavily influenced by immediate events. Also, when an estimate is developed from collective opinion, the final result may be more the opinions of a few influential or persuasive individuals rather than those from which it was drawn.

The Delphi technique is designed to remedy some of the problems which arise in consensus forecasts. The technique attempts to maximize the advantages of group dynamics while minimizing the problems caused by dominant personalities and silent experts. An iterative procedure is employed to develop forecasts from forecasters (experts) on an individual by individual basis. Each expert develops his forecast to a well-defined event individually, without contact with other experts. The responses are summarized statistically and returned to the experts. The experts revise their forecasts, and the procedure is repeated until consensus is achieved. The Delphi technique has been used in forecasting future technological events, but it can also be adapted to other forecasting problems.

Formal, statistical approaches are more appropriate for routine, short-term demand forecasting. Soliciting opinions is not particularly suited for this application, since it takes too long to develop a forecast for each time and the cost per forecast is prohibitive. Thus this technique is applied more succussfully to predict long-term trends, for new product forecasting, or for aggregate product groups.

ECONOMIC INDICATORS

Economic indicators are frequently used to predict future demand. The knowledge of one variable is used to predict the value of another (prediction by association). The decision maker searches for an economic indicator (gross national product, personal income, bank deposits, freight car loadings, etc.) that has a relationship with the forecast variable.[4] A cause-effect relationship is not necessarily implied between the indicator and the forecast variable.

The simplest type of relationship is a linear association. Regression analysis by the least squares method will fit a straight line to a plot of data from two variables. The line fitted by the method of least squares will be such that the sum of the squares of the deviations about the line is less than the sum of the squares of the deviations about any other line. A linear function has the form

$$Y=\alpha+\beta X,$$

where

Y= dependent variable (variable to be forecasted),

X= independent variable (economic indicator),

α= intercept,

β= slope.

The parameters α and β are estimated from the following formulas:

$$\alpha=\bar{Y}-\beta\bar{X}=\frac{\sum Y-\beta\sum X}{n},$$

$$\beta=\frac{n\left(\sum XY\right)-\left(\sum X\right)\left(\sum Y\right)}{n\sum X^2-\left(\sum X\right)^2}.$$

With the simple regression analysis, the forecaster seeks to discover those variables which have the greatest impact on the forecast variable. What

[4]Sources of information on economic indicators include the Federal Reserve Board, Department of Commerce, Department of Labor, trade associations, and university bureaus of business research. Publications such as the *Survey of Current Business*, *Federal Reserve Bulletin*, and *Monthly Labor Review* are typical sources of economic indicators.

linear regression analysis does is to compute a line which comes closer to connecting the observed points than any other line which could be drawn. It may be used to estimate the relationship between any two or more variables.

A statistic that indicates how well a regression explains or fits the observed data is the correlation coefficient, which ranges between -1 and $+1$. A high absolute value indicates a high degree of association, while a small absolute value indicates little association between variables. When the coefficient is positive, one variable tends to increase as the other increases. When the coefficient is negative, one variable tends to decrease as the other increases. The correlation coefficient is given by

$$r^2=\frac{\left(\sum xy\right)^2}{\left(\sum x^2\right)\left(\sum y^2\right)},$$

where

r = simple correlation coefficient,

$x=X-\bar{X}$,

$y=Y-\bar{Y}$.

The decision maker can verify the statistical significance of any derived simple correlation coefficient by using standard statistical tests found in many texts. A simple t-test can be used to verify if a correlation coefficient differs significantly from zero.

EXAMPLE 6

Find the least square regression line and the coefficient of correlation of Y on X from the following data:

Y	68	66	68	65	69	66	68	65	71	67	68	70
X	65	63	67	64	68	62	70	66	68	67	69	71

The calculations are shown in Tables 14 and 15. We have

$$\alpha=\frac{\sum Y-\beta\sum X}{n}=\frac{811-0.476(800)}{12}=35.85,$$

$$\beta=\frac{n\left(\sum XY\right)-\left(\sum X\right)\left(\sum Y\right)}{n\sum X^2-\left(\sum X\right)^2}=\frac{12(54{,}107)-(800)(811)}{12(53{,}418)-(800)^2}=0.476,$$

$$Y=\alpha+\beta X=35.85+0.476X,$$

$$r^2=\frac{\left(\sum xy\right)^2}{\left(\sum x^2\right)\left(\sum y^2\right)}=\frac{(40.34)^2}{(84.68)(38.92)}=0.4938,$$

$r=0.7027$ = coefficient of correlation.

Table 14

Y	X	X^2	XY	Y^2
68	65	4,225	4,420	4,624
66	63	3,969	4,158	4,356
68	67	4,489	4,556	4,624
65	64	4,096	4,160	4,225
69	68	4,624	4,692	4,761
66	62	3,844	4,092	4,356
68	70	4,900	4,760	4,624
65	66	4,356	4,290	4,225
71	68	4,624	4,828	5,041
67	67	4,489	4,489	4,489
68	69	4,761	4,692	4,624
70	71	5,041	4,970	4,900
$\sum Y=811$	$\sum X=800$	$\sum X^2=53{,}418$	$\sum XY=54{,}107$	$\sum Y^2=54{,}849$

Many organizations are sensitive to broad economic trends, but finding a particular indicator of how operations will react to economic pressures can be a challenging task. Industrial sales tend to be sensitive to the GNP, but consumer sales are more sensitive to disposable income. There is even a class of products that behave oppositely to the general movement of the national economy. The availability and cost of complementary and substitute products can compound the economic indicator relationship.

An economic indicator for a given period will be known only after the period has ended, too late to permit its use to predict sales for that period. An ideal indicator is one that leads the forecast variable. If no lag exists, a forecasted value of the economic indicator can be used for prediction.

Table 15

Y	X	$x=X-\bar{X}$	$y=Y-\bar{Y}$	x^2	xy	y^2
68	65	−1.7	0.4	2.89	−0.68	0.16
66	63	−3.7	−1.6	13.69	5.92	2.56
68	67	0.3	0.4	0.09	0.12	0.16
65	64	−2.7	−2.6	7.29	7.02	6.76
69	68	1.3	1.4	1.69	1.82	1.96
66	62	−4.7	−1.6	22.09	7.52	2.56
68	70	3.3	0.4	10.89	1.32	0.16
65	66	−0.7	−2.6	0.49	1.82	6.76
71	68	1.3	3.4	1.69	4.42	11.56
67	67	0.3	−0.6	0.09	−0.18	0.36
68	69	2.3	0.4	5.29	0.92	0.16
70	71	4.3	2.4	18.49	10.32	5.76
$\sum Y=811$	$\sum X=800$			$\sum x^2=84.68$	$\sum xy=40.34$	$\sum y^2=38.92$
$\bar{Y}=67.6$	$\bar{X}=66.7$					

An indicator is referred to as leading, coincident, or lagging depending on whether it precedes, parallels, or follows in time the demand it is being used to forecast. It is desirable to use leading indicators.

Multiple linear regression deals with the relationship between the dependent variable (variable to be predicted) and two or more independent variables (variables used to make the prediction). The difference between a simple linear regression and a multiple linear regression is in the number of independent variables used in the analysis. For example, for two independent variables the linear regression equation would be

$$Y=\alpha+\beta_1 X_1+\beta_2 X_2.$$

In multiple linear regression analysis, more than one independent variable is used to forecast the dependent variable. An F-test is conducted on the multivariate model to determine if the model significantly forecasts the dependent variable.[5] In multiple linear regression analysis, the simple correlation coefficient is replaced with partial correlation coefficients. Partial correlation coefficients indicate the influence of each individual independent variable on the dependent variable while all other independent variables are held statistically constant. The significance of each independent variable is revealed by a t-test.[5] An insignificant t-test means that an independent variable does not significantly aid in the forecast of the dependent variable. In determining the multiple correlation coefficient, only those independent variables that have a significant partial correlation coefficient should be included.

With multiple regression analysis, the problem of multicollinearity can arise. Multicollinearity is the situation where there is intercorrelation between independent variables. When two or more of the independent variables are highly correlated, you are in effect using the variable twice. In this situation, the forecaster simply deletes one of the related variables.

In many cases, the relationship between variables is nonlinear or curvilinear and a more complex type of analysis is required. Straight lines, polynomials, and logarithmic functions are frequently used when trends or growth patterns are present; trigonometric functions (sines and cosines) can be used when cyclic tendencies are present.

It is seldom practical to use economic indicators for item forecasts. They are usually used to forecast product groups or aggregate dollar demand for an organization. Time series analysis is much more practical for item-by-item forecasting.

[5]The F-test and t-test determine if the regression coefficients are significant. The F-test determines if $\beta_1=\beta_2=\beta_3=\cdots=\beta_n=0$, and the t-test individually determines if $\beta_1=0$, $\beta_2=0$, $\beta_3=0,\ldots,\beta_n=0$.

ECONOMETRIC MODELS

An econometric model is usually a set of simultaneous equations that explain the interactions of variables involved in a business situation. The models attempt to show the relationships between relevant variables such as supply, demand, prices, and purchasing power of the consumer. The models can become quite complex, since they analyze the causative forces operating on the variable to be predicted. Usually, they require forecasts of a number of structural variables.

The structural relationships of econometric models can be grouped into four categories—behavioral, technical, institutional, and identities. *Behavioral* relationships include supply curves, demand curves, and other curves that reflect the behavior of particular economic units (consumers, business firms). *Technical* relationships are mainly production functions that show input-output relationships as constrained by technology. *Institutional* relationships are specified by law or regulatory agencies and indicate the boundaries of acceptable social behavior (taxes, minimum wages). *Identities* specify balance relationships such as the definition of the gross national product (GNP), which is the sum of personal consumption expenditures, gross private capital formation, government purchases of goods and services, and net foreign trade.

A variant of econometric analysis is input-output forecasting models. These models consider intraperiod as well as interperiod dependences between sectors of the economy. Econometric textbooks are devoted to model development in this area.

In order to capture all the interactions, the econometric model must have many equations. Once a model is developed, its entire structure is known and its assumptions are in full view. Over a period of time, the model can be refined by new research. An econometric model may become very complex, because the phenomenon it is attempting to describe is not simple. As more equations are added, the model becomes cumbersome in both the initial estimation and the required maintenance.

A possible way to estimate future product demand is to first determine the customers, their uses of the product, how much they need for each use, and when they will order the product. A mathematical model can then be built relating all the relevant factors. Because of the number and complexity of factors, a complete model is seldom possible. Approximate models can be built that are worthwhile. A difficulty with this approach is the cost as well as the time consumed in model development.

Econometric analysis requires a highly specialized professional staff as well as a computer. Thus it can be very expensive and is usually confined to large organizations. Of course, the selection of a forecasting technique should not be based on cost alone, but on a cost-benefit analysis.

CONCLUSION

Forecasting is predicting, projecting, or estimating some future event or condition which is outside of an organization's control. While forecasting is not planning, it is an indispensable input into planning. Planning sets goals and develops alternative strategies to attain goals. Forecasting deals with the realm of matters outside of management's control. Organizations forecast so they can plan and help shape their future. Based on forecasts of future conditions, plans and policies can be developed to respond to future opportunities and react to future problems.

A demand forecast is the link between external factors in the organization's environment and its internal structure. Determination of the types of forecasts required and the establishment of procedures governing their generation are fundamental steps in the structure of a well-conceived organization. Forecast techniques depend very much on the number of items being controlled and on the type of operating system. Forecasts need to be made on a routine basis, so the techniques must accommodate the available staff skills as limited by the available computing facilities.

The forecasting of independent demand items is required for supply to be maintained in anticipation of demand. A forecast is important when an advance commitment (to procure or to manufacture) has to be made. From the forecasts, operational plans are developed. The less flexibility there is in subsequently modifying original plans, the more important the dependability and accuracy of the forecast. There has been a substantial increase in the availability of sophisticated forecasting techniques, but increases in forecasting effectiveness have not been as pronounced. Unfortunately, poor forecasts are often a fact of life. Refinements in forecasting techniques are frequently less important than the development of operational flexibility to be able to live with poor forecasts.

Some useful generalizations about forecasting are as follows:

1. Forecasts are almost always wrong.
2. Long range forecasts are less accurate than short term forecasts.
3. Aggregate forecasts for families or groups of products are usually more accurate than item forecasts.
4. Only independent demand items should be forecasted; dependent demand items can be calculated.

A forecast is only an estimate of expected demand; actual and forecasted demand cannot be expected to agree precisely. Forecasts are only "ballpark" figures that permit the planning function to commence. Frustration should not result from the inability to predict the future precisely. However, with a properly designed forecasting system, uncertainty is kept to a measurable minimum.

Forecasters can be somewhat more confident about a range of values than about a single point forecast. A good forecast usually includes not only a single estimate, but an estimate of the magnitude of likely deviations as a guide to the comparative reliability of the forecast. Deviation is usually expressed by developing the best single estimate (expected value) and then establishing limits above and below that indicate the range of likely variation.

The tracking (forecast errors) of a forecast model is needed to verify the continued integrity of the model. Forecasting models do not ensure reliability in perpetuity and must be revised when they are no longer appropriate. The tracking of a model can provide numerous benefits to management; it can:

1. indicate the reliability of the existing model,
2. provide the criterion for forecast model selection,
3. facilitate selection of parameters (months in moving average, or EWMA smoothing constant),
4. assist in establishing safety stock levels.

Reducing forecast errors requires increasing expenditures on forecasting techniques. Eventually one reaches a point of diminishing returns, and a perfect forecast is in any case an impossibility. Frequently, a much better investment is the development of operational and production flexibility that permits a rapid redeployment of resources in light of market changes.

Forecasting is an ongoing process that requires maintenance, revision, and modifications. The most obvious time to revise a forecast is when it is in error. Some techniques have built-in warning signals that indicate a departure from some predetermined tolerance range. Other techniques require personal surveillance to give the signal. Either way, the existence of the error should be communicated along with the causal relationships.

It is impossible to design rules and forecasting models that will cover every eventuality. The design is primarily concerned with routine, repetitive situations. Unusual situations that cannot be anticipated must result in a managerial override or interrupt. The computer can handle the routine occurrences, and man (manager) can devote his skill and experience to the nonroutine ones.

The techniques outlined herein are not intended to be exhaustive, but only to summarize prevalent categories. The imagination and ingenuity of a forecaster are vital ingredients in the design of forecasting systems. Although precise mathematical formulas give the impression that forecasting is a science, it still remains an art with a tenuous scientific superstructure.

QUESTIONS

1. What is a forecast?

2. Name the four basic demand forecast techniques.

3. What is a time series?

4. Name five components into which time series data are usually decomposed for analysis.

5. Name five of the most common time series analysis techniques.

6. What are the basic limitations of the arithmetic average for forecasting?

7. Which exhibits a greater degree of linear association, a correlation coefficient of $+1$ or a correlation coefficient of -1?

8. What is meant by saying time series data are autocorrelated?

9. Why does the exponentially weighted moving average (EWMA) not require the keeping of a long historical record?

10. What is a common criterion for selecting a forecast technique?

11. Name two difficulties associated with the solicitation of opinions for forecasting.

12. Give four examples of economic indicators that might be used to predict future demand.

13. What is an econometric model?

14. Into what four categories can the structural relationships of econometric models be grouped? Give examples of each.

15. Name forecasting techniques that might be used for established products.

16. What are some of the considerations to be made in the selection of a forecasting model?

PROBLEMS

1. From the data below, determine the sum of absolute deviations for the last period demand forecasting method. What is the forecast for month 13?

Month	Demand Units	Forecast	Absolute Deviation
1	500		
2	510		
3	480		
4	600		
5	600		
6	660		
7	590		
8	700		
9	680		
10	740		
11	790		
12	760		

2. From the data in Problem 1, determine the sum of absolute deviations for the three month average forecasting method. What is the forecast for month 13?

3. From the data in Problem 1, determine the sum of absolute deviations for an EWMA with $a=0.1$ (assume forecasted demand for month 1 is the same as actual demand). What is the forecast for month 13?

4. If $\hat{Y}_{t-1}=40$ and $Y_{t-1}=30$, show the effects of the smoothing constants $a=0.1$, 0.5, and 0.8 on the new average forecast.

5. Determine the linear regression equations for the data given below:

Month	1	2	3	4	5	6
Demand	30	40	40	50	55	60

What is the forecast for month 7?

6. From the data given in Problem 5, determine the standard deviation of the regression line. What is the correlation coefficient?

7. From the demand data given below, develop a trend adjusted exponentially weighted forecasted with $a=0.2, b=0.1, T_0=0, \hat{Y}_0=75$.

19X4

Month	Demand	Month	Demand
Jan.	76	July	86
Feb.	79	Aug.	81
March	84	Sept.	84
April	87	Oct.	80
May	83	Nov.	79
June	92	Dec.	78

8. Using the data from Problem 7, forecast the trend adjusted demand for March 19X5 only. What assumption is made when forecasting several periods into the future?

9. Using the demand data below, develop an EWMA model with trend and seasonal correction for 19X4. Assume $a=0.2$, $b=0.1$, $c=0.2$, $T_0=0$, and $\hat{Y}_0=79$.

	Demand		
Month	19X2	19X3	19X4
1	76	78	80
2	79	81	82
3	84	82	86
4	87	86	91
5	83	80	87
6	92	90	99
7	86	95	96
8	81	89	89
9	84	90	90
10	80	78	93
11	79	85	84
12	78	81	82

10. Using the demand figures from Problem 9 for months 1, 2, 3, and 4 of 19X2, show the effects of the trend smoothing constants $b=0.2$, 0.6, and 0.9 on the forecast when $a=0.2$, $T_0=0$, and $Y_0=75$.

11. Using the data from Problem 9, develop a trend and seasonal adjusted forecast for month 3 of 19X5.

12. If $\hat{Y}_{t-1}=84$ and $Y_{t-1}=68$, what are the forecasts for $a=0.2$? $a=0.4$? $a=0.7$?

13. Determine the linear regression equation for the following data:

Month	1	2	3	4	5	6	7	8	9	10	11	12
Demand	41	46	46	47	48	53	55	55	60	61	63	69

What is the forecast for the next period?

14. From the data given in Problem 13, determine the standard deviation of the regression line and the correlation coefficient.

CASE 1: A ROCKY ROAD

The Hill Company is a manufacturer of weatherstripping and related products. The company was formed in 1966 to exploit a patent on an improved type of steelbound weatherstripping invented by George Hill. The company is managed by George Hill and his son, Walter. Until recently, their major product was limited to special, high-efficiency applications.

The company has 20 employees, and operations are balanced throughout the year. Traditionally, 70% of sales occurred in the fall of the year. Monthly production quotas were figured by multiplying last year's sales by 1.1 and dividing by 12. Inventories increase during the off seasons and are depleted in the fall. The 10% growth factor has worked fairly well in the past.

Recently, the rising cost of energy has increased the demand for Hill's products significantly. With new building structures requiring better insulation, sales are no longer highly seasonal in the fall. Sales in the off seasons have increased substantially. The work force has been expanded to 30 employees and the single shift operation has been maintained.

The firm was not prepared for the increase in business. Stockouts in both raw materials and finished goods have occurred, and production delays have been encountered. Walter has attempted to adapt his planning to the new conditions, but he has not been very successful. Customers have been willing to accept the inconvenience because there was very little competition available. However, another small firm in the area has started to produce competing products. The sales of the

Hill Company by season for the last four years are as follows:

		Sales			
Year	Total	Spring	Summer	Fall	Winter
19X1	$230,000	$10,000	$10,000	$160,000	$50,000
19X2	250,000	10,000	20,000	170,000	50,000
19X3	450,000	50,000	110,000	200,000	90,000
19X4	640,000	70,000	200,000	240,000	130,000
19X5	800,000[a]				

[a] Forecasted by Walter Hill: 1.25(19X4 sales).

Walter is concerned because the patent on their major product will expire in a few years. Costs are increasing dramatically and must be subjected to tighter control. George has asked his son to evaluate other forecasting approaches. He believes inadequate forecasts have made planning and control impossible. Walter believes there are other more basic difficulties facing the firm.

1. What are the major problems facing the firm?
2. What forecasting techniques might the Hill Company consider?
3. What impact will growth and competition have on the firm?

CASE 2: GO OR NO-GO

Cannon Controls Corporation has just developed a new integrated circuit design, which represents an advance in the state of the art. The new product has wide market application in the electronics industry. The device will be sold at a higher price than conventional design circuits, but it offers significant advantages in size, stability, and reliability. A patent has been applied for.

Market research and test marketing of the product have just been completed in a single test market in one geographic area. The market research was aimed at determining if a breakeven sales volume of four million units per year could be attained. The research indicated with a high level of confidence that at least four million units would be sold. Marketing officials believe that the market will be in the range of six to twelve million units, although this guess is not based on their formal research.

The two distinct industrial markets for the product are to manufacturers of consumer products and to manufacturers of industrial products. The consumer products market will be in radios, televisions, timing devices, and microwave ovens. The industrial products market will be in power generation equipment, calculators, X-ray equipment, measuring devices, and military weapon systems. The industrial products market will account for approximately 70% of sales. General economic conditions will have an important influence on the consumer products market.

Mr. Lewis, the marketing manager, has recommended that a ten million unit production facility be built. Mr. Harris, the controller, has requested that the product be market tested in other geographic areas. Additional market testing will take five months and cost $150,000. After the plant capacity is decided, it will take another six months before the plant is operational. The capital costs for the different size facilities under consideration are as follows:

Production plan	Plant capacity (units)	Estimated capital cost
A	4,000,000	$15,000,000
B	6,000,000	20,000,000
C	8,000,000	24,000,000
D	10,000,000	26,000,000

If the plant is expanded after it is built, the cost will significantly exceed the initial plant costs listed above.

1. Would you recommend that the plant be built at this time? If you do, what plant size would you recommend? Why?
2. If additional market forecasting is necessary, what specific techniques and approaches would you prescribe?
3. Why is Mr. Harris not satisfied with the market test data?

CASE 3: THE NUMBERS GAME

Four major retailing firms that compete with each other traditionally make annual industry sales forecasts. From its industry sales forecasts, each company estimates its own sales and related market share. Each company makes a number of basic forecasting assumptions concerning the general condition of the national economy.

At the end of the current year, total industry sales were $8.5 billion. Using this figure as a starting point, each of the firms will forecast industrywide sales for the coming year. Each firm bases its industrywide forecast on the following three factors:

1. an overall economic growth rate of 6% in GNP,
2. a rise in consumer income of 7%,
3. an increase in consumer credit.

Even though industry forecasts were based on the above factors, there were significant differences in the forecast of each firm. Sales projections were as follows:

Firm A: $10 billion

Firm B: $9

Firm C: $10.5

Firm D: $9.5

1. Why are the forecasts different?
2. What influence do forecasting errors have on an organization?
3. If actual sales are $10.5 billion, will Firm B experience operational difficulties?
4. If actual sales are $9 billion, how will it affect Firm C?

CASE 4: PAINT APPLICATION

Peacock Paint carries four brands of exterior paint in stock throughout the year. Two brands of a superior paint are carried in stock only on a seasonal basis. One of the superior brands, Brand X, is carried during the milder months because of cold weather application problems. The other seasonal paint, Brand Y, is carried only in the winter months, again for application reasons.

The inventory manager realizes that substantial holding cost savings can be gained during periods of zero demand if unneeded stock is eliminated. He is also aware that forecasting demand for the products is critical. He wants to stock only enough paint to last the season and not have excess paint at the end of the season.

Peacock's sales are segmented in two specific consumer categories. Seventy percent of their sales is to local paint contractors, and thirty percent is to "do it yourself" homeowners. The demand forecast for the commercial contractor has proved to be much more stable than for homeowners. This contrast is accentuated by the preference of the private consumer for prime weather conditions. A late fall or early winter can cause significant fluctuations in demand for the two types of paint.

The inventory control manager has been assigned the job of choosing or developing a forecasting technique for Brands X and Y. His first activity was to make up the following table of last year's demand for the paint products:

	Brand X		Brand Y	
Month	Contractors	Homeowners	Contractors	Homeowners
Jan	0[a]	0[a]	200[a]	160[a]
Feb	0	0	150	40
Mar	0	0	60	20
Apr	60	30	10	10
May	80	40	0	0
Jun	120	50	0	0
Jul	110	60	0	0
Aug	100	60	0	0
Sep	90	30	0	0
Oct	50	30	20	10
Nov	0	0	90	60
Dec	0	0	200	80

[a] In gallons.

The inventory manager is asking himself questions such as:

1. Could and should the same technique be applied to both consumer categories?
2. What other information may be useful in choosing a forecasting technique?
3. What technique is the best for forecasting demand for Brands X and Y?

Given this set of circumstances, what should be done to develop a valid forecasting technique for these products? What problems might arise in applying formal forecasting techniques to the paint application problem?

CASE 5: FROZEN IN TIME

The Grimes Company, a manufacturer of heating, air conditioning, and refrigeration products, has five divisions. One of the divisions is responsible for the manufacturing of truck and trailer refrigeration units. Their units are sold to customers nationwide through a dealer organization consisting of approximately 180 authorized dealers.

The continual use of refrigeration units causes parts to wear rapidly, and their replacement is a frequent occurrence. However, intense usage tends to be seasonal. Grimes finds the demand for refrigeration units to coincide with the demand for replacement parts and it uses historical data to forecast both requirements. The type and number of replacement parts to order for the upcoming period is obtained by ordering the number of items sold during that period in the previous year.

Grimes receives component parts from various suppliers: for example, clutches from one supplier, engines from another, and compressors from a third. Components must meet Grimes's specifications. It is often impossible to order parts from another supplier in case of an emergency, because an alternative supplier's part usually does not match the specifications.

Dealer orders for parts are filled from stock carried at Grimes. Grimes orders at quarterly intervals from suppliers. It is common for suppliers not to immediately fill orders. When this happens, Grimes often has backorders to fill for the dealers. During the waiting periods, the dealers have been prone to panic. Because of their uneasiness, the dealers have been increasing, even doubling, their orders to Grimes and are consequently carrying more stock.

Grimes receives component parts from various suppliers: for example, clutches from one supplier, engines from another, and compressors from a third. Components must meet Grimes's specifications. It is often impossible to order parts from another supplier in case of an emergency, because an alternative supplier's part usually does not match the specifications.

1. Is Grimes using an effective method for forecasting demand?
2. What problems are occurring at Grimes?
3. What are the possible solutions?

CASE 6: ABBREVIATED DISCS

Hot Records has been a giant in the music industry since the mid 1960s and has proven to be the leader in annual record sales in the rock and hard rock categories. Hot is the foremost representative for artists introduced in the United States on a nationwide scale. Lately, the company has incurred financial setbacks because of lower than expected album sales. The executives believe that Hot's previously impressive sales growth trend has ended, because they have been unable to sign new artists or get signed artists successfully introduced.

The music industry is suffering for many reasons. A sluggish and inflation-ridden economy, record counterfeiting, rival tape producing companies, high costs of producing and cutting records, and poor quality of records have contributed to the losses. However, the major reason for the decline is the large price charged for long-playing albums. Hot's customers have been wary of expensive albums, even those by major artists. The recordings by new artists arouse even more caution. The average customer is young and unable to afford luxuries during economically hard times.

To resolve the drop in album sales Hot plans to introduce a line of ten-inch records called "shorts." The new product will feature four to six songs, have a running time of twelve to fifteen minutes, and contain previously unreleased material. Hot hopes this shorter format will overcome resistance to purchasing the more expensive long-plays. Figuring that these new records will be eye-catching in their reduced size, less expensive ($3.98 rather than $7.95), and a better quality with a cotton substitute for the expensive petroleum additive, Hot believes it has a winner.

The sole purpose of shifting attention to the ten-inch records is to increase total sales. The expected increase is not precisely known. The executives at Hot feel they can capture a large part of the album buyer's market with their value-oriented addition. They also believe the new discs will serve to introduce new artists who will later record on the expensive long-plays. Even though there is a consensus that the "shorts" are a solution to the sales dilemma, the management staff would like to know how successful this undertaking will be. The staff has decided that forecasting should be done prior to the release. As to the type of forecasting technique, they are perplexed.

Since this is an entirely new line, they realize an exact forecast is impossible. They cannot use any of the methods in practice for their established lines, but they wonder if a modification of one might suffice. One executive has suggested that multiple linear regression, which is used with the regular album line, would be suitable. He feels that the independent variables that affect regular discs, such as the population of the young age group, would be equally significant indicators for the new line. However, he welcomes more input from the managers.

1. Discuss some difficulties in developing forecasts for new products.
2. Could multiple linear regression be a practical forecasting technique for the new line? What other independent variables could be used in the prediction?
3. What other forecasting methods could be applied in this situation?
4. What new product features or considerations could affect the forecast?

SELECTED BIBLIOGRAPHY

Brown, R. G. *Smoothing, Forecasting, and Prediction of Discrete Time Series*, New York: Prentice-Hall, 1963.

———. *Statistical Forecasting for Inventory Control*, New York: McGraw-Hill, 1959.

Bowerman, B. L., and R. T. O'Connell. *Time Series and Forecasting*, North Scituate, MA: Duxbury Press, 1979.

Box, G. E. P., and G. M. Jenkins. *Time Series Analysis: Forecasting and Control*, San Francisco: Holden-Day, 1976.

Chambers, J. C., et al. "How to Choose the Right Forecasting Technique," *Harvard Business Review*, July–August 1971.

Chisholm, R. K., and G. R. Whitaker, Jr. *Forecasting Methods*, Homewood, IL: Irwin 1971.

Fuller, W. A. *Introduction to Statistical Time Series*, New York: Wiley, 1976.

Landau. E. "On the Non-Statistical Aspects of Statistical Forecasting," *American Production and Inventory Control Society Conference Proceedings*, 1976.

Makridakis, S., and S. Wheelwright. *Forecasting Methods and Applications*, New York: Wiley/Hamilton, 1978.

Nelson, C. R. *Applied Time Series for Managerial Forecasting*, San Francisco: Holden-Day, 1973.

Tersine, R. J., and W. Riggs. "The Delphi Technique: A Long Range Planning Tool," *Business Horizons*, Vol. 19, No. 2, 1976.

Tersine, R. J. "Forecasting: Prelude to Managerial Planning," *Managerial Planning*, July–August 1975.

Trigg, D. W., and A. G. Leach. "Exponential Smoothing with an Adaptive Rate," *Operations Research Quarterly*, March 1977.

Wheelwright, S., and S. Makridakis. *Forecasting Methods for Management*, New York: Wiley, 1977.

Whybark, D. C. "A Comparison of Adaptive Forecasting Techniques," *The Logistics and Transportation Review*, Vol. 8, No. 3, 1973.

MATHEMATICAL ABBREVIATIONS AND SYMBOLS USED IN CHAPTER 2

a	Mean exponential smoothing constant between 0 and 1
b	Trend exponential smoothing constant between 0 and 1
c	Seasonal exponential smoothing constant between 0 and 1
EWMA	Exponentially weighted moving average
I_t	Seasonal index for time period t
MAD	Mean absolute deviation
m	Number of periods in seasonal pattern
n	Number of time periods
r	Simple correlation coefficient
S_r	Standard deviation of the regression line
t	Time period
$\bar{t}$	Mean time period
T_t	Trend adjustment for period t
Y_t	Actual demand for period t
$\hat{Y}_t$	Forecasted demand for period t
Y	Dependent variable (variable to be forecasted)
α	Intercept
β	Slope
X	Independent variable (economic indicator)
$\bar{X}$	Mean independent variable

3 Fixed Order Size Systems: Deterministic Models

This chapter introduces quantity-based models for inventory systems that are appropriate when an organization is faced with fairly uniform independent demand and wants to maintain an inventory of the item most of the time. One major reason for having inventory is to enable an organization to buy or produce items in economic lot sizes. The models presented in this chapter determine the economic lot size to obtain when the item is purchased from a vendor or produced internally.

This chapter deals with a special collection of inventory models that are deterministic. The rate of demand for units is assumed to be known with certainty. The replenishment lead time is also a constant without variation and independent of demand. The real world is seldom as well behaved as in deterministic models. Real-world situations are more reasonably described in probabilistic terms. However, deterministic models are frequently excellent approximations or, at least, a good starting point for describing inventory phenomena.

It is often easier to work analytically with inventory models if the variables can be treated as continuous. In numerous cases, inventory demand is sufficiently high that problems caused by discreteness can be ignored and all variables can be treated as continuous. With continuous variables, it is possible to take derivatives instead of dealing with differences.

To determine the optimum inventory policy, information is needed regarding the following parameters:

1. Appropriate costs
2. Forecasts of demand
3. Knowledge of lead times

Figure 1. Fixed order size system.

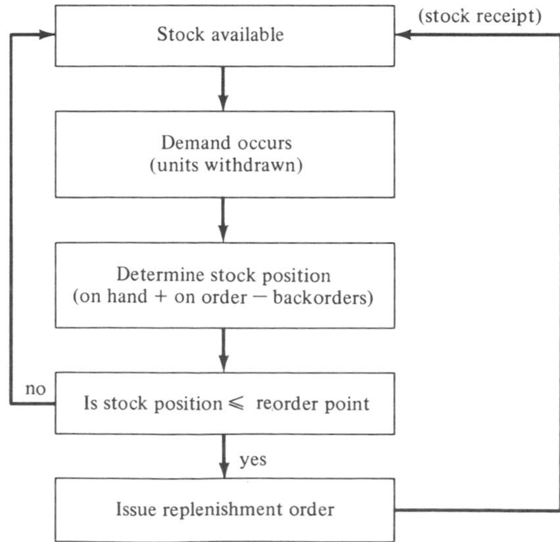

In a fixed order size system, which is also referred to as a perpetual inventory system, the same number of units is always ordered, and the demand rate is constant. An order for a fixed number of units is placed whenever the inventory position reaches a reorder point. A typical fixed order size system is depicted in Figure 1. The fixed order size system is termed a Q-system, since the size of the order (Q) is fixed for each replenishment.

ECONOMIC ORDER QUANTITY (EOQ)—SINGLE ITEMS

The size of an order that minimizes the total inventory cost is known as the economic order quantity (EOQ). The classical inventory model assumes the idealized situations shown in Figure 2, where Q is the order size.[1] Upon receipt of an order, the inventory level is Q units. Units are withdrawn from inventory at a constant demand rate which is represented by the negative-slope lines. When inventory reaches the reorder point, a new order is placed for Q units. After a fixed lead time period, the goods are received and placed in inventory. The vertical lines indicate the receipt of a lot into inventory. The new lot is received just as the inventory level reaches zero, so the average inventory is $(Q+0)/2$ or $Q/2$.

If stockouts are not permitted, the total inventory cost per year is graphically depicted by Figure 3 and by the following formula:[2]

Total annual cost = (purchase cost) + (order cost) + (holding cost)

$$\mathrm{TC}=RP+\frac{RC}{Q}+\frac{QH}{2},$$

where

R = annual demand in units,

P = purchase cost of an item,

C = ordering cost per order,

$H=PF$ = holding cost per unit per year,

Q = lot size or order quantity in units,

F = annual holding cost as a fraction of unit cost.

In effect, the total annual cost equation determines the annual purchase cost by multiplying the annual demand by the purchase cost per unit. The annual order cost is obtained by multiplying the number of orders per year (R/Q) by the cost of placing an order (C). The annual holding cost is the average inventory ($Q/2$) times the annual unit holding cost (H). The sum of the three costs (purchase, order, and holding) will be the total inventory cost per year for any given item.

[1]The classical inventory model is frequently referred to as a sawtooth diagram because of the series of right triangles.

[2]Although we have selected a time period of one year, any time period can be used as long as R and H are on the same time period basis. The model assumes that stockouts will not occur.

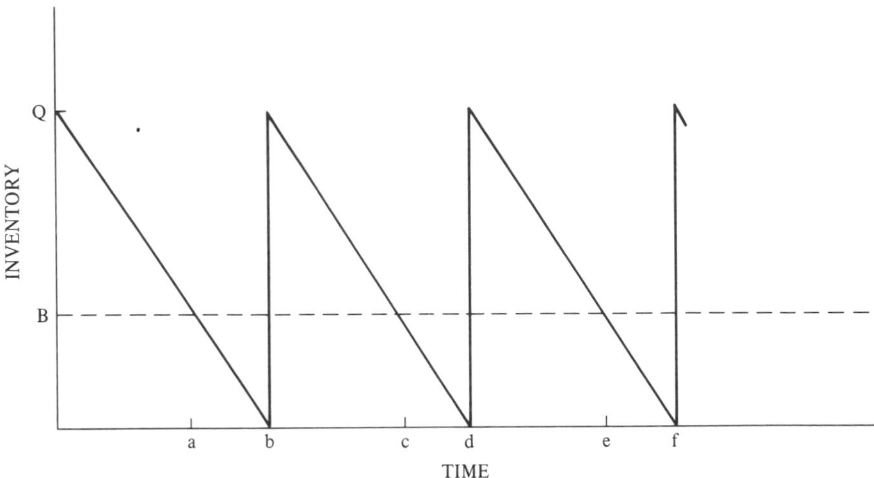

Figure 2. Classical inventory model.
Key: Q=lot size; $Q/2$=average inventory; B=reorder point; ac=ce=interval between orders; ab=cd=ef=lead time.

Figure 3. Annual inventory costs.

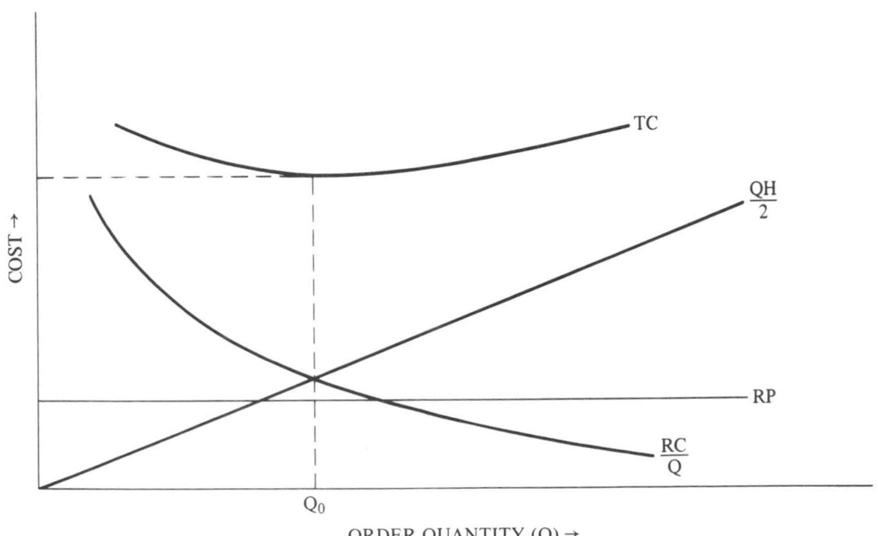

To obtain the minimum cost lot size (EOQ), take the first derivative of total annual cost with respect to the lot size (Q) and set it equal to zero:[3]

$$\frac{d\text{TC}}{dQ}=\frac{H}{2}-\frac{CR}{Q^2}=0.$$

Solving the equation for Q, we get the EOQ formula:

$$Q_0=\sqrt{\frac{2CR}{H}}=\sqrt{\frac{2CR}{PF}}=\text{economic order quantity.}$$

The EOQ results in items with high unit cost being ordered frequently in small quantities (the saving in inventory investment pays for the extra orders); items with low unit cost are ordered in large quantities (the inventory investment is small and the repeated expense of orders can be avoided). If the order cost C is zero, orders are placed to satisfy each demand as it occurs, which results in no holding cost. If the holding cost H is zero, an order (only one) is placed for an amount that will satisfy the lifetime demand for the item. The EOQ formula is based on the assumption that the entire lot is added to stock at one time, and that the stock will be withdrawn at a constant rate.

Once the economic order quantity is known, the expected number of orders placed during the year, n, and the average time between orders, T, can be determined:

$$\text{Expected number of orders during year}=n=\frac{R}{Q_0}=\sqrt{\frac{HR}{2C}},$$

$$\text{Average order interval}=T=\frac{1}{n}=\frac{Q_0}{R}=\sqrt{\frac{2C}{RH}}.$$

The reorder point is obtained by determining the demand that will occur during the lead time period. When the stock position [(on hand)+(on order)−(backorders)] reaches the reorder point, an order will be placed for Q_0 units, the economic order quantity. The following formula gives the reorder point when the lead time L is expressed in months:

$$B=\frac{RL}{12}=\text{reorder point in units.}$$

If the lead time L is expressed in weeks, the reorder point is expressed as

$$B=\frac{RL}{52}=\text{reorder point in units.}$$

The goods are assumed to be received when the last item leaves the inventory, and the inventory level is restored to a level equal to the amount ordered. If the lead time is less than the average order interval ($L<T$), there will never be more than a single order outstanding. If the lead time is

[3]See Appendix A for further clarification of the minimization of a continuous single-variable function.

greater than the average order interval ($L > T$), there will always be at least one order outstanding.

The minimum total cost per year is obtained by putting Q_0 for Q in the total annual cost equation. The following formula for the minimum total cost per year results:

$$\mathrm{TC}_0 = RP + HQ_0.$$

The classical EOQ model assumes a constant demand rate, constant lead time, constant price per unit, fixed order cost per order, fixed holding cost per unit, and the instantaneous receipt of an order. It is based on the situation where demand, lead time, and all relevant costs are known and constant over time. Further, no stockouts will occur—which is reasonable, since the demand and lead time are known and the entire order is received at one time.

EXAMPLE 1

The Williams Manufacturing Company purchases 8000 units of a product each year at a unit cost of $10.00. The order cost is $30.00 per order, and the holding cost per unit per year is $3.00. What are the economic order quantity, the total annual cost, the number of orders to place in one year, and the reorder point when the lead time is 2 weeks?

$$Q_0 = \sqrt{\frac{2CR}{H}} = \sqrt{\frac{2(30)8000}{3}} = 400 \text{ units},$$

$$\mathrm{TC}_0 = RP + HQ_0 = 8000(10) + 3(400) = \$81{,}200,$$

$$n = \frac{R}{Q_0} = \frac{8000}{400} = 20,$$

$$B = \frac{RL}{52} = \frac{8000(2)}{52} = 307.7 \text{ units}.$$

ECONOMIC ORDER QUANTITY (EOQ)—MULTIPLE ITEMS

When numerous items are subjected to EOQ determination, the optimal policy is the sum of the optimal policies for the individual items. The EOQ determination is based on the uniqueness and independence of inventory items. By establishing the EOQ for each item independently of all others, the optimal policy for the total inventory is obtained.

For computerized applications, it is desirable to utilize a real-time computer system. This means that as withdrawals are made from stock, immediately (or nearly so) this information is fed into the computer to reestablish the stock position on each item. When the stock position drops to the reorder level, a purchase requisition is triggered. The age of information is crucial in preventing delays that result in shortages.

BACKORDERING

In the backordering situation, a firm does not lose the sale when its inventory is depleted. The customer waits until the outstanding order arrives and he is served from it. Backordering occurs with loyal, patient, or captive customers. If there were no costs associated with incurring backorders, no inventory would be held. If backorders were very expensive, they would never be incurred. However, there is an intermediate range of backordering costs where it is optimal to incur some backorders towards the end of an inventory cycle.

In this treatment of backordering we assume that all shortages are satisfied from the next shipment. This is referred to as captive demand, as opposed to the situation where unsatisfied demand is totally or partially lost. When the stockout (shortage) cost is finite, an economic advantage may be gained by permitting stockouts to occur. In many cases, the increase in cost due to acceptance of a shortage is more than compensated by the reduction in holding cost.

Figure 4 depicts the backordering inventory model. An order for Q units is placed when the stock on hand reaches the reorder point. The size of the stockout is $Q-V$ units, and the maximum inventory level is V units. The average size of a stockout is $(Q-V)/2$ for each order period. The backordering cost per unit is K.

During time period t_3 one order is placed, so the order cost is C. The average holding cost during period t_1 is given as follows:

$$H\frac{V}{2}t_1=\frac{HV^2}{2R},$$

Figure 4. Backordering inventory model.

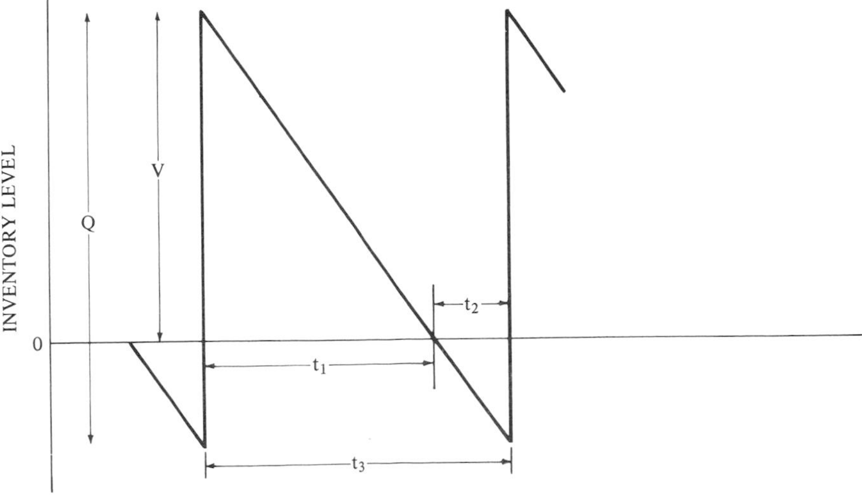

since

$$\frac{R}{1\text{ yr}}=\frac{V}{t_1}; \qquad \text{then} \quad t_1=\frac{V}{R}$$

by similar triangles. t_1 is the time period during which there is a positive inventory balance, and t_2 is the stockout time period. The average backordering cost during t_2 is as follows:

$$\frac{K(Q-V)t_2}{2}=\frac{K(Q-V)^2}{2R},$$

since

$$\frac{R}{1\text{ yr}}=\frac{Q-V}{t_2}; \qquad \text{then} \quad t_2=\frac{Q-V}{R}$$

by similar triangles. Therefore, the total cost for one time period of length t_3 is

$$QP+C+\frac{HV^2}{2R}+\frac{K(Q-V)^2}{2R}.$$

There are R/Q order periods of length t_3 in a year, so the total annual cost is obtained by multiplying the above equation by R/Q, which results in

$$\text{Total annual cost}=(\text{purchase cost})+(\text{order cost})$$
$$+(\text{holding cost})+(\text{backorder cost}),$$

$$\text{TC}=RP+C\frac{R}{Q}+\frac{HV^2}{2Q}+\frac{K(Q-V)^2}{2Q},$$

where

R = annual requirement in units,
P = purchase cost of an item,
C = ordering cost per order,
Q = lot size or order quantity,
H = holding cost per unit per year,
V = maximum inventory level in units,
K = backordering cost per unit per year,
R/Q = number of orders per year.

To obtain optimal values for Q and V, partial derivatives of the total cost with respect to Q and V are equated to zero. The following optimum formulas result:[4]

$$Q_0 = \sqrt{\frac{2CR}{H}}\sqrt{\frac{H+K}{K}},$$

$$V_0 = \sqrt{\frac{2CR}{H}}\sqrt{\frac{K}{H+K}}.$$

The inclusion of backordering cost increases the economic order quantity Q_0, but it also results in a smaller average inventory. When the backordering cost (K) approaches infinity, $\sqrt{(H+K)/K}$ approaches one, and the economic order quantity corresponds to the classical case when there is no backorder, or

$$Q_0 = \sqrt{\frac{2CR}{H}},$$

$$Q_0 - V_0 = 0.$$

When the backordering cost (K) approaches zero, $\sqrt{K/(H+K)}$ approaches zero, and the maximum inventory level becomes zero. This is the situation where all items are backordered or handled on a special order basis, since V_0 equals zero.

When backorders are permitted to exist, the reorder point calculation is modified (reduced by the size of the backorder). The reorder point is the lead time demand minus the number of units backordered, or

$$\text{Reorder point} = (\text{lead time demand}) - (\text{backorders}),$$

$$B = \frac{RL}{N} - (Q - V),$$

where

N = number of operating days per year,

L = lead time in days.

Observe that the reorder point could be negative if the lead time demand were less than the size of the backorder. This situation would result in an order not being placed until a certain number of backorders were obtained. Although the reorder point may be positive or negative with backordering, there will always be a time period in which there is no stock available. When the backordering cost is finite, the reorder point will always be less than the lead time demand.

[4]See Appendix C for derivation of the formulas.

EXAMPLE 2

From the information given in Example 1, what happens to the economic order quantity if backordering is possible and the stockout cost per unit per year is $1.00?

$$Q_0=\sqrt{\frac{2CR}{H}}\sqrt{\frac{H+K}{K}}=\sqrt{\frac{2(30)8000}{3}}\sqrt{\frac{3+1}{1}}=800 \text{ units},$$

$$V_0=\sqrt{\frac{2CR}{H}}\sqrt{\frac{K}{H+K}}=200 \text{ units},$$

$$B=\frac{RL}{52}-(Q-V)=\frac{8000(2)}{52}-600=-292 \text{ units}.$$

The EOQ doubled in size from 400 units to 800 units, but the maximum inventory decreased from 400 to 200 units. No order would be placed until 292 backorder units were accumulated.

QUANTITY DISCOUNTS

In order to induce larger purchases, a supplier often offers a reduced price if amounts greater than some minimum are ordered. This means the price per unit is lower if a large enough order is placed. Should such a discount be taken? There is no problem in the situation where the order quantity exceeds the minimum amount necessary to obtain the discount. In this event, the discount is automatically obtained.

When the order quantity is smaller than the amount necessary for the discount, calculations are necessary to determine if there is a net benefit in increasing the size of the order to obtain the discount. The discount will be taken if the total costs which result from taking the discount are less than those that result from ordering the EOQ. The ordering cost per year will decrease with a discount because less orders will be required, there being more units in each order. The smaller unit price will reduce cost, but the larger number ordered results in more units in inventory. Figure 5 shows a hypothetical situation with two quantity discounts. The advantages of quantity discount purchases are lower unit cost, lower ordering cost per year, fewer stockouts, lower shipping costs, and a hedge against price increases. The disadvantages of quantity discount purchases are a larger inventory, slower inventory turnover, and an older stock.

The basic economic lot size formula assumes a fixed purchase price per unit. With quantity discounts, the traditional EOQ formulation is not adequate. When quantity discounts are offered, the objective function is still to find the minimum cost point on the total cost curve. However, the total cost curve is not continuous, so the first derivative does not indicate the minimum cost point as readily as it does without discounts. The quantity

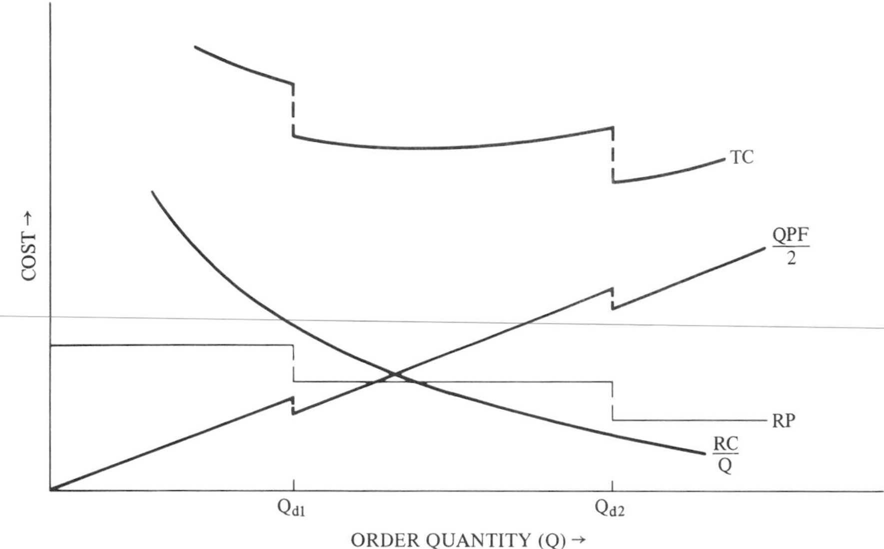

Figure 5. Inventory costs: quantity discounts.

discount creates a discontinuity or disjunction in the total cost curve. The minimum cost point will be either at the point of discontinuity or where the derivatives equal zero as determined by the EOQ.

Figure 6 shows three possible conditions that might exist with a single price quantity discount. Only the solid portion of the total cost curve is relevant; the dashed portion of the curve is not realizable. The solid curve shows the cost function which applies over the entire quantity range. The dashed curve represents extensions of the cost function into nonapplicable

Figure 6. Quantity discounts.
Decision rule: Order the quantity with the lowest cost. *Case 1*: order $> Q_d$; *case 2*: order $= Q_d$; *case 3*: order $< Q_d$.

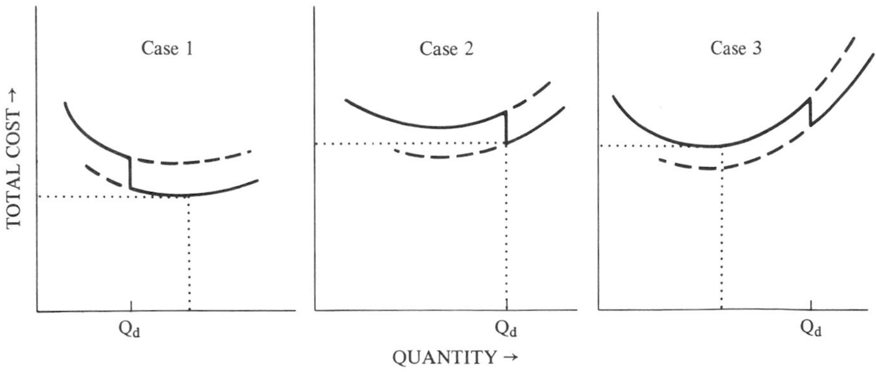

regions. The problem is reduced to finding the lowest point on the curve formed by the solid portions. Because of the discontinuous nature of the curve, the least cost quantity cannot be found by differentiation.

The following procedure indicates how to obtain the minimum cost order quantity when multiple (one or more) quantity discounts are available.[5]

1. Starting with the lowest unit cost, calculate the EOQ at each unit cost until a valid EOQ is obtained (an EOQ is valid if its quantity is equal to or greater than its price-break quantity).
2. Calculate the total annual cost for the valid EOQ and all price-break quantities larger than the valid EOQ. (A price-break quantity is the lowest quantity for which the price discount is available. For the highest unit cost, the price-break quantity is zero.)
3. The minimum cost order quantity is the quantity with the lowest total cost in step 2 above.

It is possible to obtain the economic order quantity with quantity discounts by graphing total cost versus lot size and selecting the minimum cost point. However, the graphical approach is a tedious and time-consuming process.

Quantity discounts do not affect reorder point calculations.

EXAMPLE 3

The Smith Company purchases 8000 units of a product each year. The supplier offers the units for sale at \$10.00 per unit for orders up to 500 units and at \$9.00 per unit for orders of 500 units or more. What is the economic order quantity if the order cost is \$30.00 per order and the holding cost is 30% per unit cost per year?

The total cost for the single price break quantity of 500 units is as follows:

$$\mathrm{TC}_d = RP + \frac{RC}{Q} + \frac{Q(P)F}{2} = 8000(9) + \frac{(8000)30}{500} + \frac{500(0.30)9}{2},$$

$$\mathrm{TC}_d = \$72{,}000 + \$480.00 + \$675.00 = \$73{,}155.00.$$

The EOQ for each unit price is as follows:

$$Q_{10} = \sqrt{\frac{2CR}{PF}} = \sqrt{\frac{2(30)8000}{10(0.3)}} = 400 \text{ units},$$

$$Q_9 = \sqrt{\frac{2CR}{PF}} = \sqrt{\frac{2(30)8000}{9(0.3)}} = 422 \text{ units}.$$

The EOQ with \$10 is valid. The EOQ with \$9 is invalid, since it is not available for

[5]See Appendix B for an excellent approximation approach to quantity discounts.

quantities less than 500 units. The total cost of the valid EOQ with \$10 is as follows:

$$TC_{10} = RP + HQ_0 = (8000)10 + 10(0.3)400 = \$81{,}200.00.$$

Comparing the total costs of the single price-break quantity and the valid EOQ, the minimum cost order quantity is 500 units.

SPECIAL SALE PRICES

When a supplier temporarily discounts the unit price of an item during a regular replenishment cycle, management must determine the size of the order to place. Reasons for such a price reduction range from competitive price wars to attempted inventory reduction. The logical reaction to finding an item on sale during a regular replenishment cycle is to order additional units to take advantage of the lower unit price. Thus, the order quantity is increased to take advantage of the short-lived price reduction.

Assume that when an order is being placed, it is discovered that the supplier is temporarily reducing the price of the item. The regular price of the item is P, but current purchases can be made at $P-d$, where d is the unit price decrease. Subsequent to the temporary sale, the price of the item

Figure 7. Special sale price.

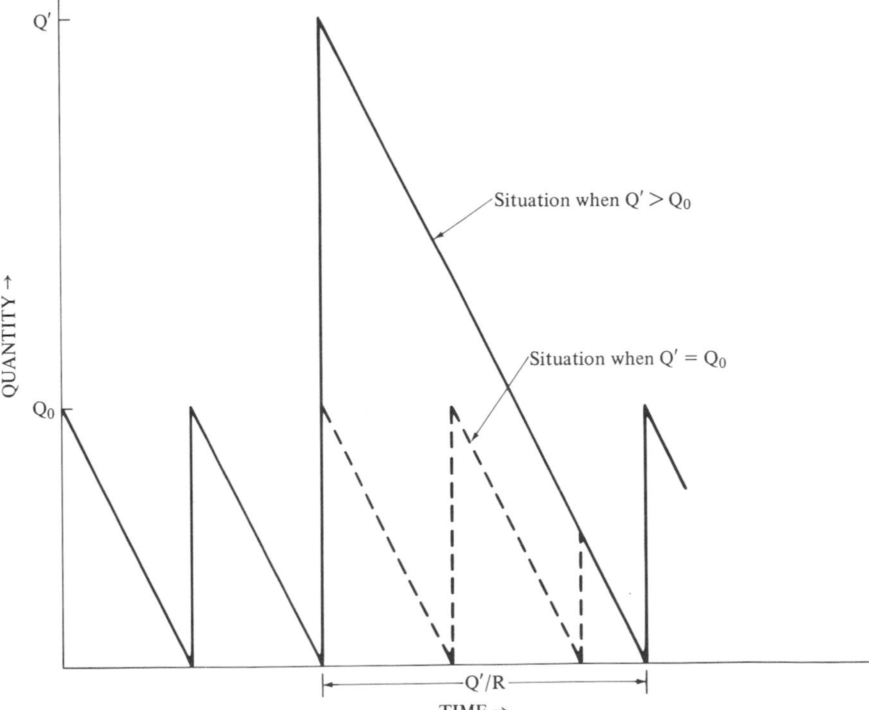

will return to P. Order quantities prior to and after the price decrease are

$$Q_0=\sqrt{\frac{2CR}{PF}}\,.$$

Management's responsibility is to determine the special one-time order size Q' to purchase. To obtain the optimal special order size, it is necessary to maximize the cost difference during the time period Q'/R with and without the special order. The inventory situation is graphically depicted in Figure 7, where the dashed lines indicate the condition if no special order is placed.

The total cost of the system during the period Q'/R, when a special order $(Q'>Q_0)$ is purchased at the unit price of $P-d$, would be as follows:

$$\text{Total cost}=\text{purchase cost}+\text{holding cost}+\text{order cost},$$

$$\mathrm{TC}'=(P-d)Q'+\frac{Q'}{2}(P-d)\frac{FQ'}{R}+C$$

$$=(P-d)Q'+\frac{(P-d)F(Q')^2}{2R}+C.$$

If no special order is placed during the period Q'/R, the total cost of the system when the first order is made at $P-d$ and all subsequent orders are made at P would be as follows:

$$\text{Total cost}=\text{purchase cost}+\text{holding cost}+\text{order cost}$$

$$\mathrm{TC}_{,}=(P-d)Q_0+P(Q'-Q_0)+\frac{Q_0}{2}(P-d)F\frac{Q_0}{R}$$

$$+\frac{Q_0}{2}PF\frac{(Q'-Q_0)}{R}+\frac{CQ'}{Q_0}$$

$$=PQ'-dQ_0+\frac{(P-d)FQ_0^2}{2R}+\frac{PFQ_0Q'}{2R}-\frac{PFQ_0^2}{2R}+\frac{CQ'}{Q_0}$$

where

P = unit purchase price before the discount,
d = unit price decrease,
Q' = special order size in units,
C = order cost per order,
F = annual holding cost fraction,
R = annual demand in units,
Q_0 = economic order quantity in units,
$P-d$ = unit purchase price with the discount,
Q'/Q_0 = number of orders during time period Q'/R.

To find the optimal one-time order size Q_0', the difference between TC_r and TC′ must be maximized and the derivative set equal to zero:

$$g = \text{TC}_r - \text{TC}' = \text{special order cost saving},$$

$$g = dQ' - dQ_0 - \frac{dFQ_0^2}{2R} + \frac{PFQ_0Q'}{2R} - \frac{(P-d)F(Q')^2}{2R} + \frac{CQ'}{Q_0} - C,$$

$$\frac{dg}{dQ'} = d + \frac{PFQ_0}{2R} - \frac{(P-d)FQ'}{R} + \frac{C}{Q_0} = 0,$$

$$Q_0' = \frac{dR}{(P-d)F} + \frac{PQ_0}{P-d} = \text{optimum special order size.}$$

Note that when the price discount is zero ($d=0$), the optimum special order size formula reduces to the EOQ formula ($Q_0' = Q_0$) and the cost saving is zero ($g=0$). By replacing Q' with Q_0' in the cost saving formula for g, the optimum cost saving is obtained.

EXAMPLE 4

The supplier in Example 1 is offering a special discount and has temporarily reduced his unit price from \$10.00 to 9.00. What amount should be purchased to take advantage of the discount?

$$Q_0' = \frac{dR}{(P-d)F} + \frac{PQ_0}{(P-d)}$$

$$= \frac{1(8000)}{(10-1)(0.3)} + \frac{10(400)}{(10-1)}$$

$$= 3407 \text{ units.}$$

A special order for 3,407 units should be purchased. The amount will last for 0.426 years ($3407/8000 = 0.426$). Thereafter the order quantity should be the EOQ of 400 units. The resultant cost saving would be

$$g = dQ' - dQ_0 - \frac{dFQ_0^2}{2R} + \frac{PFQ_0Q'}{2R} - \frac{(P-d)F(Q')^2}{2R} + \frac{CQ'}{Q_0} - C$$

$$= 1(3407) - 1(400) - \frac{1(0.3)(400)^2}{2(8000)} + \frac{10(0.3)400(3407)}{2(8000)}$$

$$- \frac{(10-1)0.3(3407)^2}{2(8000)} + \frac{30(3407)}{400} - 30,$$

$$g = \$1526.27.$$

KNOWN PRICE INCREASES

When a supplier announces that a price increase for an item will take place on some future date, management must determine the size of order to place before the higher price becomes effective. Assume the price of an item will be increased by an amount k as of some date t_1. Unit purchases before t_1 will cost P, but purchases after t_1 will cost $P+k$. It is necessary to decide what amount should be purchased before time t_1. Purchase quantities prior to the supplier's announced price increase are

$$Q_0=\sqrt{\frac{2CR}{PF}}=\text{EOQ before price increase.}$$

If an amount Q' is purchased at t' ($t'\leq t_1$) with the stock level at t' equal to q, the next purchase will occur at time t_3 after an elapse of $(Q'+q)/R$ units of time. The inventory situation is graphically depicted in Figure 8. All subsequent purchases will be made at the new price $P+k$, and the optimal lot size will be

$$Q_0^*=\sqrt{\frac{2CR}{(P+k)F}}=\text{EOQ after price increase.}$$

Figure 8. Known price increase.

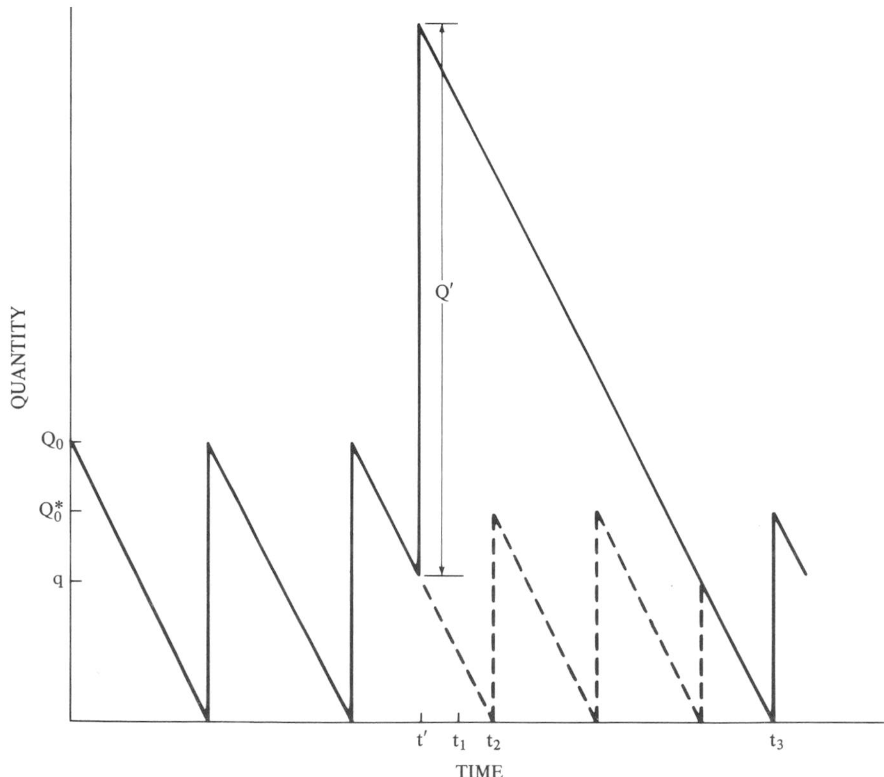

Management's responsibility, when a known future price increase is imminent, involves the determination of the special one-time order size (Q') to purchase prior to the increase. To obtain the optimal special order size, it is necessary to maximize the cost difference during the time period ($t_3 - t'$) with and without a special one-time order.

The total cost of the system during the period t' to t_3 when a special order Q' is purchased at the unit cost P would be as follows:

$$\text{Total cost} = \text{purchase cost} + \text{holding cost} + \text{order cost},$$

$$\text{TC}' = PQ' + Q'PF\frac{q}{R} + \frac{Q'}{2}PF\frac{Q'}{R} + \frac{q}{2}PF\frac{q}{R} + C$$

$$= PQ' + \frac{PFqQ'}{R} + \frac{PF(Q')^2}{2R} + \frac{PFq^2}{2R} + C.$$

If no special order is placed prior to t_1, the total cost of the system during the period t' to t_3 when several purchases of Q_0^* are made at the new price $P+k$ would be as follows:

$$\text{TC}_1 = (P+k)Q' + \frac{Q_0^*}{2}(P+k)(F)\frac{Q'}{R} + \frac{q}{2}PF\frac{q}{R} + \frac{CQ'}{Q_0^*}.$$

Substituting the economic order quantity relationship at the higher price into the above equation for Q_0^*, the total cost of the system during the period t' to t_3 if no special order is placed would be as follows:

$$\text{TC}_1 = (P+k)Q' + Q'\sqrt{\frac{2CF(P+k)}{R}} + \frac{PFq^2}{2R},$$

where

k = known price increase in dollars,
P = unit price in dollars before the price increase,
Q' = special order size in units,
C = order cost per order,
F = annual holding cost fraction,
R = annual demand in units,
Q_0 = economic order quantity before price increase,
Q_0^* = economic order quantity after price increase,
q = stock level in units when special order is placed,
t_1 = effective time of price increase,
t' = time the special order is placed,
t_3 = time when special order is depleted,
q/R = amount of time required to deplete stock-on-hand in years,
Q'/R = amount of time to deplete special order in years,
Q'/Q_0^* = number of orders of size Q_0^* during $t_3 - t_2$.

To find the optimal one-time order size Q_0', the difference between TC_1 and TC' must be maximized and the derivative set equal to zero:

$$g=\mathrm{TC}_1-\mathrm{TC}'=\text{special order cost saving}$$

$$=Q'\left[k+\sqrt{\frac{2CF(P+k)}{R}}-\frac{PFq}{R}\right]-\frac{PFQ'^2}{2R}-C,$$

$$\frac{dg}{dQ'}=k+\sqrt{\frac{2CF(P+k)}{R}}-\frac{PFq}{R}-\frac{PFQ'}{R}=0.$$

The above expression can then be solved for Q' to obtain the optimal special order size:

$$Q_0'=Q_0^*+\frac{k(FQ_0^*+R)}{PF}-q=\text{optimum special order size.}$$

By replacing Q' with Q_0' in the cost savings formula for g, the optimum cost saving is obtained.

Note that when the price increase is zero ($k=0$), $Q_0'=Q_0$ and $g=0$. The formula reduces to the EOQ formula and there is no cost saving. The reorder point will be the same after the price increase as it was before the increase.

EXAMPLE 5

The supplier in Example 1 will increase his unit price from \$10 to \$11 on 1 January. What amount should be purchased on 31 December before the price increase is effective if the stock position is 346 units? What will be the cost saving of the special purchase?

$$Q_0^*=\sqrt{\frac{2CR}{(P+k)F}}=\sqrt{\frac{2(30)8000}{(10+1)0.3}}=381.4\text{ units,}$$

$$Q_0'=Q_0^*+\frac{k(FQ_0^*+R)}{PF}-q=381.4+\frac{1[(0.3)(381.4)+8000]}{10(0.3)}-346$$

$$=381.4+2704.8-346$$

$$=2740\text{ units,}$$

$$g=Q'\left[k+\sqrt{\frac{2CF(P+k)}{R}}-\frac{PFq}{R}\right]-\frac{PFQ'^2}{2R}-C$$

$$=2740\left[1.00+\sqrt{\frac{2(30)(0.3)11}{8000}}-\frac{10(0.3)346}{8000}\right]-\frac{10(0.3)(2740)^2}{16{,}000}-30$$

$$=2740[1.00+0.157-0.129]-1407.68-30.00,$$

$$g=\$1379.04.$$

On 31 December, 2740 units should be purchased. The amount will last for 0.342 years (2740/8000=0.342). The cost saving of the purchase is $1379.04. Thereafter, the order quantity should be 381 units at the unit price of $11.

EOQ SENSITIVITY

Sensitivity analysis determines how the output of a model will be influenced by changes or errors in the input data (parameters). If an input can assume a wide range of values without appreciably affecting the output, the model is insensitive. If a small change in an input can appreciably affect the output, the model is sensitive. The sensitivity of a model will dictate the precision of parameters required for the model. The EOQ model assumes that annual demand R, holding cost H, and order cost C are deterministic and without variation. Errors by management in determining these parameters will cause variations in output (EOQ and total variable cost). This section will analyze the impact of estimation errors.

In a fixed order size system, the order quantity which minimizes the total variable cost per year dictates the optimum inventory policy.[6] The pertinent mathematical relationships are as follows:

$$Q_0=\sqrt{\frac{2CR}{H}}=\text{EOQ},$$

$$\begin{aligned}\text{TVC}_0&=(\text{order cost})+(\text{holding cost})\\&=\frac{RC}{Q_0}+\frac{Q_0H}{2}=\text{optimum total variable cost per year.}\end{aligned}$$

Assume there are errors in the estimation of the parameters R, C, and H by the respective error factors of X_R, X_C, and X_X. The model becomes

$$Q=\sqrt{\frac{2CR}{H}\frac{X_RX_C}{X_H}}=Q_0\sqrt{\frac{X_RX_C}{X_H}},$$

$$\frac{Q-Q_0}{Q_0}=\sqrt{\frac{X_RX_C}{X_H}}-1=\text{order quantity error fraction,}$$

where

Q = order quantity with parameter errors,

Q_0 = economic order quantity,

$$X_R=\frac{\text{estimated demand}}{\text{actual demand}}=\text{demand error factor,}$$

[6]In previous sections, total annual cost has been the measure of effectiveness. The total variable cost per year does not include the purchase cost of the item. It is assumed that no quantity discounts are available and stockouts are not permitted. When quantity discounts are not available, purchase cost ceases to be a relevant incremental cost, and it can be deleted from the formulation.

$$X_C = \frac{\text{estimated order cost}}{\text{actual order cost}} = \text{order cost error factor},$$

$$X_H = \frac{\text{estimated holding cost}}{\text{actual holding cost}} = \text{holding cost error factor}.$$

To examine the effects of errors in estimates of the parameters (R, C, and H), two of the error factors will be set equal to 1 while the third is varied. When all the error factors are equal to 1, the error effect is zero (as you would suspect), and $Q = Q_0$. Thus, with X_C and X_R equal to 1 while X_H is variable, the effect on the EOQ is as follows:

$$\frac{Q - Q_0}{Q_0} = \sqrt{\frac{1}{X_H}} - 1.$$

Similarly, with X_R and X_H equal to 1 while X_C is variable, the effect on the EOQ is as follows:

$$\frac{Q - Q_0}{Q_0} = \sqrt{X_C} - 1.$$

Finally, with X_R varied and X_C and X_H equal to 1, the effect is as follows:

$$\frac{Q - Q_0}{Q_0} = \sqrt{X_R} - 1.$$

Under the single parameter variations just outlined, the effects of errors in estimates of R, C, and H on the sensitivity of the economic order quantity (Q_0) are shown in Table 1. It is readily apparent that errors in parameters are attenuated or dampened when translated into changes in the economic order quantity. For example, if holding costs are in error by a factor of 2, the error in the order quantity is less than 30%. If annual demand (or order cost) is miscalculated by a factor of 2, the error in the order quantity is only 41.4%.

To determine the sensitivity of the total variable cost per year to errors in input parameters, a similar procedure of inserting error factors into the cost formula is used. This model becomes

$$\text{TVC} = \frac{RC}{Q} + \frac{QH}{2}$$

$$= \frac{RC}{\sqrt{(2RC/H)(X_R X_C/X_H)}} + \frac{H\sqrt{(2RC/H)(X_R X_C/X_H)}}{2},$$

which mathematically simplifies to

$$\text{TVC} = \left[\frac{\text{TVC}_0}{2}\right] \frac{X_H + X_R X_C}{\sqrt{X_R X_C X_H}},$$

$$\frac{\text{TVC} - \text{TVC}_0}{\text{TVC}_0} = \frac{X_H + X_R X_C}{2\sqrt{X_R X_C X_H}} - 1 = \text{TVC error fraction}.$$

Table 1. Effects of Errors in *R*, *C*, and *H* on the EOQ

Error Factor X_H[a]	Effect on Q_0(%)[b]	Error Factor X_R or X_C[a]	Effect on Q_0(%)[c]
0.1	+216.2	0.1	− 68.4
0.2	+123.6	0.2	− 55.3
0.3	+ 82.4	0.3	− 45.3
0.4	+ 58.1	0.4	− 36.8
0.5	+ 41.4	0.5	− 29.3
0.6	+ 28.8	0.6	− 22.5
0.7	+ 19.5	0.7	− 16.4
0.8	+ 11.8	0.8	− 10.6
0.9	+ 5.3	0.9	− 5.2
1.0	0.0	1.0	0.0
1.2	− 8.8	1.2	+ 9.5
1.4	− 15.5	1.4	+ 18.3
1.6	− 20.9	1.6	+ 26.4
1.8	− 25.5	1.8	+ 34.2
2.0	− 29.3	2.0	+ 41.4
2.2	− 32.5	2.2	+ 48.3
2.4	− 35.5	2.4	+ 54.9
2.6	− 37.9	2.6	+ 61.2
2.8	− 40.3	2.8	+ 67.3
3.0	− 42.3	3.0	+ 73.2
4.0	− 50.5	4.0	+100.0

[a]Estimated *H*, *R*, or *C* divided by actual value.

[b]No errors in *R* and *C*.

[c]No errors in *C* and *H* (or no errors in *R* and *H*).

When all the error factors are equal to 1, the TVC error factor is zero and $\mathrm{TVC}=\mathrm{TVC}_0$. To examine the influence of errors in parameter estimates, two of the error factors will be set equal to 1 while the third is varied. Thus, with X_C and X_R set equal to 1 and X_H variable, the effect on TVC_0 is as follows:

$$\frac{\mathrm{TVC}-\mathrm{TVC}_0}{\mathrm{TVC}_0}=\frac{1+X_H}{2\sqrt{X_H}}-1.$$

Similarly, with X_R and X_H set equal to 1 and X_C variable, the effect on TVC_0 is as follows:

$$\frac{\mathrm{TVC}-\mathrm{TVC}_0}{\mathrm{TVC}_0}=\frac{1+X_C}{2\sqrt{X_C}}-1.$$

Finally, with X_C and X_H set equal to 1 and X_R variable, the effect on TVC_0 is as follows:

$$\frac{\mathrm{TVC}-\mathrm{TVC}_0}{\mathrm{TVC}_0}=\frac{1+X_R}{2\sqrt{X_R}}-1.$$

It is obvious from the above formulations that for single parameter variations, the effect on TVC_0 is the same irrespective of the parameter (R, C, or H). Under the single parameter variations set forth above, the influence of errors in estimates of R, C, and H on the sensitivity of TVC_0 is shown in Table 2.

It is readily apparent that errors in parameters are attenuated oı dampened when translated into their impact on total incremental cost. For example, if holding costs are in error by a factor of 2, the error in TVC_0 is only 6.1%.

To determine the sensitivity of the total variable cost per year to errors in the EOQ, a similar procedure for inserting error factors into the cost formula is used. The model becomes

$$TVC_0 = \frac{RC}{Q_0} + \frac{Q_0 H}{2} = HQ_0,$$

$$TVC = \frac{RC}{X_Q Q_0} + \frac{X_Q Q_0 H}{2},$$

Table 2. Effects of Errors in R, C, and H on TVC_0 [a]

Error Factor X_a [b]	Increase in TVC_0 (%)
0.1	74.0
0.2	34.2
0.3	18.8
0.4	10.7
0.5	6.1
0.6	3.3
0.7	1.6
0.8	0.6
0.9	0.2
1.0	0.0
1.2	0.4
1.4	1.4
1.6	2.8
1.8	4.4
2.0	6.1
2.2	7.9
2.4	9.7
2.6	11.7
2.8	13.6
3.0	15.4
4.0	25.0

[a] a is any of the three parameters, and there are no errors in the other two. Thus, if a were R, then C and H would have no errors.

[b] (Estimated a)/(actual a).

where

$$X_Q = \frac{\text{estimated EOQ}}{\text{actual EOQ}} = \text{EOQ error factor.}$$

The error fraction in the total variable cost is as follows:

$$\frac{\text{TVC}-\text{TVC}_0}{\text{TVC}_0} = \frac{\dfrac{RC}{X_Q Q_0} + \dfrac{X_Q Q_0 H}{2} - HQ_0}{HQ_0}$$

$$= \frac{X_Q^2 - 2X_Q + 1}{2X_Q} = \text{TVC error fraction.}$$

When the EOQ error factor is equal to 1, the TVC error factor is zero and TVC $=\text{TVC}_0$. The influence of errors in the EOQ on the sensitivity of TVC_0 is shown in Table 3. Errors in the order quantity are dampened when translated into their impact on total variable cost. For example, if the economic order quantity is in error by 40% on the high side ($X_Q = 1.40$), it results in only a 5.7% increase over the theoretically possible minimum total variable cost. Errors on the low side are somewhat more costly. An economic order quantity that is in error by 40% on the low side ($X_Q = 0.6$) results in an increase of 13.4% over the theoretically possible minimum total variable cost.

Table 3. Effect of Errors in Q_0 on TVC_0

EOQ Error Factor X_Q	Increase in TVC_0 (%)
0.1	405.0
0.2	160.0
0.3	81.7
0.4	45.0
0.5	25.0
0.6	13.4
0.7	6.4
0.8	2.5
0.9	.6
1.0	0.0
1.2	1.7
1.4	5.7
1.6	11.3
1.8	17.8
2.0	25.0
2.2	32.8
2.4	40.9
2.6	49.3
2.8	57.9
3.0	66.7
4.0	112.5

Basic inventory models are sometimes viewed with suspicion because of their restrictive assumptions. Rarely can a situation be found where demand is constant and known with certainty while costs are known precisely. Fortunately, basic inventory models are not very sensitive to errors in the measurement of parameters. Wide variations in demand level and cost parameters do not result in wide variations in model outputs.

Over a considerable range, the total variable cost curve is fairly flat, which indicates that substantial changes in demand, order cost, or holding cost will be attenuated. When EOQs are computed with imprecise estimates, the errors are muted by the presence of the square root function. Therefore, the usefulness of these models is not diluted if exact precision is not available. Within a range of 0.4 to 2.5 times the parameter, the total variable cost is very insensitive and changes by less than 11% (see Table 2).

The insensitivity of the basic inventory models to parameter errors is a very advantageous property. Since the total cost is only slightly increased by substantial departures from optimum conditions, the basic models do not require frequent revision (recalculation). Many components of cost parameters are difficult to measure, but the insensitivity renders broad estimates to operational usefulness. All that is needed is to get into the "right ballpark," and good solutions can be obtained with fairly crude cost data. EOQs can be rounded off without a significant loss in economies. Order sizes can be increased or decreased to the nearest pack or container size; order intervals can be lengthened or shortened to the next convenient time interval.

ECONOMIC PRODUCTION QUANTITY (EPQ)—SINGLE ITEMS

The EOQ formulations assume that the entire order for an item is received into inventory at a given time. Whenever the order is received in increments, the EOQ model must be revised to account for the change in assumptions. These revisions are necessary whenever consumption and production simultaneously decrease and increase the stock level. In situations where an item is produced rather than purchased, a variant of the EOQ model is often necessary because the lot may not be made available instantaneously.[7]

If a firm produces a product with a constant demand that is entered into inventory instantaneously, the production order quantity should be determined by the EOQ model with order cost replaced by setup cost.[8] The economic production quantity (EPQ) models make the implicit assumption that units are added to inventory while production is in process. As the

[7]When the entire purchase or production order quantity is received into inventory at one time, the replenishment rate is called infinite. If the entire order quantity is not received at the same time, the replenishment rate is called finite.

[8]The setup cost is essentially the cost of the time required to prepare the equipment or work station to do the job and to dismantle it after the job is finished. Plant output can be substantially affected by the number and length of setups.

units are produced, they are taken to the storeroom and added to the inventory stock. The EOQ model assumes discrete instantaneous additions to stock, whereas the EPQ assumes continuous gradual additions to stock over the production period.

The demand for an item justifies a procurement and/or production action. The item may be obtained through purchasing (including intrafirm transfer) or production. In either case, the unit cost is usually the most important single cost. If the item is purchased, price determination is usually the responsibility of the purchasing department. If the item is manufactured, price determination is the responsibility of cost accounting. For manufactured items, the unit production cost will consist of direct labor, direct materials, and factory burden. Direct labor consists of those labor charges conveniently identified with a specified item. Direct material is the substance from which the item is made. Factory burden includes all manufacturing costs other than direct material and direct labor, such as indirect labor, indirect material, depreciation, taxes, insurance, power, maintenance, supervision, and so forth.

The assumption that the entire order is received into inventory at one time is often not true for in-house production runs. Frequently, replenishment is continuous, and the stock of inventory is being depleted even while the production of an order takes place (finished goods go into inventory gradually). The major decision involves the determination of the size of the production run. The size of the production run that minimizes the total inventory cost is known as the economic production quantity (EPQ).

Figure 9 depicts a typical cycle for the replenishment of inventory over a time period t_p. Production starts at time zero and ends at time t_p. For the time period from t_p to t, no production occurs and the inventory stock is depleted. At time t, a new production run is started. If there were no demand during the period zero to t_p, inventories would have risen at a rate p. Hence, $t_p = Q/p$. Since there is a demand at rate r, inventories will increase at a rate $p-r$, where p is greater than r.[9] During the production period, zero to t_p, inventories accumulate at a rate equal to the production rate minus the demand rate, $p-r$. The maximum inventory level is $t_p(p-r)$, or the time of production times the rate of inventory buildup. The average inventory is one-half the maximum inventory, or $t_p[(p-r)/2]$. Since $t_p = Q/p$, the average inventory is given by the following formula:

$$\text{Average inventory} = \frac{Q(p-r)}{2p}.$$

The average inventory is not just $Q/2$, but is $Q(p-r)/2p$. The factor r/p represents the fractional amount of the lot size withdrawn from stock during the time the item is being produced. The factor $(p-r)/p$ represents

[9]When $p=r$, the production rate equals the demand rate. In this situation, there are no ordering or holding costs, since production is continuous and perfectly matched with demand.

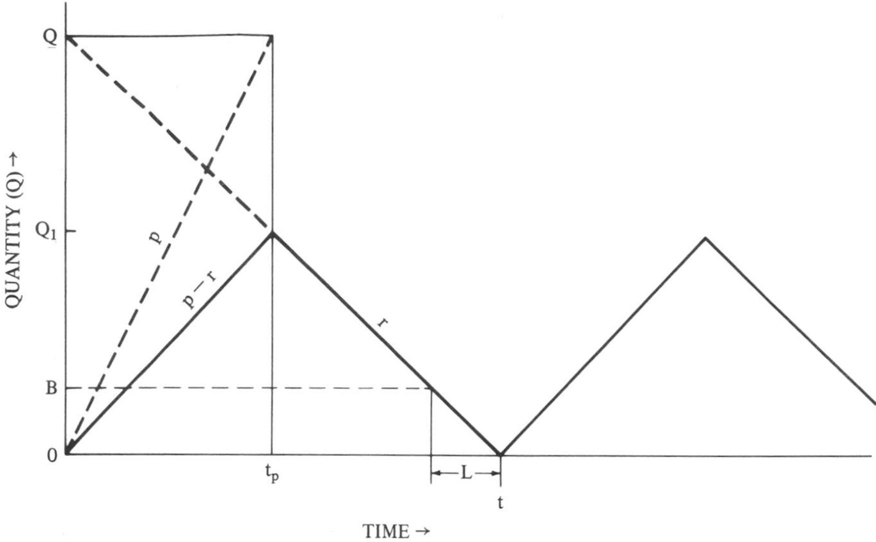

Figure 9. Production order quantity.
Key: p=production rate; r=demand rate ($r<p$); t_p=production time period; t=time between production runs; $Q_1=t_p(p-r)$=maximum inventory; $Q=t_p p$= production run quantity; $Q_1/2=[t_p(p-r)]/2=[Q(p-r)]/2p$=average inventory; $p-r$=inventory buildup rate; B=reorder point; L=lead time.

the fractional amount of the lot size remaining in stock at the end of the production period. Since the stock level ranges between a minimum of zero and a maximum of $Q(p-r)/p$, the average inventory is simply one-half of the maximum inventory. If stockouts are not permitted, the total annual inventory cost is as follows:[10]

Total annual cost = (production cost) + (setup cost) + (holding cost),

$$TC = RP + \frac{RC}{Q} + \frac{Q(p-r)H}{2p},$$

where

R=annual demand in units,
P=unit production cost,
Q=size of production run or production-order quantity,
p=production rate,
r=demand rate,
C=setup cost per production run,
H=holding cost per unit per year.

[10] The model assumes that stockouts will not occur.

To obtain the minimum cost production order quantity (EPQ), take the first derivative of total annual cost with respect to the production order quantity Q and set it equal to zero:

$$\frac{d\text{TC}}{dQ} = -\frac{RC}{Q^2} + \frac{(p-r)H}{2p} = 0.$$

Solving the equation for Q, the EPQ formula is obtained:

$$Q_0 = \sqrt{\frac{2CRp}{(H)(p-r)}}$$
$$= \text{economic production quantity.}$$

Once the economic production quantity is known, the optimum length of the production run can be obtained as well as the production reorder point. If it is assumed that there are N operating days per year, the following relationships apply:

$$\text{Optimum length of production run} = \frac{Q_0}{p},$$
$$\text{Production reorder point in units} = B$$
$$= \frac{RL}{N} = rL,$$

where L is the scheduling and production setup time in days and r is the daily demand rate.

Replacing Q in the total annual cost formula by Q_0, the following formula for the minimum total annual cost results:

$$\text{TC}_0 = RP + \frac{(p-r)HQ_0}{p}.$$

EXAMPLE 6

The demand for an item is 20,000 units per year, and there are 250 working days per year. The production rate is 100 units per day, and the lead time is 4 days. The unit production cost is \$50.00, the holding cost is \$10.00 per unit per year, and the setup cost is \$20.00 per run. What are the economic production quantity, the number of runs per year, the reorder point, and the minimum total annual cost?

$$r=\frac{R}{N}=\frac{20{,}000}{250}=80 \text{ units per day},$$

$$Q_0=\sqrt{\frac{2CRp}{(H)(p-r)}}=\sqrt{\frac{2(20)(20{,}000)(100)}{(10)(100-80)}}=632,$$

$$n=\frac{R}{Q_0}=\frac{20{,}000}{632}=31.6 \text{ runs per year},$$

$$B=\frac{RL}{N}=\frac{20{,}000(4)}{250}=320 \text{ units},$$

$$\mathrm{TC}_0=RP+\frac{(p-r)HQ_0}{p}=(20{,}000)(50)+\frac{(100-80)10(632)}{100},$$

$$\mathrm{TC}_0=\$1{,}001{,}264.$$

Backordering

If stockout costs are finite, the total annual cost must be modified to include their influence. The total annual cost will include the stockout cost as well as production cost, setup cost, and holding cost. If the stockouts are backordered (no lost demand is encountered), all shortages will be satisfied from the next production run. With infinite stockout costs, shortages were not permitted, and they were not included in the total annual cost model. With finite stockout costs, their inclusion is mandatory.

The economic production quantity with finite backorder cost is obtained from the following formula:[11]

$$Q_0=\sqrt{\frac{2CRp}{H(p-r)}}\sqrt{\frac{H+K}{K}}=\text{economic production quantity}.$$

The reorder point is obtained from the following formula when the lead time is expressed in days:

$$B=\frac{RL}{N}-\sqrt{\frac{2CR(p-r)}{pK(H+K)}},$$

where

K = backordering cost per unit per year,

L = lead time in days,

B = reorder point in units,

N = number of operating days per year.

[11] See W. J. Fabrycky and Jerry Banks, *Procurement and Inventory Systems: Theory and Analysis*, New York: Reinhold Publishing Corp., 1967, pp. 64–68, for the derivation of the formulas.

EXAMPLE 7

If the stockout cost in Example 6 is finite and stockouts are all backordered, what changes occur in the final solution with a backorder cost of $5 per unit?

$$Q_0=\sqrt{\frac{2CRp}{H(p-r)}}\sqrt{\frac{H+K}{K}}=632\sqrt{\frac{10+5}{5}}=1095 \text{ units},$$

$$n=\frac{R}{Q_0}=\frac{20{,}000}{1095}=18.3 \text{ runs/year},$$

$$B=\frac{RL}{N}-\sqrt{\frac{2CR(p-r)}{pK(H+K)}}=\frac{20{,}000(4)}{250}-\sqrt{\frac{2(20)(20{,}000)20}{100(5)(10+5)}}$$

$$=320-45=275 \text{ units}.$$

ECONOMIC PRODUCTION QUANTITY (EPQ)—MULTIPLE ITEMS

When a number of products are to be made on a regular cycle (one after the other) on the same equipment, the overall cycle length can be established in a manner similar to the single product case. If the optimum production run is determined for each product independently of other products, it is very likely that there will be scheduling conflicts on the use of the equipment unless it is highly underutilized. The use of single product economic production quantities (EPQ) implies that the equipment will be available when it is needed. On a highly utilized piece of equipment, there will be difficulty scheduling to meet the requirements of single product EPQs. The multiple product scheduling problem can be solved by determining the cycle length which will minimize total costs. The cycle length is the time to make one run through all the products.

The methodology for multiple products is similar to that for single products. The maximum inventory for a given product is $(p_i-r_i)t_p$, and the average inventory is one-half this amount. It has been established that $Q_i=p_it_p=R_i/n$, where n is the number of cycles (production runs) per year. Therefore, the average inventory is given by the following formula, where i is a designated product and there are a total of m products:

$$\frac{(p_i-r_i)t_p}{2}=\frac{(p_i-r_i)R_i}{2np_i}=\text{average inventory}.$$

If stockouts are not permitted, the total annual cost is given by the following formula:

$$\text{Total cost}=(\text{production cost})+(\text{setup cost})+(\text{holding cost})$$

$$\text{TC}=\sum_{i=1}^{m}R_iP_i+n\sum_{i=1}^{m}C_i+\frac{1}{2n}\sum_{i=1}^{m}\frac{(p_i-r_i)R_iH_i}{p_i}.$$

When $m=1$, the system reduces to the equation for the single product EPQ with $n=R/Q$. To obtain the minimum cost number of production runs, we take the first derivative of the total annual cost with respect to the number of production runs and set it equal to zero:

$$\frac{d\mathrm{TC}}{dn}=\sum_{i=1}^{m} C_i-\frac{1}{2n^2}\sum_{i=1}^{m}\frac{(p_i-r_i)R_iH_i}{p_i}=0.$$

Solving the equation for n, the optimum number of runs per year is obtained:

$$n_0=\sqrt{\frac{\displaystyle\sum_{i=1}^{m}\frac{(p_i-r_i)R_iH_i}{p_i}}{\displaystyle 2\sum_{i=1}^{m} C_i}}.$$

The production run size for a given product i is determined by the following formula:

$$Q_i=\frac{R_i}{n_0}.$$

Replacing n in the total annual cost formula by n_0, the following minimum total cost formula is obtained:

$$\mathrm{TC}_0=\sum_{i=1}^{m} R_iP_i+\frac{1}{n_0}\sum_{i=1}^{m}\left[\frac{(p_i-r_i)R_iH_i}{p_i}\right]=\sum_{i=1}^{m} R_iP_i+2n_0\sum_{i=1}^{m} C_i.$$

EXAMPLE 8

Determine the best production cycle for the group of products in Table 4, assuming 250 working days per year. What is the minimum total annual cost?

Table 4

Product	Annual Demand	Unit Production Cost P_i	Daily Production Rate p_i	Annual Holding Cost H_i	Setup Cost per Run, C_i
1	5,000	\$6.00	100	\$1.60	\$40.00
2	10,000	5.00	400	1.40	25.00
3	7,000	3.00	350	.60	30.00
4	15,000	4.00	200	1.15	27.00
5	4,000	6.00	100	1.65	80.00

Table 5

Product	Production Rate p_i	Demand Rate r_i	$\frac{(p_i - r_i)R_i}{p_i}$	H_i	(Col. 4) ×(Col. 5)	Setup Cost C_i
1	100	20	4,000	$1.60	6,400	$ 40
2	400	40	9,000	1.40	12,600	25
3	350	28	6,440	.60	3,864	30
4	200	60	10,500	1.15	12,075	27
5	100	16	3,360	1.65	5,544	80
Total					40,483	$202

The demand per day is obtained by dividing 250 into the annual demand (see Table 5):

$$n_0 = \sqrt{\frac{\sum_{i=1}^{5} (p_i - r_i) R_i H_i / p_i}{2 \sum_{i=1}^{5} C_i}} = \sqrt{\frac{40{,}483}{2(202)}} = 10.0,$$

$n_0 = 10.0$ runs per year.

The production run size for each product is $Q_i = R_i / n_0$, and it is given in Table 6. We have

$$\begin{aligned} TC_0 &= \sum_{i=1}^{m} R_i P_i + 2 n_0 \sum_{i=1}^{m} C_i \\ &= (30{,}000 + 50{,}000 + 21{,}000 + 60{,}000 + 24{,}000) + 2(10)202 \\ &= \$189{,}040. \end{aligned}$$

This section has described a theoretical way of scheduling production run sizes on one machine or department.[12] Not included in the calculations have been such unknowns as machine breakdowns, operator deficiencies, production of scrap, tooling failures, or quality difficulties. The scheduler must modify any such theoretical model to fit real-world emergencies and contingencies.

[12] It should be noted that the total number of days for all production runs will usually not equal the total number of annual operating days available. In the case where the days required exceed the operating days available, production capacity is not sufficient to meet the demand for all products. Therefore, some alternative method for meeting demand must be devised. In the case where the days required are less than the operating days available, all of the production capacity is not utilized. Therefore, excess production capacity is available during the year.

Table 6

Product	R_i	n_0	Q_i
1	5,000	10	500
2	10,000	10	1000
3	7,000	10	700
4	15,000	10	1500
5	4,000	10	400

MAKE OR BUY DECISIONS

Make or buy decisions must be made periodically by nearly every manufacturing organization. Normally, the ultimate decision may be assumed to rest upon an analysis of comparative costs. However, there are a number of factors other than product cost that may be of overriding significance. The relevant manufacturing short-term costs are only the incremental (out-of-pocket) costs associated with the make alternative.

Frequently a production or materials manager must make a decision whether to purchase or to manufacture an item. There are numerous factors to consider before a decision can be made, and many of them are difficult to quantify. Some influencing factors might be idle plant capacity, in-house capabilities (personnel, equipment, future capabilities), reliability of supply, reciprocity, employment stabilization, alternative resource uses, and economic advantage. No simple rule can be applied to all cases of make or buy. Each case must be decided on its own merits, and the important issues may vary in different cases or at different times.

If items are purchased externally, the order quantity can be obtained from EOQ analysis. If items are to be produced internally, the order quantity can be obtained from EPQ analysis. A comparison of the make (EPQ) analysis with the buy (EOQ) analysis can determine the most desirable economic alternatives. From a cost standpoint, inventory analysis can help to solve the make versus buy problem. A simple example will illustrate the method.

EXAMPLE 9

An item may be purchased for \$25 per unit or manufactured at a rate of 10,000 units per year for \$23. If purchased, the order cost will be \$5, compared to a \$50 setup cost for manufacture. The annual demand for the item is 2500 units, and the holding cost is 10%. Should the item be purchased externally or produced internally?

1. Purchase:

$$Q_0=\sqrt{\frac{2CR}{PF}}=\sqrt{\frac{2(5)(2500)}{0.10(25)}}=100 \text{ units},$$

$$\text{TC}_0=RP+HQ_0=2500(25)+2.50(100)=\$62{,}750.$$

2. Manufacture:

$$Q_0=\sqrt{\frac{2CRp}{PF(p-r)}}=\sqrt{\frac{2(2500)50(10{,}000)}{0.10(23)(10{,}000-2500)}}=381,$$

$$\text{TC}_0=RP+\frac{(p-r)HQ_0}{p}$$

$$=(2500)23+\frac{(10{,}000-2500)(2.30)381}{10{,}000}=\$58{,}156.$$

The item should be manufactured, since this is the least cost alternative, which results in a saving of \$4594 (\$62,750 − \$58,156) per year.

When searching for potential supply sources, an organization should always consider its own production facilities. The establishment of a new product or a substantial modification of an old product are typical situations requiring make or buy investigations. Make or buy analysis should be an integral part of new product development procedures. If quality, quantity, and service factors are equal, cost considerations are of paramount concern.

In general, a growing new company will tend to buy more items than a mature company. The new organization understandably concentrates its efforts on increasing its output by emphasizing its major product lines. A mature company tends to have facilities, capital and personnel that can more readily be used for making rather than buying. Thus the growing and mature companies are expanding in a mode most appropriate to their circumstances.

CONCLUSION

An important result of deterministic inventory analysis is the realization that economic order quantities do not vary directly with demand but as the square root of demand. This nonlinear relationship could explain why many organizations experience inventory problems. Intuitive inventory policies are undermined by difficult-to-grasp nonlinearities.

Although the models developed in this chapter are evidently applicable to many situations, they are fraught with many limiting assumptions. The reasonableness of model assumptions and their sensitivity to actual conditions determines the utility of any particular model. For example, all of the models assume that the demand for an item is known with certainty. There are few items that enjoy such a preordained future. Stockouts (shortages) either are not permitted to exist or are backordered and satisfied when replenishments are received.

It is further assumed that holding cost per unit per year is known. Typically, it is not known and it is subjected to gross estimation. In addition, the order cost is treated as a fixed dollar amount per order placed. Actual situations are not usually so simple. Lead times are assumed to be constant (another less than accurate characterization).

These limitations and shortcomings are not highlighted as an attempt to discourage the use of basic models. Quite the contrary, a better understanding of relevant matters can increase the use of models within their range of applicability. Fortunately, sizable deviations of the order quantity from the optimum value produce rather small cost errors. This robustness of the EOQ and EPQ helps justify their widespread use in practice. When deterministic models are insensitive to parameter changes, they provide an excellent approximation to real-world phenomena.

QUESTIONS

1. What parameters must be known to develop an optimum inventory policy?

2. What is an economic order quantity?

3. When is the practice of backordering economically feasible?

4. What parameters must be developed to define a fixed order size system?

5. What is the economic production quantity (EPQ)?

6. What impact do quantity discounts have on order quantities? Why?

7. Outline the impact of sensitivity analysis on inventory models.

8. Distinguish between sensitive and insensitive inventory models.

9. What model inputs do the basic inventory models assume to be without variation?

10. Are EOQ inventory models justifiably viewed with suspicion because of their restrictive assumptions? Explain.

11. Name three limitations of the basic inventory models.

12. Why is the EOQ model frequently unsatisfactory in determining production order quantities?

13. If a high-technology manufacturer believed that possible advances in the state of the art precluded the holding of large inventories, how could he incorporate this belief into his inventory models?

14. Name several factors which may influence a make or buy decision.

PROBLEMS

1. The Star Equipment Company purchases 54,000 bearing assemblies each year at a unit cost of $40. The holding cost is $9 per unit per year, and the order cost is $20. What is the economic order quantity? How many orders will be placed in one year?

2. The Hercules Machine Company purchases 38,000 units of a component each year at a price of $4.00 per unit. The ordering cost is $9.00 per order, and the holding cost is estimated at 25% of the unit value. What is the economic order quantity? What is the total annual cost?

3. What is the reorder point for Problem 1 if the lead time is 1 month? What is the reorder point for Problem 2 if the lead time is 2 weeks?

4. A mobile home fabricator has an annual demand of 10,000 units for a small refrigerator. The supplier sells the units for $100 in order quantities below 125, and for $95 in order quantities above 124 units. The order cost is $5.00, and the annual holding cost is 10% of unit value. In what quantities should the item be purchased?

5. What happens to the economic order quantity in Problem 1 if backordering is possible and the shortage cost per unit per year is $3.00?

6. The Never-Die hospital purchases gauze in lots of 1500 boxes, which is a 6 month supply. The cost per box is $10; the ordering cost is $25 per order; and holding cost is estimated at 25% of unit value. What is the total cost of the existing inventory policy? How much money could be saved if the economic order quantity were applied to the purchase of gauze? What should be the reorder point if the lead time is 2 weeks?

7. The Snap Company makes metal snaps for brassieres. Demand for the following year is projected at 64,000 snaps. The machine setup cost is $100, and the cost of manufacture is $1.00 per snap. Holding costs are estimated at 20% of unit cost. What is the economic production quantity?

8. A tire manufacturer plans to produce 40,000 units of a particular type of tire next year. The production rate is 200 tires per day, and there are 250 working days available. The setup cost is $200 per run and the unit production cost is $15. If holding costs are $11.50 per unit per year, what is the EPQ? How many runs should be made per year? If the production lead time is 5 days, what is the reorder point?

9. An electronics company uses 20,000 electron tubes each year. The supplier offers the following prices:

Quantity Ordered	Unit Price
1–799	$11.00
800–1199	10.00
1200–1599	9.00
≥1600	8.00

The cost of an order is $50, and the hold cost is 20% per unit per year. What size order should be placed to minimize cost?

10. A firm has an annual demand for a component of 3000 units. A fixed cost of $250 is incurred each time an order is placed, and holding costs are computed at 25%. Source *A* will sell the component for $10 regardless of the order size. Source *B* will only accept orders of at least 600 units, with a unit price of $9.50. Source *C* charges $9.00 per item, with a minimum order of 800 units. What source should be selected, and what quantity should be purchased?

11. A processing plant has a requirement for salt in the amount of 45 bags per week. The holding cost is $.10 per bag per week, and no shortages are permitted. Vendor *A* will supply the salt for $1.05 per bag with an order cost of $16 per order. Vendor *B* involves an order cost of $14 per order and quotes the following price schedule:

Bags	Price per Bag
0– 99	$1.15
100–199	1.12
200–399	1.08
400 or more	1.05

What is the minimum cost order size and the best source?

12. The Streak Paint Company purchases 100,000 one-gallon paint cans with lids each year at a cost of $.75 each. The holding cost is $.20 per unit per year, and the order cost is $15. What is the economic order quantity? How many orders will be placed in one year? What is the reorder point if the lead time is 1 month?

13. The Ajax Bicycle Company plans to manufacture 25,000 ten-speed bicycles next year. Each bicycle requires four cable sets—two for hand brakes and two for gear changers. Ajax policy is to order an additional 10% of planned requirements for the year. The price per cable set is $2.40, and the holding cost per cable set is $.50 per year. If the order cost is $18.00, what is the economic order quantity? How many orders will be placed next year? What is the reorder point if the lead time is 3 weeks?

14. If the holding cost per unit in Problem 13 is 40% of unit value per year, what is the effect on the economic order quantity? The number of orders to be placed next year? The reorder point?

15. What happens to the economic order quantity in Problem 13 if backordering is possible and the shortage cost per unit per year is $.95?

16. Ace Auto Supply purchases gaskets in lots of 500 boxes, which is a 3-month supply. The cost per box is $12.50, and the order cost is $15. The holding cost is estimated at 20% of unit value. What is the total cost of the existing inventory policy? How much money could be saved by employing the economic order quantity?

17. The demand forecast for a product during the next year is given in the table below. The lead time for the product is 3 days, and the demand rate is uniform during any one month. The order cost is $30 per order, and the annual holding cost is 30% of the unit cost. The purchase cost is $5.00 per unit for lot sizes less than 500, and $4.90 for lot sizes over 500 units. The organization has a policy of ordering units in lot sizes of 1-month, 2-month, or 3-month supply. What is the lowest cost policy from the three alternatives?

Month	Demand (Units)	Month	Demand (Units)
1	180	7	130
2	220	8	360
3	190	9	110
4	140	10	280
5	270	11	250
6	210	12	160

18. A firm produces five products on a single assembly line. The available information is shown in the table. If there are 250 working days available, what is the best production cycle? What is the optimum production run size for each product?

Item	Annual Demand	Unit Production Cost P_i	Daily Production Rate p_i	Annual Holding Cost H_i	Setup Cost C_i
1	6,000	$6.00	300	$2.10	$ 80
2	20,000	4.00	500	1.40	40
3	8,000	6.00	160	1.80	100
4	8,000	2.00	200	.50	50
5	15,000	4.00	200	1.50	50

19. A company produces six products on a single machine. The information available on the products is shown in the table. What is the optimum production cycle if there are 250 working days available? What are the product production run sizes?

Item	Annual Demand	Unit Production Cost P_i	Daily Production Rate p_i	Annual Holding Cost H_i	Setup Cost C_i
1	3,000	$8.00	100	$2.00	$ 70
2	8,000	8.00	200	1.80	100
3	5,000	4.00	100	1.20	120
4	5,000	2.00	250	.60	80
5	12,000	5.00	600	1.50	250
6	6,000	2.00	100	.50	160

20. From the information given in Problem 18, what is the length of a complete production cycle in days? From the information given in Problem 19, what is the length of a complete production cycle in days?

21. Suppose setup costs in Problem 19 were actually overestimated by 20%. How much difference would the error make in the production run sizes for each product? What difference would the error make in the length of a complete production cycle?

22. The demand for an item is 9 units per period. The holding cost is $.10 per unit per period. The demand can be met by either purchasing or manufacturing, as described by the following data:

	Purchase	Manufacture
Item cost	$ 8.00	$ 7.50
Order/setup cost	$20.00	$200.00
Replenishment rate	∞	18 units/period

What are the minimum cost source and order quantity?

23. A chemical processor uses 500 gallons/day of a solvent. The holding cost is $.002 per gallon per day. The processor is thinking about synthesizing the solvent in house. Relevant data are as follows:

	Purchase	Manufacture
Item cost	$14.00	$ 13.90
Order/setup cost	$ 8.00	$100.00
Replenishment rate	∞	2100 gallons/day

What are the minimum cost source and order quantity for the solvent?

CASE 1: A LITTLE KNOWLEDGE

A welding distributor has been buying its office supplies from the same supplier for some time. George Ouch, the salesman for the office supply company, has been calling on Hot Tips Incorporated for over three years. Much to George's dismay, it has always been the practice of Hot Tips to buy the smallest lot size available of a particular four-part preprinted billing form at a cost of $611 for 10,000 forms. The rationale for this particular buying policy was to expend the least amount of money possible (at any one time) on office supplies, for reasons of liquidity.

Tom Erudite, in an effort to enhance his position with the company, has been attending evening classes. Recently, he took a course which dealt with inventory systems and materials management. Tom was anxious to save the company money (and also look good himself) by applying the techniques he learned in class to his job.

When George contacted Tom he was amazed to discover that he wished to purchase the largest lot size available of the four-part billing form. It was 30,000 forms at $1,700. George could not believe the sudden change in policy. Upon questioning Tom, he found that he used something called an EOQ model. Tom explained that by analyzing all the relevant costs, he could save $80 annually by purchasing the larger quantity of billing forms.

1. What is your opinion of this sudden change in inventory policy?
2. Should office supplies always be purchased in the largest quantity available? Why?
3. Explain the annual cost saving of the larger order.

CASE 2: MAKE OR BUY

The Alphabet Valve Company is a small plumbing supply firm which produces several small items for a local market. The firm manufactures some of its subassemblies and relies on contractors for others. Final assembly operations take place on the premises of Alphabet. One of the products, a common exterior water valve, is presently under study by the company officials.

The company has an agreement with one of its contractors to produce the handles for the valve under consideration. The handle is milled from stainless steel to the company's specifications and shipped to a supply point at Alphabet. The handle is attached to the valve body. The entire assembly is then given a coat of corrosion-resistant paint and packaged for shipment. The other major components of the valve are made in Alphabet's plant (presently operating at 80% of capacity).

The reason the valve has come under study is a price increase announced by the handle company. The contractor has a new price of $2.25 per handle. Alphabet's president does not believe that the market will support a price increase for the valve and he wishes to evaluate alternative sources.

The purchasing agent has researched the problem and has located a used milling machine (price $7000; life 5 years, no salvage value). He estimates that the machine will cost $1000 per year to operate and that they can produce the valve handle for $1.50 (variable cost per unit) with a volume of 4000 valves per year. The purchasing agent has placed the problem before the other officers of the firm and is soliciting their recommendations.

1. What recommendation would you make to the president?
2. If the handle is manufactured in house, should it be the same handle as was purchased?

CASE 3: MR. OLDER VERSUS MR. YOUNGER

Mr. Thomas, president of Thomas Manufacturing Company, and Mr. McDonnell, vice president, were discussing how future economic conditions would affect their product, which is vacuum cleaners. They were particularly concerned about inflation, which was causing their costs to increase at an alarming rate. They had increased the prices of their products last year, and felt another price increase would have an adverse affect on sales. They wondered if there was some way to reduce costs in order to maintain the existing price structure.

Mr. McDonnell had attended a meeting the previous night and heard a presentation by the president of a hand tool company on how they were solving the inflation problem. Apparently, they had just hired a purchasing agent with a business degree who was reducing costs by 15%. Mr. McDonnell thought some new ideas might be applicable to Thomas Manufacturing. The present purchasing agent, Mr. Older, had been with the company for 25 years and they had no complaints. Production never was stopped for lack of material. Yet a 15% cost reduction, in the present economy, was a possibility which could not be ignored. Mr. Thomas suggested that Mr. McDonnell look into this area and come up with a recommendation in 3 weeks.

Mr. McDonnell contacted several business schools in the area. He said he would be interested in hiring a new graduate, majoring in purchasing. One of the requirements of the applicants was a paper on how they felt they could improve the company's purchasing function. Several applicants visited the plant and analyzed the purchasing department before they wrote their papers. The most dynamic paper was submitted by Tim Younger. He recommended:

1. Lower the stock reorder levels from 60 to 45 days for many items, thus reducing inventory.
2. Analyze the product specifications on many parts of the vacuum cleaners with an idea toward using plastics instead of metals.
3. Standardize many of the parts on the vacuum cleaners to reduce the number of items kept in stock.

4. Analyze items to see if more products can be purchased by blanket purchase orders with the ultimate goal of reducing the purchasing staff.
5. Look for new and lower cost sources of supply.
6. Increase the number of requests for bids, in order to get still lower prices.
7. Be more aggressive in negotiations. Make fewer concessions.
8. Make sure all trade, quantity, and cash discounts are taken.
9. Buy from the lowest price source, disregarding local public relations.
10. Stop showing favoritism to customers who also buy from the company. Reciprocity comes second to price.
11. Purchase as current requirements demand, instead of according to market conditions. Too much money is tied up in inventory.

After reading all the papers Mr. McDonnell was debating with himself what he should recommend to Mr. Thomas. Just last week at the department meeting Mr. Older was recommending many of the opposite actions. In particular he recommended an increase in inventory levels, anticipating rising prices. Mr. Older also stressed the good relations the company had with all its suppliers and how they can be relied upon for good service and possible extension of credit if the situation warrants it. Most of their suppliers bought their vacuum cleaners from Thomas Manufacturing. Yet, Mr. Younger said this practice was wrong and should be eliminated. Mr. McDonnell was hesitant as to what action he should recommend. He had only one day to make his decision.

1. What recommendation would you make if you were Mr. McDonnell? Why?
2. Analyze Mr. Younger's recommendations. Do you agree or disagree with them?

CASE 4: HEALTHY INDIGESTION

Nutrition Specialists, Inc. is a chain store operation in the retail health food business. NSI operates a number of small retail health food stores which are located within mall complexes throughout a southern metropolitan area. The outlets are generally small in size but offer a full line of health food items. The broad assortment of items is presently being purchased for the chain. The items are delivered to a central warehouse and then distributed to the outlets almost on an as-needed basis.

Over the past few years the NSI managers, Joe and Mike Minardo, have gained an awareness of the competitive nature of their business and the need for efficient operating practices. They have discovered that they are in a much better position than the smaller independent retail health food stores, due to their significant purchasing power and computerized inventory system. NSI has actively engaged in price competition and placed major emphasis on cost control. Thus far, its strategies have proven correct. The company has been expanding and recently has opened two new outlets.

From its inception NSI has adhered to the policy of dealing primarily with one supplier in order to achieve sales volume discounts. The major supplier furnishes the company with most of their staple health food items, such as vitamin pills, packaged teas and herbs, health food literature, beauty products, grains, fruit juices, and dairy items. This supplier, like others in the industry, hesitates to extend credit because of the nature of the industry. NSI has been one of the few that is able to overcome this reluctance.

Presently, NSI is encountering two pressing problems. Stockouts within the individual outlets occur frequently. When this happens store managers send customers elsewhere, and institute a special order for the item from the central warehouse. Because of space constraints in the warehouse, NSI is considering a possible expansion, or alternatively, purchase of a second facility.

Joe Minardo, the younger of the two managing brothers, feels measures should be taken to prevent shortages and to increase the internal efficiency of the firm. His position comes as a reaction to an announced price increase from the major supplier. Due to inflationary pressures on his costs, the supplier announced an across-the-board increase of 10% on all items to become effective in four weeks. Joe, therefore, feels that the company should stock up on all items before the increase comes into effect. He wants to increase all order quantities beyond normal lot sizes and to initiate special orders for items that would not typically be ordered before the price increase. Joe maintains that this action would delay purchase of the items at higher prices and thereby provide a substantial cost saving to the company. He also asserts that the additional stock would be a temporary solution to stockout problems and would postpone a facility decision if the larger orders could be expedited to the outlets.

Mike opposes Joe's assertions vehemently, on the basis that Joe would be taking a risky step during times when forecasts for the industry as well as the economy are grim. Mike refuses to authorize orders for larger lot sizes or place orders ahead of schedule. He insists that the gains that Joe is promising are questionable and an unworkable solution to their problems. Mike thinks Joe has finally gone too far with his cost cutting schemes.

1. What purchasing and inventory factors should be considered in order to resolve the conflict?
2. What types of risks are involved in Mike's position?
3. Does Joe have a valid argument? Mike?
4. What recommendations would you make to the brothers?

CASE 5: INGENIOUS CONTRIVANCES

I & C, Inc. produces a myriad of stainless steel and aluminum kitchen utensils as well as several patterns of stainless steel flatware. Its product lines are in continuous flux, because the company is constantly adding new kitchen gadgets to its already overwhelming number of contrivances. I & C takes great pride in its ability to create an item suitable for every conceivable kitchen need. There is heavy emphasis on product innovation and market leadership. The firm has been quite successful at entering the kitchen convenience market with a "never heard of before" but "can't live without" device.

Currently, I & C is undergoing new product development for an aluminum vegetable steamer and is in the process of formulating production decisions for the device. The steamer can be inserted in different size cooking pots, enabling the user to steam various quantities of food with the same implement. It consists of eight pieces of aluminum mesh that can expand to the size of the cooking appliance and collapse for storage.

Since I & C has a wide array of products, it is imperative that the items be produced on a regular cycle. The company stresses the need for full utilization of its equipment. Given the short product life of many items, as well as small yearly sales of others, I & C avoids purchasing equipment that would be dedicated to a specific product. Fortunately, the engineering and production managers have determined that the steamer is producible on existing equipment, since it is simply a modification of a straining utensil that has been in production for several years.

The critical decision now is the scheduling of production for the steamer. A determination must be made for the size and the frequency of the production run. Various members of the management team have been consulted. Marketing is excited about the prospects for the steamer, due to the popularity of steamed vegetables. They expect sales during the first year to be 50,000 units. The production manager has issued the following estimates: \$200 setup cost, \$5 per unit production cost, and 300 units per day production capability for the 250 day working year. The firm's inventory analyst estimates an annual holding cost of \$.80 per unit. Applying the concept of scheduling production in economic quantities to initial figures, the analyst stipulates a production run of 8660 units approximately 5.8 times a year. He feels that this size and frequency of runs meet the forecasted demand most efficiently.

Mr. Kaiser, the general manager, has reservations. He has just finished reviewing a product proposal for an item that would compete for machining time with the steamer and the strainer. He also is having difficulty ascertaining his actual production capability and questions the validity of the capacity figures he has been receiving. He is beginning to wonder if basic operating principles are being overlooked.

1. Should I & C adopt the initial figures as its production plan?
2. Has any necessary information been overlooked? Should the theoretical model be modified?
3. What production, operating, and marketing factors could alter or influence this type of decision?

MATHEMATICAL ABBREVIATIONS AND SYMBOLS USED IN CHAPTER 3

b	Price reduction fraction
B	Reorder point in units
C	Ordering cost or setup cost
d	Unit price discount in dollars
EOQ	Economic order quantity
EPQ	Economic production quantity
F	Annual holding cost fraction
g	Cost saving of special order
H	Holding cost per unit per year

K	Backordering cost per unit per year
k	Unit price increase in dollars
L	Lead time
m	Number of products
n	Number of annual orders or production runs
n_0	Optimum number of annual orders or production runs
N	Number of annual operating days
p	Daily production rate
P	Unit purchase or production cost
P_d	Unit purchase cost with discount
q	Stock level in units at a given time
Q	Order quantity in units
Q'	Special-order quantity in units
Q_d	Quantity discount break quantity
Q_0	Optimum order quantity
Q_0^*	EOQ after price increase
r	Daily demand rate
R	Annual demand in units
T	Order interval
TC	Total annual inventory cost
TC_0	Optimum total annual cost
TVC	Total variable cost per year
TVC_0	Optimum total variable cost per year
V	Maximum inventory level in units
V_0	Optimum maximum inventory level in units
X_C	Order cost error factor
X_H	Holding cost error factor
X_R	Annual demand error factor
X_Q	EOQ error factor

APPENDIX A. DETERMINATION OF SINGLE VARIABLE MAXIMUM AND MINIMUM POINTS

The determination of a maximum or minimum value for a continuous differentiable function of one variable is easily handled by differential calculus. The slope of a curve at a point is simply the derivative at that point. At a maximum or minimum point on a curve, the slope is zero.

Therefore, the maximum or minimum point can be determined by setting the first derivative of the function equal to zero. If a function is defined by

$$y=f(x),$$

the maximum or minimum point is where

$$\frac{dy}{dx}=0.$$

To determine if the point is a maximum or a minimum, it is necessary to take the second derivative. After the second derivative is taken, the value of x obtained from the first derivative is substituted into the equation for the second derivative, and the sign indicates if the point is a maximum or a minimum. The point is a maximum if the second derivative is negative; it is a minimum if the second derivative is positive.

Whenever

$$\frac{dy}{dx}=0,$$

y has a maximum value if

$$\frac{d^2y}{dx^2}<0;$$

y has a minimum value if

$$\frac{d^2y}{dx^2}>0.$$

APPENDIX B. EOQ QUANTITY DISCOUNT APPROXIMATION

The basic decision with quantity discounts is whether a larger quantity should be ordered to take advantage of a unit-price reduction.

When the order cost (C) is very small compared to the purchase cost (PQ) of an order, an approximation formula can be used to decide on the discount. The formula will determine the maximum quantity that economically could be purchased with the discount. If the quantity necessary to qualify for the discount is larger, do not take the discount; if smaller, order the optimum quantity or just enough to qualify for the discount. The maximum quantity that can economically be ordered to qualify for a quantity discount is as follows:[13]

$$Q_m=\frac{2bR}{F}+(1-b)Q_0=\text{maximum discount order quantity},$$

[13]See Robert G. Brown, *Decision Rules for Inventory Management*, Holt, Rinehart and Winston, 1967, pp. 199–200 for the mechanics of the derivation.

where

R = annual demand in units,

F = annual holding cost fraction,

Q_0 = economic order quantity without the quantity discount,

$b = (P - P_d)/P$ = price reduction fraction,

P = unit price without quantity discount,

P_d = unit price with quantity discount.

Note that when there is no discount ($b=0$), the maximum quantity is equal to the EOQ ($Q_m = Q_0$). The above formula applies when the order cost is very small compared to the total invoice cost ($C \ll P_d Q$). An example can illustrate the use of the discount procedure.

EXAMPLE B-1

A supplier sells copper elbows to a refrigerator manufacturer. The list price is \$.80 per unit, with a discount price of \$.76 per unit in lots of 2000 or more. The annual demand is for 10,000 elbows, and the order cost is \$10 per order. If the holding cost fraction is 25%, should the discount be taken? What should be the order quantity?

$$Q_0 = \sqrt{\frac{2CR}{PF}} = \sqrt{\frac{2(10)10{,}000}{0.80(0.25)}} = 1{,}000 \text{ units},$$

$$b = \frac{P - P_d}{P} = \frac{0.80 - 0.76}{0.80} = 0.05,$$

$$Q_m = \frac{2bR}{F} + (1-b)Q_0 = \frac{2(0.05)10{,}000}{0.25} + (0.95)1{,}000 = 4{,}000 + 950,$$

$$Q_m = 4950 \text{ units}.$$

The discount should be taken, and the order quantity should be 2000 units. Note that the order cost is much less than the purchase cost of an order.

APPENDIX C. DERIVATION OF EOQ WITH BACKORDERING

The total annual inventory cost is as follows:

$$\mathrm{TC} = RP + \frac{CR}{Q} + \frac{HV^2}{2Q} + \frac{K(Q-V)^2}{2Q},$$

$$\mathrm{TC} = RP + \frac{CR}{Q} + \frac{HV^2}{2Q} + \frac{KQ}{2} - KV + \frac{KV^2}{2Q},$$

where

R = annual requirement in units,

P = purchase cost of an item,

C = ordering cost per order,
Q = lot size or order quantity in units,
H = holding cost per unit per year,
V = maximum inventory level in units,
K = stockout cost per unit per year.

To obtain optimal values for Q and V, the partial derivatives of the total annual cost with respect to Q and V are equated to zero. The two resulting equations are solved simultaneously to obtain the optimal values for Q and V. The partial derivative of total annual cost with respect to Q is as follows:

$$\frac{\partial \mathrm{TC}}{\partial Q} = -\frac{CR}{Q^2} - \frac{HV^2}{2Q^2} + \frac{K}{2} - \frac{KV^2}{2Q^2} = 0,$$

$$\frac{1}{Q^2}\left(-CR - \frac{HV^2}{2} - \frac{KV^2}{2}\right) + \frac{K}{2} = 0,$$

$$Q^2 = \frac{2CR}{K} + \frac{HV^2}{K} + V^2.$$

The partial derivative of total annual cost with respect to V is as follows:

$$\frac{\partial \mathrm{TC}}{\partial V} = \frac{HV}{Q} - K + \frac{KV}{Q} = 0,$$

$$\frac{1}{Q}[HV + KV] - K = 0, \qquad \frac{V(H+K)}{Q} = K,$$

$$Q = \frac{HV}{K} + V, \qquad V = \frac{KQ}{H+K}.$$

The optimal value for V is obtained by substituting the above value of Q into the previously derived relationship:

$$Q^2 = \frac{2CR}{K} + \frac{HV^2}{K} + V^2 = \left[\frac{HV}{K} + V\right]^2,$$

$$\frac{2CR}{K} + \frac{HV^2}{K} + V^2 = \frac{H^2V^2}{K^2} + \frac{2HV^2}{K} + V^2,$$

$$\frac{2CR}{K} = \frac{H^2V^2}{K^2} + \frac{HV^2}{K},$$

$$\frac{2CR}{K} = \frac{V^2H}{K}\left[\frac{H}{K} + 1\right] = \frac{V^2H}{K}\left[\frac{H+K}{K}\right],$$

$$V^2 = \frac{2CR}{H}\left[\frac{K}{H+K}\right],$$

$$V_0 = \sqrt{\frac{2CR}{H}}\sqrt{\frac{K}{H+K}}$$

= optimum maximum inventory level.

By substituting the optimal value of V into the previously developed relationship for V, we can obtain the optimal value of Q:

$$V=\frac{KQ}{H+K}=\sqrt{\frac{2CR}{H}}\sqrt{\frac{K}{H+K}},$$

$$Q=\left[\frac{H+K}{K}\right]\sqrt{\frac{2CR}{H}}\sqrt{\frac{K}{H+K}}=\sqrt{\frac{2CR}{H}}\sqrt{\frac{(H+K)^2K}{K^2(H+K)}},$$

$$Q_0=\sqrt{\frac{2CR}{H}}\sqrt{\frac{H+K}{K}}=\text{optimum order quantity.}$$

4 Fixed Order Size Systems: Probabilistic Models

The previous chapter dealt with a collection of inventory models that are deterministic. This chapter will deal with the same type of inventory models except that they will be described in probabilistic terms. If demand and lead time are treated as *constants*, they are called deterministic; if they are treated as *random variables*, they are called probabilistic or stochastic. The models in this chapter assume that it is possible to state the probability distribution of demand for any specified time period. In particular, since the lead time is the usual period of concern, attention is focused on the distribution of demand during the lead time.

Traditional inventory models (economic order quantity and economic production quantity) do not account for risk and uncertainty in their formulation. Some of their common assumptions (limitations) are as follows:

1. The demand is known, uniform, and continuous.
2. The production rate is known, uniform, and continuous.
3. The lead time is known and constant.
4. The ordering/setup cost is known and constant.
5. The holding cost is known, constant, and linear.
6. There are no resource limitations (dollar limits or space limits).
7. Stockouts are usually not permitted (infinite stockout cost).
8. The cost of the inventory analysis is negligible.

Inventory of independent demand items can be divided into working stock and safety stock. Working stock is what is expected to be used during a given time period. The average working stock is one-half the order quantity (lot size), which may be determined by the EOQ formula or some variant of it. Working stock varies with the square root of annual usage. Safety stock, unlike working stock, does not usually depend on lot sizes. It is not held because an organization expects to use it, but because it might. It is held because an organization believes in the long run it is more efficient (it will generate more revenue or reduce costs). Safety stock is determined *directly* from a forecast. Since forecasts are seldom exact, the safety stock protects against higher than expected demand levels.

SAFETY STOCK

Risk and uncertainty enter the inventory analysis through many variables, but the most prevalent are variations in demand and lead time. Variations in demand and lead time are absorbed by provision for safety stocks, also referred to as buffer stocks or fluctuation stocks. Safety stocks are extra inventory kept on hand as a cushion against stockouts due to random perturbations of nature or the environment. They are needed to cover the demand during the replenishment lead time in case actual demand exceeds expected demand, or the lead time exceeds the expected lead time. Safety stock has two effects on a firm's cost: it decreases the cost of stockouts, but it increases holding costs.

Under the fixed order size system (Q-system), there is a fixed order quantity that is ordered every time the reorder point is reached. Safety stock is needed to protect against a stockout after the reorder point is reached and prior to receipt of an order. This time period during which a stockout could occur is known as the lead time. The fixed order quantity Q and the reorder point B completely define the fixed order size system. Safety stock is an important constituent of the reorder point. In fixed order size systems, the reorder point B is composed of the mean lead time demand $\overline{M}$ plus the safety stock S.

In an ideal inventory system, as shown in Figure 1, the average demand pattern always prevails with no variance. In actual inventory systems, as shown in Figure 2, the pattern of demand over time will be discrete and irregular. Figure 2 shows three cycles of an inventory system. In the first cycle, the demand during the lead time is so great that it results in a stockout. In the second cycle, the demand during the lead time is less than expected, and the replenishment is received before the safety stock is reached. In the third cycle, the demand during the lead time is greater than expected, but the safety stock is sufficient to absorb the demand.

Safety stocks are needed because forecasts or estimations are less than perfect and suppliers sometimes fail to deliver goods on time. There should

Figure 1. Ideal inventory model.

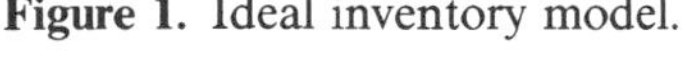

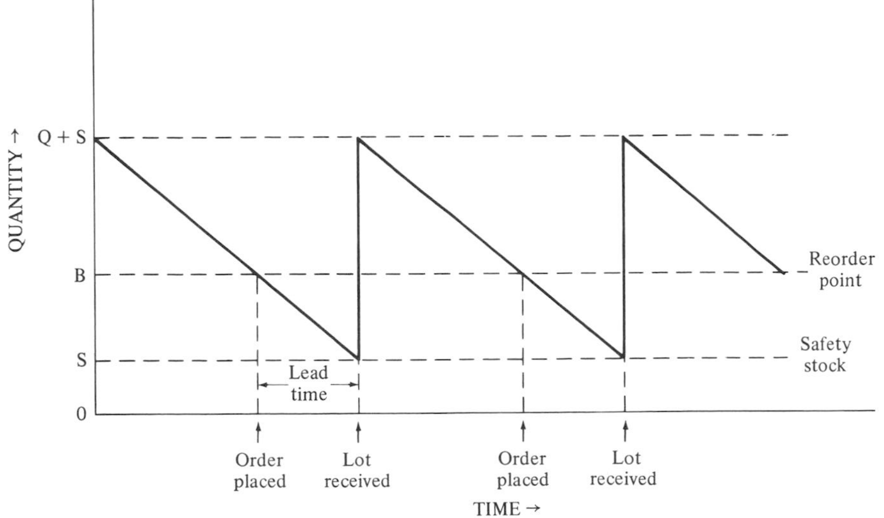

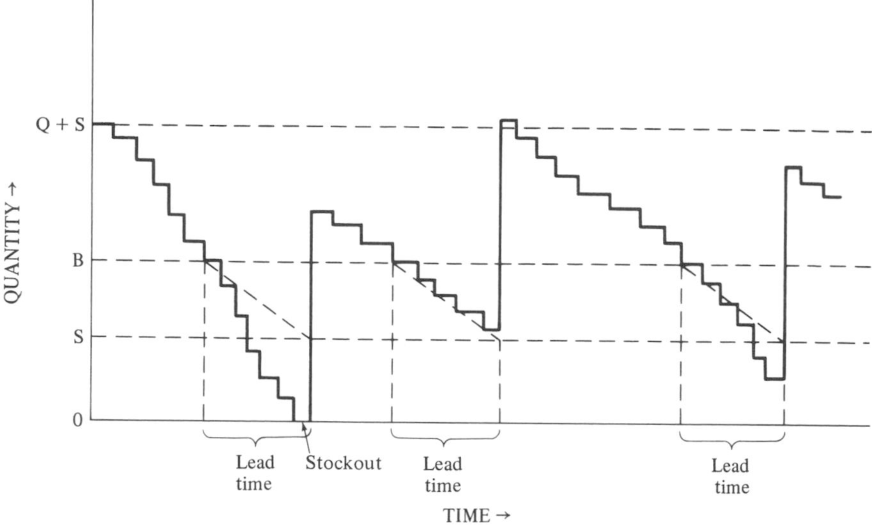

Figure 2. Realistic inventory model.

be some protection against these two unfavorable contingencies:

1. A higher rate of use than was forecasted
2. A late delivery of goods

Either or both of these situations can lead to a stockout in absence of safety stock. Each additional increase in safety stock provides diminishing (decreasing) benefit. The first unit of stock in excess of expected demand provides the largest increment of protection against stockout; the second unit provides less protection than the first unit, and so on. As the size of the safety stock is increased, the probability of a stockout decreases. At some safety stock level, the cost of storing additional units plus the expected stockout cost is at a minimum. This level is the optimum level, and a net loss results from moving in either direction.

Warehouses and retail outlets maintain safety stocks to be able to supply customers when their rate of demand is irregular or unpredictable. Factories maintain safety stocks to be able to replenish retail and field warehouse stocks when their demand is above average. Extra stock in a semifinished form is carried to normalize production among manufacturing departments when work loads are unbalanced. These additional stocks are often part of a business philosophy of serving customer and internal needs without delay in order to assure the long-run effectiveness of the organization.

It would be fallacious to believe that additional stock is maintained for altruistic purposes. Stockouts result in external and internal shortages. External shortages can result in backorder costs, present profit loss (loss of potential sales), and future profit loss (goodwill erosion). Internal shortages can result in lost production (idle men and machines) and a delay in a completion date (cost penalty).

The customer's reaction to a stockout (shortage) condition can result in a backorder or a lost sale. With a backorder, the sale is not lost, but only delayed in shipment. Typically, a company will institute an emergency expediting order to get the item, or the customer will be served from the next order of items to arrive. The backorder results in expediting costs, handling costs, and frequently extra shipping and packaging costs. With a lost sale, the customer's demand for the item is lost and presumably filled by a competitor. The stockout cost for a lost sale ranges between the lost profit on the sale to some unspecified loss of goodwill. A goodwill loss can result in a customer not returning to the outlet to purchase other items in the future. A stockout can result in an extremely high cost if it is in a raw material for a production line that must then be shut down. Often, the cost of a stockout for a manufacturing company is so great that none can be tolerated. It can be seen that the stockout cost (whether due to a backorder or to a lost sale) can vary considerably for different items, depending on customer or internal usage.

When referring to stockout cost it is necessary to be explicit to avoid confusion. A stockout can result in a backorder or a lost sale. In the backorder case, the customer has his demand satisfied upon initial receipt of an order (e.g., a captive market, as in a factory). In the lost sale case, the demand is not satisfied and it is lost forever. At the retail level, a stockout of an item usually results in a lost sale, since the customer will go elsewhere to make the purchase. At the manufacturing level, a supply bin stockout of an item usually results in a backorder. In the backorder case, the customers are patient; in the lost sales case, the customers are impatient and purchase from other sources.

Just after a shipment (order quantity) is received, the inventory level is high. Just before the next shipment is received, the inventory level is low. The average inventory level on hand just before the receipt of a replenishment order is the safety stock (over many cycles, the inventory level will sometimes be more than the safety stock and sometimes less, but it will average to the safety stock). There is no problem in giving good service just after a shipment arrives, for stocks are high and demand can be filled promptly. The only time there is danger of not meeting demand is just before the next shipment is received (during the lead time). Of course, the larger the order quantity, the fewer the annual orders, which means the fewer the opportunities (lead times) for stockouts to occur.

Safety stock can be considered a fairly permanent investment in inventory. On an average, safety stock is always on hand—similar to a fixed asset. In deterministic fixed order size models, the average inventory is approximated as $Q/2$. When safety stock is held, the approximate average inventory becomes $S+Q/2$, where S is the safety stock quantity and Q is the order quantity.

Safety stocks (and thus the reorder point) will be larger for

1. Higher stockout costs or service levels
2. Lower holding costs
3. Larger variations in demand
4. Longer lead times
5. Larger variations in lead time

The relationship between safety stock and service level is shown in Figure 3. It shows safety stock or investment along the vertical axis and service level along the horizontal axis. For a single item, the relationship is straightforward: the curve slopes upward throughout, indicating that additional safety stock (investment) will always increase the level of customer service. The curve gives no indication of what the level of service or investment should be. Management must decide if the additional expenditure is justified in a particular case. As the customer service level is raised by larger safety stock, the investment increases. Thus, the customer service level directly affects safety stock but does not affect working stock. Usually the investment in working stock is determined before considering safety stock.

There is no fixed formula or rigid procedure to follow in determining the safety stock. The calculations of different methods available are based on

Figure 3. Safety stock versus service level.

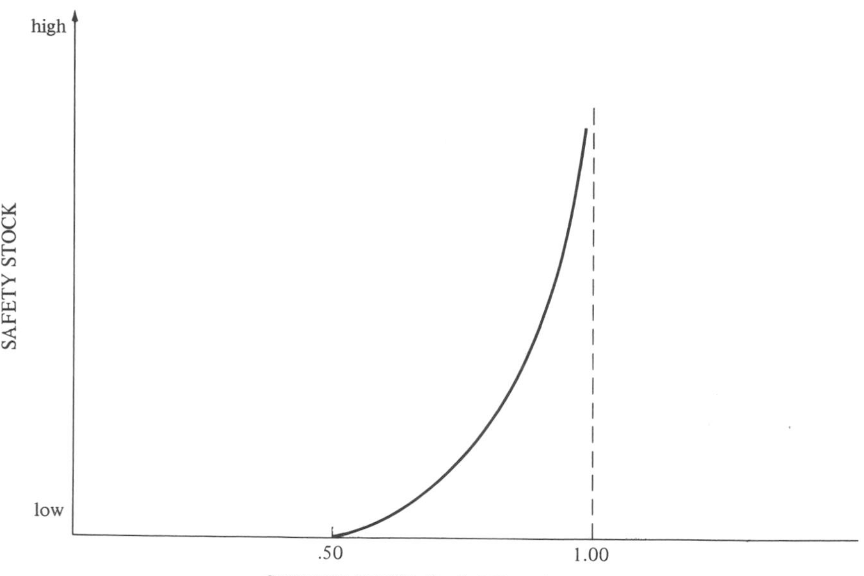

demand, lead time, and stockout costs. The information known about these variables determines the complexity of the calculations. The safety stock is simply the difference between the stock available for the replenishment period (reorder point) and the average demand during the replenishment period. The reorder point is defined as the stock position at which an order is triggered. In the formulations to be developed in this chapter, it will be assumed that the order quantity can be determined by an economic balance of the relevant inventory costs, but it will be assumed independent of the reorder point.[1]

There are two schools of thought on how to establish safety stocks (and reorder points) for a fixed order size system. The first approach deals with known stockout costs: explicit costs can be allocated to shortages. The second approach deals with unknown stockout costs: management specifies a service level based on some probability distribution of demand during the lead time. Both of these approaches will be outlined and investigated. The remainder of the chapter will emphasize safety stock and reorder point determination. The demand and lead time will be assumed independent and distributed in future time periods with time invariant parameters.

STATISTICAL CONSIDERATIONS

When the demand is probabilistic (not deterministic), rather than minimize cost, it is necessary to minimize the expected cost. If the demand distribution is discrete, the expected cost is obtained by summing the different costs for each strategy weighted (multiplied) by their respective probabilities and then selecting the strategy (demand level) with the lowest expected cost. If the demand distribution is continuous, the minimum expected cost expression is obtained by taking the derivative of expected cost with respect to the variable and then setting it equal to zero.

Two of the best-known and most widely used statistics for describing distributions are the arithmetic mean and the standard deviation. The arithmetic mean is a measure of central tendency, while the standard deviation is a measure of dispersion of a distribution. The arithmetic mean $\overline{M}$ for a continuous distribution is

$$\overline{M}=\int_0^\infty Mf(M)\,dM=\text{mean lead time demand,}$$

and the standard deviation σ is the square root of the variance,

$$\sigma^2=\int_0^\infty (M-\overline{M})^2 f(M)\,dM=\text{variance of lead time demand.}$$

[1]See Appendix B for the procedures for obtaining optimality when the order quantity and reorder point are dependent. With dependence, the expressions are difficult, cumbersome, and iterative. Fortunately, the exact minimum cost solution based on dependence is closely approximated by the simpler solution methods based on independence of the order quantity and reorder point.

For discrete data, the following formulations apply:[2]

$$\overline{M}=\sum_{M=0}^{M_{\max}} MP(M)=\text{mean lead time demand},$$

$$\sigma^2=\sum_{M=0}^{M_{\max}} (M-\overline{M})^2 P(M)=\text{variance of lead time demand},$$

where

M = lead time demand in units (a random variable),
$f(M)$ = probability density function of lead time demand,
σ = standard deviation of lead time demand,
$P(M)$ = probability of a lead time demand of M units,
$M_{\max}$ = maximum lead time demand in units.

The probability of a stockout for a given item is simply the probability that the demand during the lead time will exceed the reorder point. When continuous distributions are employed, the stockout probability is the first definite integral of the probability density function of demand during the lead time from the reorder point to infinity, or

$$P(M>B)=P(s)=\int_B^{\infty} f(M)\,dM.$$

The expected stockout quantity during the lead time is the second definite integral of the probability density function of demand during the lead time from the reorder point to infinity, or

$$E(M>B)=\int_B^{\infty}\left[\int_M^{\infty} f(M)\,dM\right]dM=\int_B^{\infty}(M-B)f(M)\,dM.$$

For discrete data, the following formulations apply:

$$P(M>B)=P(s)=\sum_{M=B+1}^{M_{\max}} P(M),$$

$$E(M>B)=\sum_{M=B+1}^{M_{\max}} (M-B)P(M),$$

where

$P(M>B)=P(s)$ = probability of a stockout,
B = reorder point in units,
$f(M)$ = probability density function of demand during the lead time,
$E(M>B)$ = expected stockout in units during lead time.

[2] For discrete distributions, replace integrals with summations and density functions $f(M)$ with probabilities $P(M)$.

The normal, Poisson, and negative exponential distributions have been found to be of considerable value in describing demand functions. The normal distribution has been found to describe many demand functions at the factory level; the Poisson, at the retail level; and the negative exponential, at the wholesale and retail levels. Of course, these distributions should not be automatically applied to any demand situation. Statistical tests should establish the basis for any standard distribution assumption concerning a demand function.

Standard distributions should not be employed in inventory analysis merely for their computational efficiency. Before any standard distribution is employed, it should be verified by a goodness-of-fit test that the distribution is a reasonable representation for the demand or lead time. One such test is the chi-square test of fit. Appendix A at the end of this chapter outlines the chi-square goodness-of-fit test.

Normal Distribution

When demand is treated as continuous, the most frequently used distribution is the normal (also called the Gaussian) distribution. The normal distribution is easy to work with, and it is well tabulated. More importantly, the normal distribution tends to reasonably approximate phenomena encountered in practice. It has two defining parameters, the mean and standard deviation.

The normal distribution is a symmetrical bell-shaped curve with the three measures of central tendency (mean, median, and mode) equal. To the extent that these three measures of central tendency are the same or nearly identical, a frequency distribution can be approximated as normal. A basis for prediction with a normal distribution is the standard deviation of observations about the measures of central tendency. For a normal distribution 68.27% of all events occur within ± 1 standard deviation, 95.45% occur within ± 2 standard deviations, and 99.73% occur within ± 3 standard deviations of the mean. In inventory analysis, the standard deviation provides a means of estimating the safety stock required to provide a specific degree of protection above the average demand.

The normal distribution can take on an infinite number of symmetrical shapes about its mean, but in all of them demands are equally likely to be above or below the mean. The shape in any individual case is dictated by the standard deviation. For low levels of average demand, the normal distribution is inadequate, since its symmetrical nature would dictate the possibility of negative demand. Since negative demand is impossible, other distributions such as the Poisson are used for low levels of demand.

The general formula for the normal distribution is cumbersome and difficult to use. Fortunately, standardized normal distribution tables have been developed which simplify use. When demand is normally distributed, the reorder point can be obtained from the following formula:

$$B=\overline{M}+S=\overline{M}+Z\sigma=\text{reorder point in units},$$

where

$\overline{M}$ = average lead time demand in units,

S = safety stock in units,

Z = standard normal deviate,

σ = standard deviation of lead time demand.

The standard deviation is frequently cumbersome to calculate; it is adequately estimated as 1.25 times the mean absolute deviation (MAD) of forecast errors.

Poisson Distribution

For items of low demand, the discrete Poisson distribution is a very likely candidate for the demand distribution. The Poisson distribution is defined by a single parameter, the mean. The mean rate of demand can be determined by dividing the total number of units demanded over the relevant historical period by the length of the time interval. The standard deviation of the Poisson distribution is simply the square root of the mean ($\sigma=\sqrt{\overline{M}}$).

The Poisson distribution is not symmetrical with respect to the mean; there are more values to the right of (greater than) the mean than to the left. For this reason, the Poisson distribution is said to be skewed to the right. If average demand is large, the Poisson distribution is indistinguishable from the normal distribution.

The Poisson distribution is not commonly applicable to distributions with mean values above 20. Only slow-moving retail items are commonly described by this distribution. As a general rule, the smaller the mean, the greater the degree of skewness in the distribution. There are instances where demand is sporadic, discontinuous, and not particularly symmetrical. The Poisson distribution can be very helpful when these conditions occur. It is a good fit for small, infrequent demand where the demand rate is fairly constant.

Negative Exponential Distribution

The negative exponential distribution has been found to describe demand for some retail and wholesale situations. This continuous distribution is a single-parameter distribution, being completely defined by its mean. The standard deviation of the negative exponential distribution is also its mean ($\sigma=\overline{M}$).

The normal, Poisson, and negative exponential distributions have been reduced to tables. These statistical tables simplify the solution to inventory problems. Statistical tables will be introduced later in the chapter.

KNOWN STOCKOUT COSTS

Stockout cost is usually the most difficult inventory cost to ascertain. Stockout cost may be due to backorders or lost sales, and it may be expressed on a per unit basis, a per outage basis, or some other basis. The diversity of ways of stating stockout cost adds to the difficulty, which is compounded by uncertainty about the effect of dissatisfied customers' actions on future demand. This section will develop solution techniques for establishing the reorder point and safety stock when stockout costs are known (stockout costs will include backorder cost per unit, backorder cost per outage, lost sales cost per unit, and lost sales cost per outage) and the demand and lead time may be constant or variable.

When demand and lead time are variable, it is necessary to describe the relevant variation in some numerical fashion such as a frequency distribution. Unless dynamic factors are known to exist (trends, seasonals, and cyclics), the variation is assumed static and due to random or chance causes. When a distribution is used to describe demand, it is assumed that trends, seasonals, or cyclic effects are not present or they have been removed by standard statistical techniques. The distribution should contain only random variations. Dynamic variations which are due to nonrandom causes can be treated by adaptive forecasting techniques.

Constant Demand and Constant Lead Time

If demand and lead time are constant, there will be no safety stock, since inventory decisions are made under certainty. Since there is perfect knowledge of demand and lead time, a manager simply plans the inventory level to match demand. Under these conditions, the inventory will be at the zero level when the replenishment order is received. This assumption of perfect knowledge of demand and lead time is usually unrealistic. But in certain cases, some products may exhibit a high degree of regularity which permits the deterministic treatment as outlined in Chapter 3. Traditional inventory models frequently assume constant demand and lead time.

Variable Demand and Constant Lead Time

The assumption of constant lead time is frequently realistic for many items. When the variation in lead time is small in relation to the average lead time, probabilistic lead times can be closely approximated by a constant lead time. Also, contractual stipulations can render the lead time nearly certain.

When the supply is from an internal source (one department or division supplying items for another department or division of the same organization), the lead time is controllable. Figure 4 exemplifies the variable demand, constant lead time situation.

If a historical distribution of demand is available, the safety stock can be determined by selecting a safety stock level that results in the lowest expected cost. It is easy to determine the safety stock using this method. The objective is to minimize the sum of the cost of holding the safety stock and the cost of the stockouts. As the size of the safety stock increases, the holding costs increase but the stockout costs decrease. As the safety stock is decreased, the stockout costs increase but the holding costs decrease. The danger of a stockout occurs only during the lead time. There are R/Q lead times per year.

Frequently, the demand distribution is expressed on a time basis that is different from the lead time. Under these conditions, it is necessary to modify the demand distribution so it specifies lead time demand. The technique of modifying demand for varying-length time periods is termed convolution. Probability distribution convolutions are described at the end of this chapter in Appendix C.

Figure 4. Inventory risk.
Key: $B-S$=expected lead time demand; $B-J$=minimum lead time demand; $B-W$=maximum lead time demand; B=reorder point; Q=order quantity; L= constant lead time; $P(s)$=probability of a stockout; $1-P(s)$=probability of no stockout; S=safety stock.

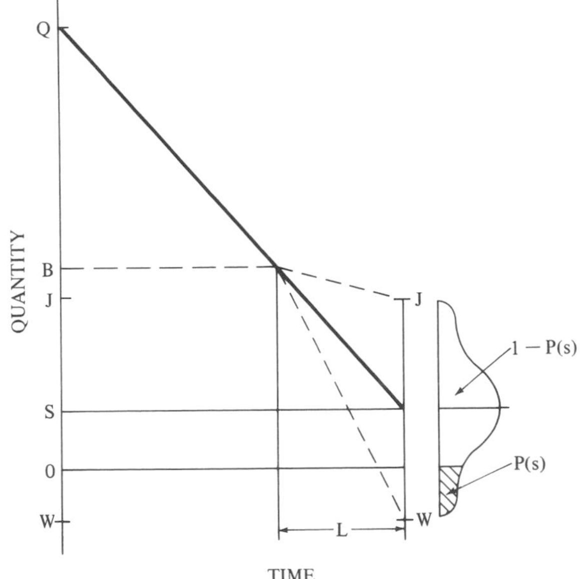

Backorder Case: Stockout Cost Per Unit

With backorders, there is no loss of sales, since the customer awaits the arrival of the order if stock is not available. The expected safety stock is defined as

$$S=\int_0^{\infty}(B-M)f(M)\,dM=B\int_0^{\infty}f(M)\,dM-\int_0^{\infty}Mf(M)\,dM=B-\overline{M},$$

where $\overline{M}$ is the expected lead time demand, and the number of backorders per lead time is zero if $M-B<0$ and $M-B$ if $M-B>0$. The expected number of backorders per lead time is

$$E(M>B)=\int_B^{\infty}(M-B)f(M)\,dM.$$

The appropriate mathematical notation is as follows for a continuous distribution when the stockout cost is on a per unit basis:

Annual safety stock cost = (holding cost) + (stockout cost),

$$\begin{aligned}\mathrm{TC}_s&=SH+\frac{AR}{Q}\int_B^{\infty}(M-B)f(M)\,dM\\&=H(B-\overline{M})+\frac{AR}{Q}\int_B^{\infty}(M-B)f(M)\,dM\\&=H(B-\overline{M})+\frac{ARE(M>B)}{Q},\end{aligned}$$

where

TC_s = expected annual cost of safety stock,
$B=\overline{M}+S$ = reorder point in units,
S = safety stock in units,
H = holding cost per unit of inventory per year,
A = backordering cost per unit,
R = average annual demand in units,
Q = lot size or order quantity in units,
M = lead time demand in units (a random variable),
$\overline{M}$ = average lead time demand in units,
$f(M)$ = probability density function of lead time demand,
$M-B$ = size of stockout in units.

By taking the derivative of the expected annual cost of safety stock with respect to the reorder point and setting it equal to zero, the following

Table 1

Lead Time Demand M	Probability $P(M)$	Probability of Demand $> M$, $P(s)$
48	0.02	0.98
49	0.03	0.95
50	0.06	0.89
51	0.07	0.82
52	0.20	0.62
53	0.24	0.38
54	0.20	0.18
55	0.07	0.11
56	0.06	0.05←
57	0.03	0.02
58	0.02	0.00
	1.00	

optimizing relationship results:[3]

$$P(M>B)=P(s)=\frac{HQ}{AR}=\text{optimum probability of a stockout.}$$

The above formula can be applied to both discrete and continuous probability distributions of lead time demand. Knowing the probability distribution permits the determination of the value of B which has the minimum expected annual cost. When discrete distributions are employed, the exact optimum stockout probability is frequently unattainable because of the discrete nature of the data. When the optimum stockout probability cannot be attained, the next lower attainable stockout probability is selected. A simple example will illustrate the procedure.

EXAMPLE 1

What is the optimal reorder point for the inventory problem specified below and in Table 1?

$R=1800$ units/year,

$C=\$30.00$ per order,

$F=15\%$,

$P=\$2.00$/unit,

$A=\$1.00$ per unit backordered.

[3]See L. A. Johnson and D. C. Montgomery, *Operations Research in Production Planning, Scheduling, and Inventory Control*, Wiley, 1974, pp. 59–62, for the mechanics of the derivation. If $HQ/AR>1$, it indicates the cost of a stockout is so small that it is desirable to incur backorders.

To solve the above problem, it is necessary to determine the economic order quantity and then the optimum probability of a stockout:

$$Q_0 = \sqrt{\frac{2CR}{PF}} = \sqrt{\frac{2(30)1800}{2(0.15)}} = 600 \text{ units},$$

$$P(M>B) = \frac{HQ}{AR} = \frac{0.30(600)}{1(1800)} = 0.10.$$

By consulting the last column in Table 1 for $P(s)=0.10$, we see the computed value is between 0.05 and 0.11. Selecting the smallest value (0.05), the reorder point is 56 units. The fixed order size system would function with $Q=600$ units and $B=56$ units.

Backorder Case: Stockout Cost per Outage

The formulations previously developed for the backorder case have been for determining safety stock when the stockout cost is on a per unit basis. The stockout cost may also be on an outage basis. An outage is a condition with one or more stockouts during the lead time period. Only one outage can occur per lead time period, and the stockout cost is independent of the size of the outage. The number of times the organization is exposed to a stockout of an item is equal to the number of times an order is placed. In an annual period there are R/Q opportunities for a stockout. When the stockout cost is a constant amount for each outage without reference to the number of units out of stock, the following formulation applies for a continuous distribution:

Annual cost of safety stock = (holding cost) + (stockout cost),

$$\mathrm{TC}_s = SH + G\frac{R}{Q}\int_B^{\infty} f(M)\,dM$$

$$= H(B-\overline{M}) + \frac{GRP(M>B)}{Q},$$

where

TC_s = expected annual cost of safety stock,

$B=S+\overline{M}$ = reorder point in units,

S = safety stock in units,

H = holding or carrying cost per unit per year,

G = backordering cost per outage,

R = average annual demand in units,

Q = lot size or order quantity in units,

$f(M)$ = probability density function of lead time demand,

$\overline{M}$ = average lead time demand in units.

If the derivative of the expected annual cost of safety stock with respect to the reorder point is taken and set equal to zero, the following relationship is obtained:[4]

$$f(B)=\frac{HQ}{GR}.$$

The above optimum relationship was developed for a continuous distribution, but frequently only integer values of inventory are possible. When the optimum reorder point lies between two integer values, select the integer with the larger $f(B)$.

For the standard normal distribution the optimum reorder point is *not* obtained from the above formula, since the ordinate $f(B)$ undergoes a change of scale when it is transformed to the standard normal distribution. Thus, if we are to find where $f(B)=0.05$, we must find where the standard normal distribution has an ordinate of 0.05σ. The standard normal deviate Z for the optimum stockout probability can be obtained directly from the standard normal table if $\sigma f(B)$ is known (see Table 2 on p. 142).

If the demand follows a normal distribution, the optimizing safety stock can be determined from Table 2 and the following formulas:

$$Z=\frac{B-\overline{M}}{\sigma}=\frac{B-\overline{D}L}{\sigma_D\sqrt{L}}=\frac{S}{\sigma_D\sqrt{L}},$$

$$S=Z\sigma=Z\sigma_D\sqrt{L},$$

where

Z = standard normal deviate,

$B=\overline{D}L+S$ = reorder point in units,

$\overline{M}=\overline{D}L$ = average lead time demand,

σ = standard deviation of lead time demand,

L = lead time,

S = safety stock in units,

σ_D = standard deviation of demand for a time period other than the lead time.

EXAMPLE 2

Weekly demand is normally distributed with a mean of 20 units and a standard deviation of 4. What is the optimum reorder point if holding costs are \$5.00 per

[4]See Martin K. Starr and David W. Miller, *Inventory Control: Theory and Practice*, Englewood Cliffs, NJ: Prentice-Hall, 1962, p. 63 for the mechanics of the derivation.

year, the backorder cost is \$10.00 per outage, the order quantity is 26 units, and the lead time is 1 week?

$$\sigma f(B)=\frac{\sigma HQ}{GR}=\frac{4(5)26}{10(52)20}=0.05$$

From Table 2 an ordinate of 0.05 gives Z of 2.03. Thus

$$S=Z\sigma=2.03(4)=8.12, \text{ or } 8 \text{ units},$$

$$B=\overline{M}+S=20+8=28 \text{ units}.$$

The optimum safety stock is 8 units, with a reorder point of 28 units.

If demand follows a Poisson distribution, the optimizing inventory policy can be obtained from Poisson tables such as Table 3. A simple example can best illustrate the use of the Poisson table.

EXAMPLE 3

The weekly demand for an item is Poisson distributed with a mean of 5 units. What is the optimum reorder point level if holding costs are \$5.00 per unit per year, the backorder cost is \$5.00 per outage, the lead time is 1 week, and the order quantity is 13 units?

$$f(B)=\frac{HQ}{GR}=\frac{5(13)}{5(52)5}=.05.$$

In the Poisson table for a lead time demand of 5 units, we find .05 between .036 and .065. Selecting the largest $f(B)$, the optimal reorder point is 8 units and the safety stock is 3 units.

Lost Sales Case: Stockout Cost per Unit

The treatment of lost sales does not differ substantially from that of the backorder cost. With lost sales, all stockouts (shortages) are lost and not recovered. The average number of annual cycles is no longer R/Q but is $R/(Q+tR)$, where t is the average length of time per cycle when the system is out of stock. Usually t is a small fraction of the total cycle time, so we will assume the average number of annual cycles is still R/Q.

The only difference between the lost sales case and the backorder case is in the safety stock expression. The expected amount of safety stock on hand when a new order arrives has previously been established as

$$S=\int_0^{\infty}(B-M)f(M)\,dM=B-\overline{M},$$

Table 2. Standard Normal Distribution

Standard Normal Deviate Z	Probability of a Stockout $P(s)$	Ordinate $\sigma f(B)$	Partial Expectation $E(Z)$
−4.00	.9999	.0001	
.00	.5000	.3989	.3989
.05	.4801	.3984	.3744
.10	.4602	.3969	.3509
.15	.4404	.3945	.3284
.20	.4207	.3910	.3069
.25	.4013	.3867	.2863
.30	.3821	.3814	.2668
.35	.3632	.3752	.2481
.40	.3446	.3683	.2304
.45	.3264	.3605	.2137
.50	.3086	.3521	.1978
.55	.2912	.3429	.1828
.60	.2743	.3332	.1687
.65	.2579	.3229	.1554
.70	.2420	.3123	.1429
.75	.2267	.3011	.1312
.80	.2119	.2897	.1202
.85	.1977	.2780	.1100
.90	.1841	.2661	.1004
.95	.1711	.2541	.0916
1.00	.1587	.2420	.0833
1.05	.1469	.2300	.0757
1.10	.1357	.2179	.0686
1.15	.1251	.2059	.0621
1.20	.1151	.1942	.0561
1.25	.1057	.1826	.0506
1.30	.0968	.1714	.0455
1.35	.0886	.1604	.0409
1.40	.0808	.1497	.0367
1.45	.0736	.1394	.0328
1.50	.0669	.1295	.0293
1.55	.0606	.1200	.0261
1.60	.0548	.1109	.0232
1.65	.0495	.1023	.0206

Table 2 *(continued)*

Standard Normal Deviate Z	Probability of a Stockout $P(s)$	Ordinate $\sigma f(B)$	Partial Expectation $E(Z)$
1.70	.0446	.0940	.0183
1.75	.0401	.0863	.0162
1.80	.0360	.0790	.0143
1.85	.0322	.0721	.0126
1.90	.0288	.0656	.0111
1.95	.0256	.0596	.0097
2.00	.0228	.0540	.0085
2.05	.0202	.0488	.0074
2.10	.0179	.0440	.0065
2.15	.0158	.0396	.0056
2.20	.0140	.0355	.0049
2.25	.0122	.0317	.0042
2.30	.0107	.0283	.0037
2.35	.0094	.0252	.0032
2.40	.0082	.0224	.0027
2.45	.0071	.0198	.0023
2.50	.0062	.0175	.0020
2.55	.0054	.0154	.0017
2.60	.0047	.0136	.0015
2.65	.0040	.0119	.0012
2.70	.0035	.0104	.0011
2.75	.0030	.0091	.0009
2.80	.0026	.0079	.0008
2.85	.0022	.0069	.0006
2.90	.0019	.0059	.0005
2.95	.0016	.0051	.00045
3.00	.0015	.0044	.00038
3.10	.0010	.0033	.00027
3.20	.0007	.0024	.00018
3.30	.0005	.0017	.00013
3.40	.0004	.0012	.00009
3.50	.0003	.0009	.00006
3.60	.0002	.0006	.00004
3.80	.0001	.0003	.00002
4.00	.00003	.0001	.00001

Table 3. Poisson Distribution

Reorder Point B^b	$f(B)^a$										
	$\overline{M}^c=$ 2	3	4	5	6	7	8	9	10	11	12
2	.271										
3	.180	.224									
4	.090	.168	.195								
5	.036	.101	.156	.176							
6	.012	.050	.104	.146	.161						
7	.003	.022	.059	.104	.138	.149					
8	.001	.008	.029	.065	.103	.130	.139				
9		.003	.013	.036	.069	.101	.124	.131			
10		.001	.005	.018	.041	.071	.099	.119	.125		
11			.002	.008	.023	.045	.072	.097	.114	.119	
12			.001	.003	.011	.026	.048	.073	.095	.109	.114
13				.001	.005	.014	.029	.050	.073	.093	.106
14					.002	.007	.017	.032	.052	.073	.091
15					.001	.003	.009	.019	.035	.053	.072
16						.001	.005	.011	.022	.037	.054
17							.002	.006	.013	.024	.038
18							.001	.003	.007	.015	.026
19								.001	.004	.008	.016
20									.002	.005	.010
21									.001	.002	.006
22										.001	.003
23											.002
24											.001

[a] The fractions in the table are the probabilities associated with exactly B demands during a lead time with an average demand of $\overline{M}$ units.

[b] $B=$ reorder point $=\overline{D}L+S=M_a$.

[c] $\overline{M}=$ average lead time demand $=\overline{D}L$.

but since the safety stock is zero whenever $M \geq B$, the expression can be rewritten as

$$
\begin{aligned}
S &= \int_0^B (B-M) f(M)\, dM \\
&= \int_0^\infty (B-M) f(M)\, dM - \int_B^\infty (B-M) f(M)\, dM \\
&= B\int_0^\infty f(M)\, dM - \int_0^\infty M f(M)\, dM - \int_B^\infty (B-M) f(M)\, dM \\
&= B - \overline{M} + \int_B^\infty (M-B) f(M)\, dM.
\end{aligned}
$$

Note that in the backordering case (no lost sales), the safety stock was simply $B-\overline{M}$, or the reorder point minus the lead time demand. In the lost sales case, the safety stock is greater than $B-\overline{M}$ by the expected number of lost sales for each cycle. The expected number of lost sales per cycle is precisely the same as the expected number of backorders per cycle in the previous analysis. The expected number of lost sales per lead time is

$$E(M>B)=\int_{B}^{\infty}(M-B)f(M)\,dM.$$

The appropriate mathematical notation is as follows for a continuous distribution with stockout cost on a per unit basis:

$$\text{Annual cost of safety stock}=(\text{holding cost})+(\text{stockout cost}),$$

$$\mathrm{TC}_s=HS+\frac{AR}{Q}\int_{B}^{\infty}(M-B)f(M)\,dM$$

$$=H(B-\overline{M})+\left(\frac{AR}{Q}+H\right)\int_{B}^{\infty}(M-B)f(M)\,dM,$$

$$\mathrm{TC}_s=H(B-\overline{M})+\left(\frac{AR}{Q}+H\right)E(M>B),$$

where

TC_s = expected annual cost of safety stock,
S = safety stock in units,
B = reorder point in units,
H = holding cost per unit of inventory per year,
A = lost sales cost per unit,
R = average annual demand in units,
Q = order quantity in units,
M = lead time demand in units (a random variable),
$\overline{M}$ = average lead time demand in units,
$f(M)$ = probability density function of lead time demand,
$M-B$ = size of stockout in units.

By taking the derivative of the expected annual safety stock cost with respect to the reorder point and setting it equal to zero, the following relationship results:[5]

$$P(M>B)=P(s)=\frac{HQ}{AR+HQ}.$$

[5]See Lynwood A. Johnson and Douglas C. Montgomery, *Operations Research in Production Planning, Scheduling and Inventory Control*, New York: John Wiley and Sons, 1974, pp. 64–65 for the mechanics of the derivation.

The above formula gives the optimum probability of a stockout. It can be applied to both discrete and continuous probability distributions of lead time demand. Knowing the probability distribution permits the determination of the value of B which has the minimum expected cost.

EXAMPLE 4

An organization orders an item in lots of 1000 units for which it has a 5000 unit yearly demand. The holding cost per unit per year is \$10, and the lost sales cost per unit is \$50. Determine the minimum cost reorder point from the demand history in Table 4 during a constant lead time period.

Table 4

Demand M	Demand Probability $P(M)$	Probability of Demand $>M$, $P(s)$
150	.01	.99
200	.04	.95
250	.21	.74
300	.55	.19
350	.09	.10
400	.07	.03 ←
450	.03	.00

$$P(s)=\frac{HQ}{AR+HQ}=\frac{10(1000)}{50(5000)+10(1000)}=0.038.$$

The optimum probability of a stockout is 0.038, which is between the probabilities of 0.10 and 0.03 associated with 350 and 400 units. The reorder point should be set at 400 units.

Lost Sales Case: Stockout Cost per Outage

The appropriate mathematical notation for a continuous distribution with stockout cost on an outage basis is

$$\mathrm{TC}_s=SH+\frac{GR}{Q}\int_B^\infty f(M)\,dM,$$

$$\mathrm{TC}_s=H(B-\overline{M})+H\int_B^\infty (M-B)f(M)\,dM+\frac{GR}{Q}\int_B^\infty f(M)\,dM,$$

$$\mathrm{TC}_s=H(B-\overline{M})+HE(M>B)+\frac{GRP(M>B)}{Q},$$

where G is the lost sales cost per outage. To minimize the above expression, the derivative of the expected annual safety stock cost with respect to B is set equal to zero:

$$\frac{d\,\mathrm{TC}_s}{dB}=0=H-HP(M>B)-\frac{GR}{Q}f(B),$$

$$f(B)=\frac{HQ[1-P(M>B)]}{GR}.$$

Constant Demand and Variable Lead Time

When the lead time is variable, it is possible to establish the reorder point in terms of the minimum lead time, average lead time, or maximum lead time. With respect to the minimum or maximum limits, the reorder points would be substantially different. A reorder point based on the minimum lead time would tend to provide inadequate protection, and one based on the maximum lead time would result in excessive stock levels. If the impact of a variable lead time is not evaluated statistically, the most common practice is to base the reorder point on the average lead time. If substantial variation in lead time is experienced, a more formal statistical analysis is warranted.

When the demand is constant and the lead time is variable, the solution techniques are similar to the variable demand, constant lead time case. The basic difference is that the demand during the lead time is obtained by multiplying the constant demand by the frequency distribution for lead time. The mathematical formulations and computations are similar.

EXAMPLE 5

An organization has a yearly demand of 260 units for a product purchased in lots of 25 units. The weekly demand is constant at 5 units. The holding cost per year is $10, and the backorder cost per unit is $10. What is the optimum reorder point if the weekly lead time is defined by the distribution shown in Table 5?

Table 5

Lead Time L	Probability $P(L)$
3	0.25
4	0.35
5	0.25
6	0.10
7	0.05
	1.00

The optimum stockout probability for backordering with stockout cost on a per unit basis is obtained as follows (see Table 6):

$$P(s)=\frac{HQ}{AR}=\frac{10(25)}{10(260)}=0.096.$$

Table 6

Lead Time Demand M	Probability $P(M)$	$MP(M)$	Probability of Demand $>M$, $P(s)$
15	0.25	3.75	0.75
20	0.35	7.00	0.40
25	0.25	6.25	0.15
30	0.10	3.00	0.05←
35	0.05	1.75	0.00
	1.00	$\overline{M}=21.75$	

The optimum reorder point is associated with a stockout probability of 0.096, which is between the probabilities 0.15 and 0.05 associated with demand levels of 25 and 30. The optimum reorder point is 30 units, which results in a safety stock of 8 units.

It is desirable for an organization to have short average lead times and consistent lead times. Both conditions permit safety stock levels to be at a minimum.

Variable Demand and Variable Lead Time

When both demand and lead time are variable, there is an increase in problem complexity. As in the previous sections, however, the objective is to set the reorder point at its lowest expected cost.

It is in fact rare to find a situation in practice where the lead time is known exactly. The factors that make up the lead time are subject to random variation, so that lead time is better described by a probability distribution than by a point estimate. In the case where both demand and lead time uncertainties are accounted for simultaneously, a joint probability distribution can be created that gives the probabilities for various combinations of demand level and lead time length. The range of the joint probability distribution is from the level indicated by the product of the smallest demand and the shortest lead time to the level indicated by the product of the largest demand and the largest lead time. The joint probability distribution is then used with the formulas developed in the previous section for the lead time demand. To deal with the joint probability approach in a rigorous mathematical manner is extremely difficult, and consequently, only models of limited applicability have been developed. See Appendix D at the end of this chapter for further elaboration on the analytical joint probability approach.

Where the demand and lead time distributions are independent, the variance of the demand during the lead time is given by[6]

$$\sigma^2 = \bar{L}\sigma_D^2 + \bar{D}^2\sigma_L^2,$$

where

$\bar{L}$ = average lead time length in days,

$\bar{D}$ = average demand per day,

σ_D = standard deviation of demand distribution,

σ_L = standard deviation of lead time distribution,

σ = standard deviation of demand during lead time,

$\bar{D}\bar{L}$ = average demand during lead time.

If the demand and lead time distributions are not independent, the variance of the demand during the lead time is given by

$$\sigma^2 = \bar{L}^2\sigma_D^2 + \bar{D}^2\sigma_L^2 + \sigma_D\sigma_L.$$

If it is not desirable to use the analytical joint probability approach, an equally appropriate approach is Monte Carlo simulation.[7] The Monte Carlo method approximates the solution to the problem by sampling from a random process. Monte Carlo simulation will be outlined in a subsequent chapter.

In summary, for fixed order size systems with known stockout costs, a comparison can be made between deterministic and probabilistic formulas. For deterministic systems, the demand and lead time are constant. The order quantity and reorder point formulas for deterministic systems are contained in Table 7. For probabilistic systems demand and lead time can either or both be variable. The order quantity and reorder point formulas for probabilistic systems are contained in Table 8.

SERVICE LEVELS

Perhaps the most common situation is when an organization does not know its stockout costs or feels very uneasy about estimating them. Under these conditions, it is common for management to set service levels from which reorder points can be ascertained. A service level indicates the ability to meet customer demands from stock.

[6]See Robert G. Brown, *Smoothing, Forecasting, and Prediction of Discrete Time Series*, Prentice-Hall, 1963, pp. 366–367.

[7]See Claude McMillan and Richard F. Gonzales, *Systems Analysis: A Computer Approach to Decision Models*, Homewood, IL: Richard D. Irwin, 1968, Chapter 7, for the analytical and Monte Carlo simulation approaches to establishing joint distributions.

Table 7. Fixed Order Size System Formulas (Deterministic Case)

Stockout Case[b]	Stockout Cost per Unit[a]	
	Economic Order Quantity Q_0	Reorder Point B
No stockouts permitted	$\sqrt{\frac{2CR}{H}}$	RL
Backordering	$\sqrt{\frac{2CR}{H}}\sqrt{\frac{H+K}{K}}$	$RL-(Q-V)$
Lost sales	—[c]	—[c]

[a]Symbols: H=holding cost per unit per year, R=annual demand in units, C=order cost per order, K=backorder cost per unit, L=lead time in years, V=maximum inventory level in units, $Q-V$=number of backordered units.

[b]When no stockouts are permitted, the stockout cost is infinite; when stockouts are permitted, the stockout cost is finite.

[c]With a deterministic fixed order size system, no lost sales will occur, since the demand is known and can be satisfied.

Table 8. Fixed Order Size System Formulas (Risk Case)

Stockout Case	Known Stockout Cost			
	Economic Order Quantity Q_0[a]		Reorder Point B[b]	
	Stockout Cost per Unit	Stockout Cost per Outage	Stockout Cost per Unit	Stockout Cost per Outage[c]
Backordering	$\sqrt{\frac{2CR}{H}}$	$\sqrt{\frac{2CR}{H}}$	$P(M>B)=\frac{HQ}{AR}$	$f(B)=\frac{HQ}{GR}$
Lost sales	$\sqrt{\frac{2CR}{H}}$	$\sqrt{\frac{2CR}{H}}$	$P(M>B)=\frac{HQ}{AR+HQ}$	$f(B)=\frac{HQ[1-P(M>B)]}{GR}$

[a]It is assumed that the deterministic EOQ is an adequate approximation because of its insensitivity. See Appendix B for more exact mathematical relationships without the deterministic assumption.

[b]The formulas in the table give the optimum reorder point for the appropriate lead time demand distribution.

[c]For the standard normal distribution, the ordinate of the distribution is $\sigma f(B)$.

There are several ways to measure a service level. It can be computed on units, dollars, transactions, or orders. It is frequently defined for some specified time period when orders are normally filled from stock. It may be specified in general as the percentage of demand filled "on time," that is, within a specified time period after receipt of the customer's order. No one service level measure will be appropriate for all the items in inventory. Different levels of control may be desirable for different classes of inventory items.

The establishment of service levels is a subjective management judgment that is based on convenience rather than scientific justification. The choice by management of a service level implies a cost attributed intuitively or indirectly to service failure.

If a customer always receives his order when demanded, the service level is 100%. Anything less than 100% means some disservice or stockout. The service level and the stockout level sum to 100%. Not only is it extremely difficult to guarantee that demand will always be satisfied, but also it is likely that such a guarantee will be far too costly. A policy of never having a stockout is generally not economical. The principle of diminishing returns applies. As the service level approaches 100%, the investment in safety stock often increases drastically. It may not cost much to increase from 85 to 90%, but going to 99% may be prohibitively expensive. Thus, most organizations consider a "reasonable" number of stockouts acceptable because of the high cost of trying to eliminate them altogether.

There are environments where service levels at or near 100% are necessary. In manufacturing organizations failure to provide a needed part could potentially bring a production line to a halt. Inventory in this environment is better suited to an MRP system than to a fixed order size system.

The service level takes on different meanings depending upon how it is stated as a decision criterion. Four commonly used service levels are:

1. Frequency of service per order cycle
2. Frequency of service per year
3. Fraction of units demanded
4. Fraction of operating days

The reorder points or safety stocks developed under the different service concepts will be different. The selection of the type and level of service is a management policy decision.

Service per Order Cycle

A service level based on frequency of service per order cycle will indicate the probability of not running out of stock during the replenishment (lead time) period. This approach does not concern itself with how large the shortage is, but with how often it can occur during the lead time (order cycle). It is defined as the fraction of replenishment cycles without depletion of stock:

Service level fraction per cycle

$$= 1 - \frac{\text{number of order periods with a stockout}}{\text{total number of order periods}}$$

$$= 1 - P(M > B),$$

$$P(M>B) = P(s)$$

$$= 1 - (\text{service level fraction per cycle})$$

$$= \frac{\text{number of order periods with a stockout}}{\text{total number of order periods}}.$$

The term $P(s)$ is the stockout level fraction per order cycle or the probability of at least one stockout while awaiting a supplier's delivery. It is also a measure of the fraction of lead time periods during which the demand will exceed the reorder point. The magnitude of the stockout is ignored with this approach.

The safety stock is determined as follows when a service per order cycle is adopted:

$$\text{Safety stock} = S = M_a - \overline{M} = M_a - \overline{D}L,$$

where

$M_a = B =$ lead time demand at acceptable service level in units,
$\overline{M} =$ average lead time demand in units,
$L =$ constant lead time in days,
$\overline{D} =$ average daily demand in units.

EXAMPLE 6

What should be the order quantity and reorder point for the inventory problem specified below and in Table 9?

Stockout level fraction per order cycle $= 0.125$,
$R = 18{,}000$ units/year,
$C = \$200$ per order,
$H = \$5$ per unit per year,
$L = 1$ day.

$$Q_0 = \sqrt{\frac{2CR}{H}} = \sqrt{\frac{2(200)18{,}000}{5}} = 1200 \text{ units},$$

$$\text{Average demand} = \overline{M} = \Sigma MP(M) = 60 \text{ units}.$$

Table 9

Lead Time Demand in Units, M	Probability $P(M)$	$MP(M)$	Probability of Demand $>M$, $P(s)$
30	0.025	0.75	0.975
40	0.100	4.00	0.875
50	0.200	10.00	0.675
60	0.350	21.00	0.325
70	0.200	14.00	0.125←
80	0.100	8.00	0.025
90	0.025	2.25	0
	1.000	60.00	

Consulting Table 9 for $P(s)=0.125$, we obtain

$$M_a=B=70 \text{ units},$$

$$\text{Safety stock}=S=M_a-\overline{M}=70-60=10 \text{ units}.$$

The order quantity would be 1200 units and the reorder point 70 units.

EXAMPLE 7

From the information given in Example 6, what would be the reorder point under the conservative method (100% service level)?

$$S=M_{\max}-\overline{M}=90-60=30 \text{ units},$$

$$B=M_{\max}=90.$$

Reorder point determination can be simplified considerably if the demand follows some known distribution such as the normal, Poisson, or negative exponential. Since these distributions have no upper bound, the 100% service level or conservative method cannot be used with them. The stockout service level can be readily used with a standard distribution.

The normal distribution is completely defined by its mean $\overline{D}$ and standard deviation σ_D. A service level of 95% indicates that you will be out of stock 5% of the cycles. Table 10 indicates how the demand at an acceptable service level is obtained when the normal distribution applies.

EXAMPLE 8

If the distribution given in Example 6 is assumed normal with a standard deviation σ_D of 20 units, what will be the safety stock if a 95% service level per order cycle is desired?

$$M_a = B = \bar{D}L + 1.64\sigma_D\sqrt{L} = 60(1) + 1.64(20)\sqrt{1} = 92.8,$$

$$\text{Safety stock} = S = M_a - \bar{D}L = 92.8 - 60 = 32.8 \approx 33 \text{ units}.$$

Table 10. Standard Normal Distribution

Reorder Point $M_a = B$	Probability of Stockout $P(s)$
$\bar{D}L + 3.09\sigma_D\sqrt{L}$	.001
$\bar{D}L + 2.58\sigma_D\sqrt{L}$	.005
$\bar{D}L + 2.33\sigma_D\sqrt{L}$	.010
$\bar{D}L + 1.96\sigma_D\sqrt{L}$	.025
$\bar{D}L + 1.64\sigma_D\sqrt{L}$	.050
$\bar{D}L + 1.28\sigma_D\sqrt{L}$	.100
$\bar{D}L + 1.04\sigma_D\sqrt{L}$	.150
$\bar{D}L + 0.85\sigma_D\sqrt{L}$	.200
$\bar{D}L + 0.67\sigma_D\sqrt{L}$	.250

EXAMPLE 9

If the annual demand for an item is a normally distributed random variable with a mean of 8000 units and a standard deviation of 1000 units, what should the safety stock and reorder point be if the lead time is $\frac{1}{2}$ month? (Assume management has decided it is willing to be out of stock in 5% of the order cycles.)

Since the mean and standard deviation are expressed on an annual basis and the lead time is on a monthly basis, the mean and standard deviation are adjusted to a monthly basis:

$$\bar{D} = \frac{R}{12} = \frac{8000}{12} = 667,$$

$$\sigma_D = \sigma\sqrt{\tfrac{1}{12}} = 1000\sqrt{\tfrac{1}{12}} = 288,$$

$$B = M_a = \bar{D}L + 1.64\sigma_D\sqrt{L} = 667(0.5) + 1.64(288)\sqrt{0.5} = 669,$$

$$S = M_a - \bar{D}L = 669 - (667)0.5 = 335 \text{ units}.$$

The safety stock is 335 units, and the reorder point is 669 units.

The Poisson distribution is completely defined by its mean $\bar{D}$. The standard deviation of the Poisson distribution is the square root of its mean ($\sigma_D = \sqrt{\bar{D}}$), so knowledge of average demand is sufficient to describe the distribution. To use an order cycle service level with the Poisson distribution assumption requires the use of a statistical table of the summed Poisson distribution. Table 11 is an abbreviated summed Poisson table. To use the

Table 11. Cumulative Poisson Distribution

Reorder Point B^b	Stockout Probability[a]									
	$\bar{M}^c =$ 2	3	4	5	6	7	8	9	10	12
2	.323									
3	.143	.353								
4	.053	.185	.371							
5	.017	.084	.215	.384						
6	.004	.033	.111	.238	.394					
7	.001	.012	.051	.133	.256	.401				
8		.004	.021	.068	.153	.271	.407			
9		.001	.008	.032	.084	.169	.283	.413		
10			.003	.014	.043	.098	.184	.294	.417	
11			.001	.005	.020	.053	.112	.197	.303	
12				.002	.009	.027	.064	.124	.208	.424
13				.001	.004	.013	.034	.074	.135	.319
14					.001	.006	.018	.041	.083	.228
15						.002	.008	.022	.049	.156
16						.001	.004	.011	.027	.101
17							.002	.005	.014	.063
18							.001	.002	.007	.037
19								.001	.003	.021
20									.002	.012
21									.001	.006
22										.003
23										.002
24										.001

[a] The fractions are the stockout probabilities associated with a given reorder point and an average lead time demand.

[b] Reorder point $B=\bar{D}L+S=M_a$.

[c] Average lead time demand $\bar{M}=\bar{D}L$.

summed Poisson table, you locate the average demand column and descend on it until you obtain the stockout probability. The desired inventory level M_a is then read from the corresponding value in the first column.

EXAMPLE 10

The average daily demand for an item is 2 units, and the lead time demand is Poisson distributed. What should be the reorder point if a 96.6% service level per order cycle is desired? (Assume a lead time of 4 days.)

From the summed Poisson table for an average lead time demand of 8 units, we find that B is 13 units for a stockout level of 0.034;

$$\text{Safety stock} = S = B - \bar{D}L = 13 - (2)4 = 5 \text{ units.}$$

The negative exponential distribution is also defined by its mean $\bar{D}$. The standard deviation of the distribution is equal to its mean ($\sigma_D = \bar{D}$). To use a service level policy with the negative exponential distribution requires the use of a statistical table. Table 12 is useful in determining the reorder point when the demand follows a negative exponential distribution.

EXAMPLE 11

If the average daily demand for an item is 2 units and the lead time demand is negative exponentially distributed, what should be the reorder point if a 95% service level per order cycle is desired? Assume a lead time of 4 days.

Table 12. Negative Exponential Distribution

$\frac{B}{\bar{D}L} = \frac{M_a}{\bar{M}} = \frac{\bar{D}L+S}{\bar{D}L}$	Stockout Probability $P(s)$	$\frac{B}{\bar{D}L} = \frac{M_a}{\bar{M}} = \frac{\bar{D}L+S}{\bar{D}L}$	Stockout Probability $P(s)$
0	1.000	2.80	0.061
0.10	0.905	2.90	0.055
0.20	0.819	3.00	0.050
0.50	0.607	3.10	0.045
0.75	0.472	3.20	0.041
1.00	0.368	3.30	0.037
1.10	0.333	3.40	0.033
1.20	0.301	3.50	0.030
1.30	0.273	3.60	0.027
1.40	0.247	3.70	0.025
1.50	0.223	3.80	0.022
1.60	0.202	4.00	0.018
1.70	0.183	4.20	0.015
1.80	0.165	4.40	0.012
1.90	0.149	4.60	0.010
2.00	0.135	4.80	0.008
2.10	0.122	5.00	0.007
2.20	0.111	5.20	0.006
2.30	0.100	5.40	0.005
2.40	0.091	5.60	0.004
2.50	0.082	5.80	0.003
2.60	0.074	6.00	0.002
2.70	0.067		

A stockout level of 0.05 gives $M_a/\overline{M}=3.00$, from Table 12; thus

$$\text{Reorder point}=M_a=3\overline{M}=3\overline{D}L=3(2)4=24 \text{ units},$$

$$\text{Safety stock}=S=M_a-\overline{M}=24-4(2)=16 \text{ units}.$$

A service level based on the frequency of service per order cycle does not indicate how frequently stockouts will occur over a given time period for all products. This unfortunate situation exists because the order cycle will vary from product to product. If an organization replenishes stock monthly with a 90% service level, there will be 1.2 (12×0.1) stockouts in a year, whereas if a firm replenishes stock weekly with a 90% service level, there will be 5.2 (52×0.1) stockouts per year. The more frequently stock is replenished in a given time period, the larger the number of expected stockouts.

Service per Year

A service level based on frequency of service per year allows for uniform treatment of different products. When the service level is based on the order cycle (as in the previous section), the stockout frequencies of different products are not comparable, since each product may have a different lead time. Fortunately, it is easy to convert from service per order cycle to service per year. The service level fraction per year is obtained by raising the service level fraction per order cycle to the power of the number of annual order cycles (R/Q).

$$\text{Service level fraction per year} = (\text{service level fraction per cycle})^{R/Q}.$$

The stockout level fraction per order cycle is obtained as follows from the stockout level fraction per year:

$$P(M > B) = 1 - (\text{service level fraction per year})^{Q/R}.$$

EXAMPLE 12

From the information given in Example 6, what should be the reorder point if the 0.125 stockout level fraction per order cycle is changed to a 15% stockout level fraction per year?

$$P(M > B) = 1 - (\text{service level fraction per year})^{Q/R}$$
$$= 1 - (0.85)^{0.67} = 0.01$$

Consulting the $P(s)$ column in Table 9, 0.01 is between 0.025 and 0.000, so the smallest $P(s)$ is chosen, which gives $M_a = 90$:

$$B = M_a = 90 \text{ units.}$$

The order quantity would be 1200 units and the reorder point 90 units.

EXAMPLE 13

From the information given in Example 9 what will be the service level fraction per year if there are four order cycles per year?

$$\text{Service level fraction per year} = (\text{service level fraction per cycle})^{R/Q}$$
$$= (0.95)^4 = 0.81$$

Fraction of Units Demanded

Often the fraction of units demands (or dollars demanded) and instantaneously filled from stock is a meaningful service index. The service level fraction for units demanded can be defined as

$$\text{Service level fraction for units demanded} = \frac{\text{number of units supplied}}{\text{total number of units demanded}}$$

$$\text{Stockout level fraction for units demanded} = \frac{\text{number of units short}}{\text{total number of units demanded}}.$$

The above relationships must be measured over some time period, which may be a week, a month, a year, or the duration of the lead time.

The expected number of stockouts during an order cycle has already been developed earlier in the chapter as

$$E(M>B) = \int_B^{\infty} (M-B) f(M)\, dM.$$

To obtain the stockout level fraction for units demanded during the order cycle, it is necessary to divide by the quantity demanded (Q) during the order cycle:

$$\text{Stockout level fraction for units demanded} = \frac{E(M>B)}{Q}.$$

For the standard normal distribution, the expected number of stockouts during an order cycle is the partial expectation $E(Z)$ times the standard deviation, or

$$E(M>B)=\sigma E(Z),$$

which results in

$$\text{Stockout level fraction for units demanded}=\frac{\sigma E(Z)}{Q}$$

for the standard normal distribution. By knowing the stockout level fraction, the standard deviation of the lead time demand, and the order quantity, the partial expectation $E(Z)$ can be determined. By consulting a standard normal table (see Table 2), the standard normal deviate Z can be obtained for the derived partial expectation, and the reorder point obtained from the following formula:

$$B=\overline{M}+Z\sigma.$$

EXAMPLE 14

What is the order quantity and reorder point for the following problem (see Table 13)?

$$\begin{aligned}\text{Stockout level fraction for units demanded}&=0.01,\\ R&=1800 \text{ units/year},\\ C&=\$3.00 \text{ per order},\\ H&=\$3.00 \text{ per unit per year?}\end{aligned}$$

We have

$$Q_0=\sqrt{\frac{2CR}{H}}=\sqrt{\frac{2(3)1800}{3}}=60 \text{ units},$$

$$\begin{aligned}E(M>B)&=Q\text{ (stockout level fraction for units demanded)}\\ &=60\ (0.01)=0.60 \text{ units}.\end{aligned}$$

The expected lead time stockout is 0.60 units, which in Table 14 is between 0.36 and 0.74 units. Selecting the smaller value, the reorder point is 54 units. The order quantity is 60 units, and the reorder point is 54 units.

EXAMPLE 15

If the distribution given in Example 14 is assumed normally distributed with a mean of 53 and a standard deviation of 2 units, what should be the reorder point?

$$E(Z)=\frac{Q}{\sigma}\text{(stockout level fraction for units demanded)}=\frac{60(0.01)}{2}=0.30.$$

Table 13

Lead Time Demand M	Probability $P(M)$	$P(s)$
48	.02	.98
49	.03	.95
50	.06	.89
51	.07	.82
52	.20	.62
53	.24	.38
54	.20	.18
55	.07	.11
56	.06	.05
57	.03	.02
58	.02	.00
	1.00	

Table 14

Reorder Point B	Probability $P(B)$	$\sum_{M=B+1}^{M_{max}} (M-B)P(M)=E(M>B)$
58	.02	0
57	.03	$1(0.02)=0.02$
56	.06	$1(0.03)=0.03$
		$2(0.02)=0.04$
		0.07
55	.07	$1(0.06)=0.06$
		$2(0.03)=0.06$
		$3(0.02)=0.06$
		0.18
54	.20	$1(0.07)=0.07$
		$2(0.06)=0.12$
		$3(0.03)=0.09$
		$4(0.02)=0.08$
		0.36 ←
53	.24	$1(0.20)=0.20$
		$2(0.07)=0.14$
		$3(0.06)=0.18$
		$4(0.03)=0.12$
		$5(0.02)=0.10$
		0.74
52	.20	$1(0.24)=0.24$
		$2(0.20)=0.40$
		$3(0.07)=0.21$
		$4(0.06)=0.24$
		$5(0.03)=0.15$
		$6(0.02)=0.12$
		1.36

Consulting the normal table for the partial expectation $E(Z)=0.30$, a standard normal deviate Z of 0.20 is obtained. The reorder point can be obtained as follows:

$$B=\overline{M}+Z\sigma=53+0.2(2)=53.4 \text{ units}.$$

Fraction of Operating Days

Another measure of stockout or shortage is the length of time an out-of-stock situation exists. Stockouts may be defined as the fraction of days out of stock. This results in a service level policy based on the time out of stock, and it can be written as

Service level fraction for operating days

$$=\frac{\text{number of operating days without stockout}}{\text{total number of operating days}}$$

$$=1-\frac{\text{number of operating days with stockout}}{\text{total number of operating days}},$$

Stockout level fraction for operating days

$$=\frac{\text{number of operating days with stockout}}{\text{total number of operating days}}.$$

If an item is out of stock 10% of the time, it is reasonable to assume that 10% of the time demand is unsatisfied. Thus the service level based on the fraction of operating days is very similar to the service level based on the fraction of units demanded. For practical purposes, the two approaches can be considered equivalent.

Before we leave the topic of service levels, a word of caution is in order. Some organizations set safety stock levels at some average time supply for each item. That is, they use a specified number of days or weeks of supply as the criterion for determining the amount of safety stock. This is a poor practice that should be avoided. The fallacy in using a fixed time supply is that safety stock is set as a function of the level of demand, whereas it should be set as a function of the variability of demand. A fixed time supply gives too much protection to high volume items with relatively predictable demands and not enough protection to low volume items with more variable demands. In actual practice, high volume items tend to exhibit less relative variability of demand.

Imputed Service Level Stockout Costs

Whenever an organization uses a service level to establish a reorder point because of an inability to determine stockout cost, it really does establish a stockout cost. Associated with a given service level is an imputed or implicit

Table 15. Imputed Stockout Costs

Stockout Level (1-Service Level)	Stockout Cost[a] Backorder Cost/Unit	Stockout Cost[a] Lost Sales Cost/Unit
Stockout level per order cycle, $P(s)$	$\frac{HQ}{AR}$	$\frac{HQ}{AR+HQ}$
Stockout level per year, $1-[1-P(s)]^{R/Q}$	$1-\left[1-\frac{HQ}{AR}\right]^{R/Q}$	$1-\left[1-\frac{HR}{AR+HQ}\right]^{R/Q}$
Stockout fraction of units demanded,[b] $E(M>B)/Q$	$\frac{HQ}{AR}$	$\frac{HQ}{AR+HQ}$

[a] The formulas in the table give the optimum probability of a stockout. To obtain the appropriate stockout cost, solve the formula for A.
[b] For the stockout fraction of units demanded, it is necessary to solve for $E(M>B)$ and find the associated $P(s)$ before the appropriate formula can be solved for the stockout cost.

stockout cost. It is a simple matter to determine the imputed stockout cost for a given service level from previously developed optimum formulations for the probability of a stockout. Table 15 outlines the formulations for determining the imputed stockout costs from the various service level concepts. A few examples can best illustrate the procedure.

EXAMPLE 16

From the information given in Example 6, what is the imputed backorder cost per unit?

$$P(s)=\frac{HQ}{AR}=0.125=\frac{5(1200)}{A(18{,}000)},$$

$$A=\frac{5(1200)}{0.125(18{,}000)}=\$2.67 \text{ per unit backordered.}$$

EXAMPLE 17

If the stockout level fraction per order cycle of 0.125 in Example 6 were changed to a stockout level fraction per year, what would be the imputed backorder cost per unit? What would be the imputed lost sales cost per unit?

$$\text{Stockout level per year} = 1 - \left[1 - \frac{HQ}{AR}\right]^{R/Q}$$

$$0.125 = 1 - \left[1 - \frac{5(1200)}{A(18{,}000)}\right]^{15}$$

$$A = \$37.04 \text{ per unit backordered;}$$

$$0.125 = 1 - \left[1 - \frac{HQ}{AR + HQ}\right]^{R/Q}$$

$$= 1 - \left[1 - \frac{5(1200)}{A(18{,}000) + 5(1200)}\right]^{15}$$

$$A = \$36.70 \text{ per unit lost.}$$

EXAMPLE 18

From the information given in Example 14, what is the imputed backorder cost per unit? What is the imputed lost sales cost per unit?

$$0.01 = \frac{E(M>B)}{Q}, \quad E(M>B) = 0.01(Q) = 0.01(60) = 0.6.$$

From the information in Example 14, the reorder point associated with 0.6 is 54 units, which has a stockout probability of 0.18. Thus

$$P(s) = \frac{HQ}{AR} = 0.18 = \frac{3(60)}{A(1800)},$$

$$A = \frac{3(60)}{0.18(1800)} = \$.56 \text{ per unit backordered;}$$

$$P(s) = \frac{HQ}{AR + HQ} = 0.18 = \frac{3(60)}{A(1800) + 3(60)},$$

$$A = \frac{3(60) - 0.18(3)60}{0.18(1800)} = \$.46 \text{ per unit lost.}$$

CONCLUSION

The fixed order size system is completely defined by the order quantity Q and the reorder point B. The risk of stockout occurs after the reorder point is reached and before the next incoming order is received. Although the risk of stockout is dependent on both the order quantity and reorder point (with large order quantities, there is less exposure over a time horizon to potential stockouts), near-optimum results can usually be obtained by treating the order quantity and reorder point as independent. In this manner, risk is only considered in establishing the reorder point. The order quantity does not enter into the risk adjustment, and it is set by deterministic procedures (EOQ and EPQ) outlined in previous chapters. Safety stock is the risk adjustment to the reorder point to protect against stockouts. The reorder point consists of the mean lead time demand plus the safety stock. Safety stock levels can be obtained by the minimization of the expected cost of safety stock (holding and stockout costs) or by the creation of service levels. The fixed order size system under risk is schematically represented in Figure 5.

There are two approaches to establishing risk adjusted reorder points, depending on whether stockout costs are known or unknown. If stockout costs are known or can be ascertained, optimizing formulas can be derived depending on the stockout case (backorder or lost sale) and on the cost category (stockout cost per unit or per outage), as outlined in Table 8. If stockout costs are unknown, management can set service levels indicating the ability to meet customer demands from stock. The more typical kinds of service levels are service per order cycle, service per year, fraction of units demanded, and fraction of operating days. Since stockout costs are difficult to determine, service levels are more commonly used. The type of service level adopted depends on the industry, organizational peculiarities, ease of application, and type of products involved.

The treatment of risk in fixed order size systems involves the analysis of the demand distribution (continuous or discrete) over the relevant lead time. Empirically derived distributions or standard distributions (normal, Poisson, negative exponential, etc.) can be employed to describe the demand pattern. Standard distributions that are well tabulated provide the benefit of easy calculation and development. Of course, standard distributions should not be employed unless they adequately describe the demand phenomenon.

In establishing optimal solutions, numerous assumptions were made which rendered the models mere approximations to the optimal solution.

Figure 5. Risk: fixed order size systems.
Key: FOSS = fixed order size systems; EOQ = economic order quantity; EPQ = economic production quantity.

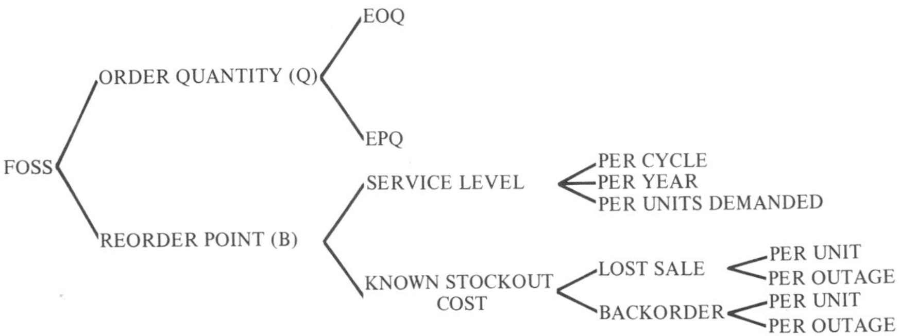

While these approximations cast some doubt on the models, they should not limit their use. Within the range of parameter estimates required to utilize any inventory model, the assumptions establish an excellent first approximation. In many cases, because of the insensitivity of total inventory cost to changes in parameters and variables, the approximations are near optimal.

QUESTIONS

1. What are some common assumptions of traditional inventory models?
2. What are the most prevalent variables through which risk and uncertainty enter the inventory analysis?
3. What provisions are usually made for absorbing variations in demand and lead time?
4. What two variables completely define the fixed order size system?
5. Give two reasons why safety stocks may be needed.
6. Under what conditions should safety stocks be large?
7. What three statistical distributions are used in describing demand functions? Where can they be used?
8. Why is the normal distribution inadequate for low levels of average demand?
9. What level of safety stock should be maintained when both demand and lead time are constant?
10. What distribution is used for low levels of average demand? Is this distribution applicable to high levels of average demand?
11. In a situation of constant demand and variable lead time, what problems would result from reorder points centered on the minimum lead time? The maximum lead time?
12. Define service level.
13. What are four commonly used types of service level?
14. What is the limitation on a service level based on the frequency of service per order cycle?
15. How does an organization establish a stockout cost when it uses the service level concept to determine the reorder point?

PROBLEMS

1. An industrial distributor sells water pumps and other related supplies. A particular water pump is purchased for $60 from the manufacturer. The average sales per day are 5 units, and the annual holding cost is 25% of unit cost. The annual demand for the pump is 1500 units, and the order quantity is 300 units. The backorder cost per unit is $50, and the lead time is 20 days. The demand during lead time is given in the table below. How much safety stock should be carried? What is the reorder point?

Demand	Number of Occurrences
70	3
80	3
90	4
100	80
110	6
120	4
	100

2. An automotive parts dealer sells 1200 carburetors a year. Each carburetor costs $25, and the average demand is 4 units/day. The order quantity is 120 units, and the lead time is 25 days. The backorder cost per unit is $20, and annual holding cost is 20% of unit cost. The lead time demand is given in the table below. Determine the safety stock level and the reorder point.

Demand	Number of Occurrences
90	25
95	25
100	5
105	20
110	15
115	10
	100

3. If the distribution given in Problem 1 is assumed to be a normal probability distribution with a mean of 100 and a standard deviation of 5, what should be the reorder point and safety stock?

4. What should be the safety stock in Problem 2 if the lost sales cost per unit is $20?

5. A pet shop's monthly demand for Angora cats is normally distributed with a mean of 20 and a standard deviation of 4. Holding costs are $50 per cat per year, the backorder cost per outage is $60, the order quantity is 25, and the lead time is 1 month. Determine the reorder point for Angora cats.

6. A pet shop's monthly demand for black snakes is Poisson distributed with a mean of 2 snakes. The order quantity is 6 snakes, holding costs are $5.00 per snake per year, the backorder cost per outage is $12.00, and the lead time is 2 months. At what level should the snakes be reordered?

7. A gasoline service station's daily demand for regular gasoline is normally distributed with a mean of 1200 gallons and a standard deviation of 400 gallons. If the lead time is 4 days, what reorder point should be set so as to be out of regular gasoline during only 1% of the order cycles?

8. A discount store's daily demand for its basic electronic calculator is Poisson distributed with a mean of 3 units. The reorder time period is 4 days. What should be the reorder point if the desired stockout probability per order cycle is 0.10?

9. The city of Connubial's demand for marriage licenses is negative exponentially distributed with a mean of 5 per day. The printer's lead time is 5 days. What should be the reorder point on marriage licenses if a service level per order cycle of 99% is desired?

10. A pizza-parlor owner is concerned about maintaining an optimum stock of pie crust, since a stockout would mean a loss of customers. He has consulted a local business student, who has sampled the pizza demand over a period of weeks and found that it was normally distributed with a mean of 106 per week and a standard deviation of 23. The owner informed the student that the lost sales cost would be $20 per unit, and the cost of maintaining a supply of pie crusts is $10 per crust per year (crusts are ordered in quantities of 100 with a lead time of 3 weeks). What is the optimum reorder point for pizza crust?

11. A commercial crabber who fishes 350 pots per day orders bait in quantities of 50 crates per order. Because of weather conditions, he is unable to fish his pots with any regularity, so his weekly demand for bait is normally distributed with a mean of 25 crates and a standard deviation of 5. Since the bait must be refrigerated, the annual holding costs are $10 per crate, with backorder costs of $15 per outage. If it takes him a week to have bait ordered and delivered, what should be his reorder point?

12. Smith Concrete has an average monthly demand for 1000 bags of cement. Replenishment orders of 2000 bags require a lead time of 1 week. Holding costs are $5.00 per bag per year, and lost sales costs are $10 per bag. If the weekly demand for concrete is as given in the table below, what should be the reorder point?

Demand M	Demand Probability $P(M)$	Probability of Demand $> M$
100	.01	.99
125	.04	.95
150	.11	.84
175	.14	.70
200	.40	.30
225	.12	.18
250	.10	.08
275	.06	.02
300	.02	.00

13. A plant that produces executive office chairs has a yearly demand of 5200 with a constant weekly demand of 100. The managers have experienced some inventory difficulties with the leather covering, which must be ordered from an outside supplier. Because of a manufacturing irregularity with the supplier, their delivery time has been variable over the past year. Leather is ordered in precut strips of 500, with annual holding costs of $20 per strip. The plant wants to ensure a suitable inventory on hand, since the backorder cost per strip is $15. What is the optimum reorder point if the weekly lead time is defined by the following distribution?

Lead Time (Weeks)	Probability
1	10
2	20
3	35
4	26
5	9
	100

14. The daily demand for an item is represented by the empirical distribution given below. What safety stock should the plant maintain to ensure that stockouts will not be incurred in more than 5.5% of the order cycles if the lead time is 1 day? What would be the safety stock under the conservative method?

Daily Demand D (Units)	Frequency f
5	10
10	35
15	65
20	32
25	8
	150

15. A grocer stocks several different brands of cereal. Because of the large number of boxes on hand, storage both on the display shelf and in the stockroom has become a problem. He has begun to analyze the demand for each brand, and he is willing to run short of a particular brand in 10% of the order cycles. He has found that the annual demand for a certain brand is a normally distributed random variable with a mean of 1000 boxes and a standard deviation of 150 boxes. What should his safety stock and reorder point be if it takes him $\frac{3}{4}$ month to get a new delivery?

16. A large business machine wholesaling company was experiencing a variation in both the demand for typewriters and the lead time in ordering them. In order to establish an efficient inventory level, an analysis of the demand and lead times was conducted, yielding a weekly demand that was normally distributed with a mean of 50 typewriters and a standard deviation of 10. The lead time was also normally distributed, with a mean of 16 days and a standard deviation of 5 days. If weekly demand and lead time are independent, what reorder point should be established to provide a 97.5% service level per order cycle?

17. The demand for an item averages 100 units per month. Actual demand data for the last 10 months are given in the table below (no seasonal, trend, or cyclical effects are in the data). The lead time is 2 months to replenish the inventory. What reorder point will ensure a service level per order cycle of 94%?

Month	1	2	3	4	5	6	7	8	9	10
Demand	100	90	80	110	90	120	130	70	100	100
Error	0	−10	−20	10	−10	20	30	−30	0	0

18. The weekly demand for a product is given in the table below. The lead time is 2 weeks. What is the probability distribution for the lead time demand?

Demand	Probability
0	.05
1	.40
2	.30
3	.25

19. An item has the following characteristics:

$$P=\$13.00/\text{unit}, \qquad F=20\%,$$
$$R=130 \text{ units/year}, \qquad L=3 \text{ weeks},$$
$$C=\$9.00/\text{order}, \qquad \sigma_R=26 \text{ units}.$$

The annual demand is normally distributed. If the manager will tolerate only one backordering outage per year, compute the economic order quantity and reorder point for the item.

CASE 1: HIGHER SERVICE LEVELS

Hopson Steel is a distributor of steel and metal products. It has sales territories in twelve states which are serviced from six warehouses. Each warehouse is autonomous and carries enough inventory to cover sales in two states.

Profits and sales at Hopson Steel have not changed appreciably over the last five years. To the dismay of the major stockholders, the profits of competitors have increased. In an effort to institute change, Mr. Benton, the President, has replaced the company's general manager with Mr. Arnold Cohen. With considerable effort and a substantial salary offer, Mr. Cohen was persuaded to leave his position with a sporting goods firm.

Upon arrival at the firm, Mr. Cohen examined sales records and market forecasts for the steel industry. He predicted a substantial increase in demand for several products. After commenting several times that increased sales were the salvation for Hopson Steel, he issued the following directives to each of his six material managers.

1. Purchase and stock at each warehouse *all* items listed in the general supply catalogue.
2. Purchase large quantities of products for inventory so quantity discounts can be utilized.
3. If economically possible, purchase economic order quantities (EOQs).

4. Inventory levels will rise, but the larger holding cost will be offset by increased sales (the higher service level will increase sales).
5. All managers who exceed last year's performance will receive bonuses.

Within a few months, sales increases were reported along with predictions of even greater increases by year end. The warehouses reported the largest stock of steel products in the company's history. Labor negotiations between the steel industry and labor unions were at an impasse and it appeared that a strike was imminent. Fearing that a strike would deplete inventory levels when sales were increasing, Mr. Cohen urged the procurement of even larger quantities of steel products from any source available.

Although a strike did occur, it lasted for only a week. At the end of the year, Mr. Benton reported a sales increase for the company but a loss on operations. He attributed the poor performance to high inventory levels and other unexpected costs. Although with some reservation, Mr. Benton predicted a brighter year ahead with increased sales and a return to profitability. He reaffirmed his complete trust in Mr. Cohen's ability.

1. Discuss the merits of each of Mr. Cohen's directives to his material managers. Do you agree with them?
2. Do you share Mr. Benton's trust in Mr. Cohen?
3. As a stockholder, what are your opinions about the president's comments on the future of the company? Do you foresee any major problems?

CASE 2: KNOT HOLES

Woodcraft, Inc. produces sundry items that are made primarily from wood and wood by-products. Their line of products includes baker's racks, wine racks, paper towel holders, chopping blocks, bread boxes and canister sets, and other wooden storage items. Although the basic material for all the products is wood, each item is made from a certain grain and grade, and the raw materials are not considered interchangeable. Woodcraft purchases most of its materials from a North Carolina supplier who ships them to the Maryland plant in numerous precut sizes.

Mr. Ash, the production manager, has the responsibility of purchasing and controlling the raw materials inventory. This has proved to be a tedious task. The supplier is unable to promise delivery dates and has been unreliable in his estimates of delivery schedules. The lead times of certain grains and grades run the gamut from speedy deliveries to seemingly endless delays. The volatility of lead times is due to the infrequency of lumber cuttings and the difficulties of cutting, preparing, and shipping the wood.

Mr. Ash, however, feels that he has finally developed an infallible system for dealing with lead time fluctuations. The infallibility rests on his success at avoiding production stoppages because of materials outages. Mr. Ash orders the lumber in economic order quantities. He has set the reorder points at arbitrarily high levels resulting in the establishment of large safety stocks. He boasts that inventory levels may be high, but his production schedule always runs smoothly.

Mr. Teak is a subordinate in Mr. Ash's department. He agrees that Woodcraft needs to ensure adequate inventory levels, but he challenges Mr. Ash's wasteful methods. Mr. Teak cites the astronomical inventory carrying costs as testimonies of poor inventory practices. More obvious evidences of exceedingly high stock levels are the stacks of rotten lumber stored in the lot adjacent to the manufacturing facility.

Mr. Teak told his superior that he is appalled at the gross mismanagement of natural resources. As a starting place, he has decided to establish more efficient inventory policies for the company's most popular product, a 12″×16″ counter-top cutting board. The board has a very stable demand and is produced evenly throughout the year. It is made from a medium grade of oak that arrives from the supplier in uniformly cut sizes.

Because the oak has been consistently difficult to obtain, the supplier has suggested an alternative type of material. The alternative wood is of lesser quality and is slightly more porous. However, the supplier has been able to ship it to a custom counter-top maker in Baltimore from 3 to 7 weeks after order receipt.

The choice between the two materials is clear-cut to Mr. Ash. He is eager to start purchasing the new precut material but is somewhat stupified on the application of the EOQ formulation. He knows that to minimize his total costs he should order in 150 unit lot sizes, but he is uncertain as to when to initiate his orders. Because there would still be variability in the lead time, he has decided to set the reorder point by a trial and error method. He will reduce the reorder point from the previously high level set by Mr. Ash and decrease it incrementally until it is in an acceptable range. This method, he hopes, will reduce the safety stock level and still allow for manufacturing regularity.

1. Is Mr. Teak's solution logical? Is it an oversimplification of the problem?
2 Is Mr. Ash's method in error? Should the order quantity and reorder point be established independently?
3. Describe the inventory situation for the cutting board and recommend a method for establishing appropriate inventory policies.

CASE 3: MANAGING MOLLUSKS

Tando's Restaurant of Virginia Beach offers one of the most varied and unusual menus in the resort city. The restaurant has acquired a fine reputation for exquisite and unique dishes. They are best known for three entrees that are ethnic adaptations of sea scallops. Due to the unusual preparation of the scallop dishes this seafood has become the largest selling menu item.

The scallops are not purchased locally but are shipped from a purveyor who services a sister operation, Tando's of Branford, Connecticut. The scallops are not bought from local dealers for quality and price reasons. The owners find that transportation charges are minimal compared to the value derived from the other factors. The New England purveyor has an established route to other local operations, and he has been able to fill an order within a three-day period.

Daniel Speas, one of the proprietors, was an operations management major and has always tried to utilize the inventory management tools he learned as an M.B.A. student. Dan had been ordering the scallops by an intuitive method until he could become familiar with the beach trade. He has been dissatisfied with the results. Tando's has experienced spoilage and shortages too frequently. Dan is certain that now is the time to test theoretical inventory methods.

Dan has spent the greater part of a week determining the cost data for the scallops and has itemized his results as follows:

$R = 2500$ doz./yr, $P = \$7$/doz.,
$C = \$25$ per order, $A = \$3.50$/doz.,
$F = .50$.

Knowing that customers are unpredictable, Dan cringes at estimating daily demand. Even though scallops are a perennial favorite, the demand is erratic. Based on scanty documentation Dan has constructed a table of the daily demand distribution for the mollusk.

Demand (doz./day)	Frequency
6	35
7	35
8	15
9	10
10	5

Dan assumes this distribution does not differ significantly from the Poisson distribution. Assured that the theoretical distribution is an adequate surrogate for his distribution, Dan's computations are simplified. His calculations yield a reorder point of 16 dozen units with an apparent safety stock of 3 dozen scallops.

1. Has Dan done a thorough and precise job?
2. How should inventory policies for sea scallops be established? What permutations could alter or destroy the formulations?
3. What type of inventory problems may be unique to restaurateurs? What types of analysis should be recommended to them?
4. Briefly describe selection of demand distributions for this menu item.

CASE 4: FLORIDA FLORA IN GEORGIA

Ashley Wynne operates a greenhouse, The Southern Nursery, in Augusta, Georgia. The name is a misnomer, because the company does not grow any of its plants from seedlings nor propagate any new plants. All of the plants are shipped from Florida and are cared for in Southern's greenhouses until sold. The only part of the operation that resembles a nursery is the greenhouse that is designated for unhealthy or diseased plants.

The lush ferns that Ashley buys in Florida are his prime product. Ashley had a 1600 unit demand for the ferns last year. The demand is increasing, because the area is becoming a tourist attraction. Many are taken home as examples of Georgian greenery. The ferns arrive in baskets suitable for hanging and are sold individually or in bulk purchases to commercial customers. At times, Ashley has also sold his baskets to other nurseries depending on his supply and the success of price negotiations with the nurserymen. Because of the diversity of his clientele, Ashley's prices vary widely.

Ashley intends to continue his practice of serving many markets; he enjoys the bartering process. However, his pricing policy, or lack of one, complicates the establishment of stockout costs. Ashley assumes he can use $3.00 per unit, but feels very uncertain that it is a valid stockout cost for ferns. He finds estimating the holding cost less complex. He has assigned a $2.00 holding cost per plant.

The time between order initiation and delivery is uncertain. The Florida supplier usually delivers the order within 5 days, and the ordering cost is $15.00. Ashley sold his ferns during the past year according to the following lead time distribution:

Lead Time Demand	Probability
21	.03
22	.04
23	.07
24	.12
25	.09
26	.20
27	.22
28	.13
29	.06
30	.04

Ashley has raised the possibility that his reordering policies and practices need revision. He figured his operation is currently servicing only about 85% of his demand. He would like to be able to service approximately 95% of customer demand for ferns.

To achieve a higher service level Ashley is contemplating becoming his own supplier. He is examining the steps necessary to cultivate the luxuriant ferns himself. Expansion seems to be the key to approaching a 95% service level or better; Ashley is intrigued with the idea of vertical integration.

1. Discuss Ashley's plans.
2. Can Ashley revise his reordering policies and accomplish his goal without vertically integrating?
3 How can Ashley compute stockout costs?
4 Discuss inventory problems that are probably occurring at The Southern Nursery.

CASE 5: INHARMONIOUS ACCORD

Radio Hut sells a large variety of products, from small transistor radios to very expensive and sophisticated component stereo systems. It is apparent that Radio Hut has been making mistakes in the determination of safety stock levels for small tape recorders. The demand for the recorders is erratic and difficult to predict; it peaks during the Christmas season. Even though the suppliers are reliable, the lead time is quite long; so the risk of stockouts is high, and outages frequently occur. Radio Hut's policy is to satisfy the customers to avoid losing them to competitors.

These conditions force Radio Hut to maintain a high safety stock. However, the space available for storage is not large enough to satisfy actual demand. Faced with these problems, Radio Hut's manager, Fidel High, appointed two assistant managers to establish the correct level of safety stock necessary to meet actual demand.

Manager One decided that the best way to determine the safety stock was to determine the stockout cost. He assumed that at the retail level a stockout would result in a lost sale, because customers choose to purchase from a competitor rather than wait. He calculated the sum of losses of present sales and losses of future sales to obtain a stockout cost per unit of $7.00. The annual demand is approximately 1200 units; the ordering cost is $30.00; the holding cost just increased from 20% to 25% of the purchase price of $65; and the leadtime demand is distributed according to the following table:

Lead Time Demand	Probability
20	.08
25	.16
30	.24
35	.22
40	.19
45	.07
50	.04

After conducting computations, he came up with a safety stock of 15 units.

Manager Two thought that determining a stockout cost was much too uncertain and involved too many variables. He based his study on the service level per order cycle. He estimated a service level of 95% would be adequate and found a safety stock of 20 units would be appropriate at this level.

Now Radio Hut faces several problems:

1. Which safety stock level would be best?
2. Should an average be taken?
3. Why are there discrepancies between the two estimates?
4. How can Radio Hut account for the peak demand at Christmas?

Solutions to these questions are still in the initial phases, yet Mr. High has decided to throw more suggestions at the two assistants. He wants them to investigate the probability of reducing stockouts by shortening lead time or by increasing lot sizes, the possibility of informing suppliers of Radio Hut's expected annual demand so that they could manage to deliver the tape recorders in the quantity needed at the moment required, and the chance of using local or multiple suppliers as a partial solution.

Given the information and the additional suggestions:

1. What should Radio Hut do?
2. Are Mr. High's suggestions likely to solve the inventory problem? If so, then how?
3. Discuss the effects of stiff competition and seasonality on the establishment of safety stock levels.

MATHEMATICAL ABBREVIATIONS AND SYMBOLS USED IN CHAPTER 4

A	Stockout cost per unit
B	Reorder point in units
C	Ordering cost per order
D	Daily demand in units (a random variable)
$\bar{D}$	Average daily demand in units
D_a	Daily demand at acceptable service level in units
D_{max}	Maximum daily demand in units
$E(M>B)$	Expected lead time stockout in units
EOQ	Economic order quantity
f	Frequency of occurrence
$f(M)$	Probability density function of lead time demand
G	Stockout cost per outage
H	Holding cost per unit per year
L	Lead time in days
$\bar{L}$	Average lead time in days
L_a	Lead time at acceptable service level in days
L_{max}	Maximum lead time in days
M	Lead time demand in units (a random variable)
$\bar{M}$	Average lead time demand in units
M_a	Lead time demand at acceptable service level in units
M_{max}	Maximum lead time demand in units
MAD	Mean absolute deviation
P	Unit purchase cost
$P(D)$	Probability of a daily demand of D units
$P(L)$	Probability of a lead time of L days
$P(M)$	Probability of a lead time demand of M units
$P(M>B)$	$=P(s)$, probability of a stockout during lead time
Q	Order quantity in units
Q_0	Economic order quantity in units
R	Average annual demand in units
S	Safety stock in units
TC	Expected annual cost of inventory
TC_s	Expected annual cost of safety stock
Z	Standard normal deviate
σ	Standard deviation of lead time demand in units
σ_D	Standard deviation of daily demand in units
σ_L	Standard deviation of lead time in days

APPENDIX A. CHI-SQUARE GOODNESS-OF-FIT TEST

When the standard statistical distributions can be used in inventory analysis, they can simplify the analysis and reduce the computational effort. Before standard distributions such as the normal, Poisson, and negative exponential are employed, it is necessary to establish the goodness of fit of the distribution. A test based on the chi-square distribution can determine if any real difference exists between an empirical (actual) distribution and the standard distribution it is assumed to represent. The chi-square goodness-of-fit test will indicate if the difference between two distributions (empirical and theoretical) is statistically significant.

To measure the compatibility of actual (observed) and theoretical (expected) frequencies, it is necessary to calculate the chi-square statistic. The calculated chi-square statistic is compared with a value obtained from a chi-square table for a given level of significance and number of degrees of freedom. If the calculated chi-square statistic is less than the value obtained from the statistical table, the theoretical distribution is accepted as an adequate surrogate for the actual distribution. A chi-square statistic of zero represents a perfect fit; the larger the chi-square statistic, the poorer the fit. Chi-square tables can be found in any statistics book.

The chi-square statistic is obtained from the following formula:

$$\chi^2 = \sum \frac{(f_0 - f_e)^2}{f_e} = \text{chi-square},$$

where

$$f_0 = \text{observed frequencies},$$

$$f_e = \text{expected frequencies}.$$

The most frequently used levels of significance are 0.05 and 0.10. The degrees of freedom are $k-3$ for the normal distribution and $k-2$ for the Poisson distribution (k is the number of frequency classes). A few simple examples can illustrate the test.

Poisson Distribution Example

The demand per day for an item is given in Table A-1. Determine whether the daily demand can be considered Poisson distributed at 0.10 level of significance.

$$\bar{D} = \frac{\sum fD}{\sum f} = \frac{100}{100} = 1.$$

The arithmetic mean $\bar{D}$ of the above distribution is 1 unit. By consulting a

Table A-1

Demand per Day D	Observed Frequency
0	40
1	30
2	20
3	10
	100

Poisson distribution table for a mean of 1 unit, the probabilities of each expected demand level are obtained and transformed to expected frequencies in Table A-2.

Consulting a chi-square table for level of significance 0.10 and 2 degrees of freedom ($k-2=4-2$), we find $\chi^2=4.605$. Since the computed value (2.17) is less than the table value, the Poisson distribution can be used to describe daily demand.

Normal Distribution Example

The lead time demand for an item is shown in Table A-3. Before the data were grouped, the mean and standard deviation were calculated to be 52.5 and 6.6 units respectively. Determine if the lead time demand can be approximated by a normal distribution at the 0.05 level of confidence.

The expected frequencies are obtained in the following manner:

1. $Z=\frac{M-\overline{M}}{\sigma}=\frac{39.5-52.5}{6.6}=-1.97.$

Table A-2

Demand per Day, D	Frequency of Demand f_0[a]	f_e[b]		f_0-f_e	$(f_0-f_e)^2$	$\frac{(f_0-f_e)^2}{f_e}$
0	40	36.8		3.2	10.24	0.28
1	30	36.8		−6.8	46.24	1.25
2	20	18.4		1.6	2.56	0.14
3	10	6.1	8.0	2.0	4.0	0.50
4	0	1.5				
5	0	0.3				
6	0	0.1				
						2.17

[a]For 100 days.

[b]$f_e=100P(D)$.

Table A-3

Lead Time Demand M	Frequency f
≤ 39	12
40–44	26
45–49	80
50–54	130
55–59	104
60–64	42
≥ 65	6
	400

From the normal table a Z of 1.97 gives 0.47558.

$$f_e = (0.5000 - 0.47558)400 = 9.768.$$

2. $Z = \dfrac{M - \overline{M}}{\sigma} = \dfrac{44.5 - 52.5}{6.6} = -1.21.$

From the normal table a Z of 1.21 gives 0.38686.

$$f_e = (0.47558 - 0.38686)400 = 35.488.$$

3. $Z = \dfrac{M - \overline{M}}{\sigma} = \dfrac{49.5 - 52.5}{6.6} = -0.45.$

From the normal table a Z of 0.45 gives 0.17364.

$$f_e = (0.38686 - 0.17364)400 = 85.288.$$

4. $Z = \dfrac{M - \overline{M}}{\sigma} = \dfrac{54.5 - 52.5}{6.6} = 0.30.$

From the normal table a Z of 0.30 gives 0.11791.

$$f_e = (0.17364 - 0.11791)400 = 116.62.$$

5. $Z = \dfrac{M - \overline{M}}{\sigma} = \dfrac{59.5 - 52.5}{6.6} = 1.06.$

From the normal table a Z of 1.06 gives 0.35543.

$$f_e = (0.35543 - 0.11791)400 = 95.008.$$

6. $Z = \dfrac{M - \overline{M}}{\sigma} = \dfrac{64.5 - 52.5}{6.6} = 1.82.$

From the normal table a Z of 1.82 gives 0.46562.

$$f_e = (0.46562 - 0.35543)400 = 44.08.$$

7. $Z = \dfrac{M - \overline{M}}{\sigma} = \dfrac{64.5 - 52.5}{6.6} = 1.82.$

Table A-4

Lead Time Demand M	Frequency of Demand f_0	f_e	(f_0-f_e)	$(f_0-f_e)^2$	$\frac{(f_0-f_e)^2}{f_e}$
≤ 39	12	9.8	3.2	10.24	1.045
40–44	26	35.5	−9.5	90.25	2.542
45–49	80	85.3	−5.3	28.09	0.329
50–54	130	116.6	13.4	179.56	1.539
55–59	104	95.0	9.0	81.00	0.853
60–64	42	44.1	−2.1	4.41	0.100
≥ 65	6	13.8	−7.8	60.84	4.409
	400				10.817

From the normal table a Z of 1.82 gives 0.46562.

$$f_e = (0.50000 - 0.46562)400 = 13.752.$$

Hence we have Table A-4.

Consulting a chi-square table for level of significance 0.05 and 4 degrees of freedom ($K-3=7-3$), we find $\chi^2=9.488$. Since the computed value (10.817) is greater than the table value, the normal distribution does not adequately describe the actual distribution.

APPENDIX B. ORDER QUANTITY AND REORDER POINT DEPENDENCE

In fixed order size inventory models involving uncertainty, it becomes apparent that the order quantity and reorder point are interdependent. The interaction is frequently and justifiably ignored to simplify inventory control. Analysis is needed, however, to check this assumption. The risk of stockout occurs only after the reorder point is reached. The size of the order quantity will determine how frequently the reorder point is reached. The larger the order quantity, the less frequent the exposure to stockouts (the risk of depletion varies inversely with the size of the order quantity).

Backorder Case: Stockout Cost Per Unit

The possibility of a stockout only occurs during the lead time (after the reorder point is reached).[8] In an annual period, if there is no more than one order outstanding at any given time, the number of time periods during which a stockout could occur is R/Q, or the annual demand divided by the order quantity. To account for the dependence between the order quantity

[8] The lead time demand is the total demand that occurs during the lead time. For deterministic models, it is simply the product of the demand rate and the lead time. When demand and lead time are independent random variables, the lead time demand is a random variable.

and reorder point, the expected annual cost formula for a continuous distribution with backordering can be written as

$$\begin{aligned}\text{Expected annual cost} &= (\text{purchase cost}) + (\text{order cost}) \\ &\quad + (\text{holding cost}) + (\text{stockout cost}), \\ \text{TC} &= RP + \frac{RC}{Q} + H\left[\frac{Q}{2} + \int_0^\infty (B-M)f(M)\,dM\right] \\ &\quad + \frac{AR}{Q}\int_B^\infty (M-B)f(M)\,dM,\end{aligned}$$

where

$$\begin{aligned}R &= \text{average annual demand in units,}\\ P &= \text{purchase cost per unit,}\\ C &= \text{ordering cost per order,}\\ Q &= \text{order quantity in units,}\\ H &= \text{holding cost per unit per year,}\\ B &= \text{reorder point in units,}\\ M &= \text{lead time demand in units (a random variable),}\\ A &= \text{stockout cost per unit,}\\ f(M) &= \text{probability density function of lead time demand,}\\ S &= B - \overline{M}\\ &= \int_0^\infty (B-M)f(M)\,dM = \text{expected safety stock in units,}\\ E(M>B) &= \int_B^\infty (M-B)f(M)\,dM\\ &= \text{expected lead time stockout in units,}\\ AE(M>B) &= \text{expected lead time stockout cost.}\end{aligned}$$

The expected annual cost formula can be simplified to the following:[9]

$$\text{TC} = RP + \frac{R}{Q}[C + AE(M>B)] + H\left[\frac{Q}{2} + B - \overline{M}\right].$$

The first term gives the annual purchase cost of the item. The second term gives the fixed cost per order cycle (order cost plus stockout cost) times the

[9]The formula developed assumes that sales are delayed (not lost) in a backorder situation. In most situations the differences between results obtained from backorders and from lost sales are slight.

number of annual cycles (R/Q). The final term is the holding cost, which amounts to half the order quantity plus the safety stock $(B-\overline{M})$.

By taking partial derivatives of the expected annual cost with respect to Q and B and setting them equal to zero, optimum expressions for Q and B can be obtained:[10]

$$\frac{\partial \mathrm{TC}}{\partial Q}=\frac{-R}{Q^2}[C+AE(M>B)]+\frac{H}{2}=0,$$

$$Q_0=\sqrt{\frac{2R[C+AE(M>B)]}{H}}$$

$$=\text{economic order quantity in units,}$$

$$\frac{\partial \mathrm{TC}}{\partial B}=-\frac{RAP(M>B)}{Q}+H=0,$$

$$P(M>B)=P(s)=\frac{HQ}{AR}=\text{optimum probability of a stockout.}$$

Lost Sales Case: Stockout Cost Per Unit

When stockouts result in lost sales, the expected annual cost formula is modified as follows:

$$\mathrm{TC}=RP+\frac{R}{Q}[C+AE(M>B)]+H\left[\frac{Q}{2}+(B-\overline{M})+E(M>B)\right].$$

The first term gives the purchase cost of an item times the units demanded. The second term gives the fixed cost per order cycle (order cost plus stockout cost) times the number of annual order cycles (the number of order cycles is slightly less than R/Q because of lost sales, but that effect is assumed negligible). The third and final term is the holding cost, which includes one-half the order quantity plus safety stock plus lost demand. The stock remaining when Q arrives is expected to be $(B-\overline{M})$; however, if shortages occur, the expected depletion will be less than $\overline{M}$ by the expected number of units short, $E(M>B)$. Thus, the average inventory will be larger by the shortage quantity.

By taking partial derivatives of the expected annual cost with respect to Q and B and setting them equal to zero, optimum expressions for Q and B can

[10]For derivations of optimal expressions, see Harold Bierman, Charles Bonini, and Warren H. Hausman, *Quantitative Analysis for Business Decisions*, Homewood, IL: Irwin, 1969, pp. 169–177; Martin K. Starr and David W. Miller, *Inventory Control: Theory and Practice*, Englewood Cliffs, NJ: Prentice-Hall, 1962, pp. 120–124; and Lynwood A. Johnson and Douglas C. Montgomery, *Operations Research in Production Planning, Scheduling, and Inventory Control*, New York: Wiley, 1974, pp. 59–66.

be obtained:

$$\frac{\partial \mathrm{TC}}{\partial Q} = -\frac{R}{Q^2}[C+AE(M>B)] + \frac{H}{2} = 0,$$

$$Q_0 = \sqrt{\frac{2R[C+AE(M>B)]}{H}}$$

$$= \text{economic order quantity in units,}$$

$$\frac{\partial \mathrm{TC}}{\partial B} = -\frac{RAP(M>B)}{Q} + H - HP(M>B) = 0,$$

$$P(M>B) = P(s)$$

$$= \frac{HQ}{AR+HQ}$$

$$= \text{optimum probability of a stockout.}$$

Summary

For the backordering case, the optimum formulas for the fixed order size system with dependence were derived and are as follows:

$$Q_0 = \sqrt{\frac{2R[C+AE(M>B)]}{H}} = \mathrm{EOQ},$$

$$P(M>B) = P(s)$$

$$= \frac{HQ}{AR}$$

$$= \text{probability of a stockout.}$$

For the lost sales case, the optimum formulas for the fixed order size system with dependence were derived and are as follows:

$$Q_0 = \sqrt{\frac{2R[C+AE(M>B)]}{H}} = \mathrm{EOQ},$$

$$P(M>B) = P(s) = \frac{HQ}{AR+HQ} = \text{probability of a stockout.}$$

To obtain the optimum values when order quantity and reorder point are dependent, an iterative procedure can be used which converges to the optimum solution. The procedure, which uses the formulas developed, is as follows:

1. Select appropriate case (backorder or lost sales formulas).
2. Compute Q with $E(M>B)=0$.
3. Use computed Q to obtain $P(M>B)$ and B.

4. Use computed B to obtain a value for $E(M>B)$.
5. Recompute Q with $E(M>B)$.
6. Repeat steps 3, 4, and 5 until convergence occurs.

The above procedure is a cumbersome but simple task, and usually not more than one iteration is required to obtain convergence. Because of insensitivity, the independence assumption usually provides an excellent approximation to optimality. A simple example can best illustrate the technique.

EXAMPLE B-1

Determine the parameters for a fixed order size system from the data given below and in Table B-1:

$$R = 1800 \text{ units/year},$$
$$C = \$30/\text{order},$$
$$F = 15\%,$$
$$P = \$200/\text{unit},$$
$$A = \$8.00 \text{ per unit backordered}.$$

To solve the above problem, we use the procedure outlined in the previous section and find the deterministic economic order quantity:

$$Q_0 = \sqrt{\frac{2CR}{PF}} = \sqrt{\frac{2(30)1800}{200(0.15)}} = 60 \text{ units},$$

$$P(M>B) = P(s) = \frac{HQ}{AR} = \frac{30(60)}{8(1800)} = 0.125.$$

By consulting Table B-1 for $P(s) = 0.125$, we see that the computed value is between

Table B-1

Lead Time Demand M	Probability $P(M)$	Probability of Demand$>M$, $P(s)$
48	.02	.98
49	.03	.95
50	.06	.89
51	.07	.82
52	.20	.62
53	.24	.38
54	.20	.18
55	.07	.11
56	.06	.05
57	.03	.02
58	.02	.00
	1.00	

0.11 and 0.18. Selecting the smaller value, we obtain a reorder point of 55 units. The next step is to compute $E(M>B)$, the expected lead time stockout in units:

$$E(M>B)=\sum_{M=B+1}^{M_{\max}}(M-B)P(M)$$

$$=(56-55)0.06+(57-55)0.03+(58-55)0.02=0.18.$$

It is now necessary to recompute the order quantity using $E(M>B)$ as follows:

$$Q_0=\sqrt{\frac{2R[C+AE(M>B)]}{PF}}=\sqrt{\frac{2(1800)[30+8(0.18)]}{200(0.15)}}$$

$$=61.4,\text{ or }61\text{ units,}$$

$$P(M>B)=\frac{HQ}{AR}=\frac{30(61)}{8(1800)}=0.127.$$

Consulting Table B-1 for $P(s)=0.127$, we obtain the reorder point of 55 again. The problem is solved. Since the reorder point has not changed, it will result in the same economic order quantity, 61 units. Convergence has been obtained. The optimum inventory policy for the fixed order size system is $Q_0=61$ and $B=55$ units.

Although convergence will not always be as easy as in the above example, the independent treatment is frequently an excellent approximation to the optimum solution. In the above example, the independent solution was $Q_0=60$ and $B=55$, while the optimum dependent solution was $Q_0=61$ and $B=55$. If the stockout cost per order cycle, $AE(M>B)$, approaches or exceeds the order cost per cycle, C, then the assumption of independence between the order quantity Q and the reorder point B weakens. In that case the order quantity and reorder point should be determined jointly.

APPENDIX C. PROBABILITY DISTRIBUTION CONVOLUTIONS

Frequently, it is necessary to know the probability distribution of the demand for varying-length time periods. If demand is stationary with no integral time series modifications and if the demand in subsequent periods is independent of the demand level in previous periods, then the probability distribution of the demand for varying-length time periods can be easily obtained. The revised probability distribution of demand is derived by convolutions of the original probability distribution with itself.[11] The convolution process permits the extension of a probability distribution of demand for a given fixed time period to the demand distribution for any integral multiple of that time period.

[11]For a more complete discussion of convolutions see G. Hadley and T. M. Whitin, *Analysis of Inventory Systems*, Englewood Cliffs, NJ: Prentice-Hall, 1963.

Table C-1

Demand	Probability
0	.10
1	.40
2	.30
3	.20

For a discrete distribution, the binomial expansion can be utilized to obtain the desired convolution. For example, suppose the demand distribution shown in Table C-1 applies to an item for a weekly period. What would be the demand distribution for a 2-week period? The 1-week demand can be written in binomial expansion terms as follows:

$$.1+.4X+.3X^2+.2X^3,$$

where the exponent of X equals the demand ($X^0=1$), and the coefficient of X is the probability of the respective demand level. To obtain the probability distribution of demand for n weeks, we raise the expression to the nth power and read the results using the same convention. Thus, the demand distribution for two weeks is obtained as follows:

$$(.1+.4X+.3X^2+.2X^3)^2=.01+.08X+.22X^2+.28X^3$$
$$+.25X^4+.12X^5+.04X^6,$$

which results in the two-week demand distribution shown in Table C-2.The use of the binomial expansion in developing convolutions, while correct, can become mathematically tedious. For this reason it is desirable to use standard distributions (normal, binomial and Poisson) which are well behaved in relation to convolutions. When normal, binomial, or Poisson distributions are convoluted, the same respective distribution results, regardless of the number of convolutions.

For a stationary distribution with mean $\overline{X}$ and standard deviation σ, n convolutions will result in a mean of $n\overline{X}$ and a standard deviation of $\sigma\sqrt{n}$. Thus, we can easily determine the demand for any integral multiple of a

Table C-2

Demand	Probability
0	.01
1	.08
2	.22
3	.28
4	.25
5	.12
6	.04

time period if the demand distribution is normally distributed in the time period.

APPENDIX D. JOINT PROBABILITY DISTRIBUTIONS

When demand and lead time are two independent distributions, the distributions can be combined to form a single distribution of the demand during the lead time. Unless a computer is used, the forming of joint probability distributions is an arduous manual task even for the simplest of discrete distributions. This section will illustrate the statistical technique for developing a joint probability distribution.

Develop a joint probability distribution of demand during lead time for the independent distributions shown in Table D-1.

From the two distributions it is apparent that the demand during the lead time could be as low as 0 and as high as 9 (a demand of 3 units on each of 3 lead time days). The joint probability distribution will range from 0 to 9 units. To determine the probability of each given lead time demand, it is necessary to sum the various probabilities of ways a specific lead time demand could occur.

Lead time demand=0:

1. first day	0 demand	0.40(0.25)	=0.1000
2. first day	0 demand	0.40(0.40)0.50	=0.0800
second day	0 demand		
3. first day	0 demand	0.40(0.40)0.40(0.25)	=0.0160
second day	0 demand		
third day	0 demand		
Total			=0.1960

Lead time demand=1:

1. first day	1 demand	0.30(0.25)	=0.0750
2. first day	1 demand	0.30(0.40)0.50	=0.0600
second day	0 demand		

Table D-1

Daily Demand D (Units)	Probability $P(D)$	Lead Time L (Days)	Probability $P(L)$
0	.40	1	.25
1	.30	2	.50
2	.20	3	.25
3	.10		1.00
	1.00		

3. first day	1 demand	0.30(0.40)(0.40)0.25	=0.0120
second day	0 demand		
third day	0 demand		
4. first day	0 demand	0.40(0.30)0.50	=0.0600
second day	1 demand		
5. first day	0 demand	0.40(0.30)(0.40)0.25	=0.0120
second day	1 demand		
third day	0 demand		
6. first day	0 demand	0.40(0.40)(0.30)0.25	=0.0120
second day	0 demand		
third day	1 demand		
Total			=0.2310

Lead time demand=2:

1. first day	2 demand	0.20(0.25)	=0.0500
2. first day	0 demand	0.40(0.20)(0.50)	=0.0400
second day	2 demand		
3. first day	2 demand	0.20(0.40)0.50	=0.0400
second day	0 demand		
4. first day	0 demand	0.40(0.40)(0.20)0.25	=0.0080
second day	0 demand		
third day	2 demand		
5. first day	0 demand	0.40(0.20)(0.40)0.25	=0.0080
second day	2 demand		
third day	0 demand		
6. first day	2 demand	0.20(0.40)(0.40)0.25	=0.0080
second day	0 demand		
third day	0 demand		
7. first day	1 demand	0.30(0.30)(0.50)	=0.0450
second day	1 demand		
8. first day	1 demand	0.30(0.30)(0.40)0.25	=0.0090
second day	1 demand		
third day	0 demand		
9. first day	1 demand	0.30(0.40)(0.30)0.25	=0.0090
second day	0 demand		
third day	1 demand		
10. first day	0 demand	0.40(0.30)(0.30)0.25	=0.0090
second day	1 demand		
third day	1 demand		
Total			=0.2260

Lead time demand=3:

1. first day	3 demand	0.10(0.25)	=0.025
2. first day	3 demand	0.10(0.40)0.50	=0.0200
second day	0 demand		
3. first day	0 demand	0.40(0.10)0.50	=0.0200
second day	3 demand		

4. first day	3 demand	0.10(0.40)(0.40)0.25	=0.0040
second day	0 demand		
third day	0 demand		
5. first day	0 demand	0.40(0.10)(0.40)0.25	=0.0040
second day	3 demand		
third day	0 demand		
6. first day	0 demand	0.40(0.40)(0.10)0.25	=0.0040
second day	0 demand		
third day	3 demand		
7. first day	2 demand	0.20(0.30)0.50	=0.0300
second day	1 demand		
8. first day	1 demand	0.30(0.20)(0.50)	=0.0300
second day	2 demand		
9. first day	2 demand	0.20(0.30)(0.40)0.25	=0.0060
second day	1 demand		
third day	0 demand		
10. first day	2 demand	0.20(0.40)(0.30)0.25	=0.0060
second day	0 demand		
third day	1 demand		
11. first day	1 demand	0.30(0.20)(0.40)0.25	=0.0060
second day	2 demand		
third day	0 demand		
12. first day	1 demand	0.30(0.40)(0.20)0.25	=0.0060
second day	0 demand		
third day	2 demand		
13. first day	0 demand	0.40(0.20)(0.30)0.25	=0.0060
second day	2 demand		
third day	1 demand		
14. first day	0 demand	0.40(0.30)(0.20)0.25	=0.0060
second day	1 demand		
third day	2 demand		
15. first day	1 demand	0.30(0.30)(0.30)0.25	=0.0067
second day	1 demand		
third day	1 demand		
Total			=0.1797

Lead time demand=4:

1. first day	3 demand	0.10(0.30)0.50	=0.0150
second day	1 demand		
2. first day	1 demand	0.30(0.10)0.50	=0.0150
second day	3 demand		
3. first day	3 demand	0.10(0.40)(0.30)0.25	=0.0030
second day	0 demand		
third day	1 demand		
4. first day	3 demand	0.10(0.30)(0.40)0.25	=0.0030
second day	1 demand		
third day	0 demand		

5. first day	2 demand	0.20(0.20)0.50	=0.0200
second day	2 demand		
6. first day	2 demand	0.20(0.20)(0.40)0.25	=0.0040
second day	2 demand		
third day	0 demand		
7. first day	2 demand	0.20(0.40)(0.20)0.25	=0.0040
second day	0 demand		
third day	2 demand		
8. first day	2 demand	0.20(0.30)(0.30)(0.25)	=0.0045
second day	1 demand		
third day	1 demand		
9. first day	1 demand	0.30(0.10)(0.40)0.25	=0.0030
second day	3 demand		
third day	0 demand		
10. first day	1 demand	0.30(0.40)(0.10)0.25	=0.0030
second day	0 demand		
third day	3 demand		
11. first day	1 demand	0.30(0.20)(0.30)0.25	=0.0045
second day	2 demand		
third day	1 demand		
12. first day	1 demand	0.30(0.30)(0.20)0.25	=0.0045
second day	1 demand		
third day	2 demand		
13. first day	0 demand	0.40(0.10)(0.30)0.25	=0.0030
second day	3 demand		
third day	1 demand		
14. first day	0 demand	0.40(0.30)(0.10)0.25	=0.0030
second day	1 demand		
third day	3 demand		
15. first day	0 demand	0.40(0.20)(0.20)0.25	=0.0040
second day	2 demand		
third day	2 demand		
Total			=0.0935

Lead time demand=5:

1. first day	3 demand	0.10(0.20)0.50	=0.0100
second day	2 demand		
2. first day	3 demand	0.10(0.20)(0.40)0.25	=0.0020
second day	2 demand		
third day	0 demand		
3. first day	3 demand	0.10(0.40)(0.20)0.25	=0.0020
second day	0 demand		
third day	2 demand		
4. first day	3 demand	0.10(0.30)(0.30)0.25	=0.00225
second day	1 demand		
third day	1 demand		

5. first day	2 demand	0.20(0.10)0.50	=0.0100
second day	3 demand		
6. first day	2 demand	0.20(0.10)(0.40)0.25	=0.0020
second day	3 demand		
third day	0 demand		
7. first day	2 demand	0.20(0.20)(0.30)0.25	=0.0030
second day	2 demand		
third day	1 demand		
8. first day	2 demand	0.20(0.30)(0.20)0.25	=0.0030
second day	1 demand		
third day	2 demand		
9. first day	2 demand	0.20(0.40)(0.10)0.25	=0.0020
second day	0 demand		
third day	3 demand		
10. first day	1 demand	0.30(0.10)(0.30)0.25	=0.00225
second day	3 demand		
third day	1 demand		
11. first day	1 demand	0.30(0.20)(0.20)0.25	=0.0030
second day	2 demand		
third day	2 demand		
12. first day	1 demand	0.30(0.30)(0.10)0.25	=0.00225
second day	1 demand		
third day	3 demand		
13. first day	0 demand	0.40(0.10)(0.20)0.25	=0.0020
second day	3 demand		
third day	2 demand		
14. first day	0 demand	0.40(0.20)(0.10)0.25	=0.0020
second day	2 demand		
third day	3 demand		
Total			=0.0478

Lead time demand=6:

1. first day	3 demand	0.10(0.10)0.50	=0.0050
second day	3 demand		
2. first day	3 demand	0.10(0.20)(0.30)0.25	=0.0015
second day	2 demand		
third day	1 demand		
3. first day	3 demand	0.10(0.30)(0.20)0.25	=0.0015
second day	1 demand		
third day	2 demand		
4. first day	3 demand	0.10(0.10)(0.40)0.25	=0.0010
second day	3 demand		
third day	0 demand		
5. first day	3 demand	0.10(0.40)(0.10)0.25	=0.0010
second day	0 demand		
third day	3 demand		

6. first day	2 demand	0.20(0.10)(0.30)0.25	=0.0015
second day	3 demand		
third day	1 demand		
7. first day	2 demand	0.20(0.20)(0.20)0.25	=0.0020
second day	2 demand		
third day	2 demand		
8. first day	2 demand	0.20(0.30)(0.10)0.25	=0.0015
second day	1 demand		
third day	3 demand		
9. first day	1 demand	0.30(0.10)(0.20)0.25	=0.0015
second day	3 demand		
third day	2 demand		
10. first day	1 demand	0.30(0.20)(0.10)0.25	=0.0015
second day	2 demand		
third day	3 demand		
11. first day	0 demand	0.40(0.10)(0.10)0.25	=0.0010
second day	3 demand		
third day	3 demand		
Total			=0.0190

Lead time demand=7:

1. first day	3 demand	0.10(0.10)(0.30)0.25	=0.00075
second day	3 demand		
third day	1 demand		
2. first day	3 demand	0.10(0.20)(0.20)0.25	=0.0010
second day	2 demand		
third day	2 demand		
3. first day	3 demand	0.10(0.30)(0.10)0.25	=0.00075
second day	1 demand		
third day	3 demand		
4. first day	2 demand	0.20(0.10)(0.20)0.25	=0.0010
second day	3 demand		
third day	2 demand		
5. first day	2 demand	0.20(0.20)(0.10)0.25	=0.0010
second day	2 demand		
third day	3 demand		
6. first day	1 demand	0.30(0.10)(0.10)0.25	=0.00075
second day	3 demand		
third day	3 demand		
Total			=0.0053

Lead time demand=8:

1. first day	3 demand	0.10(0.10)(0.20)0.25	=0.0005
second day	3 demand		
third day	2 demand		

2. first day	3 demand	0.10(0.20)(0.10)0.25	=0.0005
second day	2 demand		
third day	3 demand		
3. first day	2 demand	0.20(0.10)(0.10)0.25	=0.0005
second day	3 demand		
third day	3 demand		
Total			=0.0015

Lead time demand=9:

1. first day	3 demand	0.10(0.10)(0.10)0.25	=0.00025
second day	3 demand		
third day	3 demand		
Total			=0.0003

At this point the reader should be convinced of the laboriousness of the enumeration approach to developing joint probability distributions for even the simplest discrete distributions. Table D-2 contains the joint probability distribution for the lead time demand for the simple example.

To avoid much of the tedium of developing joint probability distributions, Monte Carlo simulation can be directly incorporated in determining inventory management policy. The calculation of joint probability distributions of lead time demand by Monte Carlo simulation requires several hundred replications to assure a reliable estimate. Monte Carlo simulation will be discussed and outlined in a later chapter.

Table D-2

Lead Time Demand M (units)	Probability $P(M)$	Probability of Demand$>M$
0	.1960	.8040
1	.2310	.5730
2	.2260	.3470
3	.1797	.1673
4	.0935	.0738
5	.0477	.0261
6	.0190	.0071
7	.0053	.0018
8	.0015	.0003
9	.0003	.0000
	1.0000	

5 Fixed Order Interval Systems

This chapter introduces time-based models for inventory systems that are appropriate when an organization is faced with fairly uniform independent demand and wants to maintain an inventory of the item most of the time. When demand is continuous and fairly uniform, time and quantity can be considered interchangeable variables. The models presented in this chapter determine the economic order interval which indicates when an order should be placed for an item or items. Orders for items are placed on a fixed time cycle.

The fixed order interval system is a time-based inventory system; it is also called a periodic inventory system. There are only two variables whose values must be chosen for a fixed order interval system. They are the fixed review period and the maximum inventory level from which all replenishment orders are calculated. A maximum inventory level for each item is developed. After a fixed period of time (T) has passed, the stock of each item in inventory is determined, and an order is placed to replenish the

Figure 1. Fixed order interval system.

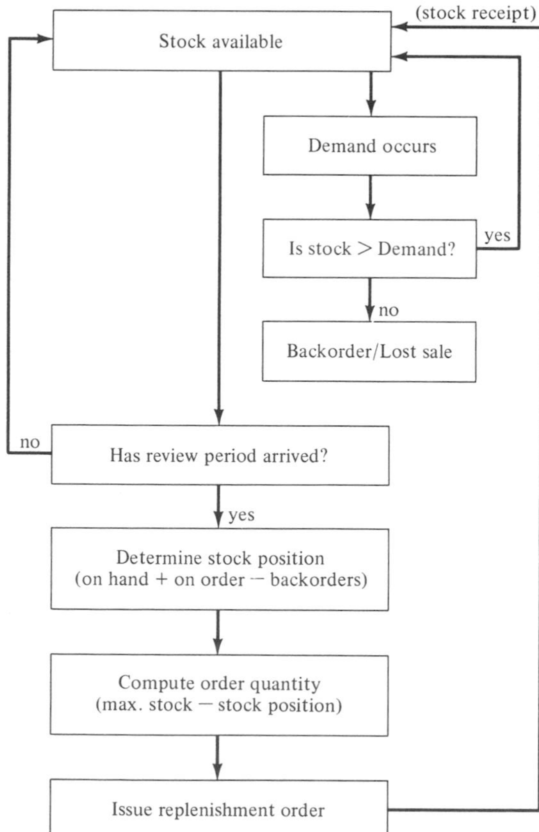

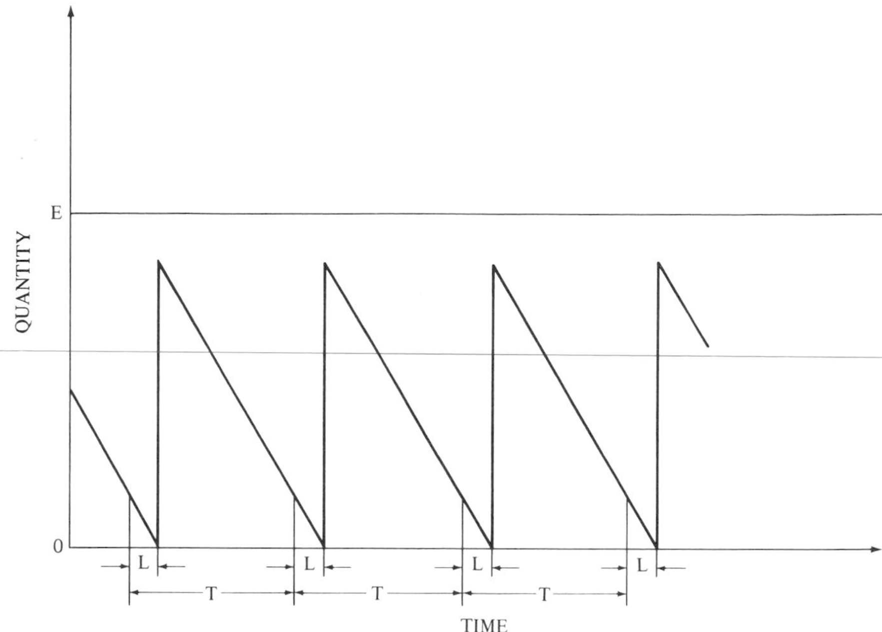

Figure 2. Fixed order interval system.

stock. The size of the order for each item is the difference between the maximum inventory level for each item and the inventory position. The fixed order interval system is termed a T-system, since the time between orders (T) is fixed.

In this system, orders are placed at equally spaced, predetermined points in time. The order quantity varies according to the fluctuations in usage between orders. The size of an order is usually the difference between the stock on hand and a desired maximum inventory. Orders may be placed weekly, monthly, or on some other cycle. A typical fixed order interval system is shown in Figures 1 and 2.

DETERMINISTIC MODELS

This section deals with a special collection of inventory models that are deterministic. The rate of demand for units is assumed to be continuous and known with certainty. The replenishment lead time is also a constant without variation and independent of demand. The real world is seldom as well behaved as in deterministic models. Real-world situations are more reasonably described in probabilistic terms. However, deterministic models are frequently excellent approximations or, at least, a good starting point for describing inventory phenomena.

Economic Order Interval (EOI)—Single Items

The basic problem in this system is determining the order interval T and the desired maximum inventory level E. The economic order interval can be obtained by the minimization of the total annual cost. If stockouts are not permitted, the total annual inventory cost is given by Figure 3 and the following formula:

$$\text{Total annual cost} = (\text{purchase cost}) + (\text{order cost}) + (\text{holding cost}),$$

$$\mathrm{TC} = RP + mC + \frac{RFP}{2m} = RP + \frac{C}{T} + \frac{RFPT}{2},$$

where

$$m = \frac{1}{T} = \text{number of orders or reviews per year},$$

$$\frac{R}{2m} = \frac{RT}{2} = \text{average inventory in units},$$

$$T = \frac{1}{m} = \text{order interval in years}.$$

To obtain the minimum cost order interval, the first derivative of the total annual cost with respect to the order interval T is set equal to zero:

$$\frac{d\mathrm{TC}}{dT} = \frac{-C}{T^2} + \frac{RFP}{2} = 0.$$

Figure 3. Annual inventory costs.

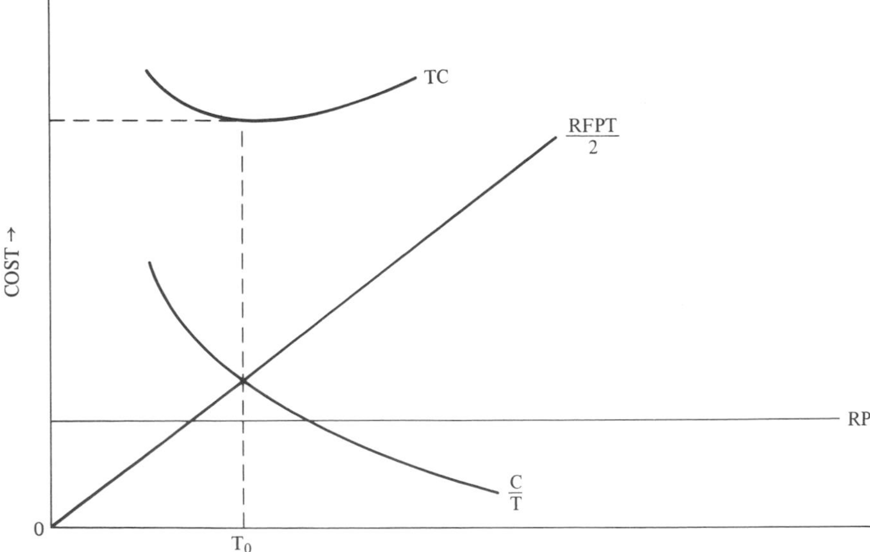

Solving the equation for T, the following formula results:

$$T_0=\sqrt{\frac{2C}{RFP}}=\text{economic order interval (EOI) in years.}$$

The minimum cost number of reviews per year (m) is simply the reciprocal of T_0, or

$$m_0=\frac{1}{T_0}=\sqrt{\frac{RFP}{2C}}.$$

In practice, the order interval tends to be determined by such factors as the number of clerks available to inspect stock records, or it is fixed at some convenient standard time such as a week or a month. In deterministic situations, there is no difference between the fixed order size system and the fixed order interval system. The order quantity for the fixed order interval is simply $Q=RT$, or

$$Q_0=RT_0=R\sqrt{\frac{2C}{RFP}}=\sqrt{\frac{2RC}{FP}}=\sqrt{\frac{2RC}{H}}.$$

The maximum inventory level E must be large enough to satisfy demand during the subsequent order interval T and also during the lead time L. The following formula gives the maximum inventory level when the order interval and lead time are expressed in years:

$$E=RT+RL=R(T+L)=Q+B=\text{maximum inventory level.}$$

The following formula gives the maximum inventory level when the order interval and lead time are expressed in days and there are N operating days in the year:

$$E=\frac{RT}{N}+\frac{RL}{N}=\frac{R(T+L)}{N}=Q+B.$$

The minimum total cost per year is obtained by putting T_0 for T in the total annual cost equation. The following formula for the minimum total cost per year results:

$$TC_0=RP+RHT_0.$$

EXAMPLE 1

The Williams Manufacturing Company purchases 8000 units of a product each year at a unit cost of \$10.00. The order cost is \$30.00 per order, and the holding cost per unit per year is \$3.00. What are the economic order interval, maximum inventory level, and the total annual cost when the lead time is 10 days and there are 250 operating days in the year?

$$T_0=\sqrt{\frac{2C}{RH}}=\sqrt{\frac{2(30)}{(8000)3}}=0.05 \text{ years}=12.5 \text{ days},$$

$$E=\frac{R(T+L)}{N}=\frac{8000(12.5+10)}{250}=720 \text{ units},$$

$$\text{TC}_0=RP+RHT_0=(8000)(10)+8000(3)0.05=\$81{,}200.$$

Every 12.5 days the inventory position would be determined and an order initiated. Note that the optimum total annual cost is exactly the same for the fixed order interval system as for the fixed order size system.

Economic Order Interval (EOI)—Multiple Items

In retailing and wholesaling, a separate order is rarely placed for each item. All items from the same source are likely to be listed together on a single order. The EOI is particularly appropriate when the stock level review can be coordinated for a number of items so that inventory maintenance is kept to a minimum. The monitoring of stock levels often is less frequent and can be scheduled to fit comfortably with other organizational activities. In addition, logistics and transportation cost savings may be possible with multiple orders because of smaller materials handling costs and weight breaks in the transportation rate structure.

Frequently, a supplier provides numerous items, and it is economical to have joint orders. In a joint order, many items are ordered from the same source or supplier. The quantity of each item to order depends on the time interval between orders for the entire group. The basic problem in this system is determining the order interval T and the desired maximum inventory level E_i for each item.

The economic order interval can be obtained by minimizing the total annual cost. Neglecting stockout cost, the formulation is as follows:

Total annual cost = (purchase cost) + (order cost) + (holding cost),

$$\text{TC}=\sum_{i=1}^{n} R_iP_i+\frac{(C+nc)}{T}+\tfrac{1}{2}TF\sum_{i=1}^{n} R_iP_i,$$

where

R_i = annual requirement for item i,

P_i = purchase cost of item i,

n = total number of joint order items,

C = order cost for the joint order,

c = order cost associated with each individual item,

T = order interval in years,

F = holding cost as a fraction of purchase cost.

The minimum cost order interval is obtained by taking the first derivative of the total annual cost with respect to the order interval (T) and setting it equal to zero:

$$\frac{d\mathrm{TC}}{dT}=\frac{-(C+nc)}{T^2}+\tfrac{1}{2}F\sum_{i=1}^{n}R_iP_i=0.$$

Solving the equation for T, the EOI formula results:

$$T_0=\sqrt{\frac{2(C+nc)}{F\Sigma_{i=1}^{n}R_iP_i}}=\text{economic order interval in years.}$$

The maximum inventory for each item must be large enough to satisfy demand during the subsequent order interval and also during the lead time L. The amount to order of each individual item is simply the maximum inventory level (E_i) minus the inventory position. The maximum inventory is determined as follows when the order interval and lead time are expressed in days, and there are N operating days in the year:

$$E_i=\frac{R_iT}{N}+\frac{R_iL}{N}=\frac{R_i(T+L)}{N}=Q_i+B_i=\text{maximum inventory for item } i.$$

EXAMPLE 2

A firm orders seven items from the same vendor. The order costs are \$1.50 per purchase order and \$.50 per item. If carrying costs are 20% per year, what is the minimum cost order interval? If lead time is 1 month, what is the maximum inventory level for each item?

See Table 1. We have

$$T_0=\sqrt{\frac{2(C+nc)}{F\Sigma_{i=1}^{n}R_iP_i}}=\sqrt{\frac{2(1.50+3.50)}{0.20(2000)}}=0.158\text{ years.}$$

The minimum cost order interval is 0.158 years or 1.9 months. Every 2 months you

Table 1

Item	Annual Demand	Unit Cost	Purchase Cost
A	150	\$1.00	\$ 150
B	400	.50	200
C	125	2.00	250
D	100	3.00	300
E	800	.50	400
F	70	5.00	350
G	175	2.00	350
			\$2000

Table 2

Item (i)	Maximum Inventory (E_i)
A	37.5 or 38
B	100
C	31.25 or 31
D	25
E	200
F	17.5 or 18
G	43.75 or 44

would enter a new order for the seven items. The maximum inventory level (Table 2) is obtained as follows:

$$E_i = \frac{R_i(T+L)}{12} = \frac{3R_i}{12} = \frac{R_i}{4}.$$

The formulas developed for the fixed order interval system assume that the demand rate, lead time, price per unit, ordering cost per order, and holding cost per unit are constant; that no stockouts are permitted; and that the complete order quantity is received at one time. In actual situations, many of these assumptions are violated. The important consideration is how useful the decision model becomes when there are assumption variances. If assumption violations are not critical, the model can be an excellent surrogate for reality.

Quantity Discounts on Individual Items

When quantity discounts are offered on individual items purchased under a fixed order interval system, the determination of the order size is more complex. With a quantity discount, the purchase price is reduced if a large enough order is placed. If the order size per item is large enough to get the discount, no computations are necessary, as the discount is obtained automatically. If the order size per item is less than the quantity discount amount, it is necessary to determine if a larger order should be purchased.

If an order size is increased to obtain a quantity discount, the purchase cost of the item decreases while the holding cost increases. If the reduction in purchase cost exceeds the increase in holding cost, the quantity discount should be taken and the order size increased to the minimum quantity discount amount. When the reduction in purchase cost does not exceed the increase in holding cost, the discount should not be taken.

Since the order size varies from review period to review period, it is necessary to determine if the discount should be taken on each review date. The normal order quantity on the review date would be the maximum inventory level (E) minus the stock on hand (I). If the stock on hand is not less than the maximum inventory level, no order will be placed. If the stock on hand is less than the maximum inventory level, an order will be placed.

The following decision rules can be followed for a single quantity discount:

1. If $Q_d \leq (E-I)$; the order size is $E-I$, where

   Q_d = quantity discount break quantity in units,

   E = maximum inventory level in units,

   I = stock on hand at the review period in units.

2. If $Q_d > (E-I)$; the order size is Q_d if

$$Q_d(P-P_d) > \bar{q}P_d FU\frac{(T+L)}{N};$$

otherwise, the order size is $E-I$. The value of U in the above equation must be an integer. If a fraction is encountered, it is simply rounded to the next whole number. The average size of the extra inventory to be held for U time periods of length $T+L$ is $\bar{q}$, and it is obtained from the following formula:

$$\bar{q} = \frac{1}{U}\sum_{i=1}^{U}\left[Q_d - (iE-I)\right],$$

where

P = unit purchase cost without the discount,

P_d = unit purchase cost with the discount,

F = unit inventory holding cost as a fraction of unit cost,

L = lead time,

T = order interval,

N = number of working periods in the year,

$P-P_d$ = unit cost saving of the discount,

$Q_d-(E-I)$ = increase in order size with the discount,

P_dF = holding cost per unit per year,

$\frac{U(T+L)}{N}$ = fraction of year that the extra units are held,

$U = \frac{Q_d-(E-I)}{E}$ = number of time periods of length $T+L$ that extra inventory will be held.

U is always an integer, and fractional values are rounded to the next whole number.

The above formulation just determines if the purchase cost saving exceeds the additional holding cost. The larger quantity is purchased if and only if the purchase cost saving exceeds the holding cost. When the next review period arrives, another decision must be made regarding the order size. The above decision rules can be used for both single items and multiple items when the quantity discount applies individually.

EXAMPLE 3

A review period indicates the stock on hand given in Table 3 for the seven items in Example 2.

Table 3

Item	Stock on Hand, I (Units)
A	15
B	40
C	12
D	10
E	20
F	7
G	18

The supplier offers quantity discounts on items A, B, and E according to the following schedules:

Item A		Item B		Item E	
Quantity	Price	Quantity	Price	Quantity	Price
0−124	\$1.00	0−199	\$.50	0−149	\$.50
≥125	.90	≥200	.48	≥150	.45

What should be the order size for each item?

For Item A:

$$U=\frac{Q_d-(E-I)}{E}=\frac{125-(38-15)}{38}=2.7, \qquad \text{so} \quad U=3.0,$$

$$\bar{q}=\frac{1}{U}\sum_{i=1}^{U}[Q_d-(iE-I)]$$

$$=\frac{[125-1(38)+15]+[125-2(38)+15]+[125-3(38)+15]}{3}$$

$$=\frac{102+64+26}{3}=64,$$

$$Q_d(P-P_d)=125(1.00-0.9)=\$12.50,$$

$$\bar{q}P_dFU\frac{(T+L)}{N}=\frac{64(0.90)0.20(3)(2+1)}{12}=\$8.64.$$

The quantity discount results in a cost saving of \$3.86 (\$12.50−\$8.64), so take the discount and order 125 units.

For item B:

$$U=\frac{Q_d-(E-I)}{E}=\frac{200-(100-40)}{100}=1.4, \qquad \text{so} \quad U=2,$$

$$\bar{q}=\frac{1}{U}\sum_{i=1}^{U}[Q_d-(iE-I)]$$

$$=\frac{[200-(100-40)]+[200-(200-40)]}{2}=90,$$

$$Q_d(P-P_d)=200(0.50-0.48)=\$4.00,$$

$$\bar{q}P_dFU\frac{(T+L)}{N}=\frac{90(0.48)0.20(2)(2+1)}{12}=\$4.32.$$

The quantity discount results in a larger holding cost, so do not take the discount; order 60 units.

For item E:

$$Q_d \le E-I, \qquad \text{so the order size is } E-I;$$
$$150<200-20.$$

The order quantity is $E-I=180$, with an automatic quantity discount.

Table 4 summarizes the order policy for all the items.

Table 4

Item	$E-I$	Order Size
A	23	125 (take quantity discount)
B	60	60 (disregard quantity discount)
C	19	19
D	15	15
E	180	180 (automatic quantity discount)
F	11	11
G	26	26

Quantity Discounts on Joint Orders

There are some suppliers who offer a quantity discount, not on individual items, but on the total dollar sales of all items delivered at one time. If the dollar order size is sufficient to qualify for the discount, it is obtained automatically. If the dollar order size is not sufficient to qualify for the discount, the decision with a fixed order interval system is whether to increase the order interval so the discount is realized with each order. If the aggregate order quantity should be increased, the increase is spread proportionately over the individual items by increasing the order interval.

With multiple items from a single supplier, the procedure requires a determination of the economic order interval. The basic formula developed in Appendix B of Chapter 3 for quantity discounts can be modified to determine if the discount should be taken by increasing the order size by lengthening the order interval. The formula will determine the maximum dollar order size that economically could be purchased with the discount. If the dollar order size necessary to qualify for the discount is larger, do not take the discount; if the dollar order size for the discount is less than the maximum dollar order size, order the larger of the optimum quantity or just enough to qualify for the discount. The maximum dollar order size that can economically be ordered to qualify for the discount is obtained as follows:[1]

$$Q_{\$}=\frac{2b\Sigma_{i=1}^{n}P_iR_i}{F}+T_0(1-b)\sum_{i=1}^{n}P_iR_i=\text{maximum dollar order size,}$$

where b is the discount fraction used as inducement for the larger order. The optimum dollar order size without the discount is as follows:

$$Q_{0\$}=T_0\sum_{i=1}^{n}P_iR_i.$$

At no time should a discount be taken if the discount is offered for more than the maximum dollar order size. If the discount is offered at less than the maximum dollar order size, it should be accepted for the optimum dollar order size or for the minimum amount to qualify for the discount, whichever is larger. If the order size is increased to obtain the discount, the new order interval is obtained as follows:

$$T=\frac{\Sigma_{i=1}^{n}P_iQ_i}{\Sigma_{i=1}^{n}P_iR_i}=\frac{\text{order size in dollars}}{\text{annual demand in dollars}}.$$

A simple example can best illustrate the procedure.

EXAMPLE 4

The supplier of the seven items in Example 2 offers a 5% discount on all orders of \$1000 or more. Should the discount be taken? What would be the new order interval and the maximum inventory level for each item?

$$\begin{aligned}Q_{\$}&=\frac{2b\Sigma_{i=1}^{n}P_iR_i}{F}+T_0(1-b)\sum_{i=1}^{n}P_iR_i\\&=\frac{2(0.05)2000}{0.20}+0.158(0.95)2000=1000+300=\$1300.\end{aligned}$$

[1]As in Appendix B of Chapter 3, the procedure assumes that the order cost $(C+nc)$ is very small compared with the purchase or invoice cost of an order. The assumption is usually true in practice.

The optimum dollar order size without the discount is

$$Q_{0\$}=T_0\sum_{i=1}^{n}P_iR_i=0.158(2000)=\$316.$$

Since the maximum dollar order size is \$1300 and the discount is offered for orders over \$1000, the dollar order size should be increased from \$316 to \$1000 by lengthening the review period. The discount should be taken with an order size of \$1000 and the order interval revised from 0.158 to the following:

$$T=\frac{\sum_{i=1}^{n}P_iQ_i}{\sum_{i=1}^{n}P_iR_i}=\frac{1000}{2000}=0.5\text{ years}=6\text{ months}.$$

The maximum inventory level for each item is revised as follows (see Table 5):

$$E_i=\frac{R_i}{12}(T+L)=\frac{R_i(6+1)}{12}=\frac{7R_i}{12}.$$

Table 5

Item (i)	Maximum Inventory (E_i)
A	87.5 or 88
B	233.3 or 233
C	72.9 or 73
D	58.3 or 58
E	466.6 or 467
F	40.8 or 41
G	102.1 or 102

Note how the discount resulted in a longer order interval and larger maximum inventory levels.

EOI Sensitivity

In fixed order interval systems, the order interval (T) which minimizes the total variable cost per year dictates the optimum inventory policy. The pertinent mathematical relationships are as follows:

$$T_0=\sqrt{\frac{2C}{RH}}=\text{EOI},$$

$$\text{TVC}_0=\frac{C}{T_0}+\frac{RHT_0}{2}=\text{optimum total variable cost per year.}$$

If there are errors in the estimation of the parameters R, C, and H with the respective error factors X_R, X_C, and X_H, the model becomes

$$T=\sqrt{\frac{2C}{RH}\frac{X_C}{X_R X_H}}=T_0\sqrt{\frac{X_C}{X_R X_H}},$$

$$\frac{T-T_0}{T_0}=\sqrt{\frac{X_C}{X_R X_H}}-1=\text{order interval error factor},$$

where

T = order interval with parameter errors,

T_0 = economic order interval,

$$X_R=\frac{\text{estimated demand}}{\text{actual demand}}=\text{demand error factor},$$

$$X_C=\frac{\text{estimated order cost}}{\text{actual order cost}}=\text{order cost error factor},$$

$$X_H=\frac{\text{estimated holding cost}}{\text{actual holding cost}}=\text{holding cost error factor}.$$

To examine the effects of errors in the estimates of the parameters (R, C, and H), two of the error factors will be set equal to 1 while the third is varied. When all the error factors are equal to 1, the error effect is zero ($T=T_0$). With X_C and X_R equal to 1 while X_H is variable, the effect on the EOI is as follows:

$$\frac{T-T_0}{T_0}=\sqrt{\frac{1}{X_H}}-1.$$

Similarly, with X_R and X_H equal to 1 while X_C is variable, the effect on the EOI is as follows:

$$\frac{T-T_0}{T_0}=\sqrt{X_C}-1.$$

Finally, with X_C and X_H equal to 1 while X_R is variable, the effect on the EOI is as follows:

$$\frac{T-T_0}{T_0}=\sqrt{\frac{1}{X_R}}-1.$$

Under single parameter variations, the effects of errors in estimates of R, C, and H on the economic order interval are as shown in Table 6. It is readily apparent that errors in parameters are attenuated in their influence on the EOI. For example, if order costs are in error by a factor of 2, the error in the order interval is only 41.4%. If annual demand is in error by a factor of 2, the error in the order interval is less than 30%.

To determine the sensitivity of total variable cost per year to errors in input parameters, error factors are inserted into the cost formula in the

Table 6. Effects of Errors in R, C, and H on the EOI

Error in C		Error in R or H	
Factor[a] X_C	Effect on T_0[b] (%)	Factor[a] X_R or X_H	Effect on T_0[c] (%)
0.1	− 68.4	0.1	+216.2
0.2	− 55.3	0.2	+123.6
0.3	− 45.3	0.3	+ 82.4
0.4	− 36.8	0.4	+ 58.1
0.5	− 29.3	0.5	+ 41.4
0.6	− 22.5	0.6	+ 28.8
0.7	− 16.4	0.7	+ 19.5
0.8	− 10.6	0.8	+ 11.8
0.9	− 5.2	0.9	+ 5.3
1.0	0.0	1.0	0.0
1.2	+ 9.5	1.2	− 8.8
1.4	+ 18.3	1.4	− 15.5
1.6	+ 26.4	1.6	− 20.9
1.8	+ 34.2	1.8	− 25.5
2.0	+ 41.4	2.0	− 29.3
2.2	+ 48.3	2.2	− 32.5
2.4	+ 54.9	2.4	− 35.5
2.6	+ 61.2	2.6	− 37.9
2.8	+ 67.3	2.8	− 40.3
3.0	+ 73.2	3.0	− 42.3
4.0	+ 100.0	4.0	− 50.5

[a] Estimated C, R, or H divided by actual value.
[b] No errors in R and H.
[c] No errors in C and H (or no errors in C and R).

following manner:

$$\mathrm{TVC}=\frac{C}{T}+\frac{RHT}{2}$$

$$=\frac{C}{\sqrt{(2C/RH)(X_C/X_R X_H)}}+\frac{RH\sqrt{(2C/RH)(X_C/X_R X_H)}}{2},$$

which mathematically simplifies to

$$\mathrm{TVC}=\left[\frac{\mathrm{TVC}_0}{2}\right]\frac{X_C+X_R X_H}{\sqrt{X_R X_C X_H}},$$

$$\frac{\mathrm{TVC}-\mathrm{TVC}_0}{\mathrm{TVC}_0}=\frac{X_C+X_R X_H}{2\sqrt{X_R X_C X_H}}-1=\text{TVC error factor.}$$

Since the above formula gives the same relationships developed for the EOQ system, it is apparent that single parameter errors have exactly the same effect on the total variable cost for the EOQ and the EOI. Thus, Table 7 is applicable to both the EOQ and the EOI model. This should be no surprise, since both the EOQ and the EOI are deterministic models that minimize the same costs.

The insensitivity of the basic inventory models to parameter errors is a very advantageous property. Since the total cost is only slightly increased by substantial departures from optimum conditions, the basic models do not require frequent revision (recalculation). Many components of cost parameters are difficult to measure, but the insensitivity renders broad estimates to operational usefulness. All that is needed is to get into the "right ballpark," and good solutions can be obtained with fairly crude cost data. EOIs can be rounded off without a significant loss in economics. Order sizes can be increased or decreased to the nearest pack or container size; order intervals can be lengthened or shortened to the next convenient time interval.

PROBABILISTIC MODELS

In the fixed order interval system (T-system), there are a fixed order period and a varying order size. At predetermined intervals, the inventory is reviewed and an order is placed. The size of the order is determined by

Table 7. Effects of Errors in R, C, and H on TVC_0[a]

Error Factor X_a[b]	Increase in TVC_0 (%)
0.1	74.0
0.2	34.2
0.3	18.8
0.4	10.7
0.5	6.1
0.6	3.3
0.7	1.6
0.8	0.6
0.9	0.2
1.0	0.0
1.2	0.4
1.4	1.4
1.6	2.8
1.8	4.4
2.0	6.1
2.2	7.9
2.4	9.7
2.6	11.7
2.8	13.6
3.0	15.4
4.0	25.0

[a] is any of the three parameters, and there are no errors in the other two. Thus, if a were R, then C and H would have no errors.

[b](Estimated a)/(actual a).

subtracting the amount on hand from a predetermined total (when the fixed order period is shorter than the lead time period, the stock on hand must include units on order but not yet received). The order interval T and the predetermined total E completely define the fixed order interval system. The operating doctrine under this system is sometimes called the "order up to E" doctrine.

In the fixed order size system (Q-system), safety stock is needed only for the lead time period. In the fixed order interval system safety stock is needed for the lead time and the order interval. With time-based systems, a stockout in a given period enhances the probability of stockout in subsequent periods. This interaction between an order for a period and subsequent periods is approximated by calculating the safety stock for the lead time plus the order interval. Intuitively, once an order is placed at time t, another order cannot be placed until time $t+T$, and the second order will not be filled until the lead time period has elapsed, at time $t+T+L$. Thus, safety stock protection is needed for the lead time L plus the order interval T.

In an ideal inventory system, as shown in Figure 4, the average demand pattern prevails with no variance (actually, the safety stock would be at the zero level). In actual inventory systems, as shown in Figure 5, the pattern of demand over time will be discrete and irregular. Figure 5 shows two complete cycles of an inventory system. In the first cycle, the demand is so great that it results in a stockout (during the first order interval T). In the second cycle, the demand is less than expected, and the safety stock is never reached (during the second order interval T). Only the start of the third cycle is graphed in Figure 5, but it shows a larger demand than expected, which requires the dispensing of some safety stock.

Figure 4. Ideal periodic inventory model.

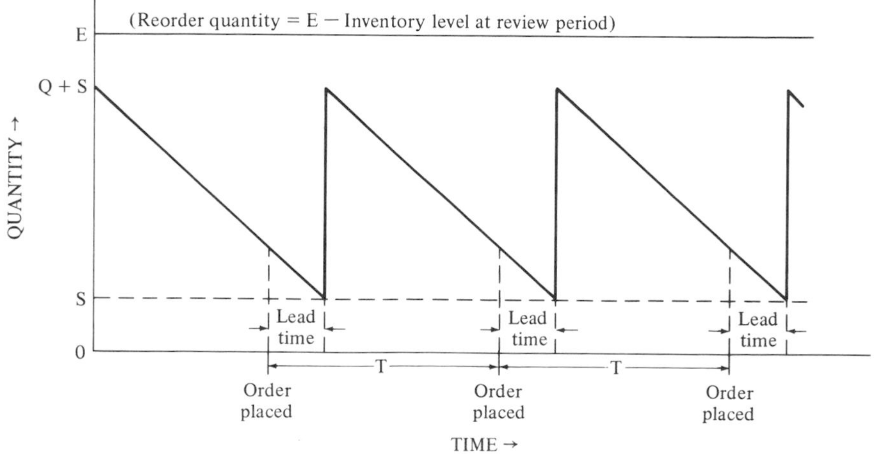

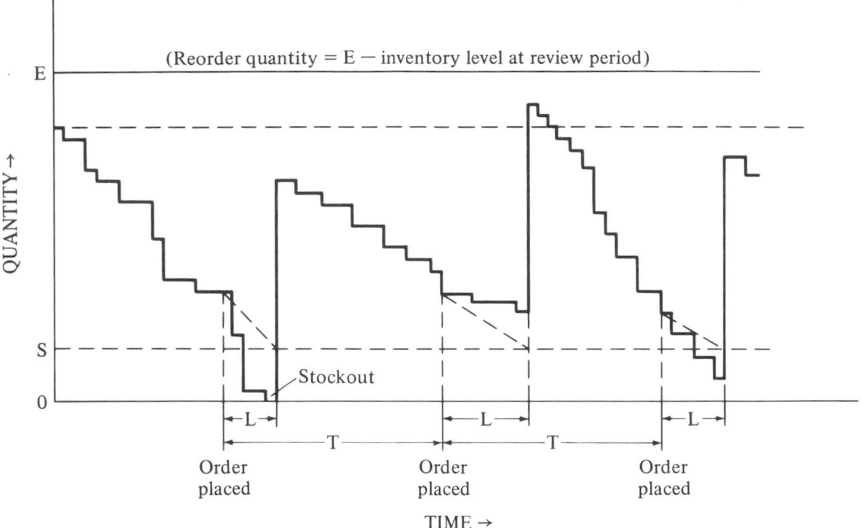

Figure 5. Realistic periodic inventory model.

The expected annual cost of operating the fixed order interval system for a single item with constant lead time is as follows:

$$\text{Expected annual cost} = (\text{purchase cost}) + (\text{order cost}) + (\text{holding cost}) + (\text{stockout cost}),$$

$$\mathrm{TC} = RP + mC + H\left[E - \left(\frac{RT}{2} + RL\right)\right] + mA\int_E^{\infty}(M-E)f(M)\,dM,$$

where

TC = expected annual cost,
R = average annual demand in units,
$m = 1/T$ = number of orders per year,
P = unit price,
C = ordering and review cost per occurrence,
H = holding cost per unit per year,
E = maximum inventory level in units,
T = order interval in years,
L = lead time in years,
A = stockout cost per unit,

M = demand during order interval and lead time (a random variable),[2]

$\overline{M} = RT + RL$ = average demand during order interval and lead time,

$f(M)$ = probability density function of demand during order interval and lead time,

$$E(M>E) = \int_{E}^{\infty} (M-E) f(M)\, dM$$

= expected stockout quantity during order interval.

After an order is placed at time t, the inventory position (units on hand and on order) is E. The expected net inventory after arrival of the order (assuming only one order is outstanding) is $E-RL$. The expected net inventory just prior to the arrival of the next order is $E-RL-RT$. The average inventory during the order interval is one-half the sum of the beginning and ending inventories:

$$\text{Average inventory} = \tfrac{1}{2}\left[(E-RL)+(E-RL-RT)\right]$$
$$= E - \left(\frac{RT}{2} + RL\right).$$

As a first approximation to an optimal periodic system, the economic order interval T is determined from the formulas deterministically developed in this chapter.[3] After the economic order interval is obtained, the maximum inventory level E can be derived. The deterministic assumption implies that the economic order interval T is independent of the maximum inventory level E. While this approach is not optimal, it is easier to do and usually represents a vast improvement over the typical intuitive inventory policies. An approximate solution will provide reasonable answers while considerably reducing the complexity of the decision problem.[4]

The maximum inventory level will consist of the safety stock plus the average demand during the order interval and lead time. The safety stock will be determined by balancing the holding costs against the stockout costs. When the stockout costs are not known, a service level policy can be prescribed.

[2] In the previous chapter, on fixed order size systems, the symbol M denoted the demand during the lead time period. Note that in this chapter, on fixed order interval systems, M denotes the demand during the order interval plus the lead time.

[3] The sensitivity analysis conducted on fixed order interval systems revealed the insensitivity of the order interval and variable costs to parameter errors. Thus, approximate solutions may very closely approach optimality.

[4] In Appendix B of the previous chapter, the optimal solution techniques were developed for dependence between the order quantity Q and reorder point B. Since fixed order interval systems apply to more than a single item (multiple items), optimal solution techniques for dependence between the order interval T and maximum inventory level E for a single item would be meaningless. Thus, they will not be developed.

The backordering case and the lost sales case must be contrasted. With backordering, the customer awaits the fulfillment of an order, and he is immediately served when the goods arrive. There is no lost sale. Backordering occurs with loyal customers or in monopoly market situations. The lost sales case occurs when the customer does not return to purchase the out of stock item. The backordering case and lost sales case will require slightly different mathematical treatments.

It will be assumed herein that stockouts occur in small quantities and the backorders are satisfied completely upon the fulfillment of the outstanding order. The cost of a stockout (whether for a backorder or a lost sale) will be assumed independent of how long it lasts. The economic order interval will be independent of the maximum inventory level. The remainder of this chapter will develop procedures for determining maximum inventory levels under conditions of known and unknown stockout costs.

Known Stockout Costs

Stockout costs can be on a per unit or an outage basis. On a per unit basis, the stockout cost indicates the loss that results from each unit of unsatisfied demand. On an outage basis, the stockout cost is constant regardless of the number of units out of stock. The specific situation usually dictates the cost basis.

Backordering Case: Stockout Cost per Unit

With backordering it can be assumed that the safety stock will be carried constantly. The appropriate mathematical notation is as follows:[5]

Annual cost of safety stock = (holding cost) + (stockout cost),

$$\mathrm{TC}_s = H(E-\overline{M}) + mA\int_E^{\infty}(M-E)f(M)\,dM,$$

where

TC_s = expected annual cost of safety stock,

$S = E - \overline{M}$ = safety stock in units,

H = holding cost per unit per year,

A = stockout cost per unit,

M = demand during order interval plus lead time (a random variable),

$\overline{M}$ = average demand during order interval plus lead time,

E = maximum inventory level in units,

$m = 1/T$ = number of orders per year.

[5]For discrete distributions, replace integrals with summations, and density functions $f(M)$ with probabilities $P(M)$.

By taking the derivative of expected annual cost of safety stock with respect to the maximum inventory level and setting it equal to zero, the following optimizing expression can be obtained:

$$\frac{d\mathrm{TC}_s}{dE}=0=H-mAP(M>E),$$

$$P(M>E)=P(s)=\frac{H}{mA}=\frac{HT}{A}=\text{optimum stockout probability.}$$

The above relationship can be used to determine the minimum cost maximum inventory level for both discrete and continuous distributions. When discrete distributions are employed, the exact stockout probability is frequently unattainable because of the discrete nature of the data. When the optimum stockout probability is not attainable for discrete data, the next lower attainable stockout probability is selected. There will be no solution if $H/mA>1$, but this cannot happen if (as we have assumed) stockouts occur infrequently. As the ratio approaches 1, numerous stockouts will be incurred. A ratio of 1 implies that the probability of a stockout is 1 and no inventory should be maintained.

EXAMPLE 5

The monthly demand for a product with a 2-month order interval and a 1-month lead time is normally distributed with a mean of 50 units and a standard deviation of 10 units. What are the maximum inventory level and safety stock if the holding cost is \$6 per unit per year and the backordering cost per unit is \$10?

$$P(s)=\frac{H}{mA}=\frac{6}{6(10)}=0.10.$$

From the standard normal table, a stockout probability of 0.10 gives $Z=1.29$ (see Table 8).

The standard deviation of 10 is for a time period of 1 month. The standard deviation required is for the order interval plus the lead time, or 3 months. The standard deviation is thus $10\sqrt{3}$, and

$$S=Z\sigma=1.29(10)\sqrt{3}=22.3 \text{ units},$$

$$E=\overline{M}+S=(2+1)50+22=172 \text{ units}.$$

Therefore, every 2 months the inventory will be checked. An order will be entered for the difference between 172 units and the stock position (units on hand plus units on order).

EXAMPLE 6

A department store replenishes inventory on a weekly basis. The replenishment lead time is also 1 week from the control warehouse. Holding costs are calculated as 25%

Table 8. Standard Normal Distribution

Standard Normal Deviate Z	Probability of a Stockout $P(s)$	Ordinate $\sigma f(E)$	Partial Expectation $E(Z)$
−4.00	.9999	.0001	
.00	.5000	.3989	.3989
.05	.4801	.3984	.3744
.10	.4602	.3969	.3509
.15	.4404	.3945	.3284
.20	.4207	.3910	.3069
.25	.4013	.3867	.2863
.30	.3821	.3814	.2668
.35	.3632	.3752	.2481
.40	.3446	.3683	.2304
.45	.3264	.3605	.2137
.50	.3086	.3521	.1978
.55	.2912	.3429	.1828
.60	.2743	.3332	.1687
.65	.2579	.3229	.1554
.70	.2420	.3123	.1429
.75	.2267	.3011	.1312
.80	.2119	.2897	.1202
.85	.1977	.2780	.1100
.90	.1841	.2661	.1004
.95	.1711	.2541	.0916
1.00	.1587	.2420	.0833
1.05	.1469	.2300	.0757
1.10	.1357	.2179	.0686
1.15	.1251	.2059	.0621
1.20	.1151	.1942	.0561
1.25	.1057	.1826	.0506
1.30	.0968	.1714	.0455
1.35	.0886	.1604	.0409
1.40	.0808	.1497	.0367
1.45	.0736	.1394	.0328
1.50	.0669	.1295	.0293
1.55	.0606	.1200	.0261
1.60	.0548	.1109	.0232
1.65	.0495	.1023	.0206

Table 8 *(continued)*

Standard Normal Deviate Z	Probability of a Stockout $P(s)$	Ordinate $\sigma f(E)$	Partial Expectation $E(Z)$
1.70	.0446	.0940	.0183
1.75	.0401	.0863	.0162
1.80	.0360	.0790	.0143
1.85	.0322	.0721	.0126
1.90	.0288	.0656	.0111
1.95	.0256	.0596	.0097
2.00	.0228	.0540	.0085
2.05	.0202	.0488	.0074
2.10	.0179	.0440	.0065
2.15	.0158	.0396	.0056
2.20	.0140	.0355	.0049
2.25	.0122	.0317	.0042
2.30	.0107	.0283	.0037
2.35	.0094	.0252	.0032
2.40	.0082	.0224	.0027
2.45	.0071	.0198	.0023
2.50	.0062	.0175	.0020
2.55	.0054	.0154	.0017
2.60	.0047	.0136	.0015
2.65	.0040	.0119	.0012
2.70	.0035	.0104	.0011
2.75	.0030	.0091	.0009
2.80	.0026	.0079	.0008
2.85	.0022	.0069	.0006
2.90	.0019	.0059	.0005
2.95	.0016	.0051	.00045
3.00	.0015	.0044	.00038
3.10	.0010	.0033	.00027
3.20	.0007	.0024	.00018
3.30	.0005	.0017	.00013
3.40	.0004	.0012	.00009
3.50	.0003	.0009	.00006
3.60	.0002	.0006	.00004
3.80	.0001	.0003	.00002
4.00	.00003	.0001	.00001

Table 9

Demand (Units)	Probability
0	0.10
1	0.40
2	0.30
3	0.20
	1.00

of unit cost. The weekly demand for a major household item that costs \$100 is given by the distribution in Table 9. If the backordering cost for the item is \$5 per unit, what maximum inventory level should be established?

$$P(s)=\frac{H}{mA}=\frac{0.25(100)}{52(5)}=0.096.$$

The above distribution is for one week. The distribution needed is for the order interval plus the lead time, or two weeks. To obtain that, the above distribution must be convoluted, which results in the distribution shown in Table 10.[6] Since the optimum stockout probability is 0.096, which is between 0.16 and 0.04, the maximum desirable inventory is 5 units. Every week, when the inventory is reviewed, the order size will be the difference between 5 and the stock position.

Table 10

Demand (Units) M	Probability $P(M)$	Probability of Demand $>M$, $P(s)$
0	0.01	0.99
1	0.08	0.91
2	0.22	0.69
3	0.28	0.41
4	0.25	0.16
5	0.12	0.04 ←
6	0.04	0.00
	1.00	

Backordering Case: Stockout Cost per Outage

With stockout cost on an outage basis, the stockout cost is assumed to be constant regardless of the size of the stockout. The stockout cost is a fixed amount if one or more units are not available for disbursement. The appropriate mathematical notation is as follows:

[6] See Appendix C to the previous chapter for the convolution procedure.

Annual cost of safety stock = (holding cost) + (stockout cost),

$$TC_s = H(E - \overline{M}) + mG\int_E^{\infty} f(M)\, dM,$$

where all symbols are the same except G, which is the stockout cost per outage (previously A was the stockout cost per unit). To minimize the above cost formula, the derivative with respect to E is set equal to zero:

$$\frac{d\,TC_s}{dE} = 0 = H - mGf(E),$$

$$f(E) = \frac{H}{mG}.$$

The above optimum relationship was developed for a continuous distribution, but frequently only integer values of inventory are possible. When the optimum maximum inventory lies between two integer values, select the integer with the larger $f(E)$.

For the standard normal distribution, the optimum maximum inventory is not obtained from the above formula, since the ordinate undergoes a change of scale when it is transformed to the standard normal distribution; however, the standard normal deviate Z for the optimum stockout probability can be obtained directly from the standard normal table if $\sigma f(E)$ is known. Again, stockout probabilities greater than one are not meaningful. A simple example can best illustrate the procedure.

EXAMPLE 7

Determine the maximum inventory level for Example 5 if the backordering cost is \$200 on an outage basis (backordering cost per outage is \$200).

$$\sigma f(E) = \frac{\sigma H}{mG} = \frac{10\sqrt{3}\,6}{6(200)} = 0.0866.$$

Looking up the ordinate of 0.0866 for a standard normal distribution, we obtain a Z of approximately 1.75. Thus, the safety stock is given by

$$S = Z\sigma = 1.75(10)\sqrt{3} = 30.1 \text{ units},$$

$$E = \overline{M} + S = (2+1)50 + 30 = 180 \text{ units}.$$

Therefore, every 2 months the inventory will be checked. An order will be entered for the difference between 180 units and the stock position.

EXAMPLE 8

The weekly demand for an item is Poisson distributed with a mean of 3 units. The order interval is 2 weeks, and the lead time is 1 week. If the holding cost is \$7 and the backorder cost per outage is \$10, what is the optimum maximum inventory level?

$$f(E)=\frac{H}{mG}=\frac{7}{26(10)}=0.027.$$

By consulting the Poisson table (see Table 11) for an average demand of 9 units during the order interval plus the lead time, we find .027 is between .019 and .032. Selecting the larger value of .032, we obtain a maximum inventory level of 14 units. When the inventory is reviewed every two weeks, the order quantity will be the difference between 14 and the stock position.

Table 11. Poisson Distribution

Maximum Inventory Level	$f(E)^a$										
E^b	$\overline{M}^c=2$	3	4	5	6	7	8	9	10	11	12
2	.271										
3	.180	.224									
4	.090	.168	.195								
5	.036	.101	.156	.176							
6	.012	.050	.104	.146	.161						
7	.003	.022	.059	.104	.138	.149					
8	.001	.008	.029	.065	.103	.130	.139				
9		.003	.013	.036	.069	.101	.124	.131			
10		.001	.005	.018	.041	.071	.099	.119	.125		
11			.002	.008	.023	.045	.072	.097	.114	.119	
12			.001	.003	.011	.026	.048	.073	.045	.109	.114
13				.001	.005	.014	.029	.050	.073	.093	.106
14					.002	.007	.017	.032	.052	.073	.091
15					.001	.003	.009	.019	.035	.053	.072
16						.001	.005	.011	.022	.037	.054
17							.002	.006	.013	.024	.038
18							.001	.003	.007	.015	.026
19								.001	.004	.008	.016
20									.002	.005	.010
21									.001	.002	.006
22										.001	.003
23											.002
24											.001

[a] The fractions in the table are the probabilities associated with exactly E demand during a time period with an average demand of $\overline{M}$ units.

[b] $E=\overline{M}+S$.

[c] $\overline{M}$ = average demand during order interval and lead time.

Lost Sales Case: Stockout Cost per Unit

The lost sales case differs little from the backordering case. The only difference is in the calculation of the safety stock. With backordering the safety stock is assumed to be $E-\overline{M}$, whereas with lost sales the safety stock also includes the expected number of stockouts. With lost sales the size of the inventory after arrival of any order is larger, since it is not reduced immediately by backorders. Consequently, the safety stock is slightly higher for the lost sales case than for the backordering case. The safety stock is determined by the following expression:

$$S=E-\overline{M}+\int_E^{\infty}(M-E)f(M)\,dM.$$

The above expression ignores the effects of lost sales during the lead time and considers lost sales as occurring only between the time one order arrives and the time the next order arrives. As long as the system is out of stock, on the average, only a small fraction of the time, the assumption is a very good approximation even when more than a single order is outstanding.

The appropriate mathematical notation for the lost sales case with stockout cost per unit is as follows:

$$\text{Annual cost of safety stock} = (\text{holding cost}) + (\text{stockout cost}),$$

$$\mathrm{TC}_s=H(E-\overline{M})+(H+mA)\int_E^{\infty}(M-E)f(M)\,dM.$$

To minimize the above expression, the derivative of expected annual cost of safety stock with respect to E is set equal to zero:

$$\frac{d\,\mathrm{TC}_s}{dE}=0=H-(H+mA)P(M>E),$$

$$P(M>E)=P(s)=\frac{H}{H+mA}=\text{optimum probability of a stockout.}$$

The above relationship can be used to determine the minimum cost maximum stock level for both discrete and continuous distributions.

EXAMPLE 9

If the stockout cost per unit in Example 5 is considered a lost sales cost per unit, what should be the maximum inventory level?

$$P(s)=\frac{H}{H+mA}=\frac{6}{6+6(10)}=0.091.$$

From the standard normal table, a stockout probability of 0.091 gives $Z=1.34$. Thus

$$S=Z\sigma=1.34(10)\sqrt{3}=23.20 \text{ units},$$

$$E=\overline{M}+S=(2+1)50+23=173 \text{ units}.$$

Note how the safety stock is slightly higher for the lost sales case than for the backordering case.

EXAMPLE 10

If the stockout cost per unit in Example 6 is considered a lost sales cost per unit, what should be the maximum inventory level?

$$P(s)=\frac{H}{H+mA}=\frac{0.25(100)}{0.25(100)+52(5)}=0.088.$$

The optimum stockout probability of 0.088 is between 0.16 and 0.04, so the maximum inventory level is 5 units. Every week, when the inventory is reviewed, the order size will be the difference between 5 and the stock position.

Lost Sales Case: Stockout Cost per Outage

With the lost sales case and stockout cost per outage, the appropriate mathematical notation is as follows:

$$\text{Annual cost of safety stock}=(\text{holding cost})+(\text{stockout cost}),$$

$$\mathrm{TC}_s=H(E-\overline{M})+H\int_E^{\infty}(M-E)f(M)\,dM+mG\int_E^{\infty}f(M)\,dM.$$

To minimize the above expression, the derivative of expected annual safety stock cost with respect to E is set equal to zero:

$$\frac{d\,\mathrm{TC}_s}{dE}=0=H-HP(M>E)-mGf(E),$$

$$f(E)=\frac{HF(E)}{mG}=\frac{H[1-P(s)]}{mG}.$$

Variable Demand and Variable Lead Time

So far in this chapter we have assumed that the lead time is constant. When lead time is also variable, the problem complexity increases. If it can be assumed that both demand and lead time are normally distributed and independent of each other, the following formulations can be utilized to obtain the maximum inventory level and safety stock:

$$E=\overline{M}+S=\overline{M}+Z\sigma,$$

$$\sigma=\sqrt{(T+\overline{L})\sigma_D^2+\overline{D}^2\sigma_{T+L}^2},$$

where

$\overline{M}=\overline{D}(T+\overline{L})=$ average demand during order interval and lead time,

$E=$ maximum inventory level in units,

S = safety stock in units,
Z = standard normal deviate,
T = order interval in days,
$\bar{L}$ = average lead time in days,
σ = standard deviation of demand during order interval and lead time,
σ_D = standard deviation of demand per day,
σ_{T+L} = standard deviation of order interval and lead time in days,
$\bar{D}$ = average demand per day.

To obtain Z in the above formula, it is necessary to obtain the optimum stockout probability. The optimum stockout probability is obtained from the proper classification of the problem as one of backordering or lost sales, with stockout costs on a per unit or outage basis. The optimum formulas have already been derived in this chapter.

EXAMPLE 11

The demand for an item is normally distributed with a mean of 5 units per day and a standard deviation of 2. The lead time for the item is also normally distributed with a mean of 10 days and a standard deviation of 3 days. The order interval for the item is 24 days, and the holding cost is \$6 per unit per year. If the backordering cost per unit is \$10, what is the optimum maximum inventory level (assume there are 360 working days in a year)?

$$P(s) = \frac{H}{mA} = \frac{6}{(360/24)10} = 0.040.$$

From the normal table Z is 1.75 for $P(s) = 0.040$.

$$\sigma = \sqrt{(T+\bar{L})\sigma_D^2 + \bar{D}^2\sigma_{T+L}^2}$$

$$= \sqrt{(24+10)4 + 25(9)} = 19,$$

$$E = \bar{M} + Z\sigma = \bar{D}(T+\bar{L}) + Z\sigma = 5(24+10) + 1.75(19),$$

$$E = 170 + 33 = 203 \text{ units.}$$

For probabilistic fixed order interval systems, either the demand or the lead time or both can be variable. When stockout costs can be ascertained, optimizing formulas can be developed that specify the most desirable maximum inventory level. Table 12 summarizes the formulas for the appropriate conditions.

Table 12. Formulas for Fixed Order Interval System Under Risk

		Probability[a]	
Stockout Case	Stockout Cost:	Per Unit	Per Outage[b]
Backordering		$P(M>E)=\frac{H}{mA}$	$f(E)=\frac{H}{mG}$
Lost sales		$P(M>E)=\frac{H}{H+mA}$	$f(E)=\frac{H[1-P(M>E)]}{mG}$

[a]The formulas give the optimum maximum inventory level for the appropriate demand distribution during the lead time plus the order interval. Symbols: H=holding cost per unit per year, A=stockout cost per unit, G=stockout cost per outage, m=number of orders per year, σ=standard deviation of demand for order interval and lead time, $P(M>E)=P(s)=$ probability of a stockout during order interval.

[b]For the standard normal distribution, the ordinate of the distribution is $\sigma f(E)$.

Service Levels

Very commonly an organization does not know its stockout costs. Under these circumstances, a service level policy is utilized from which the maximum inventory level can be ascertained. Service levels are usually set subjectively by management, and they indicate the ability of the organization to meet customer demands from stock.

A policy of never having a stockout is usually uneconomical. The economic principle of diminishing returns applies. Each additional unit of safety stock reduces the probability of stockout by a smaller amount. Most organizations consider a "reasonable" number of stockouts acceptable because of the extremely high cost of trying for total elimination.

Many organizations hold a given number of weeks' demand as a safety stock level for all products. Although this is administratively simple, it is not a good practice. Safety stock should be based upon the variability of demand over the relevant time period. Having a constant number of weeks' supply for all products means that slow-moving items may have too little safety stock and fast-moving items too much. This policy ignores the number of times a year stock is replenished.

If customers always receive their orders when demanded, the service level is 100%. Anything less than 100% means some disservice or stockout. The service level plus the stockout level must sum to 100%. The service level takes on different meanings depending upon how it is stated as a decision criterion. Four commonly used service levels are:

1. Frequency of service per order interval
2. Frequency of service per year
3. Fraction of units demanded
4. Fraction of operating days

The maximum inventory levels developed under the different service concepts will be different. The selection of the type and level of service is a management policy decision. The main considerations in choosing a measure of service are that it should reflect what the customer wants and that it should be capable of being measured by statistics derived from the control system. Several kinds of safety level can be chosen and the cost-performance tradeoffs in each presented to top management. Comparisons can help to determine if extra investment is needed to improve customer service. The choice by management of a service level implies a cost attributed intuitively or implicitly to service failure.

Service per Order Interval

A service level based on the frequency of service per order interval will indicate the probability of not running out of stock during the order interval. This approach does not concern itself with the magnitude of a shortage, but only with whether a shortage of at least one unit occurred. It is defined as the fraction of order intervals without depletion of stock:

Service level fraction per interval

$$= 1 - \frac{\text{number of order intervals with a stockout}}{\text{total number of order intervals}}$$

$$= 1 - P(M > E) = 1 - P(s),$$

$$P(M > E) = P(s) = \frac{\text{number of order intervals with a stockout}}{\text{total number of order intervals}}.$$

The term $P(s)$ is the stockout level fraction per order interval, or the probability of at least one stockout during an order interval. It is a measure of the fraction of order intervals during which the demand will exceed the maximum inventory level. The safety stock is determined as follows when service per order interval is adopted:

$$S = E_a - \overline{M} = E_a - (RT + RL),$$

where

S = safety stock in units,

$\overline{M}$ = average demand during order interval and lead time,

R = average annual demand in units,

T = order interval in years,

L = lead time in years,

E_a = maximum inventory level at acceptable service level in units.

EXAMPLE 12

The monthly demand for an item with a 2-month order interval and a 1-month lead time is normally distributed with a mean of 100 units and a standard deviation of 20 units. If the organization maintains a 90% service level per order interval, what should be the maximum inventory level?

$$P(s)=0.10.$$

For the normal table,

$$Z=1.28.$$

Thus

$$E=\overline{M}+Z\sigma=\overline{D}(T+L)+Z\sigma=100(2+1)+1.28(20)\sqrt{3}$$
$$=344 \text{ units.}$$

Service per Year

A service level based on the frequency of service per year allows for uniform treatment of different products. When the service level is based on the order interval and product groups have different order intervals, the frequency of stockout among product groups is not comparable. Fortunately, it is easy to convert from service per order interval to service per year. The service level fraction per year is obtained by raising the service level fraction per interval to the power of the number of annual orders (m).

$$\text{Service level fraction per year} = (\text{service level fraction per interval})^m.$$

The stockout level fraction per order interval is obtained as follows from the stockout level fraction per year:

$$P(M>E) = 1-(\text{service level fraction per year})^{1/m}$$
$$= 1-(1-\text{stockout level fraction per year})^{1/m}.$$

EXAMPLE 13

What is the service level fraction per year for Example 12? If an annual service level fraction of 0.8 is desired, what should be the service level fraction per order interval and the maximum inventory level?

$$\text{Service level fraction per year} = (0.9)^6 = 0.53$$

$$\text{Service level fraction per interval} = (\text{service level fraction per year})^{1/m}$$
$$= (0.8)^{.167} = 0.964$$

$P(s)=0.033$ gives a Z from the normal table of 1.80. Thus

$$E=\overline{M}+Z\sigma=\overline{D}(T+L)+Z\sigma$$
$$=100(2+1)+1.80(20)\sqrt{3}=362 \text{ units.}$$

Fraction of Units Demanded

The fraction of units demanded (or dollars demanded) and immediately filled from stock can be a meaningful service index. The service level fraction for units demanded can be defined as

$$\text{Service level fraction for units demanded} = \frac{\text{number of units supplied}}{\text{total number of units demanded}},$$

$$\begin{aligned}\text{Stockout level fraction for units demanded} &= 1-(\text{service level fraction for units demanded}) \\ &= \frac{\text{number of units short}}{\text{total number of units demanded}}.\end{aligned}$$

The above relationships must be measured over some fixed time period such as the order interval.

The expected number of stockouts during an order interval has already been developed earlier in the chapter as

$$E(M>E)=\int_E^{\infty}(M-E)f(M)\,dM.$$

To obtain the stockout level fraction for units demanded during the order interval, it is necessary to divide by the quantity demanded (TR) during the order interval:

$$\text{Stockout level fraction for units demanded}=\frac{E(M>E)}{TR}.$$

For the standard normal distribution, the expected number of stockouts during the order interval is the partial expectation $E(Z)$ times the standard deviation, or

$$E(M>E)=\sigma E(Z),$$

which results in

$$\text{Stockout level fraction for units demanded}=\frac{\sigma E(Z)}{TR}$$

for the standard normal distribution. By knowing the stockout level fraction, the standard deviation of demand during the order interval plus the lead time, the order interval, and the annual demand, the partial expectation $E(Z)$ can be determined. By consulting a standard normal table (see Table

8), the standard normal deviate Z can be obtained from the derived partial expectation, and the maximum inventory can be obtained from the following formula:

$$E=\overline{M}+Z\sigma.$$

A simple example illustrates the procedure.

EXAMPLE 14

From the information given in Example 12, what should be the maximum inventory level if a 0.99 service level fraction for units demanded is to be attained?

$$\text{Stockout level fraction for units demanded}=\frac{\sigma E(Z)}{TR},$$

$$0.01=\frac{20E(Z)}{0.166(1200)},$$

$$E(Z)=0.0966.$$

From the standard normal table, $E(Z)=0.0996$ gives $Z=0.90$. Then

$$E=\overline{M}+Z\sigma=\overline{D}(T+L)+Z\sigma=100(2+1)+0.90(20)\sqrt{3}$$

$$=331 \text{ units}.$$

Fraction of Operating Days

Another measure of stockout or shortage is the length of time an outage exists. With this measure, stockouts can be defined by the fraction of days with a shortage. This service level policy relates to the time out of stock, and it can be written as

$$\text{Service level fraction for operating days} = \frac{\text{number of operating days without stockout}}{\text{total number of operating days}}.$$

It is reasonable to assume that an item shortage for 10% of the time will result in unsatisfied demand equal to 10% of demand. If so, the service level based on operating days is very similar to the service level based on units demanded. For practical purposes, the two approaches can be considered equivalent.

Imputed Service Level Stockout Costs

When an organization sets a service level to establish a maximum inventory level, it really does in effect establish a stockout cost. Associated with a given service level is an imputed or implicit stockout cost. It is a simple matter to determine the imputed stockout cost for a given service level from

Table 13. Imputed Stockout Costs

Stockout Level (1 − Service Level)	Stockout Cost[a]	
	Backorder Cost/Unit	Lost Sales Cost/Unit
Stockout level per order cycle, $P(s)$	$\frac{H}{mA}$	$\frac{H}{H+mA}$
Stockout level per year, $1-[1-P(s)]^m$	$1-\left[1-\frac{H}{mA}\right]^m$	$1-\left[1-\frac{H}{H+mA}\right]^m$
Stockout fraction of units demanded,[b] $E(M>E)/TR$	$\frac{H}{mA}$	$\frac{H}{H+mA}$

[a] The formulas give the optimum probability of a stockout. To obtain the appropriate stockout cost, solve the formula for A.

[b] For the stockout fraction of units demanded, it is necessary to solve for $E(M>E)$ and find the associated $P(s)$ before the appropriate formula can be solved for the stockout cost.

the previously developed optimum formulations for the probability of a stockout. Table 13 outlines the formulations for determining the imputed stockout costs from the various service-level concepts. A few examples will illustrate the procedure.

EXAMPLE 15

From the information given in Example 12, what is the imputed lost sales cost per unit if the holding cost is \$1 per unit per year?

$$P(s)=\frac{H}{H+mA},$$

$$0.1=\frac{1}{1+6A},$$

$$A=\$1.50/\text{unit}.$$

EXAMPLE 16

The weekly demand for an item is normally distributed with a mean of 30 units and a standard deviation of 6 units. The order interval is 3 weeks, and the lead time is 1 week. Holding costs are \$2 per unit per year, and the service level fraction for units demanded is 0.95. What is the imputed lost sales cost per unit?

$$\text{Stockout fraction of units demanded}=\frac{E(M>E)}{TR}=\frac{\sigma E(Z)}{TR},$$

$$0.05=\frac{6\sqrt{4}\,E(Z)}{(3/52)(30)52},$$

$$E(Z)=0.375.$$

From the standard normal table, $E(Z)=0.375$ gives $P(s)=0.481$. Thus

$$P(s)=\frac{H}{H+mA},$$

$$0.481=\frac{2}{2+(52/3)A},$$

$$A=\$.12/\text{unit}.$$

CONCLUSION

This chapter has studied deterministic and probabilistic models for fixed order interval systems. Only the simplest type of periodic inventory system has been treated. There are many other modifications of fixed order interval systems, but none is more prevalent than the system outlined. The fixed order interval system under risk is schematically represented in Figure 6.

Although the techniques outlined do not result in optimal solutions, they do represent good approximations of optimal solutions. Optimal solutions require much more complicated mathematics and iterative procedures for exact solutions. The extra degree of exactness is not warranted in most inventory situations. Frequently, the parameter inputs (such as appropriate costs) to optimal solution techniques are estimates whose imprecision makes optimal solution methods a kind of overkill. The insensitivity of total inventory costs to slight movements away from the optimum makes approximate solution techniques usable tools for inventory analysis.

The assumption that the order interval T is prescribed prior to establishing the maximum inventory level is a reasonable one. Frequently order intervals are dictated by the workload, the available personnel, the central warehouse, and the availability of transportation equipment. These internal and external constraints tend to favor an independently prescribed order interval.

Figure 6. Risk: fixed order interval systems.
Key: FOIS=fixed order interval system; EOI=economic order interval.

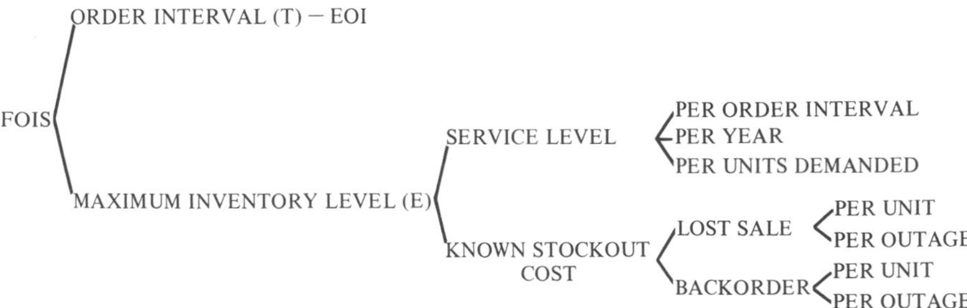

Even when optimal inventory rules can be derived, they are only optimal in reference to the assumptions made in developing the mathematical model. In practice, the inventory system must undergo revision in the light of organizational realities which are not variables in inventory models. For example, consideration must be given to the large volume of transactions, the high cost of informational systems, the necessity of forecasting demand, policies of suppliers, integration with the production system, and integration with the transportation or distribution system.

QUESTIONS

1. What two variables completely define the fixed order interval system?
2. For what periods of time are safety stocks needed in the fixed order interval system?
3. What components make up the maximum inventory level?
4. What are the basic assumptions made in using the fixed order interval system?
5. In a situation of variable demand and constant lead time, how is the optimum stockout probability obtained?
6. Define service level.
7. What are four commonly used types of service level?
8. What is the limitation on a service level based on the frequency of service per order interval?
9. By what criteria (limitations) are order intervals frequently dictated?
10. What are some typical factors to consider when analyzing an inventory system?
11. What is the difference between a backorder and a lost sale?
12. Differentiate between deterministic and probabilistic fixed order interval systems.
13. How sensitive are errors in parameters (demand, order cost, and holding cost) on the economic order interval?

PROBLEMS

1. A firm orders eight items from the same vendor, as shown in the table. The ordering costs are \$10 per purchase order and \$.25 per item. If carrying costs are 15% per year, what is the economic order interval? If the lead time is 1

month, what is the maximum inventory level for each item?

Item	Annual Demand	Unit Cost	Purchase Cost
A	175	$1.00	$175.00
B	425	.60	255.00
C	115	2.10	241.50
D	90	3.00	270.00
E	810	.75	607.50
F	70	4.00	280.00
G	190	5.00	950.00
H	210	2.00	420.00
			$3,199.00

2. A tire salesman experiences a very slow turnover of steel belted radials. The demand is found to be Poisson distributed with an average of 3 new tires sold per week. He normally orders tires every 2 weeks, since delivery takes only 1 week. His problem areas are the large expense ($52 per tire) of holding tires in stock and the backorder cost of $75 each time he runs short. What is his optimum maximum inventory level?

3. An appliance dealer is operating with a serious inventory problem because of variations in customer demand and wholesale delivery. After a study was conducted, he determined that his demand is normally distributed with a mean of 7 washing machines per week and a standard deviation of 2. He found that his delivery time is also normally distributed with a mean of 14 days and a standard deviation of 3 days. He has made a practice of ordering every 30 days, and his storage cost per washer is $50 per year. If the backordering cost per unit is $12, what is his optimum maximum inventory?

4. A service station maintains a 90% service level per order interval on auto accessories such as air filters and wiper-blade replacements. Items are ordered every 4 weeks, and an order is filled in 2 weeks. Each part shares the expense of the storage area at a rate of $10 per part per year.The weekly demand for an item is normally distributed with a mean of 6 parts and a standard deviation of 2. What maximum inventory level should be maintained, and what is the imputed backorder cost per unit?

5. From the data given in Problem 4, what is the imputed backorder cost per outage?

6. A breakdown in equipment is always caused by the failure of a special part. The monthly demand for the replacement part is normally distributed with a mean of 15 and a standard deviation of 3 units. Inventory is ordered every 3 months, and the delivery time is 1 month. The holding cost per unit per year is $40. Inventory levels are established on the basis of a 97.5% service level per order interval. What should be the maximum inventory level? What is the imputed backorder cost per unit?

7. What is the imputed backorder cost per outage in Problem 6?

8. An automobile dealer has a Poisson distributed monthly demand for an import car with a mean of 5 units. The annual holding cost is $400 per car, and the backorder cost per outage is $300. The dealer orders the car monthly, and delivery requires another month. What should be his maximum inventory level for the import car?

9. A small manufacturing plant produces generators which are sent to several electrical equipment companies. The plant orders generator kits every two months, with a delivery time of one month. The monthly demand for these generators is normally distributed with a mean of 25 and a standard deviation of 5. It costs $10 per year to maintain a generator in inventory. What should the maximum inventory be if they experience a backorder cost per outage of $50 each time they run out?

10. An art store reorders items every week, and it takes another week for delivery. Its holding costs per year are $33\frac{1}{3}$% of unit costs. The weekly demand for painting kits that cost $30 is given by the following distribution:

Demand	Probability
0	0.05
1	0.40
2	0.33
3	0.22
	1.00

If the backorder cost per kit is $4, what maximum inventory level should be established?

11. A retailer reorders supplies every 4 months, and the replenishment period is 1 month. His annual demand for a product that costs $.60 is 600 units. The annual demand is normally distributed with a standard deviation of 60 units. What maximum inventory level should be set for the product if the retailer can tolerate an outage once every 2 years?

12. An item has the following characteristics:

$$P=\$13.00/\text{unit}, \qquad F=20\%,$$
$$R=130 \text{ units/year}, \qquad L=3 \text{ weeks},$$
$$C=\$9.00/\text{order}, \qquad \sigma_R=26 \text{ units}.$$

The annual demand is normally distributed. If the manager will tolerate only one backordering outage per year, compute the economic order interval and the maximum inventory level.

CASE 1: IN THE BAG

Hitch & Blair, Inc. is a midwestern manufacturer of leather purses. Three years ago the owners, Sandy Hitch and Jane Blair, received their Fine Arts degrees in sculpture from Northwestern University. Both were directly influenced by the naturalistic lines found in modern sculpture and began to incorporate their aesthetic notions about sculpture into ladies' handbags. After receiving the encouragement from friends, they decided to show their work to buyers from two department stores, Marshall Field's of Chicago and L. S. Ayres of Indianapolis. The representatives from both stores were impressed by the quality and uniqueness of the designs and agreed to carry the items. Within six months, *Vogue* magazine and *W* had run articles on the latest fashion items and included examples of H & B's work. Demand for the handbags surged.

Today, there are over thirty artisans engaged in producing five different styles of handbags. All are premium priced ($100 and over). Each of the handbags is made from the same glove tanned cowhide and cured with their own formula of special tanning extracts. Rapid growth has presented some problems for this small firm. Shipments to their distributors have not always been timely. Not wishing to incur ill will, Sandy and Jane have been advised to exercise more efficient inventory control.

The main problem appears to be chronic shortages of the primary raw material. Hide prices have risen sharply, and leather now costs $18.00 a yard or 2.6 times what it did three years ago. In addition, commercial cattle slaughter has declined by 9–11%. Frequently, the firm must shut down production due to late shipments of cowhide.

Recently H & B hired a consultant to assist them with their problem. He established a probability distribution of lead times for cowhide based on the firm's historical data:

Lead Time (weeks)	4	5	6	7	8
Probability	.1	.2	.4	.2	.1

Jane provided the consultant with the following data pertaining to the five styles of handbags.

	Courier Pouch	Handle Clutch	Zippered Clutch	Musette Bag	Handle Portfolio
Weekly Demand	5	8	15	6	10
Amount of Cowhide per Handbag (yards)	2.3	1.6	0.5	0.7	2.1

The ordering cost for cowhide, regardless of the amount, is $50.00. The stockout cost for a yard of leather is $10.00, and holding costs sum to $8.00 per yard annually.

H & B have been using a fixed order interval inventory model, since they feel that ordering the cowhide at designated intervals meets their needs most adequately. They assume that ordering every six weeks is a feasible method and coincides conveniently with the hide industry's slaughtering, hide preparation, and delivery practices.

After accumulating this information, the consultant set upon analyzing the existing system so as to make necessary recommendations.

1. Is the existing inventory system appropriate?
2. What changes, if any, should be made?
3. What influence do rapidly rising costs have in choosing an inventory control system? Safety stock?

CASE 2: INTERNATIONALIZATION

Wiberg is the largest engineering industry in the Nordic area and its country's leading exporter, its foreign sales accounting for more than 10% of total exports. Wiberg manufactures and markets more than 100 products in 160 countries, generating more than $3.5 billion in worldwide sales annually. The product group which comprises the largest percentage of sales is transportation vehicles, and slightly more than one-half of the company's sales is in the passenger car category. Other products accounting for sales to the transportation sector are trucks, buses, and construction machinery. In addition, Wiberg's sales include marine and industrial engines, hydraulic machinery, engine heaters, and recreational products.

The company is organized into industrial groups and product units; production units; marketing units; administrative, insurance, and financing units; and consulting and service units. The Group management operates from the head office in Scandinavia. Most of the products are manufactured in 28 plants in the home country. There are also 21 wholly or partly owned facilities in 10 other countries.

The consulting/service unit coordinates Group activities and provides assistance and service in various specialized areas to other divisions. One area where they are concentrating efforts is in materials management. Two members of the consulting unit are providing assistance to the Wiberg–Gustavson Division, which assembles marine engines in the United States.

In researching the W–G production unit the consultants have found the following to be true. The W–G Division has very little direct control of quantities of inventory provided by the Wiberg Components Corporation in Scandinavia. Production plans are based on U.S. marketing forecasts as formulated by the American headquarters, are adjusted by Group management for worldwide requirements, and are compared with current inventory levels. The Group procures and ships appropriate quantities of materials to meet these production schedules. The interval between the formulation of production plans and the receipt of material is from three to six months.

Wiberg Components Corporation ships materials, not by part number, but by "module." A module is a grouping of all parts required to assemble a given number of a product or subassembly. Shipments from W. C. Corp. are received at random intervals in container size multiples. Each container shipment includes numerous pallets of various sizes; within certain pallets will be an assortment of parts; and several pallets collectively will make up a module or modules of parts.

W–G Division has direct control of orders for U.S. made materials. Lead times for these materials tend to be long (12–16 weeks) due to the relatively small size of the orders placed and to frequently encountered transportation delays. Accordingly, W–G considers a four week stock (one month's production requirements) of U.S. made materials to be an appropriate safety stock level.

All Nordic supplied parts are controlled as kits or modules based on the production plan. Each part, whether an engine block or a starter, receives essentially the same degree of management control. Similarly, all American supplied parts are purchased at production intervals to meet the following production period requirements. All parts are ordered at the same interval regardless of the supplier source. The variation and frequent changes in production plans complicate inventory planning, control, and maintenance. The recurrence of production schedule changes, coupled with long lead times for materials, induces W–G to stock excessive amounts of inventory as a precautionary measure.

W–G Division is currently in the design phase of a computerized inventory system. The American headquarter's staff is analyzing W–G's computer needs and is coordinating the findings with the inventory staff from the Group unit. The computer experts do not feel that W–G currently needs an MRP system but that it will in a few years. Therefore, they are planning toward a MRP-structured system.

1. Describe W–G's interval ordering system.
2. What are the inventory problems at W–G Division? How can they be solved?
3. Discuss the difficulties of controlling and coordinating inventories in multinational firms.

CASE 3: WORSTED WORRIES

The unpopularity of traditional style clothing pervaded the decade of the seventies. In contrast, the outlook for classical garments and fabrics in the eighties is very good. Consumers are exhibiting strong preferences for tailored attires, and there is an expected cross-sectional increase in this market segment. The dramatic shift in tastes has Michael McFarland, general manager of McFarland Company's production units, concerned. McFarland Company's ability to produce moderate quantities of conventional clothing has been proven, but its capability to meet higher levels of demand efficiently has not been tested in ten years.

McFarland Company began as a textile manufacturer in New Haven, Connecticut. The firm was established by a family of Irish immigrants and has remained under their control. Since the 1920's, McFarland has been weaving some of the finest woolen cloth available. The company expanded vertically into the production of men and women's classical styled clothing in 1949 and quickly came to be reputed as New England's foremost manufacturer of traditional garments. McFarland has always carried a very limited line and has no intention of increasing it. The firm plans to retain a standard selection of the classics in the basic solid and tartan fabrics produced perennially at the weaving plant in New Haven.

Michael is dismayed with the generally careless management of inventories, and in particular the extent of inventory shortages incurred last year for finished items. He is certain the poor operating performance is connected with his brother's control devices and the laxity with which control mechanisms are applied. He advocates a change in approach and an abandonment of the interval system now in use. He proposes a joint effort to modify current operational guidelines or replace them with specific practices. He suggests an investigation of the combined effects of inventory policies, scheduling, purchasing, and related activities expressly for the development of a reduced cost system.

Brian McFarland, manager of the weaving unit, agrees there needs to be a search for superior practices, but insists that a review of operations should be the preliminary phase—a step that might arrest Michael's suppositions that the company is functioning out of control.

McFarland purchases its raw materials (spools of wool and some synthetic thread) from a New England firm it has been trying to acquire for years. The materials are purchased bimonthly, and the stock is kept at the New Haven plant. The company has established emergency procedures to receive additional materials in approximately two days—a system that avoids stockouts and lowers safety stock levels. The emergency device is simply a periodic check by Brian whereby he estimates the number of days' supply. If the warehouse supply appears critically short, the supplier is notified and a reduced shipment is sent. The size of the shipment depends on the relative timing of the next reorder interval. The special shipment is an amount large enough to supply production until the regular reorder interval is reached. At the order interval, Brian orders quantities of materials estimated to fill the vacant shelves.

The New Haven plant is presently operating below capacity, and the production schedule at the weaving plant never varies. The adherence to stable schedules is indicative of the company's management philosophy. After the wool is dyed and woven, it is shipped either to fabric outlets or to the Guilford, Connecticut factory to be cut and sewn into finished garments. One third of all the cloth is sold in bolt lots at a lucrative profit.

When Guilford receives the woven fabric, it is stored in the consistently understocked storeroom. Guilford also believes in stable production. The company has so few styles that the 20 items in the ladies' line are made in sizes 6–16 with a specified number in each size. The men's line has 15 items with unvarying quantities produced in each size. The finished goods are sold directly to retailing establishments in the six New England states. Under existing conditions, McFarland can service about 75% of demand. Standard orders are filled for permanent customers. Considering the seasonality of the garments, McFarland has customarily stored the finished goods during the production year until the issuance of orders in late summer through early winter.

Brian is satisfied with many of these practices. He urges the continuation of the stable production but at an increased level. He is willing to adopt an economic order interval system for multiple items as the method for ordering from their primary supplier. Emphasizing the insensitivity of this model, Brian points out that his estimation processes would remain viable. The interval system in use needs only to be formalized.

Michael realizes that current procedures will have to be altered to service the increased demand. He feels Brian's focus on the inventory system is naive. He contends the firm will have to define the following before Brian can institute any system: the rate and magnitude of demand; the degree of certainty of the demand; the applicability of the interval system now in use for raw materials and for woven goods; and other economic and industry variables. Michael's cursory view has him working toward the interval system for raw materials, and a model based on stockout cost per outage or on service level fraction for units demanded for woven goods.

1. What are the apparent business conditions and problems at the McFarland Company?
2. What direction should McFarland Company take?
3. Can the McFarland Company practices of using operational guidelines and emphasizing stability be effective?
4. Could acquisition of the supplier, changes in the lines, reaching capacity, increased competition for raw materials, and discontinuation of bolt lot sales affect the selection of the inventory model? If so, then how?

MATHEMATICAL ABBREVIATIONS AND SYMBOLS USED IN CHAPTER 5

A	Stockout cost per unit
B	Reorder point in units
b	Price reduction fraction
C	Ordering and review cost per occurrence
D	Daily demand in units
$\overline{D}$	Average daily demand in units
E	Maximum inventory level in units
E_a	Maximum inventory level at acceptable service level in units
$E(M>E)$	Expected stockout quantity during order interval
$E(Z)$	Partial expectation
$f(M)$	Density function of demand during order interval and lead time
F	Annual holding cost fraction
G	Stockout cost per outage
H	Holding cost per unit per year
I	Stock on hand on review date
L	Lead time in years
M	Demand during order interval and lead time (a random variable)
$\overline{M}$	Average demand during order interval and lead time
m	Number of orders per year
n	Total number of joint order items
P	Unit purchase cost
P_d	Unit purchase cost with discount
$P(M>E)$	Probability of a stockout during order interval, $P(s)$
$\bar{q}$	Average size of extra inventory held for U time periods
Q	Order quantity in units
Q_d	Quantity discount break quantity in units
$Q_\$$	Maximum dollar order size
R	Average annual demand in units
S	Safety stock in units
T	Order interval in years
T_o	Economic order interval in years
TC	Expected total annual cost of inventory
TC_o	Optimum total annual cost of inventory

TC_s	Expected annual safety stock cost
TVC	Total variable cost per year
U	Number of time periods of length $T+L$ that extra inventory is held
X_C	Order cost error factor
X_H	Holding cost error factor
X_R	Annual demand error factor
Z	Standard normal deviate
σ	Standard deviation of demand during order interval plus lead time
σ_D	Standard deviation of demand per day
σ_{T+L}	Standard deviation of order interval and lead time in days

6 Inventory System Changes and Limitations

Inventory systems tend to develop over time. When an organization is small or in its infancy, inventories are small. Initially, elaborate systems of inventory control are unnecessary, so fairly unsophisticated methods of control are implemented. As an organization develops new product lines, the problem of control increases. All too often it results in the expansion of the existing, unsophisticated inventory system. Eventually, the inventory system becomes overloaded and extremely inefficient. At this point, it is necessary to redesign the inventory system in its entirety in light of current and future needs.

The signals for inventory system redesign can come from many sources. If the system loses orders, does not adequately indicate inventory status, results in frequent stockouts, or does not serve the purposes of its users, it is time to consider redesign. Unfortunately, management tends to believe the system is adequate if items are always available when requested and no stockouts occur. An inadequate inventory system can appear efficient through an overinvestment in inventory. This can occur because top management is usually more alerted to stockouts than to overstocks. An overstock is indicated by a large investment in inventories and low stock turnover ratio. If stockouts never occur, it is likely that the inventory investment is too high.

Poor results can emanate from inappropriate operating procedures, the system not operating as designed, an inadequate design, or personnel shortcomings. Systems which must be revised for small changes in operating conditions are of limited value. It is also untenable to require a mathematical genius for routine decisions. The relative value of alternative inventory systems can be measured by capital investment, customer service, and operating costs.

During an economic downturn or a recession, inventory systems and levels are frequently reevaluated (under duress). Organizations experiencing liquidity or cash problems usually limit their investment in inventory. Inventory systems should be periodically (perhaps yearly) evaluated as to their effectiveness in attaining organizational goals. Although inventory inefficiencies are highlighted during periods of economic stress, larger efficiencies and savings are also available during periods of economic growth.

INVENTORY SYSTEM REDESIGN

Before any changes are considered, the various objectives of the inventory system should be delineated. It is essential to define what objectives are to be sought and their relative importance. The two most important purposes are usually to increase sales and to reduce costs. The relative importance of various objectives may change over time or as dictated by economic conditions. It is practically impossible to design an effective system without a thorough understanding of the purposes it will serve.

When considering a change in an inventory system, a good starting point is to review the existing system, so as to determine whether or not to change the resident system, in what way it should be changed, and to what extent. In this respect, the decision to change an inventory system can be treated like any other capital investment analysis.

The redesign of an inventory system should be based on the resultant system's benefit to the organization. The benefit can be expressed in incremental cost savings and/or improved customer service. Since a revised system affects manpower levels, paperwork, information flow, and accounting functions as well as inventory levels, it is difficult to establish a precise point estimate of total cost savings. It is easier to determine the cost savings that result from changes in the level of average inventory. Before any revised inventory system is implemented, an incremental cost analysis should be conducted to indicate the potential benefits of redesign. The final decision should not be based solely on a cost analysis, since other intangible or unquantifiable factors also must be considered. The interested parties and personnel who use or work in the existing inventory system should be part of the redesign study.

It is generally too costly and time-consuming to analyze every item. Conclusions can be drawn from a sample of items, preferably a random sample. When relevant information is scarce or when the inventory involves thousands of items, data collection can involve all the high dollar usage items and only a sample of the remaining items.

When feasible, simulation is an excellent analysis tool for determining the impact of different system designs without actually implementing them. The principle involved in any simulation is to design a model in mathematical or symbolic terms which behaves in the same manner as the real system. Different systems with various features can be tested via simulation models, and the best system selected. Simulation will be treated more thoroughly in a subsequent chapter.

Frequently, a pilot study of the inventory system can reveal the potential benefits of redesign. It can be conducted in the following manner:

1. A representative sample of inventory items is selected and analyzed.
2. Using the appropriate inventory models, theoretical and actual performance are compared.
3. The potential cost savings and resultant benefits are determined.
4. A decision is made to continue the study, stop the study, revise the inventory system, or make no changes in the inventory system.

Another approach, which provides maximum security, is to run the new and old systems in parallel. This costly approach provides the greatest amount of comparative information.

There is no best way to implement a system conversion. A plan should be adopted with a schedule that contains milestones indicating continuation or termination. Finally the umbilical cord of the old system must be severed and the new system must stand alone.

It is sometimes advisable to install a new computerized system with a small range of items and gradually expand it to other items or locations. The gradual implementation provides time to correct errors and miscalculations. Rapid installation based on a "sink or swim" philosophy can be devastating for systems with major flaws or weaknesses that are not apparent until after installation. A stepwise installation provides time for unanticipated adjustments and modifications.

Some caution should be exercised in reviewing a new inventory system for several periods after its implementation. Stock levels and service levels are likely to be higher than planned for some time. The replenishment of understocked items will usually be more rapid than the sales of overstocked items. The net result will be a temporary increase in stock. Months or even years may be required to realize the full benefits of a control system.

A new system will not be perfect, and it will not produce optimum results. The important thing is that any new system be an improvement over present methods. It should produce schedules and plans that are reasonably good. It is unrealistic to rely on everything going right. There must be reserve built into any system in the form of contingencies to cope with emergencies or unusual events. A fallback capability or a failure mode is necessary.

EXAMPLE 1

An organization with an inventory of five items is considering the change from a periodic to a perpetual inventory system. Currently, each item is ordered at the end of the month. The ordering cost per item is \$10 per order, and the holding cost is 20% per year. Relevant item data are listed in Table 1. Should the organization adopt a perpetual inventory system?

Table 1

Item	Annual Demand R_i	Unit Cost P_i	Orders Per Year	Average Inventory $P_iR_i/24$
1	600	\$ 3.00	12	\$ 75.00
2	900	10.00	12	375.00
3	2400	5.00	12	500.00
4	12000	5.00	12	2500.00
5	18000	1.00	12	750.00
			60	\$4200.00

Table 2

Item	Optimal Dollar Order Size P_iQ_i	Orders per Year P_iR_i/P_iQ_i	Order Size Q_i
1	$ 424.26	4.24	141
2	948.68	9.49	96
3	1095.44	10.95	219
4	2449.49	24.49	490
5	1341.54	13.42	1342
	$6259.51	62.59	

The cost of the periodic inventory system is as follows:

$$\text{Periodic annual cost} = (\text{order cost}) + (\text{holding cost})$$
$$= 10(60) + 0.2(4200) = \$1440.$$

To determine the cost of the perpetual inventory system, it is necessary to calculate EOQ in dollars for each item. The optimal dollar order size for each item is obtained by multiplying the optimal order size by the unit cost, or

$$\text{EOQ in dollars} = P_iQ_i = P_i\sqrt{\frac{2R_iC}{FP_i}} = \sqrt{\frac{2P_iR_iC}{F}}.$$

Using the above expression, the optimal order size in dollars can be calculated (see Table 2). The cost of the perpetual inventory system is as follows:

$$\text{Perpetual annual cost} = (\text{order cost}) + (\text{holding cost})$$
$$= 10(62.59) + \frac{0.20(6259.51)}{2}$$
$$= 10(62.59) + 0.20(3130)$$
$$= \$1252.$$

The adoption of the perpetual system will result in annual savings of $1,440 − $1,252 = $188. The perpetual system will reduce costs by 13% from the existing periodic system.

A comparison of a perpetual and an MRP inventory system for an item with dependent demand is illustrated in Chapter 8.

RELEASING WORKING CAPITAL

If money is tight, an organization can trade off liquidity against the number of orders placed. This can be done by reducing the lot sizes and placing orders more frequently. Although placing extra orders for smaller quantities is somewhat uneconomical, it will increase liquidity by decreasing the inventory investment. As will be illustrated in the next section, the net effect of this action is to increase the holding cost fraction.

Organizations should be careful in arbitrarily reducing lot sizes for liquidity purposes. The smaller lot sizes will increase the exposure to stockouts for independent demand items and thus lower the service level. Additionally, quantity discounts may be lost. All the ramifications for operational performance should be considered before implementing such a policy. For example, if service levels are to be maintained while lot sizes are reduced, it will be necessary to increase safety stocks. All the facets of inventory management should be kept in view when attempting to change systems.

INVENTORY SYSTEM CONSTRAINTS

In determining the optimal inventory system, it has been assumed that no limitations are placed upon it. Frequently, management imposed limitations and physical limitations render the optimal system unacceptable. Since the inventory system is only a single subsystem in an organization, management may be required to suboptimize the inventory system for the overall good of the organization. Shortages of working capital may dictate less than optimal inventory policies, and storage limitations can do the same.

Stringent budget requirements can sometimes necessitate that inventory levels be less than optimal. This situation is not uncommon when the liquidity preference has increased. In essence, the liquidity condition has necessitated an increase in the holding cost fraction which negates the previously determined optimal order quantities. It is a relatively simple matter to determine the new holding cost fraction.

Suppose an organization with a perpetual inventory system and an average inventory investment of \$3130 (see Example 1) must reduce the average inventory investment to \$2000 because of liquidity necessities. If the existing holding cost fraction is 0.20, what will be the new, higher holding cost fraction? The ratio of the old average inventory investment to the new is as follows:

$$\frac{\left(\sum_{i=1}^{n} P_i Q_i/2\right)_1}{\left(\sum_{i=1}^{n} P_i Q_i/2\right)_2} = \frac{3130}{2000} = \frac{\sum_{i=1}^{n} \sqrt{P_i R_i C/2F_1}}{\sum_{i=1}^{n} \sqrt{P_i R_i C/2F_2}} = \sqrt{\frac{F_2}{F_1}},$$

$$\frac{3130}{2000} = \sqrt{\frac{F_2}{0.20}},$$

$$F_2 = 0.489.$$

The holding cost fraction has been increased from 0.20 to 0.489. The economic order quantity for each inventory item would be recalculated with the holding cost fraction of 0.489, which would ensure that the total average inventory investment would be \$2000. In the next section, the same type of problem will be solved with the more versatile mathematical technique of Lagrange multipliers.[1]

Suppose an organization with a periodic inventory system and an average inventory investment of \$4200 (see Example 1) must reduce the average inventory investment to \$3150 for liquidity reasons. If the existing economic order interval is 1 month and the holding cost fraction is 0.20, what will be the new economic order interval and the new holding cost fraction? The ratio of the old inventory investment to the new is as follows:

$$\frac{\sum_{i=1}^{n} R_i P_i T_1/2}{\sum_{i=1}^{n} R_i P_i T_2/2} = \frac{T_1}{T_2} = \frac{4200}{3150},$$

$$\frac{1}{T_2} = \frac{4200}{3150},$$

$$T_2 = 0.75 \text{ month.}$$

The review period would be decreased from 1 month to 0.75 month. The maximum inventory level would have to be recalculated for each item, using the shorter review period. The increased holding cost fraction would be determined as follows:

$$\frac{T_1}{T_2} = \frac{\sqrt{\dfrac{2C}{F_1 \sum_{i=1}^{n} P_i R_i}}}{\sqrt{\dfrac{2C}{F_2 \sum_{i=1}^{n} P_i R_i}}} = \sqrt{\frac{F_2}{F_1}},$$

$$\frac{1}{0.75} = \frac{F_2}{0.2},$$

$$F_2 = 0.27.$$

The holding cost fraction has increased from 0.20 to 0.27.

[1]For a further elaboration of Lagrange multipliers, see Appendix A at the end of this chapter.

Working Capital Restrictions

If working capital restrictions limit the size of the average inventory investment to J dollars, the determination of the best inventory levels can be determined by the Lagrange-multiplier method. Appendix A at the end of this chapter outlines the procedures for optimizing constrained functions by this method. The problem can be stated as:

$$\text{Minimize}\quad G=(\text{order cost})+(\text{holding cost})$$

$$=\sum_{i=1}^{n}\left[\frac{R_iC}{Q_i}+\frac{Q_iP_iF}{2}\right]$$

$$\text{subject to}\quad g=\sum_{i=1}^{n}\frac{P_iQ_i}{2}=J.$$

From the above minimization problem subject to a single constraint, the following Lagrangian expression can be developed:

$$h=C\sum_{i=1}^{n}\frac{R_i}{Q_i}+F\sum_{i=1}^{n}\frac{P_iQ_i}{2}+\lambda\left[\sum_{i=1}^{n}\frac{P_iQ_i}{2}-J\right].$$

To minimize the original objective function G subject to the restriction requires the minimization of h with respect to Q_i and λ. This is accomplished by taking the partial derivatives and setting them equal to zero:

$$\frac{\partial h}{\partial Q_i}=-\frac{CR_i}{Q_i^2}+\frac{FP_i}{2}+\frac{\lambda P_i}{2}=0,$$

$$\frac{\partial h}{\partial \lambda}=\sum_{i=1}^{n}\frac{P_iQ_i}{2}-J=0.$$

The simultaneous equations above can be solved for Q_i and λ:

$$Q_i=\sqrt{\frac{2CR_i}{(F+\lambda)P_i}},$$

$$\lambda=\frac{C\left(\sum_{i=1}^{n}\sqrt{P_iR_i}\right)^2}{2J^2}-F.$$

An example can best illustrate the technique.

EXAMPLE 2

The optimal average inventory investment in Example 1 is \$3130. Suppose the organization has a shortage of working capital and can only afford an average inventory investment of $2000. What is the best perpetual inventory policy, given the information in Example 1, with the restriction on the average investment of $2000?

The problem can be stated as the minimization of the cost

$$G = (\text{order cost}) + (\text{holding cost})$$
$$= 10 \sum_{i=1}^{n} \frac{R_i}{Q_i} + 0.20 \sum_{i=1}^{n} \frac{P_i Q_i}{2}$$

subject to the restriction that

$$g = \sum_{i=1}^{n} \frac{P_i Q_i}{2} = 2000.$$

To solve the problem, the Lagrange-multiplier technique must be applied, which results in the following optimum expressions:

$$\lambda = \frac{C\left(\sum_{i=1}^{n} \sqrt{P_i R_i}\right)^2}{2J^2} - F = \frac{10(625.95)^2}{2(2000)^2} - 0.20 = 0.289,$$

$$Q_i = \sqrt{\frac{2CR_i}{(F+\lambda)P_i}} = \sqrt{\frac{20R_i}{0.489P_i}}.$$

Table 3 develops the order size for each item.

For item 1, the order size is determined in the following manner:

$$Q_i = \sqrt{\frac{20(600)}{0.489(3.00)}} = 90 \text{ units}.$$

For all other items in the table, the values are obtained in a similar fashion. The cost of the constrained inventory policy is as follows:

$$G = (\text{order cost}) + (\text{holding cost})$$
$$= 10(97.86) + \frac{0.20(4003)}{2} = \$1379.$$

It can be seen that the annual cost increased from $1252 for the optimal policy to $1379 for the constrained policy. Thus, the organization has cut the average

Table 3

Item	$P_i R_i$	$\sqrt{P_i R_i}$	Order Size Q_i	Orders per Year R_i/Q_i	Dollar Order Size $P_i Q_i$
1	$ 1,800	42.43	90	6.66	$ 270.00
2	9,000	94.87	61	14.75	610.00
3	12,000	109.54	140	17.14	700.00
4	60,000	244.95	313	38.33	1565.00
5	18,000	134.16	858	20.98	858.00
		625.95		97.86	$4003.00

inventory level \$1130 (\$3130−\$2000) by an increase in the annual cost of \$127 (\$1379−\$1252). The value of λ, 0.289, has an interesting economic significance. Its value represents the increment added to the holding cost because of the inventory restriction on average investment. If the holding cost had been 0.489 (0.20+0.289) in the original problem, the optimal inventory policy would have indicated an average inventory investment of \$2000.

The procedure outlined in this section has put a limitation on average inventory investment. Sometimes the limitation would be on the total investment in inventory at any one time. The only difference in the procedure would be that the constraint would be

$$\sum_{i=1}^{n} P_i Q_i = \sum_{i=1}^{n} P_i R_i T = J.$$

The above example has illustrated the impact of a liquidity restriction on inventory. The Lagrange-multiplier method exhibited the optimum redesign of the inventory system to accommodate the capital constraint. The calculus-based Lagrange-multiplier method can be extended to other types of restrictions as well as to multiple constraints.

Storage Space Restrictions

If storage space restrictions limit the maximum inventory size to W cubic feet, the determination of the best inventory levels can be obtained by using Lagrangian multipliers. The problem can be stated as:

$$\text{Minimize} \quad G = (\text{order cost}) + (\text{holding cost})$$

$$= \sum_{i=1}^{n} \left[\frac{R_i C}{Q_i} + \frac{Q_i P_i F}{2} \right]$$

$$\text{subject to} \quad g = \sum_{i=1}^{n} w_i Q_i \leq W,$$

where

W = total storage volume for all inventory items,

w_i = storage requirement for each unit of item i.

From the above minimization problem subject to a single constraint, the following Lagrangian expression can be developed:

$$h = C \sum_{i=1}^{n} \frac{R_i}{Q_i} + F \sum_{i=1}^{n} \frac{P_i Q_i}{2} + \lambda \left[\sum_{i=1}^{n} w_i Q_i - W \right].$$

To minimize the original objective function G subject to the inequality restriction requires the simultaneous solution of the following equations:

$$\frac{\partial h}{\partial Q_i} = -\frac{CR_i}{Q_i^2} + \frac{FP_i}{2} + \lambda w_i = 0,$$

$$\lambda(g - W) = \lambda\left[\sum_{i=1}^{n} w_i Q_i - W\right] = 0,$$

where

$$\lambda = 0 \quad \text{if} \quad g - W < 0,$$

$$\lambda > 0 \quad \text{if} \quad g - W = 0.$$

From the simultaneous equations above, the following expression for Q_i can be obtained:

$$Q_i = \sqrt{\frac{2CR_i}{FP_i + 2\lambda w_i}}.$$

By testing different values of λ, it is possible to determine the optimum order quantities Q_i that meet the requirements of the constraining condition g. Manually, the enumerative process is laborious, but it is easily handled with the aid of a computer. The iterative process requires that λ be set equal to zero and small increments be added to it until the problem conditions are met. An example can best illustrate the technique.

EXAMPLE 3

If the maximum storage space available in Example 1 is 2000 cubic feet, what is the optimal perpetual inventory system? Assume the unit volume requirement in Table 4. The problem can be stated as the minimization of the following cost equation:

$$G = (\text{order cost}) + (\text{holding cost})$$

$$= 10\sum_{i=1}^{n} \frac{R_i}{Q_i} + 0.20\sum_{i=1}^{n} \frac{P_i Q_i}{2}$$

Table 4

Item i	w_i (ft^3)
1	1.0
2	1.5
3	0.5
4	2.0
5	1.0

Table 5

Item	R_i	P_i	w_i	Q_i	w_iQ_i (ft^3)
1	600	$ 3.00	1.0	117	117.0
2	900	10.00	1.5	86	129.0
3	2,400	5.00	0.5	205	102.5
4	12,000	5.00	2.0	392	784.0
5	18,000	1.00	1.0	866	866.0
					1,998.5

subject to the restriction that

$$g = \sum_{i=1}^{n} w_i Q_i \le 2000.$$

By trial and error or an enumerative computer program, the optimum value of λ is found to be 0.14. Table 5 develops the relevant order quantities for each item. For item 1, the order quantity in Table 5 was obtained in the following manner:

$$Q_1 = \sqrt{\frac{2CR_1}{FP_1 + 2\lambda w_1}} = \sqrt{\frac{2(10)600}{0.2(3) + 2(0.14)1}} = 117 \text{ units.}$$

The other order quantities were obtained in a similar manner. The storage space constraint resulted in smaller order quantities than in the unconstrained solution in Example 1. The reduction in order sizes will ensure that the maximum storage-space requirement of 2000 cubic feet is not violated. The value of λ has a useful economic interpretation. It is the marginal value of warehouse space. The cost saving per year that would result from one more cubic foot being available is $.14.

Working Capital and Storage Space Restrictions

Working capital and storage space considerations may both constrain the operation of an inventory system. If the average inventory investment is limited to J dollars and maximum inventory storage space to W cubic feet, the best inventory level can be obtained by using Lagrange multipliers with the Kuhn-Tucker conditions. The problem can be stated as:

$$\text{Minimize} \quad G = (\text{order cost}) + (\text{holding cost})$$

$$= \sum_{i=1}^{n} \left[\frac{R_i C}{Q_i} + \frac{Q_i P_i F}{2} \right]$$

$$\text{subject to} \quad g_1 = \sum_{i=1}^{n} \frac{P_i Q_i}{2} \le J,$$

$$g_2 = \sum_{i=1}^{n} w_i Q_i \le W.$$

From the above minimization problem, subject to two constraints, the following Lagrangian expression can be developed:

$$h=C\sum_{i=1}^{n}\frac{R_i}{Q_i}+F\sum_{i=1}^{n}\frac{P_iQ_i}{2}+\lambda_1\left[\sum_{i=1}^{n}\frac{P_iQ_i}{2}-J\right]+\lambda_2\left[\sum_{i=1}^{n}w_iQ_i-W\right].$$

To minimize the original objective function G subject to the two inequality restrictions requires the simultaneous solution of the following equations:

$$\frac{\partial h}{\partial Q_i}=-\frac{CR_i}{Q_i^2}+\frac{FP_i}{2}+\frac{\lambda_1 P_i}{2}+\lambda_2 w_i=0,$$

$$\lambda_1(g_1-J)=\lambda_1\left[\sum_{i=1}^{n}\frac{P_iQ_i}{2}-J\right]=0,$$

$$\lambda_2(g_2-W)=\lambda_2\left[\sum_{i=1}^{n}w_iQ_i-W\right]=0,$$

where

$$\lambda_1=0 \text{ if } g_1-J<0, \qquad \lambda_2=0 \text{ if } g_2-W<0,$$
$$\lambda_1>0 \text{ if } g_1-J=0, \qquad \lambda_2>0 \text{ if } g_2-W=0.$$

From the first equation above, the following expression for Q_i can be obtained:

$$Q_i=\sqrt{\frac{2CR_i}{FP_i+\lambda_1P_i+2\lambda_2w_i}}.$$

Substituting the Q_i expression into the two remaining simultaneous equations, the following expressions are obtained:

$$\frac{\lambda_1}{2}\left[\sum_{i=1}^{n}\sqrt{\frac{2CR_iP_i^2}{FP_i+\lambda_1P_i+2\lambda_2w_i}}-J\right]=0,$$

$$\lambda_2\left[\sum_{i=1}^{n}\sqrt{\frac{2CR_iw_i^2}{FP_i+\lambda_1P_i+2\lambda_2w_i}}-W\right]=0.$$

By testing different combinations of values of λ_1 and λ_2, it is possible to determine the optimum order quantities Q_i that meet the requirements of the constraining conditions g_1 and g_2. The enumerative process requires a computer. The process begins with λ_1 and λ_2 set equal to zero, and then one is held constant while the other is increased in increments, and vice versa. An example will illustrate the procedure.

EXAMPLE 4

Assume the maximum storage space available in Example 1 is 1500 cubic feet. If working capital is restricted and the average inventory investment must not exceed

Table 6

Item i	Volume w_i (ft^3)
1	1.0
2	1.5
3	0.5
4	2.0
5	1.0

\$2000, what is the best perpetual inventory system? The unit space requirements in Table 6 apply to each item. The problem can be stated as the minimization of the following cost equation:

$$G=(\text{order cost})+(\text{holding cost})$$
$$=10\sum_{i=1}^{n}\frac{R_i}{Q_i}+0.20\sum_{i=1}^{n}\frac{P_iQ_i}{2}$$

subject to

$$g_1=\sum_{i=1}^{n}w_iQ_i\leq 1500,$$
$$g_2=\sum_{i=1}^{n}\frac{P_iQ_i}{2}\leq 2000.$$

With an enumerative computer program, the values of $\lambda_1=0.03$ and $\lambda_2=0.37$ were obtained. Table 7 establishes the optimal order quantities for each item. For item 1, the order quantity was obtained as follows:

$$Q_1=\sqrt{\frac{2CR_1}{FP_1+\lambda_1P_1+2\lambda_1w_1}}=\sqrt{\frac{2(10)600}{0.2(3)+0.03(3)+2(0.37)(1)}}=92.$$

The other order quantities were obtained in a similar manner. Because of the inability to stock fractional units, we could not precisely attain the goal of \$2000 and 1500 cubic feet, but the solution is very close. All of the order quantities are less than in the unconstrained solution obtained in Example 1. The multiplier values ($\lambda_1=0.03$ and $\lambda_2=0.37$) indicate the marginal benefits from relaxing the constraints. The overall impact of capital and space limitations is to increase the holding cost of an item.

Table 7

Item	R_i	P_i	w_i	Q_i	w_iQ_i	$P_iQ_i/2$
1	600	\$ 3.00	1.0	92	92.0	\$ 138.0
2	900	!0.00	1.5	73	109.5	365.0
3	2,400	5.00	0.5	178	89.0	445.0
4	12,000	5.00	2.0	302	604.0	755.0
5	18,000	1.00	1.0	609	609.0	304.5
					1503.5	\$2007.5

Overview of Constraints

There are other types of constraints that can be put upon inventory systems. There could be a limitation on the total number of orders per year because of workload and manpower conditions.[2] The constraint equation would take the form

$$\sum_{i=1}^{n} \frac{R_i}{Q_i} \leq Y,$$

where Y is the maximum number of possible orders (setups) per year. Regardless of the type of limitation, the Lagrange method can be utilized to obtain the best solution.

An APICS special report developed a technique for optimizing order quantities under a number of orders (setups) limitation.[3] The technique is called "lot-size inventory management interpolation technique" or LIMIT. The LIMIT technique obtains the most economical lot sizes when there is a restriction on the number of orders (setups) which can be processed. The restriction may be imposed by the number of orders or setup men, or the amount of machine time. It reveals to management the effect on inventory of restrictions on setup times or number of orders. The LIMIT order quantities are the most economical ones possible under the limitation. The LIMIT technique applies when setup capacity is not readily available and economic order quantities (EOQ) would require too much setup time from what is available.

When constraints exist, the optimum solution techniques increase in complexity. Fortunately, constraints are frequently inactive. An inactive constraint does not modify the optimum solution by its existence. In other words, it can be ignored when solving the problem. Active constraints are those that modify the optimum solution by their existence, and they must be included in obtaining the solution to the problem.

It is a simple matter to determine if constraints are active or inactive. First, determine the order quantities by ignoring the constraints (assume all constraints are inactive). If the order quantities satisfy the constraints, the solution is optimal. If the unconstrained order quantities do not satisfy the constraints, determine the optimal solution for one constraint at a time (assume only one constraint is active) and establish its suitability. If the singly constrained order quantities satisfy all constraints, the solution is optimal. If none of the singly constrained order quantities satisfy all the constraints (more than one constraint is active), solve the problem treating multiple constraints as active, as in Example 4. The effort required to solve a problem increases rapidly with the number of constraints.

[2]An optimum policy when there are restrictions on inventory investment or the total number of orders can be obtained from an exchange curve. See M. K. Starr and D. W. Miller, *Inventory Control: Theory and Practice*, Englewood Cliffs, NJ: Prentice-Hall, 1962, pp. 93–104.

[3]James H. Greene (Ed.), *Production and Inventory Control Handbook*, New York: McGraw-Hill, 1970, pp. 16-17 to 16-22.

QUESTIONS

1. What are some of the signs of an overloaded or inefficient inventory system?

2. Can an inventory system be described as adequate solely because items are always available when requested and no stockouts occur?

3. What are three limitations which may render the optimal inventory system unacceptable?

4. What are active and inactive constraints? How do they enter into the problem of finding the optimal solution if three constraints exist, one of which is active?

5. How are optimal solutions determined for constrained inventory systems?

6. In inventory problems, what units are assigned to the Lagrange multiplier? What does it represent?

7. To what type of constraints does the Lagrange method specifically apply?

8. How are problems involving inequality constraints solved?

9. Once a constrained solution is obtained, how is its optimality verified?

10. Define a convex function for both one- and two-variable functions.

PROBLEMS

1. A firm with an inventory of five different items is considering the change from a periodic to a perpetual inventory system. Each item is currently ordered quarterly, with an order cost of $25. The holding cost per year is 30% of unit cost. Relevant data are listed below:

Item	Annual Demand R_i	Unit Cost P_i	Orders Per Year	Average Inventory $P_iR_i/8$
A	300	$ 8.00	4	$ 300
B	800	10.50	4	1050
C	1500	4.00	4	750
D	2150	4.00	4	1075
E	2600	2.60	4	845
			20	$4020

Should the organization adopt a perpetual inventory system?

2. In Problem 1, should the organization adopt a perpetual inventory system if the holding cost per year is 10% per unit?

3. The optimal average inventory investment in Problem 1 was $2537. Suppose the

firm has a shortage of working capital and can only afford an average inventory investment of \$1500. What is the best perpetual inventory policy, given the information in Problem 1 with the above restriction imposed?

CASE 1: RUNNING ON THE INSIDE TRACK

The junior sales representative for Jocko Wholesale Sporting Goods had a recent business flight from his home base in Houston to the Dallas–Fort Worth area. As his incomparable luck would have it, he was seated next to the assistant coach of Texas Technical Institute's highly successful football team. The young coach's father, by coincidence, is the Chairman of the Board of Hercules Sports Shops, an affiliate of Texas Conglomerates. Conglomerates owns the top-ranked professional football team, a chain of indoor tennis clubs, and the fastest growing franchise of roller rinks. The huge enterprise is also the prestigious sponsor of the nationally organized Middle League of Amateur Baseball.

Realizing his good fortune, the junior salesman swiftly displayed his marketing "gimmickry." Due to his occupational verbosity, wit, and charm, he was able to commission a deal to supply uniforms to Coach Schumacher's summer football camp. Even more impressive was his attainment of commercial leads. Not only was he able to personally contact the coach's father during his Dallas visit, but he obtained "inside tracks" that could result in acquisition of some of the industry's most sought-after accounts.

Upon his return to Houston, he spoke to the marketing vice president about his phenomenal success. He had negotiated a deal with one of the Conglomerate executives to supply 1500 units of merchandise to a central warehouse every week for the next two months. He is in the process of working out the details of supplying Fleet Feet, a subsidiary of Conglomerates, with a complete line of jogging shoes for the more than 30 stores. In addition, he has several large orders pending approval of other purchasing departments.

This recent wave of good fortune is not unique. Since his arrival at Jocko, the young sales wonder has bestowed unbelievable windfalls on the firm. However, the unprecedented sales have come at incongruent intervals and are causing planning difficulties for the other functional areas.

Surprisingly, the difficulties associated with the discontinuous sales seem to have trickled to his own department. During his sales report Buz is able to glean that the marketing vice president is less than exuberant about his news. This negative reaction to his accomplishments stirs the enthusiastic Hodges. Comprehending that his firm commitments, let alone his projected sales, may not be met, Buz voices the following refusal to retrench:

> If the company is unable to meet my quotas, then a company expansion plan is the only alternative. If the company wants aggressive sales, then they should prepare for them.
>
> Support for my new style of sales must come from an adequate inventory. These manufacturers should be called at once, and the shipments should be expedited. Let's get the goods here and "blast" our infernal interval ordering periods. Lead times and other delay excuses used by our manufacturers are hypocritical—I'm doing them a favor as well.

> Limitation of my sales is asinine—the only logical solution for these pending orders is instantaneous receipt of goods and prior stocking of merchandise. If the company wants to do this systematically, then we need to design a system that can do it.

The marketing vice president admits that the present system cannot support a highly aggressive marketing program. The system is simply overloaded. The company receives orders from manufacturers in economic intervals, but the present interval system is clearly inadequate. However, an abrupt change would not be well received. Some improvement over the old system might be a more realistic goal.

1. What is the relationship between the company's goals and its inventory system? What would appear to be reasonable goals for Jocko?
2. How can they handle the influx of orders? What should their policy be toward Texas Conglomerates?
3. What may be the limitations of the system? Would limitation of sales be a possibility in the short or long run?
4. Can great variations in demand affect the selection and operation of the inventory system?

CASE 2: RESTRICTED CAPITAL FLOW

David Friedman & Sons sell air conditioning and heating units in the Oklahoma City metropolitan area. Numerous members of the Oklahoma City Homebuilders Association do business with Friedman & Sons, and the most reputable builders are regular clients of the firm. The majority of its air conditioning unit sales are to residential builders, but there are some sales of special size units to commercial contractors as well as single unit sales to private homeowners.

Friedman carries 15 different models of air conditioning units in stock. The four manufacturers of the models are implementing technological changes in order to satisfy the demand for more efficient units. The rapidity of the technological changes is forcing Friedman to reevaluate its present stocking policies. The firm wants to include the updated models in its inventory ordering system and yet be flexible enough to include even more efficient models as they are developed.

The company has usually held a small inventory; keeping the inventory investment at a minimum has been an important company policy. Friedman forecasts sales on a quarterly basis. The forecast is derived by accumulating the actual orders and adjusting them with an additional amount for uncommitted, but projected, sales. These figures are kept at a conservative level so that when translated into an inventory investment the amount stays within a low range.

Friedman's purchases are based on a reorder point and economic order quantity. The firm uses a manual inventory system. Each model is inventoried on a file card with pertinent information on the model, such as price, reorder point, EOQ, and lead time. Sam Levinson calculates the EOQ periodically; he tries to keep the EOQ as accurate as possible in view of fluctuating demand. So far, the executives believe that the EOQ system is functioning fairly well.

One problem that the firm is encountering with the present system is control of the physical inventory. There are some problems in keeping track of unit serial numbers with the manual system. There are physical problems in locating and updating the status of individual units. Some of the problem is attributed to general accounting inaccuracies. The control problem often is not discovered until a unit is allotted for sale. It is not uncommon to find the unit is defective or has been dismantled so that some of the parts could be used on other units or sold as spare parts. The physical stock and the condition of the stock seldom are accounted for correctly on the file card.

An even more pressing problem is a general economic one. Management is forecasting a critically slow period for the homebuilding industry with residual effects on their own sales. New housing starts are decreasing due to spiraling inflation and record-high mortgage rates. Actual orders for air conditioning units have dropped appreciably, and the forecast is extremely bleak. Business is so bad that the firm has received the fewest firm orders in five years, and the accounts receivable are aging. The builders are operating on credit, because they are holding sizable inventory investments of their own.

It is becoming very difficult to forecast sales in the present economic situation. The forecasting problem is compounded by the change in ordering habits by the builders. The builders are giving less advance notification on much smaller orders. These changes on the demand side, coupled with the builders' needs to seek credit on their orders, are hastening Friedman's inventory dilemma and working capital shortages.

Sam Levinson's inclination is to effect a change in the depth of the instock line. He contends that the firm should reduce the number of models in all of the manufacturers' lines carried by Friedman. For instance, one of the more popular lines should include only the most frequently purchased models and a slightly larger number of each. Sam prepared a table illustrating the models in this line he would select to carry, with his estimate of each model's annual sales under present conditions:

Model	Price	Yearly Sales
Z 210	$650	170
Z 310	690	240
Z 410	740	220
X 520	750	260
X 530	780	180

David Friedman agrees that this is a good initial cutback, but would like to see a more quantitative analysis showing the plan's desirability. A further improvement would be simply to apply a working capital restriction on the investment in inventory. David feels that the limit on this particular line should approximate $30,000. He is anxious to develop a system that will cut back on inventory and enhance the liquidity of the firm.

1. Given $F=0.25$ and $C=\$30$, construct an inventory policy for the firm's most popular line.
2. What other inventory changes should be incorporated?

3. What further economic changes would affect the development of the inventory system? Will the new system correct the other inventory problems?
4. Is Levinson's reduction plan the sole solution, and should it be extended to the other lines?

CASE 3: MRP OR BUST

Rollo Fishbein, President of Alpha Electronics, has recently become a member of APICS, an organization for production and inventory control professionals. Through APICS, Rollo has gained considerable knowledge about modern production and inventory control systems. He has become particularly interested in material requirements planning (MRP) systems as solutions to many present day inventory problems—the types of problems which exist at Alpha.

Alpha Electronics is a small but rapidly growing manufacturer of electrical meters and test equipment such as voltmeters, potentiometers, ohmmeters, and galvanometers. All of the end products are high quality, expensive items sold primarily to industrial firms or to educational institutions. Alpha purchases over 1000 parts and manufactures approximately 1500 parts and assemblies of its own. Some of the parts are used on more than one instrument, and a few simpler parts are used on at least 40% of the finished items. Production lots are mostly small, as usual for precision instruments. Alpha is using a fixed order size system to control inventories of both parts and end items. EOQs and reorder points are calculated for all items.

Because of the rapid expansion of the firm, there is a recurrent cash crunch. In order to improve the liquidity position, Rollo would like to see inventories minimized. He has become enthusiastic about MRP's capability of substantially reducing production costs and inventory investments. His convictions about the relative advantages of MRP systems are so strong that he has declared that Alpha will implement an MRP system immediately with a target completion date of less than one year.

Judging from what he has heard and read, Rollo has determined that Alpha meets all the product requirements for successful implementation of an MRP system. The other requirements of the organization dictate computerized data processing methods, and the functional requirements of the production and inventory departments require a sophisticated MRP system. Rollo has deemed further investigation of alternative systems unnecessary and has chosen to bypass some of the system design phases. For instance, he has overridden the material manager's request for detailed systems design proposals from competing firms; Rollo has requested a design for an entirely new system and requisitioned information pertaining only to conversion to an MRP system. His short-cut procedure stipulates that the only detailed design is to be the selection of an MRP package. Rollo is so confident of his decision and so eager to begin the process that he has already contacted a software consultant to come in and tailor an existing MRP package to Alpha's needs.

The selection of the software consultant has anticipated the selection process for computer hardware. Rollo is circumventing the tedious process of choosing hardware and is ready to match the computer configuration to his stated system requirements and MRP software needs. Rollo has decided that the power and capabilities of the computer configuration should exceed the present system requirements by a wide margin. Thus, he is prepared to purchase more computing power for the firm and will simply select a system that is compatible with the MRP system undergoing development. Rollo is pleased that his software consultant is affiliated with a company well known for general purpose equipment. Not only is the computer company respected for its highly versatile equipment, but Rollo's APICS associates have informed him that this company could best meet his selection criteria—low cost and familiarity with the software.

As a further step toward a speedy implementation Rollo is proposing a direct conversion. This "cold turkey" approach is based on two important considerations. First, there should be an abrupt discontinuation of the old system, as it is obsolete and so drastically different from the new system that nothing could be gained from its continuation. Second, the conversion should be made quickly and inexpensively.

Rollo has assured his personnel that there will be an educational program, but it will have to come subsequent to the developmental phase. All system operators will receive on-the-job training, and all management and staff personnel will attend a session designed to explain the system outputs. In addition, management and staff will be required to attend an acceptance meeting near project completion and a follow-up meeting at project termination. Rollo has also promised that he will allocate funds for new positions; people with computer backgrounds and experience will be hired to execute a smoother transition and to ensure optimum operating efficiency.

1. Is the proposed system a good way of handling the firm's expansion problem? Realizing that perfect results are unlikely, have the potential benefits of the redesign been exaggerated?
2. What are the behavioral implications of this system conversion? Has Rollo Fishbein initiated the change in a manner that will lessen resistance?
3. What implementation approach would you suggest?
4. Is it essential that Alpha undergo a system redesign? If so, what needs to be redesigned?

MATHEMATICAL ABBREVIATIONS AND SYMBOLS USED IN CHAPTER 6

C	Order cost per order
EOQ	Economic order quantity
F	Annual inventory holding cost fraction
G	Total annual incremental cost = (order cost) + (holding cost)
n	Number of inventory items
J	Maximum size of average inventory in dollars
P_i	Unit purchase cost of item i
Q_i	Order quantity for item i in units
R_i	Annual demand for item i in units
T_i	Order interval for item i
w_i	Storage volume requirement for each unit of item i

W	Maximum total storage volume for all items
Y	Maximum number of annual orders
λ	Lagrange multiplier

APPENDIX A. OPTIMIZING CONSTRAINED FUNCTIONS

In many models developed in this text, a general cost function has been minimized. Generally, the only constraints on the solution were boundary conditions, such as that the order quantity must be nonnegative. However, it is common to find certain restrictions on controllable variables. Frequently, physical resources, such as capital and floor space, put limitations on the optimum solution. The method of Lagrange multipliers can be used to find a minimum value of a function subject to constraints.

The Lagrange method specifically applies to equality constraints. When the Lagrangian method is combined with the Kuhn-Tucker conditions, problems involving inequality constraints can be solved. However, the solutions obtained with the equality constraints and inequality constraints are only optimal if the functions meet the test of convexity for minimization problems.[4] Tests for convexity are outlined in a later section.

In inventory problems, the function f usually represents the expected annual cost, and the constraints g_i are usually capital or floor space. The Lagrange multiplier is the value or cost per unit of resource; it represents the amount by which the minimum cost can be reduced by adding one additional unit of limiting resource. The Lagrange multipliers can be considered imputed values or shadow prices of the resources.

One Equality Constraint

To minimize a function $f(X_1,\ldots, X_n)$, subject to an equality constraint $g(X_1,\ldots, X_n)=a$, where both functions are continuous and differentiable, simply minimize the unconstrained function

$$h(X_1,\ldots, X_n,\lambda)=f(X_1,\ldots, X_n)+\lambda[g(X_1,\ldots, X_n)-a],$$

where λ is a Lagrange multiplier unrestricted in sign.

To minimize the unconstrained function $h=f+\lambda(g-a)$, the partial derivatives of h with respect to X_j and λ are set equal to zero:

$$\frac{\partial h}{\partial X_j}=\frac{\partial f}{\partial X_j}+\lambda\frac{\partial g}{\partial X_j}=0, \qquad j=1,\ldots,n,$$

$$\frac{\partial h}{\partial \lambda}=g-a=0.$$

[4]For solution techniques for optimizing constrained functions when the convexity requirement does not hold, see G. Hadley and T. M. Whitin, *Analysis of Inventory Systems*, Englewood Cliffs, NJ: Prentice-Hall, 1963, pp. 433–437.

By simultaneously solving the above equations for X_j and λ, the minimum point $f(X_1,\ldots,X_n)$ is obtained. If the multiplier is positive, it indicates the rate at which f will decrease per unit increase in the parameter a.

More Than One Equality Constraint

The method for one equality constraint can be extended to more than one. To minimize a function $f(X_1,\ldots,X_n)$, subject to two equality constraints $g_1(X_1,\ldots,X_n)=a_1$ and $g_2(X_1,\ldots,X_n)=a_2$, where all the functions are continuous and differentiable, simply minimize the unrestrained function

$$h(X_1,\ldots,X_n,\lambda_1,\lambda_2)=f(X_1,\ldots,X_n)+\lambda_1[g_1(X_1,\ldots,X_n)-a_1]$$
$$+\lambda_2[g_2(X_1,\ldots,X_n)-a_2],$$

where λ_1 and λ_2 are Lagrange multipliers unrestricted in sign.

To minimize the unconstrained function $h=f+\lambda_1(g_1-a_1)+\lambda_2(g_2-a_2)$, the partial derivatives of h with respect to X_j, λ_1, and λ_2 are set equal to zero:

$$\frac{\partial h}{\partial X_j}=\frac{\partial f}{\partial X_j}+\lambda_1\frac{\partial g_1}{\partial X_j}+\lambda_2\frac{\partial g_2}{\partial X_j}=0,$$

$$\frac{\partial h}{\partial \lambda_1}=g_1-a_1=0,$$

$$\frac{\partial h}{\partial \lambda_2}=g_2-a_2=0,$$

where $j=1,\ldots,n$. By simultaneously solving the above equations for X_j, λ_1, and λ_2, the minimum point $f(X_1,\ldots,X_n)$ is obtained.

One Inequality Constraint

The Lagrangian method can be supplemented with the Kuhn-Tucker conditions to solve the minimization problem subject to a single inequality. To minimize a function $f(X_1,\ldots,X_n)$ subject to an inequality constraint $g(X_1,\ldots,X_n)\leq a$, where both functions are continuous and differentiable, simply minimize the unconstrained function

$$h(X_1,\ldots,X_n,\lambda)=f(X_1,\ldots,X_n)+\lambda[g(X_1,\ldots,X_n)-a],$$

where λ is a nonnegative Lagrange multiplier.

To minimize the unconstrained function $h=f+\lambda(g-a)$, the Kuhn-Tucker conditions for the minimization of a function subject to an inequality constraint are invoked as follows:

$$\frac{\partial h}{\partial X_j}=\frac{\partial f}{\partial X_j}+\lambda\frac{\partial g}{\partial X_j}=0, \qquad \lambda(g-a)=0,$$

where $j=1,\ldots,n$. By simultaneously solving the above equations for X_j and λ, the minimum point $f(X_1,\ldots,X_n)$ is obtained.

More Than One Inequality Constraint

The method for one inequality constraint can be extended to more than one. To minimize a function $f(X_1,\ldots, X_n)$ subject to two inequality constraints $g_1(X_1,\ldots, X_n)\leq a_1$ and $g_2(X_1,\ldots, X_n)\leq a_2$, where all the functions are continuous and differentiable, simply minimize the unconstrained function

$$h(X_1,\ldots, X_n, \lambda_1, \lambda_2)=f(X_1,\ldots, X_n)+\lambda_1[g_1(X_1,\ldots, X_n)-a_1]$$
$$+\lambda_2[g_2(X_1,\ldots, X_n)-a_2],$$

where λ_1 and λ_2 are nonnegative Lagrange multipliers.

To minimize the unconstrained function $h=f+\lambda_1(g_1-a_1)+\lambda_2(g_2-a_2)$, the Kuhn-Tucker conditions for the minimization of a function subject to two inequality constraints are invoked as follows:

$$\frac{\partial h}{\partial X_j}=\frac{\partial f}{\partial X_j}+\lambda_1\frac{\partial g_1}{\partial X_j}+\lambda_2\frac{\partial g_2}{\partial X_j}=0,$$
$$\lambda_1(g_1-a_1)=0,$$
$$\lambda_2(g_2-a_2)=0,$$

where $j=1,\ldots, n$. By simultaneously solving the above equations for X_j, λ_1, and λ_2, the minimum point $f(X_1,\ldots, X_n)$ is obtained.

Tests for Convexity

The procedures outlined herein for obtaining the optimum solution to a minimization problem only give candidates for the optimum solution. To ensure that a solution is optimum, both the objective function f and constraints g_i must be convex. A convex function always bends upward. A straight line (linear) function is both convex and concave.

A function $F(X)$ with one variable that is continuous and possesses a second derivative is convex if its second derivative is greater than or equal to zero:

$$\frac{d^2F(X)}{dX^2}\geq 0.$$

A function $F(X_1, X_2)$ with two variables that is continuous and possesses second derivatives is convex if

$$\left(\frac{\partial^2 F}{\partial X_1^2}\right)\left(\frac{\partial^2 F}{\partial X_2^2}\right)-\left(\frac{\partial^2 F}{\partial X_1\partial X_2}\right)^2>0, \qquad \frac{\partial^2 F}{\partial X_1^2}>0, \qquad \frac{\partial^2 F}{\partial X_2^2}>0.$$

For the determination of the convexity of functions with more than two variables, see McMillan.[5]

[5] Claude McMillan, Jr., *Mathematical Programming*, New York: John Wiley and Sons, 1970, pp. 419–424.

7 Single Order Quantities

The single order model is concerned with the planning and control of inventory items that are purchased only once during a time period, or for which only one production run may be initiated. The familiar inventory models (EOQ, EOI, and EPQ) do not readily apply to the single order because (1) the demand is not continuous, (2) the demand level may change drastically from time period to time period, and (3) the product's market life may be very short due to obsolescences or perishability. The single order quantity problem is frequently referred to in the literature as the Christmas tree problem or the newsboy problem.

The single order quantity model is applicable when (1) a demand exists for an item at infrequent intervals or (2) an uncertain demand exists for a short-lived item at frequent intervals. The first situation is typified by promotional and fad items ordered by retail stores, or spare parts for maintenance repair. The second situation is typified by highly perishable items (fresh fish, flowers) and short-lived, obsolescent items (newspapers, periodicals).

In this case, within the time period considered, there are no repeat orders. If the demand is greater than the order size, an opportunity-profit loss results, since there is insufficient time to replenish the stock. If the demand is less than the order size, the overstock is usually disposed of at a loss. Christmas trees, high-fashion apparel, some perishable items, and seasonal agricultural products are examples that fall into the single order category. Figure 1 indicates the different classifications for the single order inventory problem.

To determine the optimum single order quantity, it is necessary to balance two opposing costs. Order costs are irrelevant, since only one order will be placed and a single order cost incurred. Holding costs are not important, since an ongoing demand for the item is not expected. The two relevant costs for the single order are obsolescence (overage) costs and opportunity (underage) costs. Obsolescence costs are incurred when all of the stock is not sold. Excess stock may be sold at less than cost, or the stock may be discarded for a total unit loss. Opportunity costs result from not being able to satisfy customer demand. Opportunity costs include lost profit from potential sales when demand exceeds supply. If the demand exceeds the single-order quantity, there is no obsolescence cost, but only an opportunity cost; if the demand is less than the single order quantity, there is no opportunity cost, but only an obsolescence cost. The optimum condition is when demand equals supply and no opportunity or obsolescence costs are incurred.

The source of the single order quantity may be self-supply or outside supply. Self-supply exists when the organization produces the item itself, whereas outside supply exists when another organization is the supply source. With self-supply, the lead time is mainly composed of production

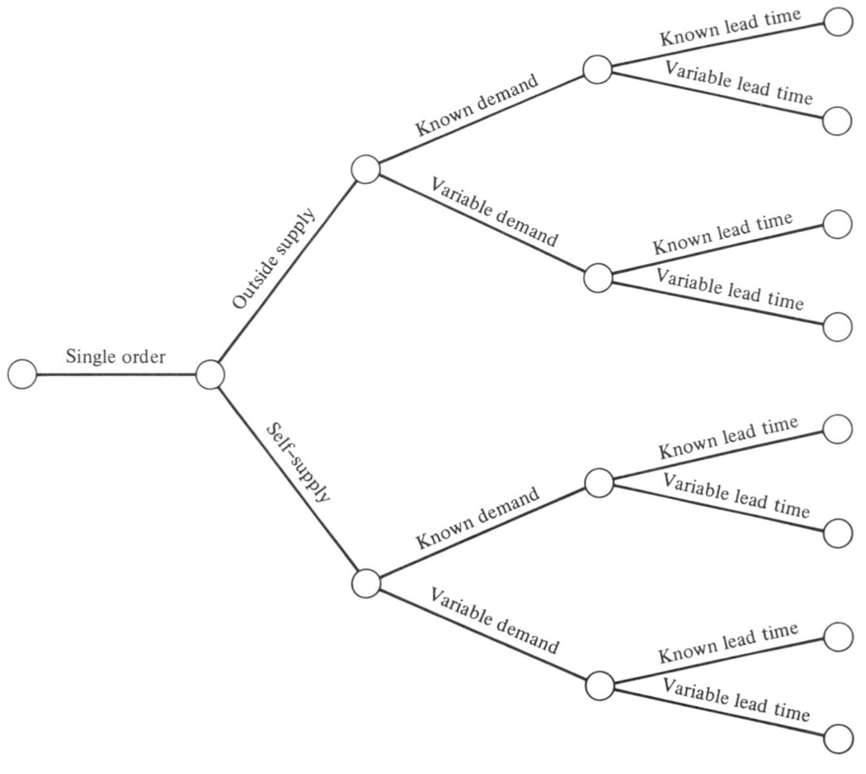

Figure 1

scheduling, manufacturing, and assembly time. With outside supply, the lead time also includes the transit and receipt times. An organization has greater control over the lead time if an item is self-supplied.

The determination or estimation of the demand is critical in dealing with a single order. If the demand is known, the problem is simplified. If the demand follows some specified or empirical distribution, the problem can be solved by decision making under risk. With no information concerning the demand, it becomes necessary to do market analysis or market research.

The lead time has a different significance with the single order than with the repeat order. With a repeat order and ongoing demand, the lead time is a complication, since demand occurs during the lead time. With a single order, there is no demand, or at any rate there is no stock available to satisfy demand, during the lead time. The lead time is thus the waiting time until goods are available to meet demand. Until the goods arrive, there is no stock available. If the lead time is longer than expected, some sales may be lost. If the lead time is shorter than anticipated, the stock is available prior to demand.

KNOWN DEMAND, KNOWN LEAD TIME

When the demand is known and the lead time is known, there is no single order inventory problem. The quantity of goods ordered matches the demand, and they arrive on the day of demand origination. A condition of certainty exists which rarely occurs in practice. For this condition to exist, all planning must be perfect with no unusual occurrences or delays.

KNOWN DEMAND, VARIABLE LEAD TIME

Since the demand is known, the size of the single order is known. With a variable lead time, the decision maker wants to ensure that the order is received prior to demand, so there is no idle production time or lost sales. If no lost sales are to be tolerated, orders are placed prior to the maximum possible lead time. If a lead time distribution can be ascertained, a lead time can be selected which has a high probability of arrival prior to demand. Alternatively, if the demand is fixed regardless of when the goods are delivered, a late delivery only delays an activity. This situation could exist in the construction of a building, where a delivery delay would only result in a construction delay.

EXAMPLE 1

The Norfolk Boys Club plans to sell Christmas trees for the building fund. Local merchants have placed orders for the trees to be delivered on specified dates, starting with the earliest lot on 1 December. When should the order be placed if an 85% chance of the trees arriving on time is desired? The lead time distribution in Table 1 is known.

Table 1

Lead Time (Days)	Number of Occurrences
10	10
11	10
12	15
13	20
14	30
15	10
16	5
	100

Table 2

Lead Time L	Probability $P(L)$	Probability of Lead Time $\leq L$
10	.10	.10
11	.10	.20
12	.15	.35
13	.20	.55
14	.30	.85 ←
15	.10	.95
16	.05	1.00

To satisfy all demand, the largest lead time would be selected, which is 16 days. The trees would be ordered 16 days prior to 1 December.

From Table 2, it is seen that if an 85% chance of the trees arriving on time is desired, the lead time must be 14 days. Trees would be ordered 14 days prior to 1 December.

When self-supply exists, the variable lead time is a result of uncertainties in scheduling and in the production processes. A service level policy on the lead time can be obtained from a PERT analysis. A description of PERT analysis is beyond the scope of this section, but it can be found in any production/operations textbook.

VARIABLE DEMAND, KNOWN LEAD TIME

When the demand is variable and the lead time is known, the single order inventory problem is in ascertaining the order size. If the demand is not known but a probability distribution of demand is available, the problem can be solved as decision making under risk. The order size that results in the largest expected profit or lowest expected cost is selected.

The procedure for decision making under risk is to determine the demand strategy with the optimum expected value. The probability that the demand will be less than or equal to the single order quantity for a discrete distribution is as follows:

$$P(M \leq Q) = \sum_{M=0}^{Q} P(M) = 1 - \sum_{M=Q+1}^{M_{\max}} P(M),$$

where

Q = single order quantity in units,

M = demand in units (a random variable),

$P(M)$ = probability of a demand of M units,

$M_{\max}$ = maximum demand in units.

The probability that the demand will exceed the single order quantity is as follows:

$$P(M>Q)=\sum_{M=Q+1}^{M_{\max}} P(M)=1-\sum_{M=0}^{Q} P(M).$$

The procedure for calculating the expected value of each discrete demand strategy Q_i is as follows:

$$E(Q_i)=P(M_0)F(Q_iM_0)+P(M_1)F(Q_iM_1)+\cdots+P(M_n)F(Q_iM_n)$$

$$=\sum_{j=0}^{n} P(M_j)F(Q_iM_j)=\text{expected value of strategy } Q_i,$$

where $F(Q_iM_j)$ is the outcome of following the demand strategy Q_i when the actual demand is the state of nature M_j. The determination of outcomes can take on two forms, depending on whether the amount ordered (Q_i) is less than or greater than the demand level (M_j). When the outcomes are expressed in profit or benefit terms, the following relationships apply:

$$F(Q_iM_j)=Q_iJ \quad \text{for} \quad Q_i \le M_j \quad \text{(understock condition)},$$
$$F(Q_iM_j)=M_jJ-(Q_i-M_j)l \quad \text{for} \quad Q_i > M_j \quad \text{(overstock condition)},$$

where

J = unit profit or benefit,
l = loss from disposition of unutilized unit,
Q_i = single order quantity of i units,
M_j = demand level of j units,
Q_i-M_j = number of units overstocked.

When outcomes are expressed in cost or sacrifice terms, the following relationships apply:

$$F(Q_iM_j)=Q_iP \quad \text{for} \quad Q_i \ge M_j \quad \text{(overproduction condition)},$$
$$F(Q_iM_j)=Q_iP+(M_j-Q_i)A \quad \text{for} \quad Q_i < M_j \quad \text{(underproduction condition)},$$

where

P = unit cost,
A = stockout cost per unit,
M_j-Q_i = size of stockout in units.

The matrix in Table 3 depicts the previously established discrete mathematical relationships.

Table 3

Strategy	Probability: State of Nature:	$P(M_0)$ M_0	$P(M_1)$ M_1	$\cdots$	$P(M_n)$ M_n	Expected Value $E(Q_i)$
Q_0		$F(Q_0M_0)$	$F(Q_0M_1)$	$\cdots$	$F(Q_0M_n)$	$E(Q_0)$
Q_1		$F(Q_1M_0)$	$F(Q_1M_1)$	$\cdots$	$F(Q_1M_n)$	$E(Q_1)$
$\vdots$		$\vdots$	$\vdots$		$\vdots$	$\vdots$
Q_m		$F(Q_mM_0)$	$F(Q_mM_1)$	$\cdots$	$F(Q_mM_n)$	$E(Q_m)$

EXAMPLE 2

A merchant wishes to stock Christmas trees for sale during the Christmas season. He must determine how many trees to order, since only one order can be filled during the short time frame. He pays $2.00 for each tree delivered, and he sells the trees for $6.00. His ordering costs are negligible, and he can sell any unsold tree for $1.00 as firewood. The merchant's probability distribution for Christmas tree demand during the season is given in Table 4. (The merchant must order trees in multiples of ten.) How many trees should the merchant order?

Table 4

Demand M	Probability $P(M)$
10	.10
20	.10
30	.20
40	.35
50	.15
60	.10
	1.00

A payoff matrix is developed (Table 5) with the profit from each strategy and state of nature. The expected value of each strategy is obtained by multiplying its probability of occurrence by the value of its outcome and summing the products. The final selection is based on the strategy with the highest expected value. The best strategy is to order 50 trees with the expected value of $127.50.

Table 5

Strategy	Probability: State of Nature:	0.10 10	0.10 20	0.20 30	0.35 40	0.15 50	0.10 60	Expected Value
10		40	40	40	40	40	40	$40.00
20		30	80	80	80	80	80	75.00
30		20	70	120	120	120	120	105.00
40		10	60	110	160	160	160	125.00
50		0	50	100	150	200	200	127.50←
60		−10	40	90	140	190	240	122.50

Marginal Analysis

Marginal analysis can be used to solve the single order problem with variable demand. When the outcome matrices are large, marginal analysis is computationally more efficient than the expected value approach. When an additional unit is obtained, there are two possible outcomes. It either will be demanded or not, and the sum of the two probabilities must be one. Additional units should be stocked so long as the expected marginal profit plus the expected marginal stockout cost saving is greater than the expected marginal loss. The expected marginal stockout cost saving is added to the expected marginal profit because the stocking of an additional unit will increase the expected profit if the unit is demanded (the stockout cost is avoided on this unit). The marginal extra unit should be stocked as long as

$$p\,\mathrm{MP}+pA-(1-p)\mathrm{ML}\geq 0,$$

$$p\geq\frac{\mathrm{ML}}{\mathrm{MP}+\mathrm{ML}+A},$$

where

MP = marginal profit,
ML = marginal loss,
p = probability of selling one or more additional units,
$1-p$ = probability of not selling one or more additional units,
A = stockout cost per unit (marginal stockout cost),
pA = expected marginal stockout cost saving,
$p\,\mathrm{MP}$ = expected marginal profit,
$(1-p)\mathrm{ML}$ = expected marginal loss.

The letter p represents the minimum probability of selling at least an additional unit required to justify the stocking of the additional unit. Additional units should be stocked so long as the probability of selling an additional unit is equal to or greater than p. Frequently, in single-order problems, there will be no stockout cost associated with excess demand. In this situation, the stockout cost per unit (A) is assumed to be zero.

EXAMPLE 3

Using the marginal approach, how many Christmas trees should be ordered from the information given in Example 2?

$$p\geq\frac{\mathrm{ML}}{\mathrm{MP}+\mathrm{ML}+A}=\frac{1}{4+1+0}=0.20.$$

Table 6

Demand M	Probability	Probability of Demand $\geq M$
10	0.10	1.00
20	0.10	0.90
30	0.20	0.80
40	0.35	0.60
50	0.15	0.25←
60	0.10	0.10
	1.00	

From Table 6, the probability of selling 50 or more units is 0.25, so 50 trees should be ordered.

EXAMPLE 4

The Evergreen Company owns acreage of shrub trees to be harvested and sold each spring. The company estimates the costs of cutting and trimming the trees to be \$2.50 per tree. The average cost of shipping the trees to the retailer is about \$.50 per tree. The company receives about \$5.00 per tree ordered by the retailer. However, if the trees are cut and not sold to the retailer, they are a total loss. Shipping costs are not incurred if trees are not sold. The historical demand distribution is shown in Table 7. How many trees should be cut in order to maximize profit if the demand occurs in lots of 10,000?

Table 7

Level of Demand M (Thousands)	Probability $P(M)$
10	.10
20	.20
30	.25
40	.30
50	.15

$$p \geq \frac{\text{ML}}{\text{MP}+\text{ML}+A} = \frac{2.50}{2.00+2.50+0} = 0.55.$$

From the data in Table 8, the probability of selling 30 or more trees is 0.70, and the probability of selling 40 or more trees is 0.45. Since 0.55 is less than 0.70 but more than 0.45, 30,000 trees should be cut to maximize profits.

Table 8

Level of Demand, M	Probability	Probability of Demand $\geq M$
10	0.10	1.00
20	0.20	0.90
30	0.25	0.70←
40	0.30	0.45
50	0.15	0.15

Cost Analysis

When items are intended for internal use with no generation of revenue, the selection of the single order size is based on the lowest expected cost. The cost components are the order cost, purchase cost, stockout cost, and salvage value. The following formula is for the expected cost of a single order for a continuous distribution:

$$\text{Expected cost} = (\text{order cost}) + (\text{purchase cost}) + (\text{expected stockout cost}) - (\text{expected salvage}),$$

$$\text{EC} = C + PQ + A\int_{Q}^{\infty}(M-Q)f(M)\,dM - V\int_{0}^{Q}(Q-M)f(M)\,dM,$$

where

C = order cost per order or setup cost,
P = unit cost,
Q = single order quantity in units,
A = stockout cost per unit,
M = demand in units (a random variable),
$M-Q$ = size of stockout in units,
$f(M)$ = probability density function of demand,
V = salvage value per unit.

To determine the minimum expected cost for a continuous distribution requires taking the derivative of the expected cost with respect to the order size and setting it equal to zero:

$$\frac{d\text{EC}}{dQ} = P - AP(s) - V[1-P(s)] = 0,$$

$$P(s) = \frac{P-V}{A-V} = P(M>Q) = \text{optimum stockout probability.}$$

Observe that if the purchase cost is equal to or greater than the stockout cost, the desired stockout probability is 1. Under these conditions, no orders would be instituted until a known demand existed. Also, if an item has no salvage value, the optimum probability of a stockout is $P(s) = P/A$. For discrete distributions where the optimum probability of a stockout is not exactly attainable, select the stock level with the next lower probability of a stockout. Thus, the above optimum expression can be used for both discrete and continuous distributions.

The expression $1-P(s)$ is the service level, and $P(s)$ is the stockout probability. Thus, if the demand for the item is normally distributed with a

Table 9. Standard Normal Distribution

Standard Normal Deviate Z	Probability of a Stockout $P(s)$	Standard Normal Deviate Z	Probability of a Stockout $P(s)$
−3.00	.999	1.20	.115
0.00	.500	1.25	.106
0.05	.480	1.30	.097
0.10	.460	1.35	.088
0.15	.440	1.40	.081
0.20	.421	1.45	.073
0.25	.401	1.50	.067
0.30	.382	1.55	.060
0.35	.363	1.60	.055
0.40	.344	1.65	.049
0.45	.326	1.70	.045
0.50	.308	1.75	.040
0.55	.291	1.80	.036
0.60	.274	1.85	.032
0.65	.258	1.90	.029
0.70	.242	2.00	.023
0.75	.227	2.25	.012
0.80	.212	2.50	.006
0.85	.198	2.75	.003
0.90	.184	3.00	.001
0.95	.171		
1.00	.159		
1.05	.147		
1.10	.136		
1.15	.125		

known mean $\overline{M}$ and standard deviation σ, the following expression determines the lowest expected cost single order quantity:

$$Q_0 = \overline{M} + Z\sigma = \text{optimum single order size},$$

where Z is the standard normal deviate obtained from the normal table for a stockout probability of $P(s)$. Table 9 exhibits the standard normal distribution which permits conversion from stockout probabilities to standard normal deviates.

EXAMPLE 5

A large department store has just purchased a new central air conditioning unit. The lifetime of the air conditioner is estimated at 12 years. The manager must decide how many spare compressors to purchase for the unit. If he purchases the compres-

Table 10

Failures M	Probability	Probability of Failures$>M$, $P(s)$
0	.30	.70
1	.40	.30
2	.25	.05
3	.05	.00

sors now, they will cost \$100 each. If he purchases them when they fail, the cost will be \$1000 each. Table 10 gives the probability distribution of the number of failures of the part during the life of the air conditioner, as supplied by the manufacturer.

The installation cost of the compressor, as well as its salvage value, is assumed to be negligible. How many compressors should be purchased if the holding cost is neglected? How many compressors should be purchased now if holding cost, which is mainly the opportunity cost of the money invested, is 10% (assume failures occur at equal intervals—the single failure occurs at the end of the 6th year, the two failures occur at the end of the 4th and 8th years, and the three failures occur at the end of the 3rd, 6th, and 9th years)?

With holding costs neglected, the cost matrix can be developed, as shown in Table 11.

Since strategy 2 has the lowest expected cost, the manager should order two spare compressors at the present time. An easier method to obtain the same solution as with the expected value approach is as follows:

$$P(s)=\frac{P-V}{A-V}=\frac{100-0}{1000-0}=0.1.$$

There are two failures associated with a 0.05 stockout probability and one failure with a 0.30 probability, so two compressors should be purchased.

In the case of a holding cost of 10%, the manager must correct his matrix costs according to the time value of money. Consulting a present value table for future single payments results in the factors shown in Table 12. A payment that must be made in the future must be multiplied by the respective time correction factor. The cost matrix of Table 13 results. For strategy 0, the cost for state of nature 1 is 0.564(1000)=564; the cost for state of nature 2 is 0.683(1000)+0.467(1000)=1150; and the cost for state of nature 3 is 0.751(1000)+0.564(1000)+0.424(1000)=1739. The costs for each strategy are obtained in a similar manner. Since strategy 2 results

Table 11

Strategy	Probability:	0.30	0.40	0.25	0.05	Expected Cost
	State of Nature:	0	1	2	3	
0		0	1000	2000	3000	\$1050
1		100	100	1100	2100	450
2		200	200	200	1200	250←
3		300	300	300	300	300

Table 12

Failure at End of Year	Factor
3	0.751
4	0.683
6	0.564
8	0.467
9	0.424

Table 13

Strategy	Probability:	0.30	0.40	0.25	0.05	
	State of Nature:	0	1	2	3	Expected Cost
0		0	564	1150	1739	\$600.25
1		100	100	567	1088	266.15
2		200	200	200	624	221.20←
3		300	300	300	300	300.00

in the lowest expected cost, the manager should order two spare compressors at the present time.

EXAMPLE 6

If the demand for an item is normally distributed with a mean of 100 and a standard deviation of 20, what should be the size of the single order if the unit cost is \$100 and the stockout cost is \$1000?

$$P(s)=\frac{P-V}{A-V}=\frac{100-0}{1000-0}=0.1,$$

$$Q_0=\overline{M}+Z\sigma$$

$$=100+1.29(20)=126 \text{ units.}$$

VARIABLE DEMAND, VARIABLE LEAD TIME

When both demand and lead time are variable, the problem is more complex. Since no product is being used during the lead time, a delay in delivery could result in lost demand. It is possible to treat demand and lead time as independent variables. The demand can be determined independently of the lead time, as in the variable demand, constant lead time case. The lead time can be set at its maximum level or at some acceptable service level, as in Example 1. The peculiarities of the single order problem would dictate what policy to follow in reference to lead time determination. Contractual stipulations can simplify the lead time problem when outside supply is utilized.

CONCLUSION

The major emphasis in inventory analysis tends to be on items for which there are repeat orders. Single items are frequently a greater source of difficulty, since errors in ordering cannot be corrected by an ongoing demand. Seasonal, religious, and cultural events have imposed the need for single order inventory analysis.

Single order models are referred to as static inventory models. Repeat order inventory items are analyzed as dynamic inventory models. The static or one time period model applies when only a single inventory decision is made in anticipation of demand. Static models have a simpler structure than their dynamic counterparts and are easier to apply. They are, however, far more sensitive to forecasting errors, since there is no opportunity to reorder or alter the operation.

For several types of activities, single order inventory analysis is the major mode of the inventory system. In job shops, construction, and special projects (shipbuilding, space vehicles, and research) single order analysis is much more important than repeat order analysis. Single order inventory analysis is likely to receive much more attention on a practical level than it has in the past as its economic significance becomes better understood and appreciated.

QUESTIONS

1. What types of inventory items can be analyzed as a single order quantity?
2. Why are familiar inventory models (EOQ, EOI, and EPQ) not readily applicable to the single order?
3. What are the two relevant costs for the single order?
4. What constitutes the lead time for a single order under self-supply? Under outside supply?
5. What is the significance of lead time with the single order?
6. What is the single order inventory problem under conditions of variable demand and known lead time?
7. In marginal analysis, what limitation should be placed on the stocking of an additional unit?

8. In cost analysis, what are the relevant costs in the selection of the single order quantity?

9. Why are models for single order quantities referred to as static inventory models? In what way are static inventory models more restrictive than dynamic inventory models?

10. What are some examples of types of activities for which single order inventory analysis is the major mode of the inventory system?

PROBLEMS

1. A wholesale bakery provides lemon cookies in gross containers to a discount food chain. The bakery is attempting to determine the number of gross containers of lemon cookies to bake each day. Any containers of cookies not sold at the end of the day are worthless. Each container costs $10.00 and is sold for $12.00 by the bakery. Over the last 100 days, the bakery has kept daily sales records, and they reveal the following distribution:

Containers Sold	Number of Days
26	10
27	20
28	40
29	20
30	10

What is the optimum number of gross containers of lemon cookies to bake each day? Solve this problem by the expected value method.

2. Solve Problem 1 by marginal analysis.

3. The owner of the bakery in Problem 1 is able to sell any unsold containers of lemon cookies to a local orphanage for $8.00 a container. What is the optimum number of gross containers of lemon cookies to bake each day? What is the optimum expected profit?

4. The Parker Flower Shop promises its customers delivery within 4 hours on all flower orders. All flowers are purchased on the prior day and delivered to Parker by 8:00 the next morning. Parker's daily demand for roses is as follows:

Dozens of Roses	Probability
7	.1
8	.2
9	.4
10	.3

Parker purchases roses for $5.00 per dozen and sells them for $15.00. All unsold roses are donated to a local hospital. How many dozens of roses should

Parker order each evening to maximize its profits? What is the optimum expected profit?

5. The Parker Flower Shop must stock some orchids for the upcoming high school prom. Most of the boys will purchase gardenias, but a few orchids will be requested. An orchid costs Parker $10.00 and sells for $25.00. Only one orchid order can be placed, and any unsold orchids will have no salvage value. Past proms' sales records reveal the data in the table. How many orchids should be ordered for the prom?

Orchid Demand	Number of Occurrences
12	5
13	5
14	10
15	15
16	30
17	20
18	15
	100

6. As president of the senior class you are responsible for planning activities for the ten-year class reunion. The planning committee has decided on a hamburger cookout. It is your task to determine the number of one pound hamburgers to purchase for the event. Demand for the dinner is normally distributed with a mean of 200 people and a standard deviation of 40. An out-of-town supplier will sell you meat at $1.50 per pound for large orders placed two weeks in advance. If you do not have enough meat you will have to purchase additional meat from a local supplier at $2.00 per pound. What should be the size of the meat order to the out-of-town supplier?

7. A food broker is trying to decide how many bushels of apples to purchase from the orchards to maximize his profits. His potential sales are estimated to be normally distributed with a mean of 1000 bushels and a standard deviation of 100 bushels. The apples can be purchased for $5.00 per bushel and sold for $7.00. Any unsold apples can be sold for $4.00 per bushel for cider. Determine by marginal analysis the quantity of apples to purchase.

8. You are having a new furnace installed. The dealer offers to sell you spare fuel pumps at $20 each if you buy them during installation. The pumps sell for $50 retail. Manufacturer's records indicate the following probability of fuel pump failures during the furnace's lifetime:

Failures	Probability
0	.1
1	.3
2	.4
3	.1
4	.1

Ignoring installation and holding costs, how many spare fuel pumps should be purchased during installation?

9. A supermarket must decide how much bread to purchase for the weekend (Friday and Saturday). Past history has shown that weekend demand can be considered normally distributed with a mean of 300 and a standard deviation of 40 loaves. A loaf of bread sells for $.50 and costs the store $.42. Any bread not sold over the weekend can be sold on Sunday for $.30 a loaf. How many loaves should be purchased to maximize expected daily profit?

10. Solve Problem 9 above if there is a goodwill loss of $.60 for every loaf of bread demanded when the store is out of stock.

11. A fashionable department store must order chocolate rabbits for the Easter season. They must be ordered three months in advance, and there is no possibility of a reorder. Each rabbit costs $5.00 and sells for $14.50. The manager feels he can sell at least 100 rabbits but not more than 500. Any number between 100 and 500 rabbits is felt to be equally likely (distribution of demand is uniform from 100 to 500 rabbits). How many chocolate rabbits should be ordered if unsold rabbits are donated to a children's hospital?

12. If all unsold rabbits in Problem 11 are sold on Easter Monday for $3.00, what is the single order quantity?

13. Spare parts for an experimental aircraft are made at the time of production. Once production is terminated, the cost of spare parts increases substantially. The experimental aircraft will have an operational lifetime of 8 years, and the demand for a specific part is Poisson distributed with a mean rate of 0.75 per year. The spare part costs $2000 per unit if ordered during production. If the spare part is purchased after production has ceased, its cost is $13,072 per unit. There will be no scrap value for any unused spare parts at the end of the aircraft's operational life. How many spares should be purchased while the aircraft is in production?

14. A buyer for a large southern department store must decide what quantity of expensive women's leather handbags to procure in Italy for the Easter season. The handbags cost the store $48 each and will retail for $75. Any unsold handbags can be sold at a sale price of $40 after the holiday. The buyer feels she is losing $2.50 additional on any unsold bags, since the money could have been invested to yield a profit. The buyer estimates demand to be normally distributed with a mean of 150 bags and a standard deviation of 30. How many leather bags should be purchased in Italy?

15. The buyer in Problem 14 believes she can sell more than 50 bags but not more than 250. If she considers the sale of any number between the limits as equally likely, how many bags should be purchased for the Easter holiday?

16. Instant Cement and Concrete Company mixes concrete for use at a nuclear

power-plant construction site. One cubic yard of concrete costs $26, and it sells for $43. Under the contract established with the site contractor, daily orders are placed for concrete to be used on the following day. Any concrete not used by the end of the day is poured into a waste pit. Records of previous jobs result in the data in the table. How any cubic yards of concrete should be planned for mixing each day?

Concrete Demand (Cubic Yards)	Number of Occurrences
250	5
260	8
270	11
280	20
290	22
300	19
310	15
	100

17. Solve Problem 16 with the additional stipulation that concrete remaining at the end of the day can be sold to a paving contractor for $20 per yard.

18. An amusement park must decide how many hot dogs to purchase for the upcoming three-day holiday weekend. Each hot dog costs the park $.12 and sells for $.35. Any hot dogs remaining at the end of the weekend are sold to employees for a nickel each. Past years have resulted in the following:

Demand M	4500	4600	4700	4800	4900	5000	5100
Probability $P(M)$	.07	.10	.18	.25	.16	.13	.11

How many hot dogs should be purchased to maximize the expected profit if there is a loss of goodwill of $.20 for each hot dog demanded when the concessions are out of stock?

19. The demand for an item is normally distributed with a mean of 1560 and a standard deviation of 80. What should be the size of the single order if the unit cost is $250 and the stockout cost is $1200?

20. If the salvage value is $50 in Problem 19, what should be the size of the single order?

CASE 1: HARBORFEST

Harborfest is the summer gala event in San Mateo in which the local residents and businesses participate in a sea-oriented extravaganza. Each year tens of thousands of people congregate at the downtown harbor to view a water spectacle. Locals and tourists come to converse, view art works and displays, watch sailing craft of all types, and witness the largest fireworks show on the coast. The event has become so famous that crews of foreign ships join American seamen in the festivities.

The highlight of the celebration is the Harborfest Seafood Feast. Large crowds come to sample crabs, scallops, shrimp, oysters, and clams. The seafood is prepared at the waterfront and distributed from booths scattered throughout the main harbor area. Only one seafood item is available at each booth, but there are usually several booths serving each item. The food is eaten in covered or open picnic areas or as one walks the boardwalk. One admission price is charged, and the customer can eat all he wants.

Until this year all the clams were shipped from a northern seaport. The festival officials have not been pleased with the size or flavor of the clams and have decided to buy the clams from a local bay fisherman. The problem of selecting the vendor and ordering the bay clams rests with Anne Cooney, the Regional Seafood Commission's home economics expert.

Anne is familiar with Captain Ben Edwards, an old-timer in the clam business. He knows the bay waters better than most and manages to locate the most succulent clams. Anne is positive that Captain Ben's catches are not overrated and a pound of his clams would contain fewer but larger and tastier clams than pounds purchased elsewhere. Anne, however, is unsure of the correct number of pounds to order.

Anne is to receive $1.50 from each ticket sold. Captain Ben has quoted her a price of $2.50 per pound. Based on past consumption, Anne estimates that $\frac{1}{3}$ pound of clams will be consumed for each ticket sold. However, her estimate is based on a correlation of past tickets sold and the number of pounds purchased. She is unable to locate statistics on the number of pounds overage or on the frequency or level of dissatisfaction due to insufficient clams. Anne does have accurate data on the number of tickets sold. She has rounded the numbers and plotted the following distribution of ticket sales for the past 25 festivals:

Tickets Sold	Probability
17,500	.10
20,000	.10
22,500	.40
25,000	.20
27,500	.15
30,000	.05

Because of his large contract with a leading soup company, Captain Ben has only a two-day opening left in his fishing schedule. The opening, however, is just prior to the festival and would enable him to provide fresh clams for the feast. Captain Ben promises Anne that he can provide up to 12,000 pounds if he allocates his fleet of resources to the project. Captain Ben needs a firm commitment from Anne within the week.

Anne's extreme apprehension over the correct number of pounds to order is not unfounded. The Harborfest Seafood Festival and the Regional Seafood Commission have both come under severe criticism. The community and the media have not been laudatory, and the credibility of both groups is at stake. Inclement weather has caused extensive overages and waste on some occasions; on others, there have been complaints of insufficient quantities. One newspaper article called the feast a hoax, because those who did not attend early went home hungry.

Because of the difficulties experienced in past Harborfests, the Festival Commission is declaring strict accountability. Each seafood item will be handled as a separate profit unit. If some items show a considerable loss this year, they may be dropped in upcoming feasts. Anne is determined to protect her reputation as well as the Commission's. She is desperate to find a quantitative method to calculate the number of pounds of clams so that she can show a profit and protect the clams from cancellation as a festival seafood item.

1. Taking into account statistical changes, do Anne's 25 years of data give a good indication of ticket sales?
2. How reliable are Anne's portion estimates?
3. What impact will adversities such as foul weather, more competition from other profit units, or strict accountability have on ordering practices?
4. What method should be used to order the clams and what quantity should be ordered?

CASE 2: LACTIC ACID

Hannifin's Dairy is under contract to four fast food chains to supply the Memphis franchises with containerized milk and milk products. While the milk products business appears undifferentiated, Hannifin's in reality does not serve a homogeneous market. Hannifin's must blend milk products to the specifications of McDonald's, Burger King, Wendy's, and Dairy Queen; each chain requires a different formula for milk shake and ice milk products.

The fast food chains make periodic checks on Hannifin's to ensure they are receiving the proper formulas. Samples are analyzed and rated for quality and consistency. Because of the sizable investments these companies have in product identification, they are unwavering in their requirements. For example, Wendy's builds a large portion of its reputation on the thickness of its "Frostie"; any consistency less than promised could obliterate the Wendy's image.

Containerized milk and coffee creamers are the only products Hannifin's distributes that are homogeneous in composition. Although the milk and creamers are packaged in the same assortment of container sizes, each company's logo is stamped on the carton, making sale to another chain impossible. In addition, some companies prefer to use some container sizes more than others. Therefore, the orders for containerized milk come in various proportions.

The milk products have shelf lives of eight days. The products are blended and packaged in a continuous process in one day for next day delivery. The standard contract that Hannifin's has with the chains does not stipulate the amount of products to be delivered within a given period; but it does specify that Hannifin's will deliver to the franchises on a bi-daily basis. When the deliverymen run their routes, they fill the orders they have received from the franchise managers.

Because their customers practice product differentiation, Hannifin's product line cannot be completely standardized. Although the chains' marketing strategies distinctly segment and lower individual product sales, the total sales potential is substantial enough for Hannifin's to require methods to supply this market efficiently. The need for efficient and economical supply of nonstandard, perishable products burdens the production and inventory planners with many problems.

In the past Hannifin's has packaged more products than it has sold; it has repeatedly had to dispose of milk products that were beyond the expiration dates. Various methods to eradicate the problem were tried unsuccessfully. Hannifin's manager, Frederick Holsteiner, appealed to his production supervisor, Charles Guernsey, to invent a solution.

Guernsey has tried rescheduling the production, but the method is proving futile. There is too much delay in receiving the feedback from the deliverymen. Aside from the delays, Guernsey is not receiving accurate information from the deliverymen on their stock levels on the trucks. Since the delivermen are paid on commission, they keep their levels inordinately high.

Even when correct inventory level data are received, their translation into a revised schedule is proving to be a rushed and disorderly means of dealing with the problem. What usually results is a jumbled schedule that cannot be followed precisely or on time. The irregularity of this method has led to gross negligence and disarray.

At this point, Holsteiner is in an extremely excitable state. The issue has become divisive; Guernsey wants to continue with his method in hopes of working out the kinks, while Holsteiner is ready to reject the rescheduling method immediately. Holsteiner wants to test other schemes before the summer season is upon them. Hannifin's has suffered some of its greatest losses during times when enormous profits were possible. The peak summer season and the numerous fast food promotional events have caught Hannifin's wholly unprepared. Holsteiner knows that if operations do not improve this season, the fast food chains may take their trade elsewhere.

1. Where does the overage problem lie? Could seasonality and forecasting be contributing factors?
2. Is the production rescheduling method a muddled plan? How could it be leading to gross negligence?
3. What type of production and inventory system does Hannifin's need?
4 What other changes could mitigate Hannifin's problem?

CASE 3: AN EDUCATED GUESS

Henning's Bookstore, located adjacent to the main campus of the University of Oklahoma, is the oldest bookstore in Norman. Its name has become synonymous with bookstore: the faculty and students use the terms interchangeably. This unqualified acceptance is due in part to the completeness of the store's stock of textbooks and course materials. Traditionally Henning's has carried all textbooks on the university textbook adoption list. For over 40 years the store and the university have had a mutually beneficial relationship.

Supplemental to textbooks and course materials, Henning's has ancillary lines of school and office supplies. Additionally, it offers an assortment of O.U. commemoratives, memorabilia, and knickknacks bearing the university insignia. One of the more popular lines of university bric-a-brac is a selection of O.U. T-shirts, sweatshirts, and other athletic wear.

Presently, Henning's is making plans for the upcoming school year and is restocking the depleted line of T-shirts and sweatshirts. In past years, the task of ordering these garments has not been viewed as an onerous job by the store owner, Harold DeWitt. Mr. DeWitt, following in the parsimonious footsteps of his predecessors, has always used the same fundamental ordering system. He has never anticipated his competitors in purchasing clothing or bric-a-brac items; he waits and sees what they buy and then tries to duplicate the selections in his fall order. His order quantity is based on an inventory expenditure allowance. Mr. DeWitt releases orders for shirts until the amount of his expenditures plus the value of the stock on hand equals a predetermined upper limit. The limit typically has been set low enough so that the bulk of the inventory has been sold by summer vacation. At that time the store closes for four weeks and then reopens to prepare for the coming year.

Upon his return this year, Mr. DeWitt has recruited the services of a stock clerk, Debbie Dodd, a management major at the university. Debbie spent many tutorial sessions with Mr. DeWitt during the last semester. She advised him on the relative benefits of adopting optimizing techniques for all areas of his operation. Debbie was able to convince Mr. DeWitt that he could minimize costs if he would order for the shirt department according to a periodic inventory system that she designed as a course project. The system is structured to work effectively in situations where there are to be reorders on basic items. Obviously, the scope of Debbie's lectures included the merits of ordering basic styles in advance of demand. Debbie coaxed Mr. DeWitt into ordering some basic shirts as well as periodically ordering newer styles as special inventory items. The system incorporated a category of eight special inventory items, and each item in this group would have a set economic order interval and maximum inventory level. However, at the order interval the inventory items were subject to style change, so that a newer style could be purchased in lieu of the existing item.

Mr. DeWitt's willingness to implement Debbie's system was a result of his priorities and Debbie's concessions. Mr. DeWitt has emphasized the textbook end of his business and always will, leaving areas of lesser importance to subordinates. Also, Debbie capitulated on two issues. First, she dropped her semester long argument against Mr. DeWitt's system for ordering textbooks, strictly according to the adoption list and in quantities that are a rigid percentage of the class sizes set by the university. Second, she admitted that her system cannot accommodate all items. In particular, a specialty item that Mr. DeWitt added to the T-shirt line two years ago defies Debbie's ordering policies.

Acting on the recommendation of a marketing major who worked for Henning's, Mr. DeWitt had decided to take an innovative step. The marketing major had had a brainstorm for capitalizing on the largest annual O.U. football event. Her idea was to sell T-shirts commemorating the O.U.–Texas game, a game that incites one of the wildest weekends of the fall season. The T-shirts colorfully displayed the O.U. logo with lettering proclaiming the big event. Last year's shirts had a design unique from the year before but advertised the same message—"O.U.–Texas Weekend". The shirts were sold at $9.00 each and were sacrifice priced at $3.00 each after the football weekend.

Mr. DeWitt has requested that Debbie apply her educated methods and devise a unique solution to the specialty item ordering problem. However, he has told Debbie that if she cannot concoct an educated guess by the time the order needs to go to the shirt printers, he will. Either Mr. DeWitt will order according to his set limit of expenditures method as previously used with the entire T-shirt line, or he will use a system similar to the one he uses in ordering textbooks. In the latter case, the quantity of shirts ordered will be a fixed fraction of the total student enrollment figure.

The important factor for Debbie to consider is an appropriate method for the determination of the order quantity and the quantity of shirts in each size. The newness of the item makes the determination very difficult, particularly since Mr. DeWitt has not used very scientific methods on past orders. The only information Debbie has is the order quantities for each of the two previous years and scanty information from Mr. DeWitt's wife as to her estimate of the number of sacrifice sales. Alternatively, Debbie is considering a change in the item itself, to something with less style dependence.

1. Evaluate Mr. DeWitt's ordering methods in practice at Henning's and their appropriateness to his needs.
2. Considering Mr. DeWitt's lack of emphasis in the sportswear line, does Debbie's system sound reasonable? Are there other factors that affect her system, such as the store's vacation schedule and the historical inventory investment policy?
3. What method should Debbie prescribe for the O.U.–Texas shirt? What assumptions must she make?
4. What qualitative factors need consideration?

MATHEMATICAL ABBREVIATIONS AND SYMBOLS USED IN CHAPTER 7

A	Stockout cost per unit
EC	Expected cost
$E(Q_i)$	Expected value of demand strategy Q_i
$F(Q_i M_j)$	Outcome of strategy Q_i when demand M_j occurs
J	Unit profit or benefit
L	Lead time in days
l	Loss from disposition of unutilized unit
M	Demand in units (a random variable)
$\overline{M}$	Average demand in units
$M_{\max}$	Maximum demand in units
ML	Marginal loss
MP	Marginal profit
P	Unit cost
$P(M)$	Probability of a demand of M units

$P(M>Q)$ $=P(s)$	Probability of a stockout
p	Probability of selling one or more units
Q	Single order quantity
Q_0	Optimum single order quantity
V	Salvage value per unit
Z	Standard normal deviate
σ	Standard deviation of demand

8 Material Requirements Planning (MRP)

Material requirements planning (MRP) is a computer-based production planning and inventory control system. It is also known as "time-phased requirements planning." MRP is concerned with both production scheduling and inventory control. It provides a precise scheduling (priorities) system, an efficient material control system, and a rescheduling mechanism for revising plans as changes occur. It keeps inventory levels at a minimum while assuring that required materials are available when needed. The major objectives of an MRP system are *simultaneously* to:

1. ensure the availability of materials, components, and products for planned production and for customer delivery,
2. maintain the lowest possible level of inventory,
3. plan manufacturing activities, delivery schedules, and purchasing activities.

It is the attainment of these objectives concurrently that makes MRP worthwhile.

Demand for an item may be independent or dependent. Independence means no relationship exists between the demand for an item and any other item, such as end items or products. Independent demand tends to be continuous and fluctuates because of random influences. In contrast, dependence means the demand for an item is directly related to or the result of the demand for a "higher level" item. For example, raw materials, parts, or subassemblies are required for manufacture of an end item. Dependent demand is not random but tends to occur in a lumpy manner at specific points in time. The lumpiness occurs because most manufacturing is in lots and all the items needed to produce the lots are usually withdrawn from inventory at the same time, not unit by unit. Thus, although the demand for the final product may be continuous and independent, the demand for lower-level, subordinate items composing the product tends to be discrete, derived, and dependent.

Demand should be forecasted only when it cannot be calculated. Independent demand items should be forecasted, while dependent demand items should be calculated via a bill of materials explosion.

The lumpy pattern of demand for dependent demand items is very unlike the constant demand rate assumption of the basic EOQ model. MRP was developed to cope better with dependent demand items. MRP works backward from the scheduled completion dates of end items to determine the dates when dependent demand components are to be ordered and the quantities to be ordered.

Dependent demand items need not be forecasted, but are calculated by the MRP system from the master schedule. Except for lot sizing economies, dependent demand items should be available when needed, not before and not after. In manufacturing organizations, most inventory items are dependent and should be controlled by an MRP system.

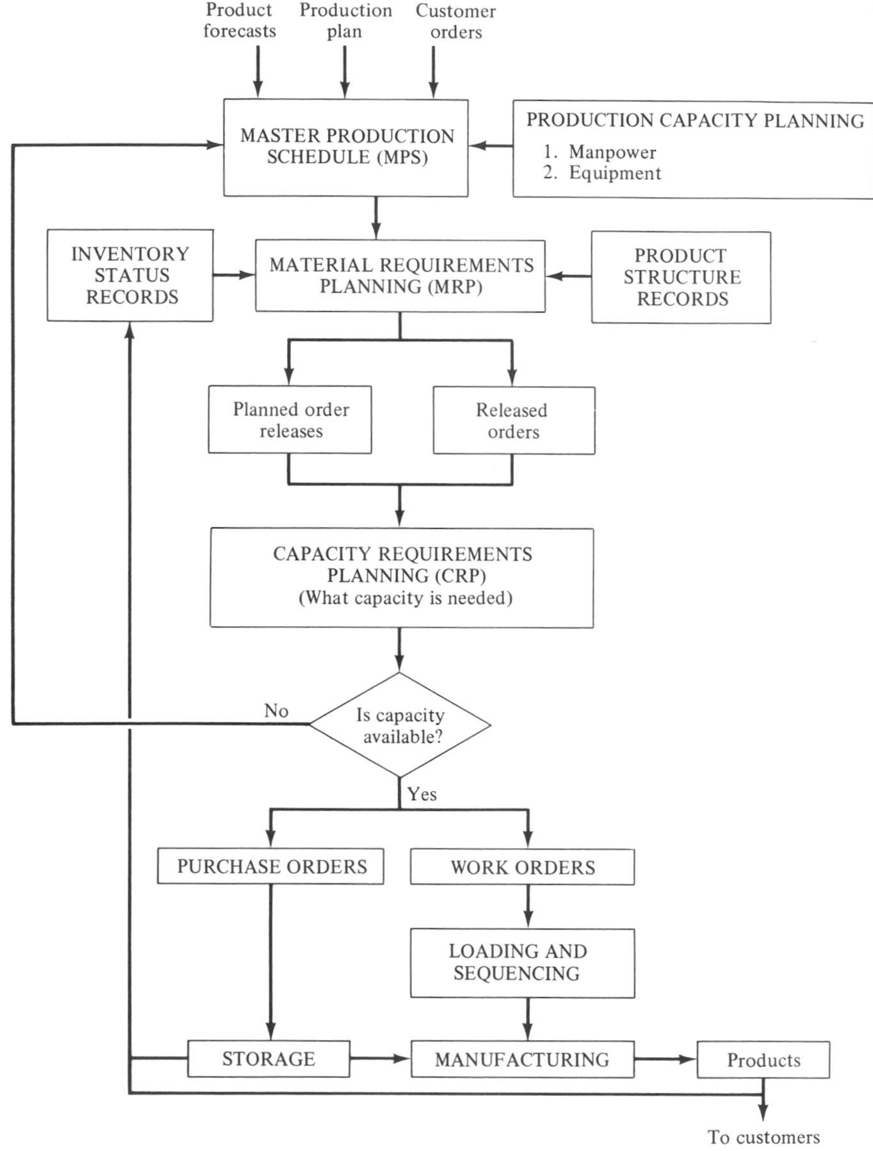

Figure 1. A closed-loop MRP system.

The key features of an MRP system are the time phasing of requirements, generation of lower-level requirements, planned order releases, and rescheduling capability. Time-phasing of requirements simply establishes the time period in which work must be accomplished (or material made available) to meet the delivery date of the end item as stipulated in the master schedule.[1] Starting with the end item, MRP generates the necessary scheduling for all lower-level requirements (assemblies, subassemblies, and components). Planned order releases indicate when orders should be placed by purchasing and manufacturing. When work cannot be accomplished on time, MRP can reschedule planned orders so priorities are realistic and meaningful. A flow diagram of how a typical MRP system may function is shown in Figure 1.

MRP INPUTS

The three major inputs of an MRP system are the master production schedule, the inventory status records, and the product structure records. Without these basic inputs the MRP system cannot function. The master production schedule outlines the production plan for all end items. The product structure records contain information on all materials, components, or subassemblies required for each end item. The inventory status records contain the on-hand and on-order status of inventory items. A flow diagram of MRP inputs is contained in Figure 2.

The demand for end items is scheduled over a number of time periods and recorded on a *master production schedule*. The master production schedule expresses how much of each item is wanted and when it is wanted. The planning horizon of the master production schedule should be large enough to cover the cumulative procurement and production lead times ("stacked" lead times) for all components and assemblies composing the end items. One-week increments have been found to be the most practical, so the planning horizon can comprise several one-week planning periods. The master production schedule is developed from end item forecasts and customer orders. It must project a realistic plan of production that is leveled to accommodate the available capacity. The MPS is not the same as the forecast; they may differ because (1) the forecast may exceed the plant capacity, (2) it may be desirable to increase or decrease inventory levels, or (3) the forecast may fluctuate while the firm may desire to operate uniformly using inventory as a buffer. Master scheduling is done at the end item level, and it is a basic input to and driving force behind the MRP system. MRP takes the master schedule for end items and translates it into individual time-phased component requirements.

The *product structure records*, also known as bills of materials (BOM) records, contain information on every item or assembly required to produce end items. The master schedule shows how much of each end item must be available on particular dates to satisfy the independent demand. The

[1] The term end item will be used in reference to the master schedule. The end item may be the final product, a product module, or a major assembly. When a product consists of numerous options, it is frequently desirable to master schedule below the product level at a lower level that disentangles the options.

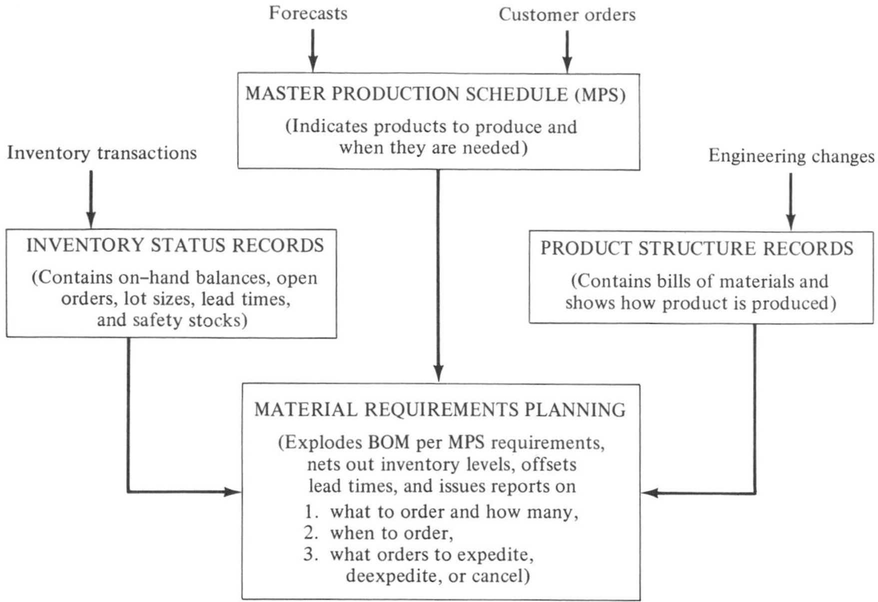

Figure 2. MRP inputs.

quantities of components required to build the end items can be derived from the bills of materials. Information on each item, such as part number, description, quantity per assembly, next higher assembly, and quantity per end item, must be available. The product structure records contain the bills of materials for the end items in levels representing the way they are actually manufactured: from raw materials to subassemblies to assemblies to end items.

The *inventory status records* contain the status of all items in inventory. All inventory items must be uniquely identified. These records must be kept up to date, with each receipt, disbursement, or withdrawal documented to maintain record integrity. They should also contain information on lead times, lot sizes, or other item peculiarities. MRP will determine from the master production schedule and the product structure records the gross component requirements; the gross component requirements will be reduced by the available inventory (on-hand plus on-order) as indicated in the inventory status records. Quantities of items in inventory at the start of a planning horizon are available for use and are referred to as "on-hand." "On-order" quantities are those that are expected to become available during a planning horizon from open work orders or open purchase orders. MRP takes into account both on-hand and on-order quantities.

These three sources (master production schedule, product structure records, and inventory status records) are the data inputs for an MRP system. Remember that the master production schedule only applies to upper level end items, so MRP is left with the task of all lower level scheduling.

MRP OUTPUTS

Thus, MRP takes the master production schedule for end items and determines the gross quantities of components required from the product structure records. Gross requirements are obtained by "exploding" the end item product structure record into its lower level requirements. The exploding process is simply a multiplication of the number of end items by the quantity of each component required to produce a single end item. The explosion identifies *what* components are required, as well as *how many*, to produce a given quantity of end items (the term explosion is used because each level in the product structure tends to create more requirements than the previous one). By referring to the inventory status records, the gross quantities will be netted by subtracting the available inventory items. Just as important as "what" and "how many" is *when*, which is determined by offsetting (setting back in time) the lead times for each component. Thus,the material requirements for each component are phased over time in a pattern determined by lead times and parent requirements.

At this point, MRP plans orders (planned order releases) for purchasing and shop scheduling for the quantity of items that must be available in each time period to produce the end items. A schematic of MRP outputs is contained in Figure 3. The planned order release provides the quantity and time period when work orders are to be released to the shop or purchase orders placed with suppliers. When the order (work or purchase) is released or placed, it changes from being "planned" to being "scheduled," "open," or "on order."

An MRP system identifies each item (part number) needed. As men-

Figure 3. MRP outputs.

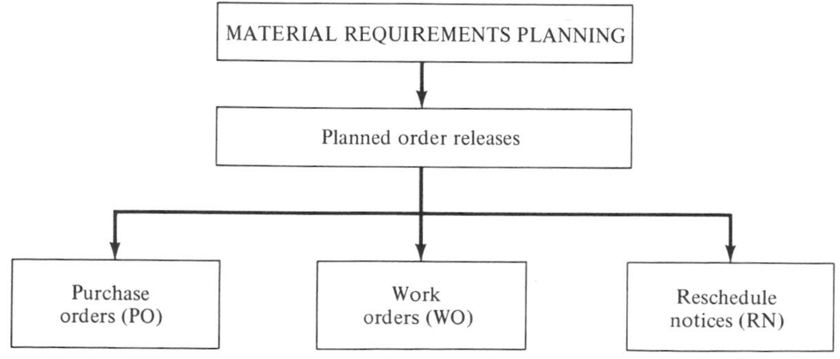

tioned, it establishes a schedule of planned orders for each item, including the specific dates for release of each order. The time-phasing of net requirements is accomplished by lead time offsetting or setbacks. For purchased components, lead time is the time interval between placement of the purchase order and its availability in inventory. For manufactured items, it is the interval between release of the work order and its completion. The planned order has to be released at the beginning of the lead time. Normally, all components to an assembly are planned to be available before the start date. Two basic purposes of planned orders are:

1. to generate material requirements at the next lower level,
2. to project capacity requirements.

The actual order quantity for an item may be adjusted to a suitable lot size, or it may simply be the net requirement.

Although MRP is an excellent planning and scheduling tool, its greatest benefit may be its ability to replan and reschedule in view of unforeseen contingencies. The MRP system can predict shortages and overages soon enough so that something can be done to prevent them. It can keep order priorities up to date by planning and replanning order due dates. MRP provides exception reporting whenever a mismatch of timing between demand and supply exists. It is a priority system: typical messages are to delay, expedite, cancel an existing order, launch a new order, etc. It attempts to make the due date and need date coincide, so operations proceed as planned while inventory investment is minimized. If a component to an assembly will not be available when planned, MRP can reschedule all other co-components to the same assembly to a later date while rescheduling shop priorities. MRP will not actually reschedule orders, but it will print messages specifying exactly where changes are appropriate. The decision to make changes remains with management personnel.

PRODUCT STRUCTURES

MRP is well suited for fabrication and/or assembly type operations. A fabricated part has had manufacturing operations performed on it such as bending, cutting, grinding, milling, drilling, blanking, polishing, or coating. An assembly is a collection of parts and/or subassemblies that are put together. A subassembly is an assembly that is used at a higher level to make up another assembly. The term "component" in MRP refers to all inventory items below the product level, including subassemblies, parts, and raw materials, whether they are produced internally or obtained from suppliers. In MRP, only assembly and component relationships are considered; other terms such as subassembly, fabricated part, purchased part, or raw material are subsumed under "components."

A bill of materials (BOM) is a list of the items, ingredients, or materials needed to produce an end item or product. It lists all of the subassemblies, parts, and raw materials that go into a parent assembly, showing the quantity of each required to make an assembly. It shows how much of what materials are needed in what order to manufacture a product. An accurate formal bill of materials is needed for every product. The BOM will contain information on each input to the product, such as part numbers, descriptions, quantity needed for each part number, and the unit of measure. All items in the BOM must be uniquely numbered and identified.

When a product is designed, an engineering drawing (blueprint) is made and the bill of materials is created at the same time. This initial design information is used by a process planner to develop route and operation sheets on how to make the product and by a purchasing agent to procure an adequate supply of parts for production. Originally, the function of a bill of materials was to define a product from a design point of view only. Unfortunately, a product may not be assembled the way it is designed. For MRP to be effective it is necessary to generate a BOM that represents the way the product is manufactured. Frequently, an existing BOM must be modified or restructured so it is a manufacturing as well as an engineering document.

Since MRP is product-oriented, bills of materials are an important basis for planning. Indeed, MRP is impossible without structured bills of materials. Without them, MRP could not successfully translate the master schedule into gross requirements below the end item level.

The traditional bill of materials for a product defines its structure by listing all the components that go into making it. A structured bill of materials specifies not only the composition of a product, but also the process stages in its manufacture. It defines the product structure in terms of levels of manufacture, each of which represents a completion stage in the buildup of the product. It shows the "as built" as opposed to the "as designed" condition. In a schematic form, a structured bill of materials is known as a product structure, product tree, or Christmas tree.

A schematic representation of a product structure is shown in Figure 4. The structure of product *A* defines the relationship among the various items that make up the product in terms of levels as well as parent/component relationships. The product has four levels of manufacture. The end product is designated, by convention, as being at level 0, its immediate components at level 1, and so forth. The parent/component relationship indicates that *A* is the parent of the components *B*, *C*, and 10; *B* is the parent of components *D* and 20; *C* is the parent of components 30, 40, and 50; and *D* is the parent of components 60 and 70. The only item that is not a component is the independent demand item, *A*. The dependent demand items, *B*, *C*, *D*, 10, 20, 30, 40, 50, 60, and 70, are components. Items *B*, *C*, and *D* are parents as well as components.

To show the presence of subassemblies or different levels of production,

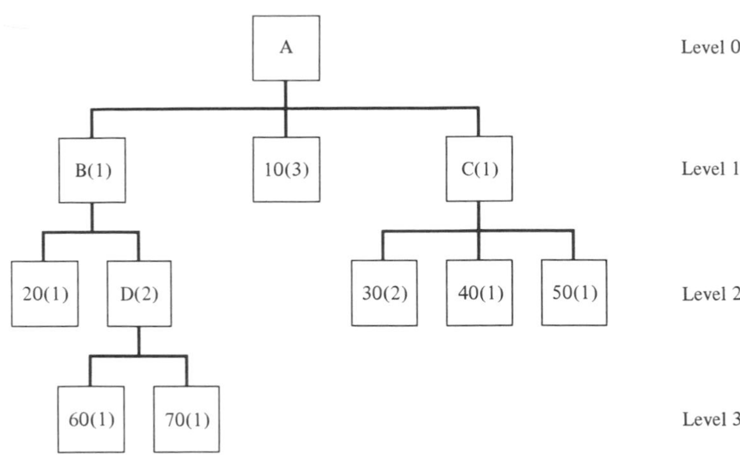

Figure 4. Typical product structure.
The letters represent assemblies/subassemblies, and the numerals represent parts. The numbers in parentheses are the quantities required for assembly.

an indented bill of materials can be used. All components of a given level are shown with their part numbers beginning in the same column. All components of a given item are listed immediately below and indented to indicate their lower level. The indented format is the most widely used method of presenting multilevel bills of materials because of its ability to represent the product in the manner in which it is manufactured. An indented bill of materials (indented parts list) for Product A, as shown in Figure 4, is shown in Table 1. The dependent relationships among components to a product are highlighted by their indentation. The quantities shown on the indented bill of materials are the quantities needed to

Table 1

Item Name	Item Number Level 0	1	2	3	Quantity per Assembly	Description
	A				—	
	.	*B*			1	
	.	.	20		1	
	.	.	*D*		2	
	.	.	.	60	1	
	.	.	.	70	1	
	.	*C*			1	
	.	.	30		2	
	.	.	40		1	
	.	.	50		1	
	.	10			3	

assemble one item at the next highest level. For example, item A is the end item and it requires one subassembly B, one subassembly C, and three part 10's. One part 20 and two subassembly D's make a single subassembly B. One part 60 and one part 70 are required to make a single subassembly D. Two part 30's, one part 40, and one part 50 make a single subassembly C.

Modular Bills of Materials

Modular bills of materials are used for complex products that have many possible configurations and are made from a substantial number of common parts. For example, in vehicle manufacturing, where choices of engines, transmissions, bodies, interiors, trim, and many other features are available, the several variations can be combined into a tremendous number of final configurations. Modularization provides a wide choice of products to the customer while keeping component inventories down. It has been used extensively in the automotive and farm equipment industries.

When a product line has many variations (optional features), their combinations can be astronomical and forecasting them for the master schedule becomes impossible. If a separate BOM is used for each unique end product for MRP purposes, the file records would be excessive (too costly to store and maintain). The solution to this problem is the modular bill of materials. A modular BOM is stated in building blocks or modules from which the final product is put together. The process of modularizing breaks down the bills of products into lower level modules. The demand for these modules can be forecasted separately with much more accuracy than the final configurations. Modules can achieve two different purposes:

1. to disentangle combinations of optional product features,
2. to segregate common parts from unique parts.

The first purpose facilitates forecasting, while the second minimizes inventory investment in components common to optional units.

An example will illustrate the concept of modularity. Suppose a manufacturer offers his customers 10 engines, 30 colors, 4 bodies, and 2 frames. By assembling the optional features in various combinations, it is possible to build (10)(30)(4)(2)=2400 models or unique configurations (Figure 5). We

Figure 5

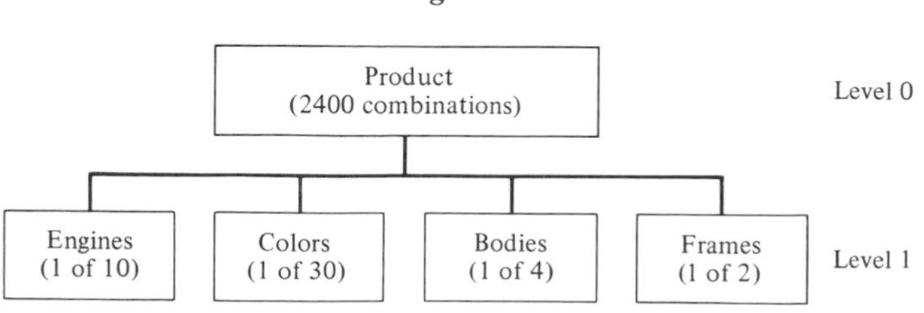

would not want to set up separate bills for each end product (level 0); we would need 2400 of them. It would be difficult to develop a master schedule showing the quantity of each model needed in specific time periods. The solution is to forecast at a high component level (major assembly unit) and not to try to forecast the end products at all. We would forecast at level 1 for each of the ten different engine variations, the thirty colors, the four types of bodies, and the two types of frames. Each of the options or modules would have a BOM. There would be a total of $10+30+4+2=46$ bills instead of 2400. From past customer orders, the percentage of orders for a given option can be ascertained. For example, past sales may indicate that 75% of orders call for frame *A* and 25% for frame *B*. If we produce 100 products per period, we would schedule orders for 75 *A* frames and 25 *B* frames.

Modularity does away with BOM at the product level (level 0) for purposes of MRP. Instead, assembly components (level 1 or lower) are promoted to end item status. This procedure establishes a new modular planning bill suitable for forecasting, master production scheduling, and MRP.

EXAMPLE 1

Suppose you are to produce 100 units of product *A* in period 8 with the product structure shown below. If no stock is on hand or on order, determine when to release orders for each component and the size of each order (Figure 6). Product *A* is made from components *B* and *C*; *C* is made from components *D* and *E*. By simple computation we can calculate our quantity requirements:

Component *B*: (1)(number of *A*'s)$=1(100)=100$,
Component *C*: (2)(number of *A*'s)$=2(100)=200$,
Component *D*: (1)(number of *C*'s)$=1(200)=200$,
Component *E*: (2)(number of *C*'s)$=2(200)=400$.

Figure 6

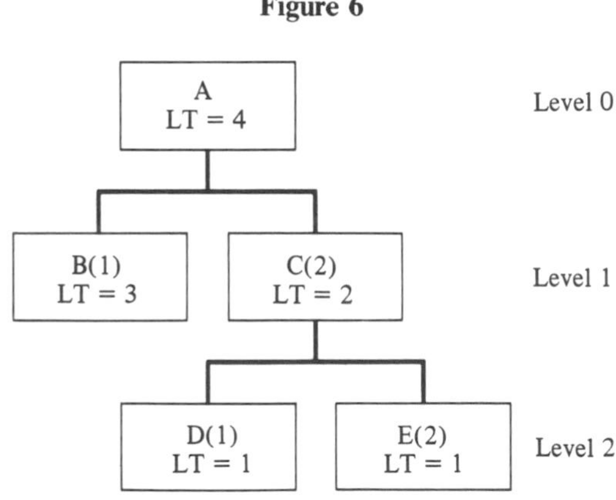

Table 2. MRP Plan for 100 Units of Product A in Period 8

Lead Time			1	2	3	4	5	6	7	8
4	*A*	Gross requirements								100
		Planned order releases				100				
3	*B*	Gross requirements				100				
		Planned order releases	100							
2	*C*	Gross requirements				200				
		Planned order releases		200						
1	*D*	Gross requirements		200						
		Planned order releases	200							
1	*E*	Gross requirements		400						
		Planned order releases	400							

Now we must consider the time element for all the items. Table 2 creates a material requirements plan based on the demand for *A*, the knowledge of how *A* is made, and the time needed to obtain each component. It time-phases the requirements by offsetting the lead times. It shows which items are needed, how many are needed, and when they are needed.

A material requirements plan has been developed for product *A* based on the product structure of *A* and the lead time needed to obtain each component. Planned order releases of a parent item are used to determine gross requirements for its component items. Planned order releases generate a requirement in the same time period for its lower level components. In order to complete 100 units of product *A* in period 8 it is necessary to release orders for 100 units of *B* in period 1, 200 units of *C* in period 2, 200 units of *D* in period 1, and 400 units of *E* in period 1. Planned order release dates are simply obtained by offsetting the lead times. A component's gross requirements time period is the planned order release period of its parent. Planned order releases indicated for the first period are those that are in "action buckets" where immediate action is mandatory. Planned order releases for two or more periods into the future do not require immediate action.

Low Level Coding

When a component is used on numerous products or appears in various levels in the BOM, it is necessary to use low level coding. Some components are used in two or more end items at various levels. When a component appears at more than one level, it is customary to assign it to its lowest level —i.e., the level farthest down the product structure (lower levels are indicated by higher numbers). Every item will have one and only one low level code. This code will indicate when to explode and net (subtract available inventory from the gross requirements) an item during MRP so it is netted only once during the generation of requirements.

The low level code determines when an item is eligible for netting (after all higher level items have been exploded and netted). It is necessary to explode the numbers of level 0 items needed in order to find out how many level 1 components are needed, because level 1 items are the ones that go directly into level 0 items. In a similar fashion, it is necessary to explode the numbers of level 1 items to find out how many level 2 components are needed. The above process is continued until all the product levels have been treated. The total gross requirement for an item is the sum of requirements from all its parents or sources.

MRP COMPUTATIONS

The computations and steps required in the MRP process are not complicated. They involve only simple arithmetic. The MRP process is outlined in Figure 7. The format for a typical MRP matrix is shown in Figure 8 along with a description of the meaning of each term. An example of MRP component computation is shown in Figure 9 along with an explanation of how the quantities were determined. A thorough understanding of the MRP matrix and component computations are necessary before MRP can be mastered. *Note:* Figures 7, 8, and 9 are shown on pp. 300–302, following Example 3.

EXAMPLE 2

In the MRP table below, indicate the projected on hand requirements, the planned order receipts, and the planned order releases. The lead time is two periods, and the lot size is the same as the net requirements (lot size = 1).

	Period								
	PD	1	2	3	4	5	6	7	8
Gross requirements		5	10	18	0	10	6	0	14
Scheduled receipts			20						
Projected on hand	20								
Net requirements									
Planned order receipts									
Planned order releases									

Solution:

	Period								
	PD	1	2	3	4	5	6	7	8
Gross requirements		5	10	18	0	10	6	0	14
Scheduled receipts			20						
Projected on hand	20	15	25	7	7	0	0	0	0
Net requirements						3	6		14
Planned order receipts						3	6		14
Planned order releases				3	6		14		

The preceding example illustrated how to net the gross requirements and establish planned order releases with lot-for-lot ordering (the order quantity is the same as the net requirements). The following example will require the same process except with a fixed lot size.

EXAMPLE 3

Redo Example 2 in the MRP table below with the lot size equal to 15 units.

	Period								
	PD	1	2	3	4	5	6	7	8
Gross requirements		5	10	18	0	10	6	0	14
Scheduled receipts			20						
Projected on hand	20								
Net requirements									
Planned order receipts									
Planned order releases									

Solution:

Gross requirements		5	10	18	0	10	6	0	14
Scheduled receipts			20						
Projected on hand	20	15	25	7	7	12	6	6	7
Net requirements						3			8
Planned order receipts						15			15
Planned order releases				15			15		

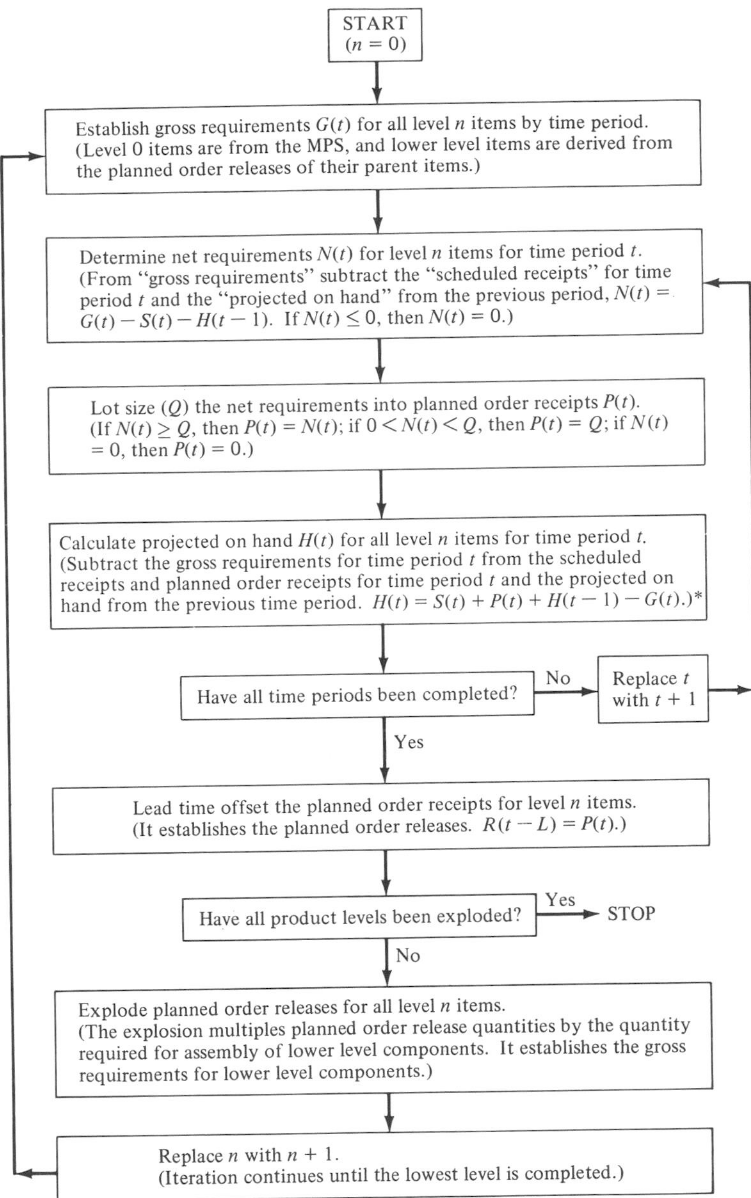
START
($n = 0$)
Establish gross requirements $G(t)$ for all level n items by time period.
(Level 0 items are from the MPS, and lower level items are derived from the planned order releases of their parent items.)
Determine net requirements $N(t)$ for level n items for time period t.
(From "gross requirements" subtract the "scheduled receipts" for time period t and the "projected on hand" from the previous period, $N(t) = G(t) - S(t) - H(t-1)$. If $N(t) \leq 0$, then $N(t) = 0$.)
Lot size (Q) the net requirements into planned order receipts $P(t)$.
(If $N(t) \geq Q$, then $P(t) = N(t)$; if $0 < N(t) < Q$, then $P(t) = Q$; if $N(t) = 0$, then $P(t) = 0$.)
Calculate projected on hand $H(t)$ for all level n items for time period t.
(Subtract the gross requirements for time period t from the scheduled receipts and planned order receipts for time period t and the projected on hand from the previous time period. $H(t) = S(t) + P(t) + H(t-1) - G(t)$.)*
Have all time periods been completed?
No
Replace t with $t + 1$
Yes
Lead time offset the planned order receipts for level n items.
(It establishes the planned order releases. $R(t-L) = P(t)$.)
Have all product levels been exploded?
Yes
STOP
No
Explode planned order releases for all level n items.
(The explosion multiples planned order release quantities by the quantity required for assembly of lower level components. It establishes the gross requirements for lower level components.)
Replace n with $n + 1$.
(Iteration continues until the lowest level is completed.)
*When safety stock is maintained and/or units are "allocated," these amounts must also be subtracted to obtain the "projected on hand."

Figure 7. The MRP process.

Lot size	Lead time	On hand	Safety stock	Allocated	Low level code	Item		Period								
								PD	1	2	3	4	5	6	7	8
							Gross requirements									
							Scheduled receipts									
							Projected on hand									
							Net requirements									
							Planned order receipts									
							Planned order releases									

Figure 8. Typical MRP matrix.

The column entries are self explanatory. The row entries have the following meaning:

Gross requirements: the total anticipated production, use, or withdrawals during each time period. For end items, this quantity is obtained from the master production schedule (independent demand items); for components (dependent demand items) it is derived from the "planned order releases" of their parents.

Scheduled Receipts: material that is already ordered (from manufacturing orders or purchase orders) that is expected to arrive (also known as on-order, open orders, or scheduled orders).

Projected on hand: the expected quantity in inventory at the end of the period, available for demand in subsequent periods. This is calculated by subtracting the "gross requirements" for the period from the "scheduled receipts" and "planned order receipts" for the same period as well as the "projected on hand" from the previous period. When "safety stock" is maintained and/or units are "allocated" to future orders, these amounts must be added to the gross requirements before calculating the "projected on hand."

Net requirements: the reduction of "gross requirements" by the "scheduled receipts" in the period plus the "projected on hand" in the previous period. This indicates the net number of items that must be provided to satisfy the parent or master schedule requirements.

Planned order receipts: the size of the planned order (the order has not been placed yet) and when it is needed. This appears in the same time period as the "net requirements," but its size is modified by the appropriate lot sizing policy. It shows when the order is needed in stock. With lot sizing, the planned order quantity will generally exceed the "net requirements." Any excess beyond the "net requirements" goes into "projected on hand" inventory. With lot-for-lot ordering, the "planned order receipts" is always the same as the "net requirements."

Planned order releases: when the order should be placed (released) so the items are available when needed by the parent. This is the same as the "planned order receipts" offset for lead times. "Planned order releases" at one level generate material requirements at lower levels. When the order is placed, it is removed from the "planned order receipts" and "planned order releases" rows and entered in the "scheduled receipts" row. "Planned order releases" show the *what*, *how many*, and *when* of MRP.

Lot size	Lead time	On hand	Safety stock	Allocated	Low level code	Item		Period								
								PD	1	2	3	4	5	6	7	8
25	2	10	0	0	1	*Z*	Gross requirements		10	15	25	25	30	45	20	30
							Scheduled receipts		10	25						
							Projected on hand	10	10	20	20	20	15	0	5	0
							Net requirements				5	5	10	30	20	25
							Planned order receipts				25	25	25	30	25	25
							Planned order releases		25	25	25	30	25	25		

Figure 9. Example of MRP component computations.

Item Z with a low level code of 1 has an on hand quantity of 10, a lead time of 2 weeks, and a lot size of 25 units. The numbers in each time period are interpreted as follows:

In the past due (PD) period, the "projected on hand" is the present on hand quantity of 10.

In period 1, the "gross requirements" are 10, which are satisfied from the 10 "projected on hand" from the previous period. The "scheduled receipts" of 10 will then become the "projected on hand."

In period 2, the "gross requirements" for 15 are satisfied by the 10 "projected on hand" from the previous period and 5 of the 25 from "scheduled receipts." The rest of the "scheduled receipts" of 20 become the "projected on hand."

In period 3, the "gross requirements" for 25 are satisfied by the 20 "projected on hand" from the previous period. The "net requirements" for 5 generate the need for "planned order receipts" of 25, the lot size. Offsetting for two weeks of lead time, the "planned order release" is for period 1.

In period 4, the situation is exactly the same as in period 3 except the "planned order release" is for period 2.

In period 5, the "gross requirements" for 30 are satisfied by the 20 "projected on hand" from the previous period. The "net requirements" for 10 generate the need for "planned order receipts" of 25, the lot size. Thus, the "planned order release" for 25 is planned for period 3. The rest of the "planned order receipts" of 15 become the "projected on hand."

In period 6, the "gross requirements" for 45 are satisfied by the 15 "projected on hand" from the previous period. The "net requirements" for 30 generate the need for "planned order receipts" of 30. Since the "net requirements" exceed the lot size, the "planned order receipts" are for the larger or the "net requirements." The "planned order release" is for period 4. Since the "planned order receipts" equal the "net requirements," the "projected on hand" becomes zero.

In period 7, the "gross requirements" of 20 become the "net requirements," since there are no units "projected on hand" from the previous period. The "net requirements" for 20 generate the need for "planned order receipts" of 25, the lot size. Thus, the "planned order release" is for period 5. The rest of the "planned order receipts" of 5 become the "projected on hand."

In period 8, the "gross requirements" of 30 are satisfied by the 5 "projected on hand" from the previous period. The "net requirements" for 25 generate the need for "planned order receipts" of 25, which is the lot size. The "planned order release" is for period 6. Since the "planned order receipts" equal the "net requirements," the "projected on hand" becomes zero.

The following example will illustrate the explosion process where gross requirements for a dependent item are derived from the parent which generates the demand for it. The planned order release of the parent is exploded into the gross requirements of its component items. It "lines up" (appears in same time period) with the gross requirements generated by it. Thus, the planned order release is responsible for the dependent item requirements.

EXAMPLE 4

Product *K* has the product structure shown below. Complete the MRP tables if the lot sizes are equal to one.

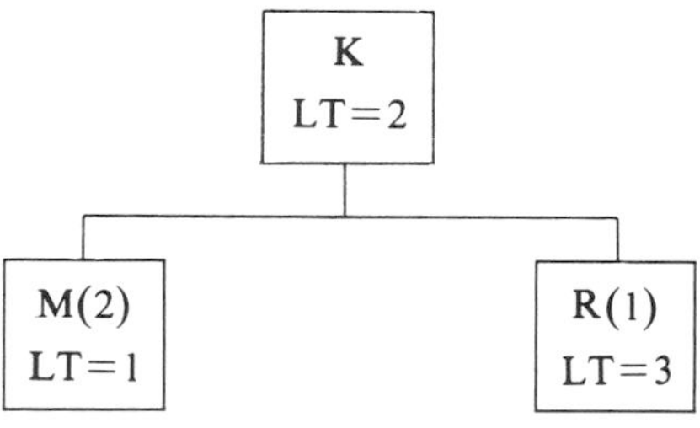

K

	Period								
	PD	1	2	3	4	5	6	7	8
Gross requirements		25	15	120	0	60	0	15	0
Scheduled receipts									
Projected on hand	50								
Net requirements									
Planned order receipts									
Planned order releases									

M

	PD	1	2	3	4	5	6	7	8
Gross requirements									
Scheduled receipts		30							
Projected on hand	225								
Net requirements									
Planned order receipts									
Planned order releases									

Solution:

K

	PD	1	2	3	4	5	6	7	8
Gross requirements		25	15	120	0	60	0	15	0
Scheduled receipts									
Projected on hand	50	25	10	0	0	0	0	0	0
Net requirements				110		60		15	
Planned order receipts				110		60		15	
Planned order releases		110		60		15			

M

	PD	1	2	3	4	5	6	7	8
Gross requirements		220		120		30			
Scheduled receipts		30							
Projected on hand	225	35	35	0	0	0	0	0	0
Net requirements				85		30			
Planned order receipts				85		30			
Planned order releases			85		30				

The preceding example illustrated the explosion process for a single product. The next example will show that a particular dependent item may have "needs" or gross requirements placed on it from more than one source. MRP will combine the gross requirements placed on items regardless of their source or number of parents.

EXAMPLE 5

Two products, J and K, have the product structures shown below. Complete the MRP tables below with the lot sizes of $J=1$, $K=1$, and $M=30$.

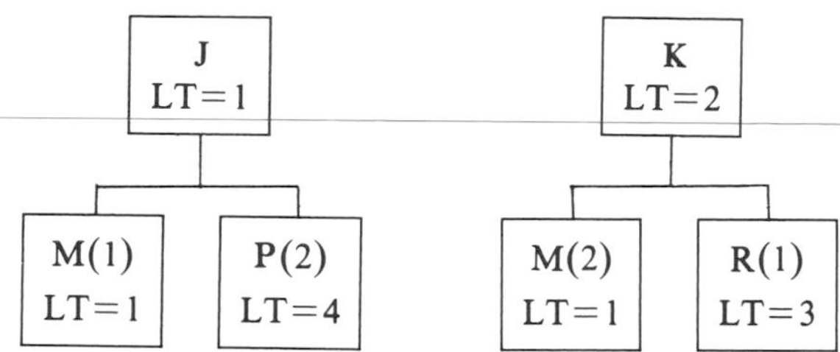

J

	PD	1	2	3	4	5	6	7	8
Gross Requirements		0	50	80	10	0	60	10	25
Scheduled Receipts									
Projected On Hand	15								
Net Requirements									
Planned Order Receipts									
Planned Order Releases									

K

	PD	1	2	3	4	5	6	7	8
Gross Requirements		25	15	120	0	60	0	15	0
Scheduled Receipts									
Projected On Hand	50								
Net Requirements									
Planned Order Receipts									
Planned Order Releases									

	Period								
	PD	1	2	3	4	5	6	7	8

M

	PD	1	2	3	4	5	6	7	8
Gross Requirements									
Scheduled Receipts		30							
Projected On Hand	225								
Net Requirements									
Planned Order Receipts									
Planned Order Releases									

Solution:

J

	PD	1	2	3	4	5	6	7	8
Gross Requirements		0	50	80	10	0	60	10	25
Scheduled Receipts									
Projected On Hand	15	15	0	0	0	0	0	0	0
Net Requirements			35	80	10		60	10	25
Planned Order Receipts			35	80	10		60	10	25
Planned Order Releases		35	80	10		60	10	25	

K

	PD	1	2	3	4	5	6	7	8
Gross Requirements		25	15	120	0	60	0	15	0
Scheduled Receipts									
Projected On Hand	50	25	10	0	0	0	0	0	0
Net Requirements				110		60		15	
Planned Order Receipts				110		60		15	
Planned Order Releases		110		60		15			

M

	PD	1	2	3	4	5	6	7	8
Gross Requirements		255	80	130	0	90	10	25	0
Scheduled Receipts		30							
Projected On Hand	225	0	0	0	0	0	20	25	25
Net Requirements			80	130		90	10	5	
Planned Order Receipts			80	130		90	30	30	
Planned Order Releases		80	130		90	30	30		

EXAMPLE 6

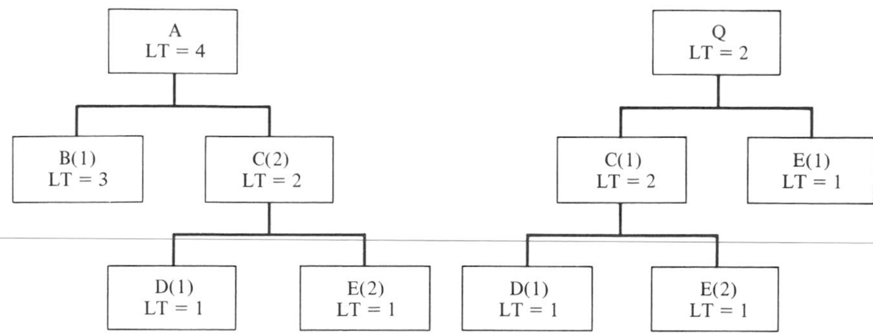

Figure 10

Develop an MRP plan for products A and Q with the product structures given in Figure 10. There are orders for 103 units of product A in period 8 and 200 units of product Q in period 7. The on hand inventory levels for each item are $A=18$, $Q=6$, $B=10$, $C=20$, $D=0$, and $E=30$. A safety stock of five units is maintained on product A and six units on product Q; there is no safety stock on other components. Additionally, ten of the eighteen units on hand of product A are already allocated. There are no open orders (scheduled receipts) on any item. The lot size for items A, Q, B, and C is the same as the net requirements (lot-for-lot ordering), while the lot size for D is 200 units and E is 500 units. What should be the size of the orders for each item, and when should the orders be released?

The low level code (LLC) for each item is as shown in Table 3. Since item E appears at level 1 and level 2 in product Q, and also at level 2 in product A, it is assigned the lowest level code of 2.

Table 3

Item	Low level code
A	0
Q	0
B	1
C	1
D	2
E	2

The MRP plan for 103 of product A and 200 of product Q is shown in Table 4. It shows "what" is needed, "how many" are needed, and "when" they are needed. The table was developed in the following manner.

1. The first step is to establish the gross requirements for items A and Q, which are given as 103 and 200 units. Items A and Q are netted, since they have low

Table 4. MRP Plan for 103 of product *A* and 200 of product *Q*

Lot size	Lead time	On hand	Safety stock	Allocated	Low level code	Item		Period PD	1	2	3	4	5	6	7	8
							Gross requirements									103
							Scheduled receipts									
1	4	18	5	10	0	*A*	Projected on hand	3	3	3	3	3	3	3	3	0
							Net requirements									100
							Planned order receipts									100
							Planned order releases					100				
							Gross requirements								200	
							Scheduled receipts									
1	2	6	6	0	0	*Q*	Projected on hand	0	0	0	0	0	0	0	0	
							Net requirements								200	
							Planned order receipts								200	
							Planned order releases						200			
							Gross requirements					100				
							Scheduled receipts									
1	3	10	0	0	1	*B*	Projected on hand	10	10	10	10	0				
							Net requirements					90				
							Planned order receipts					90				
							Planned order releases		90							

1	2	20	0	0	1	*C*	Gross requirements					200	200			
							Scheduled receipts									
							Projected on hand	20	20	20	20	0	0			
							Net requirements					180	200			
							Planned order receipts					180	200			
							Planned order releases			180	200					
200	1	0	0	0	2	*D*	Gross requirements			180	200					
							Scheduled receipts									
							Projected on hand	0	0	20	20					
							Net requirements			180	180					
							Planned order receipts			200	200					
							Planned order releases		200	200						
500	1	30	0	0	2	*E*	Gross requirements			360	400		200			
							Scheduled receipts									
							Projected on hand	30	30	170	270	270	70			
							Net requirements			330	230					
							Planned order receipts			500	500					
							Planned order releases		500	500						

level codes of 0. By lead time offsetting, planned order releases for *A* and *Q* of 100 and 200 units in periods 4 and 5 are obtained.

2. The planned order releases for *A* and *Q* in periods 4 and 5 are exploded (multiplied by use quantities of items *B*, *C*, and *E*) and accumulated as gross requirements for items *B*, *C*, and *E*. Only items *B* and *C* have a low level code of 1. Items *B* and *C* are netted. A planned order release of 90 units is scheduled for *B* for period 1. Similarly, planned order releases for 180 and 200 units are scheduled for *C* for periods 2 and 3.
3. The planned order releases for *B* and *C* in periods 1, 2, and 3 are exploded (multiplied by use quantities of items *D* and *E*) and accumulated as gross requirements for items *D* and *E*. Item *E* already has a gross requirement of 200 units in period 5 from item *Q*'s explosion. Items *D* and *E*, with low level codes of 2, are netted. Planned order releases for 200 units are scheduled for *D* for periods 1 and 2. Planned order releases for 500 units are scheduled for *E* for periods 1 and 2.

The planned order release is exploded into gross requirements of its component items. It "lines up" (appears in same time period) with the gross requirements generated by it. Thus, the planned order release is responsible for the dependent item requirements. In Example 6, note how the planned order release for 100 units of product *A* in period 4 was exploded into gross requirements of 100 units for component *B* and 200 units for component *C* in the same period 4. Similarly, in Example 6, the planned order release for 200 units of product *Q* in period 5 was exploded into gross requirements of 200 units each of components *C* and *E* in the same period. The process of planned order releases creating requirements at the next lower level continues to the end of the product structure, when all the component requirements have been satisfied.

Planned order release quantities in MRP may be lot size quantities or identical to the net requirements for a given period. Ordering the same quantity as the net requirements, as in Example 1, is called lot-for-lot ordering. Safety stocks can be used with MRP, but it does not consider them available for regular use. Safety stock is recommended at the end item level but not the component level in MRP. The need for safety stock of components is reduced by MRP, since it calculates the exact quantities and when they are needed.

Reasons of economy or convenience may dictate the ordering of inventory items in excess of net requirements. Lot sizing techniques based on balancing the costs of ordering and holding inventory are commonly used with MRP systems. There are several different types of lot sizing techniques, such as the economic order quantity (EOQ), the Wagner-Whitin algorithm, the Silver-Meal heuristic algorithms, and the part-period algorithm. These techniques are discussed in Appendix A at the end of this chapter.

It is not logical to schedule a component in a time period that has already past. With MRP logic, it is possible to have low level items scheduled "past due." The analyst might revise the master schedule for the end item to a later time period. It might also be possible to compress the lead time by expediting the item. Some managerial replanning is necessary when action is required in the past due time period.

MRP performs its procedures from the top of the product structure downward, exploding requirements level by level. There are times when it is desirable to identify the parent item that generated the component (dependent) requirement. This is possible through what is called "pegged" requirements. The pegging of requirements permits a retracing upward in the product structure to identify each parent that created the component demand. Single-level pegging locates the immediate parents; full pegging determines the end items that generated the component requirement. If a component will be delayed, it is then possible to indicate its impact on the delivery of the end item to the customer. Pegged requirements are very important in determining the significance of rescheduling alternatives.

AN EOQ-MRP COMPARISON

The MRP system has numerous advantages over the fixed order size system for control of production items. A comparison of the fixed order size and the MRP systems is contained in Table 5. Some disadvantages of the fixed order size system are as follows:

1. It requires a very large inventory investment.
2. It is unreliable with a highly varying demand rate.
3. It requires a large investment in safety stock.
4. It requires forecasts for all items.
5. It is based on past demand data.
6. Material obsolescence is more likely.

The use of EOQ or EPQ when demand is dependent can create serious

Table 5. Comparison of fixed order size and MRP systems

Fixed Order Size System (EOQ/EPQ)	MRP System
Part oriented (every item)	Product/component oriented
Independent demand	Dependent (derived)demand
Continuous item demand	Discrete/lumpy item demand
Continuous lead time demand	No lead time demand
Reorder point ordering signal	Time-phased ordering signal
Historical demand base	Future production base
Forecast all items	Forecast end items only
Quantity-based system	Quantity- and time-based system
Safety stock for all items	Safety stock for end items only

operational problems and an excessive inventory investment. For dependent demand items, demand should be calculated from a bill of materials explosion. Demand should not be forecasted when it can be calculated. Independent demand items must be forecasted, but dependent demand items should be calculated. It is much more efficient to order components from product requirements and to drive the component inventory to zero between requirements. MRP will substantially reduce inventory investment in dependent demand items while improving operational efficiency by removing the automatic (built-in) risk of shortages associated with the EOQ or EPQ. Independent demand inventory models when used for dependent demand items generate excessive inventory when it is not needed and insufficient inventory when it is needed. A few examples will illustrate the benefits of the MRP system.

EXAMPLE 7

A toy manufacturer assembles a small wagon composed of the following components (quantities): frame (1), wheels (4), axles (2), body (1), and handle (1). All of the components are maintained on an EOQ system with the service levels[2] shown in Table 6. What is the probability that all the components will be in stock when production is scheduled to commence? What must be the component service level to maintain a 90% service level for the complete wagon?

Since the EOQ system assumes independent component demand, the probability of all the components being available is obtained as follows:

$$(0.90)(0.90)(0.90)(0.90)(0.90)=(0.90)^5=0.5904, \quad \text{or} \quad 59.04\%.$$

While service appears to be high at the component level, it is not high at the assembly (product) level. Very few production managers would agree that a service level of 59% is acceptable. To maintain a 90% service level on the wagon, each component must have a service level as follows:

$$\sqrt[5]{0.90}=0.98, \quad \text{or} \quad 98\%.$$

Table 6

Component	Service level
Frame	.90
Wheels	.90
Axles	.90
Body	.90
Handle	.90

[2] The service level may be viewed as that fraction (percentage) of time components are available in the storage area (90% of the time the frame is available, and 10% of the time it is out of stock).

Now the production manager may be pleased with being able to produce a complete wagon 90% of the time, but the financial manager would argue relentlessly against a 98% service level on components because of the large quantity of safety stock required to maintain such a high service level. An extremely high level of investment would be required in safety stock. Thus, the example illustrates the operational difficulties in using independent demand EOQ as well as the large inventory investment required to make the system work. When the final product is composed of many components (many more than five used in the example), the EOQ is practically impossible to use.

EXAMPLE 8

An end item is fabricated from a single component supplied by a local distributor. The end item is produced on a cycle every fourth week, or 13 times per year, during weeks 3, 7, 11, 15, 19, 23, 27, 31, 35, 39, 43, 47, and 51. Annual demand for the end item is 52,000 units. Each component costs \$3.50, and the order cost is \$125 per lot. The annual inventory holding cost is 20% of the unit cost, and the lead time is a constant one week. What is the total annual cost with EOQ? What is the total annual cost of MRP with lot-for-lot ordering? Compare the EOQ and MRP costs.

With the EOQ model, the inventory policy would be as follows:

$$\text{EOQ} = Q_0 = \sqrt{\frac{2CR}{PF}} = \sqrt{\frac{2(125)(52{,}000)}{0.20(3.50)}} = 4310 \text{ units},$$

$$\text{Reorder point} = B = \frac{RL}{52} = \frac{52{,}000(1)}{52} = 1000 \text{ units}.$$

Figure 11

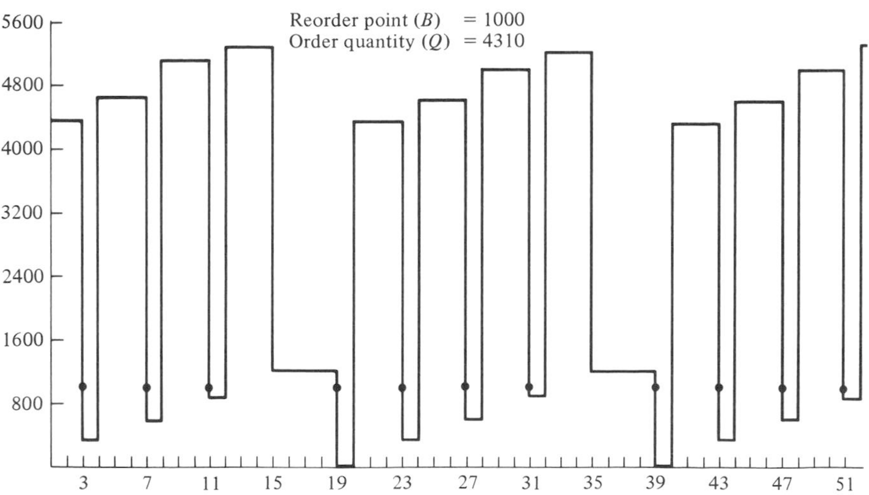

The performance of the EOQ model on inventory levels is shown graphically in Figure 11, based on production runs of 4000 units. Note how inventory levels go through a cyclical pattern every 20 weeks, with a stockout occurring at least twice and sometimes three times in a year. Instead of inventory peaks there are plateaus (for three weeks after each order is received, inventory lies dormant in the storage area awaiting production). Table 7 develops the average inventory level for the EOQ model. We have

$$\text{Average inventory} = \frac{172{,}610}{52} = 3319 \text{ units.}$$

Neglecting stockout cost, the total annual cost using the EOQ model is as follows:

$$\begin{aligned}\text{Total annual cost} &= \text{purchase cost} + \text{order cost} + \text{holding cost}\\ &= (52{,}000)(3.50) + (125)(11) + (3319)(0.20)(3.50)\\ &= 182{,}000.00 + 1375.00 + 2323.30\\ &= \$185{,}698.30.\end{aligned}$$

Table 7

Week	Inventory level	Week	Inventory level
1	4,310	27	620[a]
2	4,310	28	4,930
3	310[a]	29	4,930
4	4,620	30	4,930
5	4,620	31	930[a]
6	4,620	32	5,240
7	620[a]	33	5,240
8	4,930	34	5,240
9	4,930	35	1,240
10	4,930	36	1,240
11	930[a]	37	1,240
12	5,240	38	1,240
13	5,240	39	0[a]
14	5,240	40	4,310
15	1,240	41	4,310
16	1,240	42	4,310
17	1,240	43	310[a]
18	1,240	44	4,620
19	0[a]	45	4,620
20	4,310	46	4,620
21	4,310	47	620[a]
22	4,310	48	4,930
23	310[a]	49	4,930
24	4,620	50	4,930
25	4,620	51	930[a]
26	4,620	52	5,240
		Total	172,610 units

[a] Order placed.

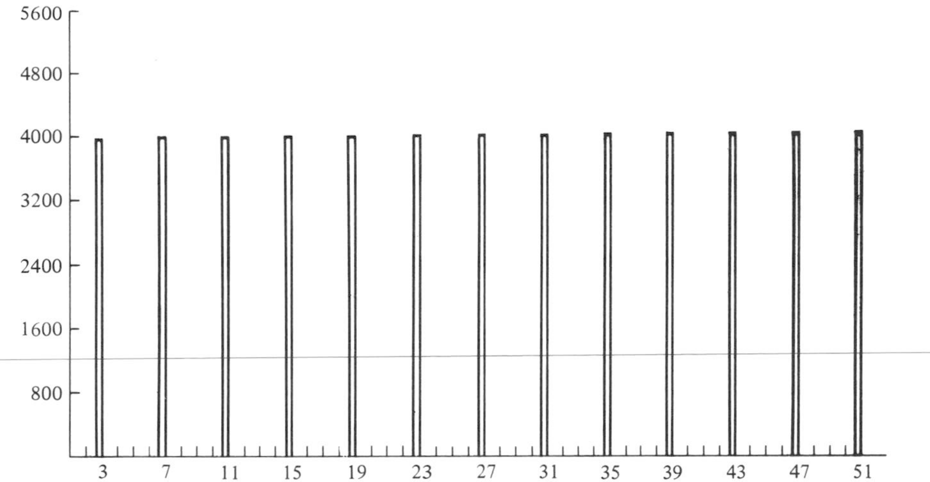

Figure 12. Inventory levels for MRP model.

Now consider an MRP system with the same variables except that orders are scheduled to arrive the day before they are needed for production. The performance of the MRP system on inventory levels is shown graphically in Figure 12. Table 8 develops the average inventory level for the MRP system. We have

$$\text{Average inventory} = \frac{52{,}000}{365} = 143 \text{ units.}$$

To avoid complicating the computations, no attempt will be made to determine if savings could be realized by combining some orders to reduce the number of orders required from 13 to some lesser amount. However, discrete lot sizing techniques could be applied. Note that with MRP no stockouts occurred. The total annual cost with MRP is as follows:

$$\begin{aligned}\text{Total annual cost} &= \text{purchase cost} + \text{order cost} + \text{holding cost}\\ &= (52{,}000)(3.50) + (125)(13) + (143)(0.20)(3.50)\\ &= 182{,}000.00 + 1625.00 + 100.10\\ &= \$183{,}725.10,\\ \text{MRP cost savings} &= \text{EOQ annual cost} - \text{MRP annual cost}\\ &= 185{,}698.30 - 183{,}725.10\\ &= \$1973.20.\end{aligned}$$

In this example, a cost saving of $1973.20 was realized through the use of MRP when compared with EOQ. In addition, no stockouts occurred with MRP. Since our example dealt with only one end item with only one component, imagine the savings that can be obtained with numerous products with several components. The advantages of MRP for dependent demand items should now be apparent.

Table 8

Week	Inventory level[a]	Week	Inventory level
1	0(7)	27	4,000(1); 0(6)
2	0(7)	28	0(7)
3	4,000(1); 0(6)	29	0(7)
4	0(7)	30	0(7)
5	0(7)	31	4,000(1); 0(6)
6	0(7)	32	0(7)
7	4,000(1); 0(6)	33	0(7)
8	0(7)	34	0(7)
9	0(7)	35	4,000(1); 0(6)
10	0(7)	36	0(7)
11	4,000(1); 0(6)	37	0(7)
12	0(7)	38	0(7)
13	0(7)	39	4,000(1); 0(6)
14	0(7)	40	0(7)
15	4,000(1); 0(6)	41	0(7)
16	0(7)	42	0(7)
17	0(7)	43	4,000(1); 0(6)
18	0(7)	44	0(7)
19	4,000(1); 0(6)	45	0(7)
20	0(7)	46	0(7)
21	0(7)	47	4,000(1); 0(6)
22	0(7)	48	0(7)
23	4,000(1); 0(6)	49	0(7)
24	0(7)	50	0(7)
25	0(7)	51	4,000(1); 0(6)
26	0(7)	52	0(7)
		Total	52,000

[a] The number of days in the week at the given level follows in parentheses.

EXAMPLE 9

An organization produces an end item from a single purchased component. The existing inventory system is based on EOQs for both the end item and the purchased component. The data in Table 9 pertain to the existing inventory system. What difference would an MRP system with lot-for-lot ordering have on the average inventory level of the purchased component? What would be the cost saving of an MRP system on the purchased component? Assume all end item stockouts are lost sales.

Figure 13 illustrates a few cycles of the end item and component inventory levels with the EOQ system. The average inventory levels for the EOQ and MRP systems are calculated in Table 10. It is assumed the end item demand is stable at 10 units per week. It is further assumed that the MRP system delivers purchased components to the storeroom one week before required. Unsatisfied end item demand results in a lost sale, while unsatisfied component demand results in a backorder. The average

Table 9

	End Item	Component
Cost/unit	$65.00	$28.80
Annual demand (units)	520	520
Setup/order cost	$100.00	$50.00
Holding cost fraction	0.25	0.25
Stockout cost/unit	$5.00	—
Lead time (weeks)	3	4
Safety stock (units)	5	5
EOQ (Q_0)	80	85
Reorder point B	35	45

weekly component inventory with the EOQ system is 55 units, whereas with the MRP system it is only 10 units. With the EOQ system, there are 18 weeks (over 11% of the time) when there are shortages in end items that result in lost sales. The end item shortages result from the EOQ system not providing sufficient quantities of purchased components for production needs. There are no end item shortages with the MRP system and component inventory levels are much smaller.

Figure 13. Inventory levels with EOQ.

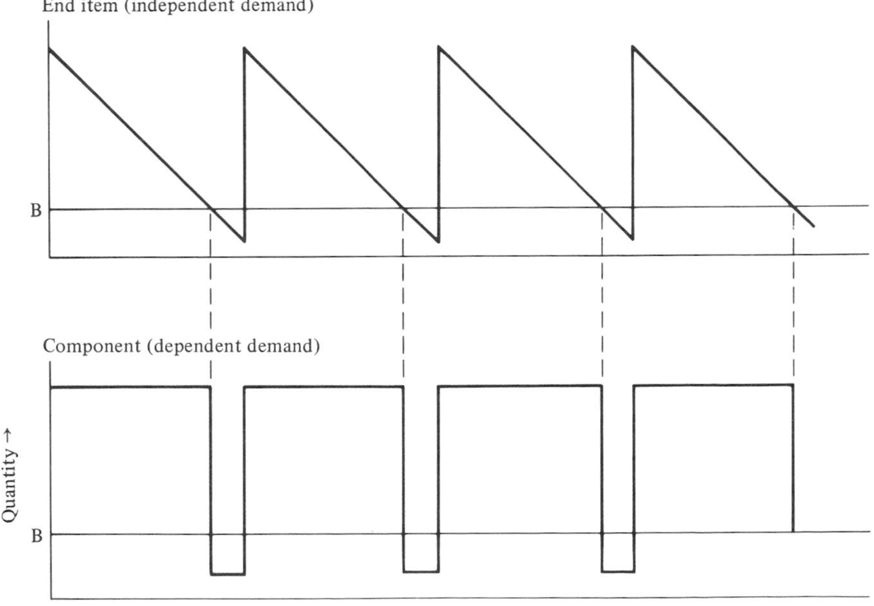

Table 10. EOQ and MRP Inventory Levels

		EOQ			MRP	
Week	End Item Demand	End Item Inventory Level	Component Demand	Component Inventory Level	End Item Inventory Level	Component Inventory Level
0	–	80	–	85	80	0
1	10	70	0	85	70	0
2	10	60	0	85	60	0
3	10	50	0	85	50	0
4	10	40	0	85	40	0
5	10	30[a]	80	5[a]	30	80
6	10	20	0	5	20	0
7	10	10	0	5	10	0
8	10	80[b]	0	5	80[b]	0
9	10	70	0	90[b]	70	0
10	10	60	0	90	60	0
11	10	50	0	90	50	0
12	10	40	0	90	40	0
13	10	30[a]	80	10[a]	30	80
14	10	20	0	10	20	0
15	10	10	0	10	10	0
16	10	80[b]	0	10	80[b]	0
17	10	70	0	95[b]	70	0
18	10	60	0	95	60	0
19	10	50	0	95	50	0
20	10	40	0	95	40	0
21	10	30[a]	80	15[a]	30	80
22	10	20	0	15	20	0
23	10	10	0	15	10	0
24	10	80[b]	0	15	80[b]	0
25	10	70	0	100[b]	70	0
26	10	60	0	100	60	0
27	10	50	0	100	50	0
28	10	40	0	100	40	0
29	10	30[a]	80	20[a]	30	80
30	10	20	0	20	20	0
31	10	10	0	20	10	0
32	10	80[b]	0	20	80[b]	0
33	10	70	0	105[b]	70	0
34	10	60	0	105	60	0
35	10	50	0	105	50	0
36	10	40	0	105	40	0
37	10	30[a]	80	25[a]	30	80
38	10	20	0	25	20	0

(continued)

Table 10. EOQ and MRP Inventory Levels (*continued*)

		EOQ			MRP	
Week	End Item Demand	End Item Inventory Level	Component Demand	Component Inventory Level	End Item Inventory Level	Component Inventory Level
39	10	10	0	25	10	0
40	10	80[b]	0	25	80[b]	0
41	10	70	0	110[b]	70	0
42	10	60	0	110	60	0
43	10	50	0	110	50	0
44	10	40	0	110	40	0
45	10	30[a]	80	30[a]	30	80
46	10	20	0	30	20	0
47	10	10	0	30	10	0
48	10	80[b]	0	30	80[b]	0
49	10	70	0	115[b]	70	0
50	10	60	0	115	60	0
51	10	50	0	115	50	0
52	10	40	0	115	40	0
53	10	30[a]	80	35[a]	30	80
54	10	20	0	35	20	0
55	10	10	0	35	10	0
56	10	80[b]	0	35	80[b]	0
57	10	70	0	120[b]	70	0
58	10	60	0	120	60	0
59	10	50	0	120	50	0
60	10	40	0	120	40	0
61	10	30[a]	80	40[a]	30	80
62	10	20	0	40	20	0
63	10	10	0	40	10	0
64	10	80[b]	0	40	80[b]	0
65	10	70	0	125[b]	70	0
66	10	60	0	125	60	0
67	10	50	0	125	50	0
68	10	40	0	125	40	0
69	10	30[a]	80	45[a]	30	80
70	10	20	0	45	20	0
71	10	10	0	45	10	0
72	10	80[b]	0	45	80[b]	0
73	10	70	0	130[b]	70	0
74	10	60	0	130	60	0
75	10	50	0	130	50	0
76	10	40	0	130	40	0
77	10	30[a]	80	50	30	80

(*continued*)

Table 10. EOQ and MRP Inventory Levels (*continued*)

Week	End Item Demand	EOQ End Item Inventory Level	EOQ Component Demand	EOQ Component Inventory Level	MRP End Item Inventory Level	MRP Component Inventory Level
78	10	20	0	50	20	0
79	10	10	0	50	10	0
80	10	80[b]	0	50	80[b]	0
81	10	70	0	50	70	0
82	10	60	0	50	60	0
83	10	50	0	50	50	0
84	10	40	0	50	40	0
85	10	30[a]	80	(−30)[a]	30	80
86	10	20	0	(−30)	20	0
87	10	10	0	(−30)	10	0
88	10	0	0	(−30)	80[b]	0
89	10	0	0	55[b]	70	0
90	10	0	0	55	60	0
91	10	0	0	55	50	0
92	10	70[b]	0	55	40	0
93	10	60	0	55	30	80
94	10	50	0	55	20	0
95	10	40	0	55	10	0
96	10	30[a]	80	(−25)[a]	80[b]	0
97	10	20	0	(−25)	70	0
98	10	10	0	(−25)	60	0
99	10	0	0	(−25)	50	0
100	10	0	0	60[b]	40	0
101	10	0	0	60	30	80
102	10	0	0	60	20	0
103	10	70[b]	0	60	10	0
104	10	60	0	60	80[b]	0
105	10	50	0	60	70	0
106	10	40	0	60	60	0
107	10	30[a]	80	(−20)[a]	50	0
108	10	20	0	(−20)	40	0
109	10	10	0	(−20)	30	80
110	10	0	0	(−20)	20	0
111	10	0	0	65[b]	10	0
112	10	0	0	65	80[b]	0
113	10	0	0	65	70	0
114	10	70[b]	0	65	60	0
115	10	60	0	65	50	0
116	10	50	0	65	40	0
117	10	40	0	65	30	80

(*continued*)

Table 10. EOQ and MRP Inventory Levels *(continued)*

		EOQ			MRP	
Week	End Item Demand	End Item Inventory Level	Component Demand	Component Inventory Level	End Item Inventory Level	Component Inventory Level
118	10	30[a]	80	(−15)[a]	20	0
119	10	20	0	(−15)	10	0
120	10	10	0	(−15)	80[b]	0
121	10	0	0	(−15)	70	0
122	10	0	0	70[b]	60	0
123	10	0	0	70	50	0
124	10	0	0	70	40	0
125	10	70[b]	0	70	30	80
126	10	60	0	70	20	0
127	10	50	0	70	10	0
128	10	40	0	70	80[b]	0
129	10	30[a]	80	(−10)[a]	70	0
130	10	20	0	(−10)	60	0
131	10	10	0	(−10)	50	0
132	10	0	0	(−10)	40	0
133	10	0	0	75[b]	30	80
134	10	0	0	75	20	0
135	10	0	0	75	10	0
136	10	70[b]	0	75	80[b]	0
137	10	60	0	75	70	0
138	10	50	0	75	60	0
139	10	40	0	75	50	0
140	10	30[a]	80	(−5)[a]	40	0
141	10	20	0	(−5)	30	80
142	10	10	0	(−5)	20	0
143	10	0	0	(−5)	10	0
144	10	0	0	80[b]	80[b]	0
145	10	0	0	80	70	0
146	10	0	0	80	60	0
147	10	70[b]	0	80	50	0
148	10	60	0	80	40	0
149	10	50	0	80	30	80
150	10	40	0	80	20	0
151	10	30[a]	80	0[a]	10	0
152	10	20	0	0	80[b]	0
153	10	10	0	0	70	0
154	10	80[b]	0	0	60	0
155	10	70	0	85[b]	50	0
				8520		1520
Weekly Average				55		10

[a] Reorder point.

[b] Stock replenishment.

The total annual cost of the component with the EOQ system is as follows:

$$\begin{aligned} TC &= \text{purchase cost} + \text{order cost} + \text{holding cost} + \text{stockout cost} \\ &= \$28.80(520) + 16(\$50)52/155 + \$28.80(0.25)55 + 180(\$5.00)52/155 \\ &= \$14{,}976.00 + \$268.39 + \$396.00 + \$301.94 \\ &= \$15{,}942.33. \end{aligned}$$

The total annual cost of the component with the MRP system is as follows:

$$\begin{aligned} TC &= \text{purchase cost} + \text{order cost} + \text{holding cost} + \text{stockout cost} \\ &= \$28.80(520) + \$50(19)52/155 + \$28.80(0.25)10 + 5(0) \\ &= \$14{,}976.00 + \$318.71 + \$72.00 + 0 \\ &= \$15{,}366.71. \end{aligned}$$

$$\begin{aligned} \text{MRP annual cost savings} &= (\text{EOQ annual cost}) - (\text{MRP annual cost}) \\ &= \$15{,}942.33 - \$15{,}366.71 \\ &= \$575.62. \end{aligned}$$

Thus, the MRP system not only provided better service (no stockouts) to production, but it reduced the inventory investment.

As was previously illustrated in Table 5, an MRP system has several advantages over an EOQ system. However, the systems are not really competing, for each has a different area of application. For continuous, uniform, and independent demand the EOQ system is desirable. For discontinuous, nonuniform, and dependent demand the MRP system is desirable. For production, manufacturing, fabrication, or assembly industries the majority of inventory items dictates an MRP approach.

Historically, many organizations have used statistical inventory control via EOQ models when they should have been using MRP. Since the statistical approach does not ensure the availability of components for production, they instituted expediters and support departments to ensure material availability. Expediters were required to make an inadequate system meet scheduling and delivery needs. In accounting for the system's shortcomings, everybody had his own idea who was the culprit, and recriminations were common. The real culprit was an inappropriate system that did not serve the needs of the organization. Not only will the wrong system hamper operations and increase costs, but it can result in serious conflicts between the various parts of the organization.

It should be apparent by now that a manual MRP system is untenable except for very simple products. Computerized MRP systems are necessary because of the massive number of lower level items and the tedium of manual computations. Numerous organizations have highly sophisticated MRP systems, which have been implemented in the last decade. Software packages are readily available to ease the pain of conversion from other systems. However, MRP systems must be tailored to meet the specific needs of an organization.

MRP TYPES

There are two basic types of MRP systems, the regenerative and the net change systems, geared to different frequencies of replanning. With *regenerative systems*, the entire MRP (full explosions) is recalculated periodically (usually once a week) based on the latest master schedule requirements. The regenerative approach is designed for low-frequency replanning and employs batch-processing techniques. Regeneration starts over with a "new slate" and reexplodes the entire master schedule. After each planning period the planning horizon is extended one more period into the future. The advantages of the regenerative system are that it permits efficient use of data processing equipment and fewer data errors are compounded over time, since it is checked and corrected on a regular basis.

With *net change systems*, the entire requirements for every component are not recalculated periodically, but only additions and subtractions from the master schedule are entered. The requirements change is then calculated for only those components affected (partial explosions). Net change can be applied instantaneously or at the end of each day. Net change is designed for high-frequency replanning. In a stable environment (master production schedule) the regenerative MRP functions satisfactorily; in a volatile environment with constant change the net change MRP is more desirable.

MRP OVERVIEW

MRP was originally seen as a superior method of ordering inventory. As it evolved, its major emphasis shifted to scheduling (establishing and maintaining valid due dates on orders). Today, MRP is considered an important but single module in a total closed-looped system of production, sometimes referred to as manufacturing resource planning. The closed-looping refers to the ability to tie into other financial, capacity, and business planning areas. Thus, the term MRP has meant different things to different people at different times. Some think of it as an inventory system, others as a scheduling system, and still others as a completely closed-loop production system. It can be all of these things, depending on the organization and the stage of its development with MRP. Most would agree that MRP tends to foster systems thinking and it tends to become the cornerstone of the production system. Within the limits of its methodology, it will reveal (1) what is needed, (2) how many are needed, (3) when they will be needed, and (4) when they should be ordered.

The time horizon in MRP is composed of equal time periods called "time buckets." The "time buckets" are usually weeks or some other convenient time increment. The length of the time horizon is usually greater than the product with the longest sequence of component lead times. It should be long enough to obtain all materials and produce all components before a planned order release for end items. It is also possible to have "bucketless MRP" where equal time periods are not used but specific dates are developed for every order.

The effective operation and efficiency of an MRP system are functions of the integrity of the files and records of relevant data. The quality is directly influenced by data accessibility, up-to-dateness, and accuracy. Lack of record integrity is a major reason for the failure of MRP systems to live up to expectations. Computer-based MRP will not perform satisfactorily with poor files and records. File integrity is not a one-time affair, but must be a constant maintenance function. Manual systems must have file integrity too. But because MRP involves the processing of data on a massive scale, low-quality input data will heavily contribute to operational failure. The outputs from a computer-based MRP system cannot be better than its inputs.

Fixed order quantity or fixed order interval systems are part-based, whereas material requirements planning systems are component-based (an end item is composed of numerous parts). MRP is based on the future, as represented in forecasts and the production schedule; other systems are based upon the past and an expected continuation of historical forces. Other systems require safety stock for all items; MRP maintains safety stock for end items only. Other systems establish a reorder point based on a fixed number of units or a fixed period of time; the reorder point in MRP is time-phased and determined by order due dates. When it can be employed, the MRP system can substantially reduce inventory levels and inventory investment.

When inventory decisions cannot be separated from production decisions, they must be considered part of aggregate planning for the total production system. Dependent demand inventory items are in this category, since they are production dependent. The function of an MRP system is to translate the overall plan of production (master production schedule) into detailed component requirements and orders. It determines what is to be manufactured and when, as well as what is to be procured and when. For end items, it is feasible to hold extra inventory to provide for customer service. To hold extra inventory of components with a dependent demand is foolish, since it serves no function.[3] While the demand for end items may be uncertain, the demand for components is certain (deterministic) and dictated by the production schedule.

[3]Safety stocks for components may be desirable to cushion uncertain purchase lead times.

When the following conditions hold, MRP is usually superior to other inventory systems:

1. The final product is complex and contains several other items.
2. The specific demand for the product in any time period is known.
3. The final product is expensive.
4. The demand for an item is tied in a predictable fashion to the demand for other items.
5. The forces creating the demand in one time period are distinguishable from those in other time periods.

CAPACITY PLANNING AND CONTROL

Capacity planning determines how many persons, machines, and physical resources are required to accomplish the tasks of production. It defines, measures, and adjusts the levels of capacity so they are consistent with the needs of production. Capacity must be planned based on some unit of measure that is common to the mix of products encountered (units, tons, meters, standard hours, etc.). The unit of measure selected must translate all products into a common equivalent unit with respect to time.

There are many factors that affect capacity. Some factors are completely under management control while others are not. The management controlled factors include:

1. land,
2. labor,
3. facilities,
4. machines,
5. tooling,
6. shifts worked per day,
7. days worked per week,
8. overtime,
9. subcontracting,
10. preventive maintenance.

Other less controllable factors include:

1. absenteeism,
2. personnel turnover,
3. labor performance,
4. equipment breakdown,
5. scrap and rework.

Thus, capacity can be modified by a change in any of the above factors.

Capacity refers to the production capability of a work center, department, or facility. It is important because (1) sufficient capacity is needed to provide the output for current and future customer demand, (2) it directly influences the efficiency (cost) of operations, and (3) it represents a sizable investment by the organization.

Operations managers must address the conflicting objectives of efficient plant operation, minimum inventory investment, and maximum customer service. They must answer the questions:

1. What should I be working on?
2. Do I have the capacity to work on it?

The first question deals with *priorities* and the second with *capacities*. It is necessary to plan and control both priority and capacity. Priority is the ranking by due date of an order relative to other orders. It determines what material is required and when it is required. MRP is a form of priority planning. Capacity is the quantity of work that can be performed at a work center and is frequently expressed in hours.

Capacity planning relates to labor and equipment requirements. It determines what labor and equipment capacity is required and when it is required. It is usually planned on the basis of labor or machine hours available within the plant. Capacity has a direct influence on customer service. Excess capacity results in low resource productivity, while inadequate capacity may mean poor customer service.

Capacity decisions really start with the production plan, which establishes the output for each time period in aggregate terms. The production plan should be leveled so it is realizable within capacity constraints. The time horizon of the production plan is usually sufficient so capacity can be changed (expanded or contracted) to meet expected demand. While the production plan deals in aggregate terms, the master schedule, which is derived from it, contains more specific detail on products and product modules. As shown in Figure 14, the production plan serves as a rough cut capacity plan within which the master schedule must be laid out.

The master schedule must also be a realizable schedule. MRP plans priorities, and it assumes that sufficient capacity is available to execute the master schedule. If the master schedule is overstated (overloaded), MRP priorities will be invalid and impossible to attain. For this reason, it is necessary to verify that sufficient capacity is available after the material requirements plan is obtained.

MRP is not a capacity plan, it does not solve capacity problems, and it does not level work loads in the shop. It tends to utilize capacity in a lumpy manner. Leveling the MPS can attenuate capacity fluctuations, but the netting of demands against existing stocks, previous order actions, and lot sizing policies tends to generate fluctuations in capacity requirements at the lower shop level.

The output from MRP will be planned order releases and released (open) orders, which are the inputs into capacity requirements planning (CRP). As

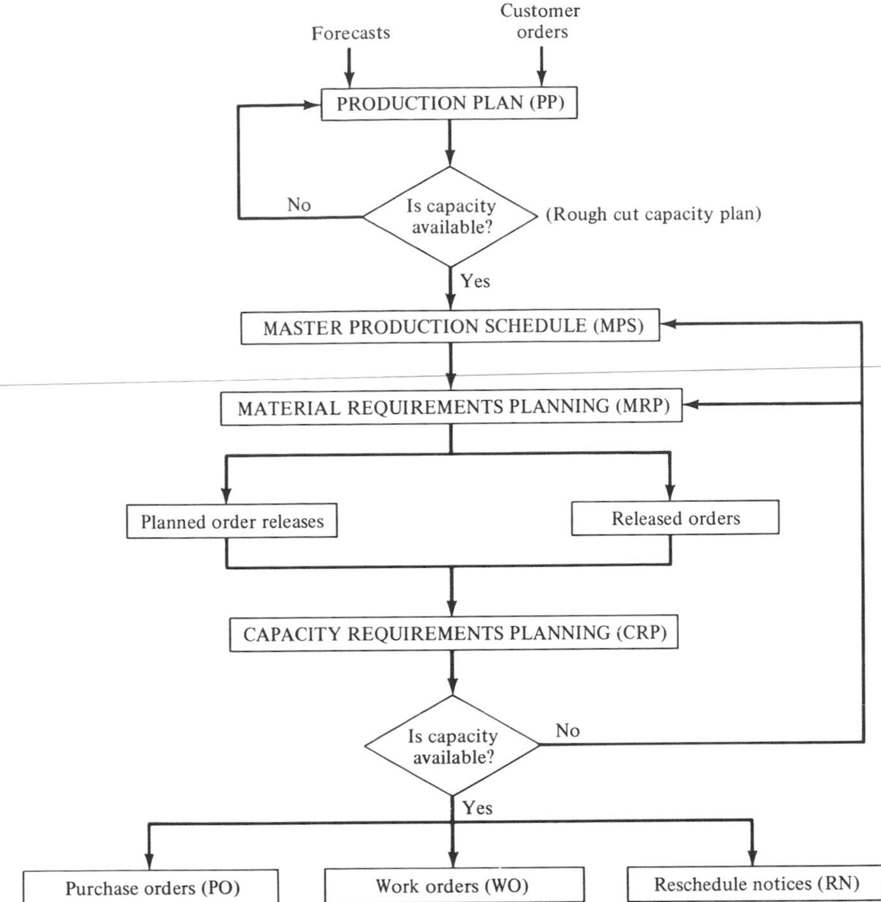

Figure 14. Capacity planning.

shown in Figure 15, the combination of planned orders and released orders will be converted into their capacity requirements by time period. From route sheets, the operations required and their standard time can be ascertained. The capacity requirements plan will calculate the standard hours of production by work center and time period required to satisfy the master schedule. The objective is to indicate if existing capacity is adequate to support the master schedule. If sufficient capacity is not available, the master schedule must be revised or capacity expanded. If sufficient capacity is available, the material requirements plan can be executed.

Thus, capacity planning is performed at various stages with different degrees of exactness. Before MRP, capacity planning is rough cut (per-

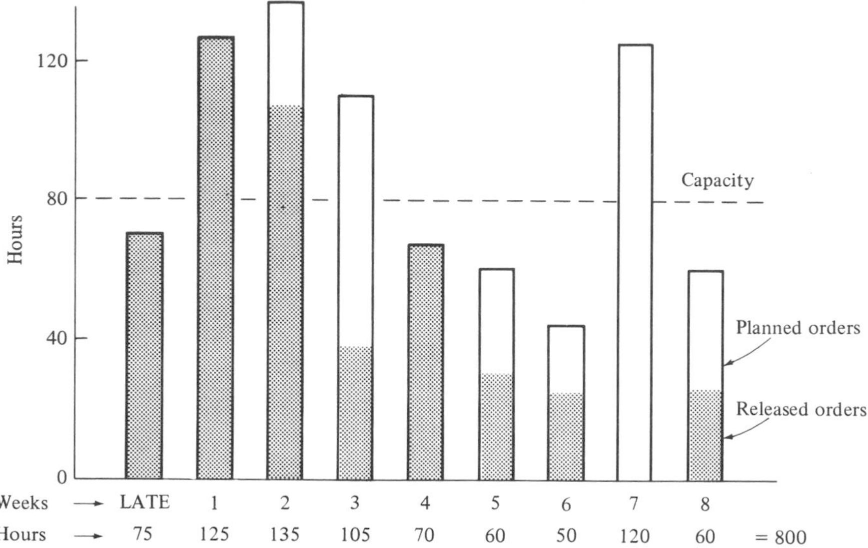

Figure 15. Capacity requirements plan.

formed in broad aggregate terms). After MRP, capacity planning, in the form of CRP, measures the work load at each work center based on both planned and released orders. Capacity planning is really an iterative process of comparing available capacity with future capacity requirements. When there is an imbalance the following steps can be taken:

1. If available capacity is less than required capacity, either increase available capacity (utilize overtime, extra shifts, subcontracting, etc.) or reduce required capacity (reduce master schedule requirements, select alternate routings, etc.).
2. If available capacity is greater than required capacity, either reduce available capacity (shift or lay off manpower, reduce shift hours, etc.) or increase required capacity (increase master schedule requirements, release orders early, reduce subcontracting, etc.).

Frequently organizations have critical work centers that limit production. Critical work centers are bottleneck work centers where capacity is limited and flow restricted. In job shops, critical work centers may change from time period to time period. Frequently, work center loading is based only on released orders. With MRP, capacity requirements on work centers are based on planned orders as well as released orders. Thus, critical work centers can be planned more effectively.

An objective of capacity management is to match the level of operations

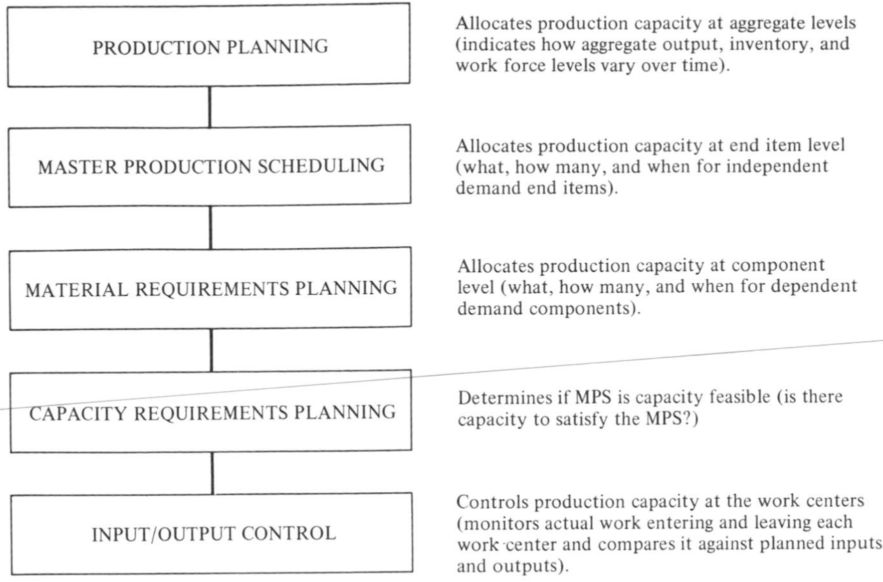

Figure 16. Production planning and control systems.

to the level of demand. The uncertainty of demand gives rise to the need for capacity management. *Capacity planning* is a medium to long range problem based on expected demand patterns for the future. *Capacity control* is a short to medium range problem based on implementation of capacity plans and deployment of resources to accommodate temporary changes in demand.

MRP is an input to capacity requirements planning, which must assess the workload at work centers and determine if capacity is sufficient. MRP systems assume that the master production schedule is feasible and adequate capacity exists to meet its requirements. If capacity is insufficient, changes must be made. Usually, capacities in key work centers are continuously monitored, for they indicate capacity limitations. Adjustments to labor and machine utilization may be necessary in critical work centers. The major modules in a production planning and control system are outlined in Figure 16.

CONCLUSION

Production planning and master scheduling establish the manufacturing plan of products or end items to be produced during a given time frame. MRP takes the master schedule for end items and calculates the plan for all dependent demand items composing the end items. Manufacturing and purchasing are responsible for executing the overall material plans.

Although MRP primarily calculates material requirements, it can be used to calculate machine time and labor needs. Once the MRP plan is established, route and operation sheets can be utilized to determine labor and machine times. This additional extension is called capacity requirements planning. Thus, MRP is a valuable tool for (1) inventory control (time phasing orders to needs), (2) scheduling (setting priorities), and (3) capacity requirements planning (determining MPS capacity feasibility).

MRP is normally implemented as a computer-based system because of the quantity of transactions and simple calculations required. It is practically impossible to plan and replan hundreds of subassemblies with many-leveled product structures on a manual basis. Without a computer it is impossible to keep up-to-date records on the status of thousands of inventory items.

QUESTIONS

1. What is MRP?
2. Differentiate between dependent and independent demand.
3. Are MRP systems more suitable for dependent or independent demand items?
4. What are the key features of an MRP system?
5. Name the major inputs to an MRP system.
6. How does MRP time-phase net requirements?
7. What is a bill of materials?
8. What is a structured bill of materials?
9. What is the purpose of an indented bill of materials?
10. Does the product (end item) have the highest or the lowest level code?
11. Do planned order release quantities indicate the exact order size for each item?
12. Differentiate between regenerative and net change MRP systems.
13. What is meant by "pegged" requirements?
14. Contrast priorities with capacities.

PROBLEMS

1. Compute the net requirements for the three items listed below:

	Item A	Item B	Item C
Gross requirements	175	30	140
On hand	35	5	70
On order	40	0	50
Safety stock	18	3	0

2. From the information given below for product A, draw the product structure.

Parent:	A	B	C
Components:	$B(1)$ $C(1)$ $E(1)$ $F(4)$	$E(2)$ $F(1)$ $G(1)$	$D(1)$ $G(3)$

3. Make an indented bill of materials with low level coding for the product in Problem 2.

4. An indented parts list for product Z is given below. How many component F's are required? How many component 50's are required?

Part Number			Quantity/assembly
Z			—
·	A		1
·	·	80	6
·	·	110	6
·	·	F	3
·	G		2
·	·	50	4
·	·	70	4
·	·	90	1
·	K		2
·	M		2
·	Q		1
·	R		1
·	·	50	4
·	·	70	4
·	·	D	1
·	50		1

5. Subic Marine, Inc. manufactures power packages for the U.S. Navy. An order for 200 power packages has been received. Each power package contains two engines, each of which contains one gearbox; each gearbox contains five gears,

and each gear is forged from high tensile strength steel. The available inventory is as follows:

Engines	13
Gear boxes	22
Gears	215
Steel forges	67

Determine the net requirements for each item.

6. After reviewing reliability data, the production manager in Problem 5 decides that a safety stock of five engines is necessary. What are the new net requirements for each item?

7. A manufacturer of one-half ton trucks offers its customers a number of options. The options available are as follows:

5 engines	15 colors
3 transmissions	4 bodies
2 rear ends	3 frames

How many unique truck configurations are possible? At what level of the product structure would the organization perform its master scheduling?

8. The lead time to purchase a steel spring from a supplier is four weeks. There are currently 42 springs available with an additional scheduled receipt of 20 springs in four weeks. The gross requirements for the steel spring over the next eight weeks are as follows:

Week	1	2	3	4	5	6	7	8
No. of units	12	17	0	14	2	28	9	18

If the order quantity is 20 units, when should orders be released for the spring?

9. An order has been received for 200 units of product *A* with the product structure shown below. If no stock is available or on order, determine the size of each order and when to release each order.

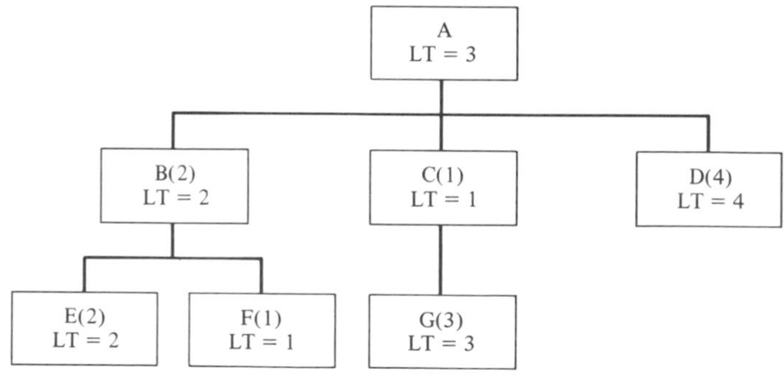

10. An order has been received for 150 units of product A with the product structure shown below. If no stock is available or on order, determine the size of each order and when to release each order.

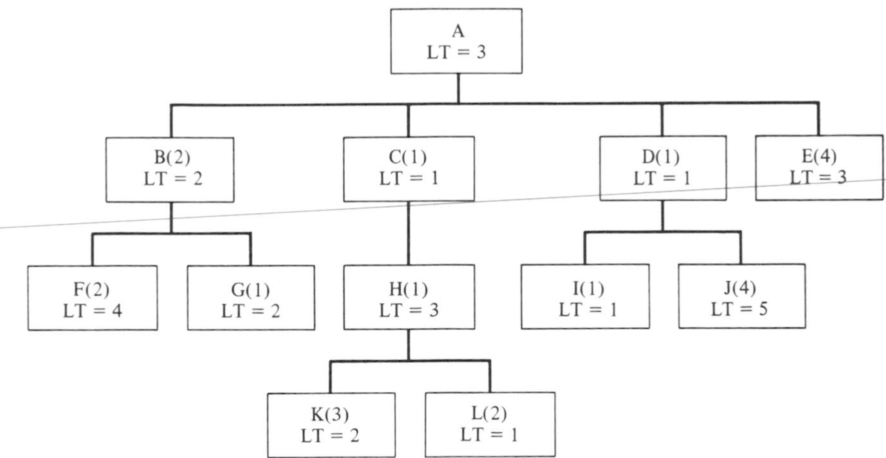

11. Orders have been received for 20 units of product A and 50 units of product R with the product structures shown below for period 8. The on hand stock levels are $A=1$, $R=4$, $B=74$, $C=19$, $D=190$, and $E=160$. What is the low level code for each item? If components are ordered as required (no fixed lot sizes), what should be the size of each order? When should orders be released for each item?

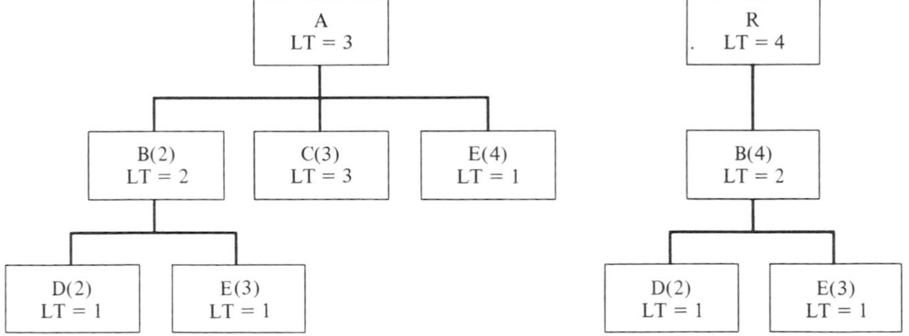

12. The A and B Manufacturing Company produces two products with the product structures shown below. It has orders for 150 units of product A in period 8 and 135 units of product B in period 7. The on hand inventory levels for each item are $A=5$, $B=2$, $C=135$, $D=300$, and $E=356$. When should orders be released for each item, and what should be the size of the order?

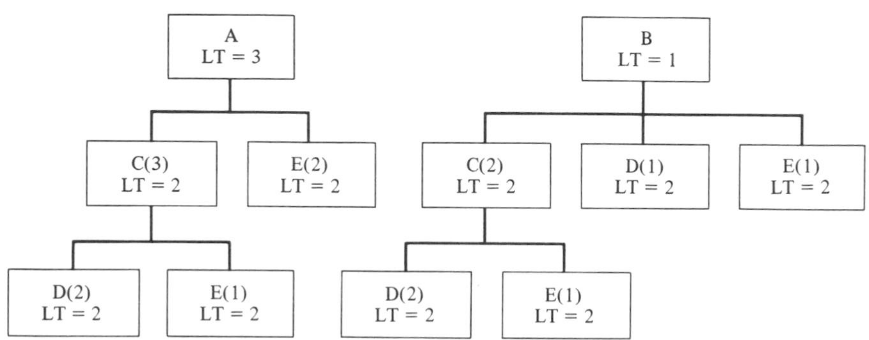

13. The XYZ Corporation assembles three products as shown in the product structures below. It has orders for 50 units of product X for period 8, 20 units of product Y for period 6, and 10 units of product Z for period 7. The on hand stocks of each item are $X=7$, $Y=3$, $Z=2$, $A=3$, $B=12$, $C=30$, $D=3$, and $E=40$. When should each order be placed, and what should be the size of each order?

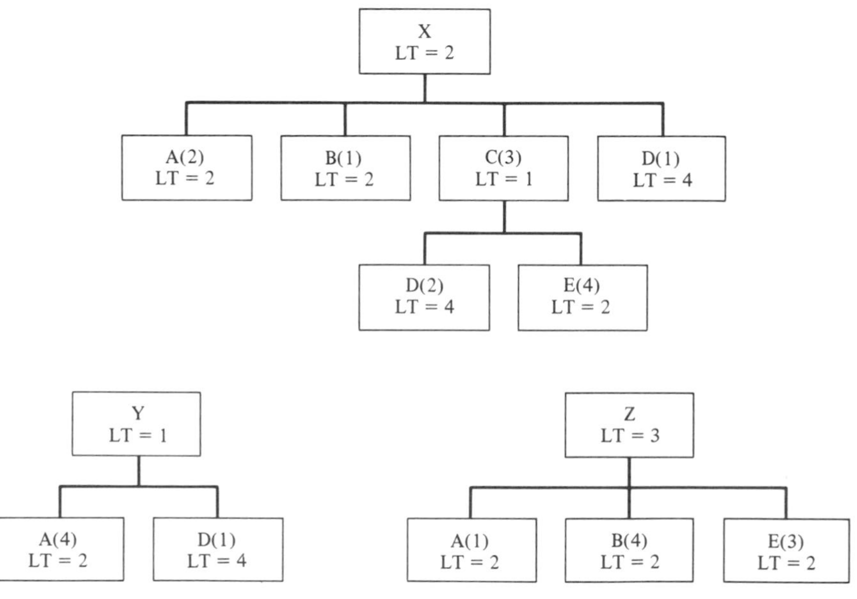

14. Joe Breakdown, the maintenance manager for XYZ Corporation, has just informed you that he will need ten item E's in period 4. How would this change affect the orders planned in Problem 13?

15. The supplier of item E in Problem 13 indicates that its lead time will be one period longer (three periods) due to strike difficulties. What impact will this change have on the delivery of the product orders?

16. An item with a unit purchase cost of \$6.00 has an ordering cost of \$30 and a holding cost fraction of 0.05. What would be the order size for the first and second replenishments using the Silver-Meal Heuristic I (see Appendix A) if the demand pattern is as follows:

Time	0	1	2	3	4	5	6	7	8
Period	1	2	3	4	5	6	7	8	
Demand	15	18	17	20	23	31	22	19	

Assume the first replenishment is at time 0.

17. An item with a unit purchase cost of \$4.00 has an ordering cost of \$20 and a holding cost fraction of 0.04. What would be the order size for the first, second, and third replenishments using the Silver-Meal Heuristic I, given the following demand pattern:

Time	0	1	2	3	4	5	6	7	8
Period	1	2	3	4	5	6	7	8	
Demand	24	18	35	12	16	40	21	37	

The initial replenishment is at time 0.

18. An item with a unit purchase cost of \$3.00 has an ordering cost of \$60 and a holding cost fraction of 0.10. What should be the order size with the Silver-Meal Heuristic II if replenishment is required at time zero and the known demand pattern for the next five months is as follows:

Time	0	1	2	3	4	5
Period	1	2	3	4	5	
Demand	20	15	18	22	31	

19. The ordering cost for an item is \$15 per order, and the holding cost per unit per period is \$.30. Determine the order quantities by the part-period algorithm if the forecasted demand follows the pattern represented by

Period	1	2	3	4	5	6	7	8	9	Total
Demand	7	5	9	8	11	10	9	7	10	76

20. The holding cost per unit per period for an item is $.50, and the order cost is $25 per order. Determine the order quantities by the part-period algorithm from the following schedule of forecasted demand:

Period	1	2	3	4	5	6	7	Total
Demand	5	20	8	11	40	10	6	100

Apply the look-ahead and look-backwards tests to refine the order quantities obtained by the simplified part-period algorithm.

21. Determine the lot sizes from the information given in Problem 20 by Groff's marginal cost algorithm.

CASE 1: SUBVERSION OR TERRITORIAL RIGHTS

Sinthetics Corporation was still attempting to work the "bugs" out of its recently installed computerized MRP system. It had been six months since the system was put into operation. Ed Explode, the production control manager, disagreed with Sue Structure, the computer programmer. It seemed that the two could not agree on the format and design of the reports the computer was to generate. Ed insisted, on behalf of his two production supervisors, that the report be printed with an additional space between lines. Each line represented a separate part number. Sue Structure argued that providing additional space would only increase the cost of the report. Sue exclaimed it would take a very good reason to convince her to modify the reports.

In an attempt to gather additional information for his argument Ed discussed the situation with his supervisors. After meeting several hours with them, he uncovered the real reason behind their request for more space in the report. It seemed the supervisors wanted the extra space so they could write in their own numbers regarding planned production and parts requirements. The supervisors apparently had little faith in the new computerized system. They both had been involved in an earlier system that was a complete failure. As he left his office to meet with Sue, Ed was not sure what position he should take.

1. What strategy would you recommend to Ed Explode?
2. Who should make the decision on the format of the reports?
3. Is the resistance of the supervisors warranted?

CASE 2: TROUBLE DOWN BELOW

Riff Manufacturing was founded twenty-four years ago and until recently had a steady record of growth in sales, assets, and profits. The company manufactures four products, and each product has over twenty options. Until three years ago, profit margins were satisfactory and the company's main objective was growth into other geographical areas. Profit margins have fallen dramatically because of higher production costs and increased competition from foreign firms.

George Riff, the founder and president, faces the additional problem of raising capital for plant expansion into the growing southeastern section of the country. Unfortunately, the company's stock is selling below book value, and interest rates are approaching an all-time high. It was in such an atmosphere that the year-end meeting was called to review the past and draw up plans for the future. After brief presentations by several managers, Mr. Riff asked for a brief statement from the production vice president on their problems in holding down costs. The following is a summary of the points presented:

a. The forecasting techniques developed should produce excellent results. Over capacity in the new computer installation has permitted extensive experimentation with exponentially weighted moving averages.
b. A production plan is now prepared for eighteen months and will be updated quarterly.
c. A master schedule is now prepared for twelve months and will be updated monthly.
d. Inventory remains excessive. Holding costs are high, and the availability of components remains a problem.
e. Manufacturing disruptions and stoppages are common.
f. Purchasing costs are high because of constant rush orders, while deliveries are erratic.

As the production vice president was sitting down, Mr. Riff wondered if their strategies were sufficient to solve the problem.

1. Are the actions by the vice president of production sufficient for effective cost control? Why or why not?
2. What action should be taken on geographical expansion into the southeast?
3. What recommendations would you make to Mr. Riff?

CASE 3: A NEW ARRIVAL

Fun Toys, Inc., has been producing toys for over 50 years. The company was originally started by John Brunch with just a few workers in a workshop behind his general store. Last year sales exceeded 17 million dollars, but only a small profit was reported. Profit performance has been dismal for the last four years. In an effort to improve operations, Richard A. Talent was hired as chief executive officer to return the firm to profitable operations.

Before even meeting his top management team, Mr. Talent walked through the production area and randomly talked with several people without revealing his true identity. One shop foreman told him his major problem was dealing with urgent, very urgent, and super-urgent job orders. Several other foremen indicated a need for a more reliable priority system that didn't change every day. Two workers recalled that there were seldom sufficient components available in inventory to complete a job without resorting to cannibalizing from other orders. A woman in the stockroom complained of undocumented stock removals by foremen on the second shift. Several expediters thought that floor supervisors were hostile toward them without sufficient justification.

As Richard left the production area, several thoughts went through his mind. He wondered what the production manager would say about his operations.

1. What do you perceive as the major problems in the production area?
2. What questions should be asked of the production manager by Richard Talent?
3. If you were the chief executive officer, what actions (if any) would you take? Why?

CASE 4: WILDCAT OPERATIONS

Gulf Coast, Inc. is a Texas manufacturer that engages in the production and distribution of equipment for the oil-producing industry. Gulf Coast is regarded as a competent manufacturer by the petroleum industry and especially so by the front-line production employees, who boast a high rate of success with G.C. products. The confidence shown in Gulf Coast is attributed to the generally faultless field installation of the company's pumping units and the outstanding performance and maintenance records of both the pumping units and the well heads. The major product lines are these two critical pieces of equipment: well heads (casing and tubing types and Christmas-tree assemblies) and pumping units (hydraulic-powered sucker-rod pumps, subsurface hydraulic pumps, and plunger lifts). Gulf Coast is adding another artificial lift to the pump line this year, an electrical submersible centrifugal pump. Production design changes are occurring very rapidly due to technological advances, and additions to the major lines are being made frequently as a result of the dynamic nature of the industry.

The petroleum industry and all its subsections are presently undertaking projects that could drastically alter current operating methods. The industry is in perpetual motion and is investing even more capital in research and development in order to evoke more technological advancement in the future. Gulf Coast is an active participant in the change process. The company is dedicated to improving oil-producing equipment both to retain its competitive edge and to keep abreast of methods that extract the precious resource by the most efficient means.

Other changes occurring in oil-producing equipment and practices are less voluntary but an outcome of external regulations. The EPA, for instance, is becoming a very strong voice against the numerous and disastrous accidents that are plaguing drilling operations. Legislation governing the allowance for depletion is being scrutinized with a view to a reduction in the percentage rate of depletion. Laws are also being enacted to regulate exploration, transport, refinement, and sale of oil products; these newer and stricter measures could have adverse effects. Further, Congress has passed legislation to levy taxes on the income of the producers, i.e. windfall profits. Those particularly vulnerable to such taxation laws appear to be the integrated companies and the independent producers, who are Gulf Coast's largest customers.

Some legislation is on the horizon that could benefit the industry. One such act that could mitigate the onslaught of deleterious regulations is a proposed measure to support secondary recovery methods. Legislation of this type could foster the acquisition of new equipment and supplies. A second move to improve conditions is the American Petroleum Institute's increasing leniency regarding the specifications that have been set as to size, grade, weight per foot, type, etc. of the many casings used throughout the industry.

All factors considered, the industry is experiencing phenomenal growth. The growth of the independent producers is unprecedented. Gulf Coast is in the remarkable position of having sold all the pieces of equipment that it could possibly produce under present conditions for the next two years. With capacity and supplier constraints both being critical, the firm is unable to promise any more equipment within this two year period. However, the firm's management is in hope of increasing the supply by the implementation of an MRP system to replace the fixed order size system now in use.

Gulf Coast executives feel that an MRP system could be a more efficient way to order and control inventory. The present method of ordering every item—even valves, gauges, casings, tubings, etc.—independently is unsatisfactory. Computerized reports are seen as better control devices. In addition, the MRP system is considered to be a superior method for production scheduling. Given the frequent design changes, the increasing costs in the oil-producing industry, and the volatility of the energy related fields, MRP seems to be the safeguard that Gulf Coast management desires. Therefore, a shift to an MRP system appears to be a solution to Gulf Coast's problems of having parts on hand at necessary times and of being able to schedule and deliver by customer due dates.

However, in conjunction with the MRP system, Gulf Coast is also considering a companion system for the spare parts division. Because of the need for a large stock of spare parts, i.e., tubings and casings, for field installations and repairs, Gulf Coast knows it would be an impossibility to supply these needs from a dependent demand system. Thus, it is expected that a scaled-down version of the present EOQ system would be operational for spare parts after implementation of an MRP system to handle orders for finished products.

1. Does Gulf Coast management seem to be considering many of their circumstances as exceptional?
2. What effects does the demand side of the industry have on Gulf Coast's situation?
3. Is an MRP system a practical solution to capacity and supply problems?
4. What purposes could an MRP system serve at Gulf Coast?

SELECTED BIBLIOGRAPHY

Brown, R. G. *Materials Management Systems*, New York: Wiley, 1977.

Orlicky, J. A. *Material Requirements Planning*, New York: McGraw-Hill, 1975.

Orlicky, J. A., et al. "Structuring the Bill of Materials for MRP," *Production and Inventory Management*, December 1972, pp. 19–42.

Plossl, G. W., and O. W. Wight. *Production and Inventory Control*, Englewood Cliffs, NJ: Prentice-Hall, 1967.

Wight, O. W. *Production and Inventory Management in the Computer Age*, Boston: Cahners Books, 1974.

APPENDIX A. MRP LOT SIZING

The lot sizing systems developed for continuous and independent demand items (EOQ, EPQ, and EOI) assume that demand occurs with certainty at a constant rate. Discrete and dependent demand items exhibit time varying demand patterns. Although the static EOQs, EPQs, and EOIs are insensitive (robust) to variations from their underlying assumptions (including demand variations), there are situations where time variations in demand are so pronounced that the constant demand rate assumption is seriously violated.

MRP is proactive in the sense that it attempts to plan for the future. Traditional inventory systems are reactive in that they base future decisions on an analysis of historical data. Reactive systems assume demand is continuous and constant over time with deviations from the average described by a single distribution. These assumptions are not valid when there is trend, seasonality, or lumpiness in demand. Thus, reactive systems are frequently not suitable for MRP.

Even when the demand rate is known with certainty, it may not occur at a constant rate. Such is the case for dependent demand items in an MRP system. Components in an MRP system tend to exhibit a deterministic, time varying demand where the demand pattern varies with time in a known fashion.

Various approaches have been devised to handle varying demand rates. The simplest approach is to ignore the variation and apply the EOQ formulation with an average demand rate. In lot-for-lot ordering, the order for each period is the exact quantity in that period. Wagner and Whitin developed a dynamic programming procedure to determine the optimum varying order size.[4] Silver and Meal developed two heuristic algorithms for order size determination.[5] Groff developed a marginal cost algorithm for lot sizing.[6] The part-period algorithm also derives varying order sizes for varying demand patterns.[7] Several of these approaches will be discussed in subsequent sections herein.

[4]H. M. Wagner, and T. W. Whitin, "Dynamic Version of the Economic Lot Size Model," *Management Science*, Vol. 5, October 1958, pp. 89–96.

[5]E. A. Silver, and H. C. Meal, "A Simple Modification of the EOQ for the Case of Varying Demand Rate," *Production and Inventory Management*, Vol. 10, No. 4, 4th Qtr., 1969, pp. 52–65; E. A. Silver and H. C. Meal, "A Heuristic for Selecting Lot Size Quantities for the Case of a Deterministic Time-Varying Demand Rate and Discrete Opportunities for Replenishment," *Production and Inventory Management*, Vol. 14, No. 2, 2nd Qtr., 1973, pp. 64–74.

[6]G. K. Groff, "A Lot Sizing Rule for Time-Phased Component Demand," *Production and Inventory Management*, Vol. 20, No. 1, 1st Qtr., 1979, pp. 47–53.

[7]J. J. DeMatteis, and A. G. Mendoza, "An Economic Lot Sizing Technique," *IBM Systems Journal*, Vol. 7, 1968, pp. 30–46.

Lot-For-Lot Ordering

Lot-for-lot ordering is the simplest approach of all. Items are purchased in the exact quantities required for each period. There is no forward buying beyond the immediate period. This approach minimizes inventory holding cost, since no items are ever held over from period to period. However, it ignores the costs of placing an order. For very expensive items or items with a highly discontinuous demand, excellent inventory control is maintained. It is also well suited to high-volume, continuous production (assembly lines).

Wagner-Whitin Algorithm

An algorithm is a procedure which will lead to a solution of a given problem by a repetitive process. An algorithm is more complex than solving an equation, and it requires considerably more computation. The Wagner-Whitin algorithm obtains an optimum solution to the deterministic dynamic order size problem over a finite horizon with the requirement that all period demands must be satisfied. The time periods in the planning horizons must be of a fixed determinate length, and orders are to be placed to assure the arrival of the goods at the beginning of a time period.

The Wagner-Whitin algorithm is a dynamic programming approach which uses several theorems to simplify the computations. The algorithm proceeds in a forward direction to determine the minimum controllable cost policy. The Wagner-Whitin algorithm will provide for minimum cost determination, but it is not widely accepted in practice because of the considerable amount of computation required. The procedure is mathematically too involved for a detailed description here. The complexity of the procedure inhibits its understanding by the layman and acts as an obstacle to its adoption in practice. An inherent weakness of the algorithm lies in its assumption that demands beyond the planning horizons are zero. The algorithm will not be developed herein, but the interested reader is directed to the originating article previously footnoted.

Silver-Meal Heuristic Algorithms

Edward Silver and Harlan Meal developed two heuristic algorithms for selecting order sizes for deterministic time-varying demand rates. The two algorithms, which are very similar, differ only in when replenishments are made. The one algorithm permits replenishments to be made at any point in time, and the other permits replenishments only at the beginning of a discrete time period. The Silver-Meal algorithms do not ensure an optimal solution, but they have been proven to provide results almost as good as the Wagner-Whitin algorithm. They are also not so computationally demanding as the Wagner-Whitin algorithm. The term "Silver-Meal Heuristic I" will be used for the algorithm with replenishment at any time, and "Silver-Meal Heuristic II" for the algorithm with beginning-of-period replenishment.

Silver-Meal Heuristic I

It is assumed that the demand rate can be different for each period, but the rate is constant during a given period. An order will be placed at time zero, and the length of time (measured in periods) that the replenishment will last is T. The selection of T will be such that

$$T=\sqrt{\frac{2C}{PhR_T}},$$

where

R_T = demand rate at time T in units per period,
C = order cost per order in dollars,
h = holding cost fraction per period,
P = unit purchase cost.

The order interval for the case of constant demand is as follows:

$$T=\sqrt{\frac{2C}{PhR}}.$$

In order to determine the time supply which should be ordered when a replenishment is required, the radical is removed by squaring each side, and the following relationship results:

$$T^2R_T=\frac{2C}{Ph}.$$

The calculations are performed iteratively by calculating the left side of the equation for steadily increasing integer values of T until

$$T^2R_T\geq\frac{2C}{Ph}$$

for the first time in period k. Then the equation

$$T=\sqrt{\frac{2C}{PhR_k}}$$

is solved to obtain the time supply. Figure A-1 contains a flow diagram of the algorithm. A simple example can illustrate the technique.

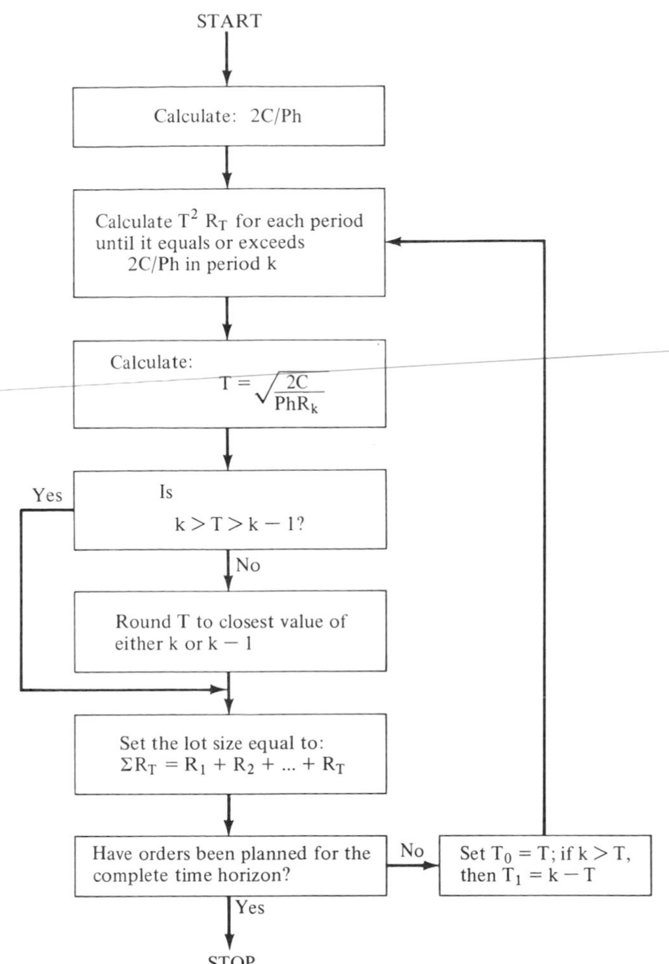

Figure A-1. Silver-Meal Heuristic I.

EXAMPLE A-1

An item has cost parameters such that $2C/Ph = 290$. What should be the order size with the Silver-Meal Heuristic I if replenishment is required at time zero and the known demand pattern for the next six months is as follows:

Time	0	1	2	3	4	5	6
Period	1	2	3	4	5	6	
Demand	8	12	15	20	70	170	

For

$$T=1, \quad R_T=8, \quad T^2R_T=1(8) <290,$$
$$T=2, \quad R_T=12, \quad T^2R_T=4(12) <290,$$
$$T=3, \quad R_T=15, \quad T^2R_T=9(15) <290,$$
$$T=4, \quad R_T=20, \quad T^2R_T=16(20)>290.$$

The T-value must be in the range between 3 and 4 periods;

$$T=\sqrt{\frac{2C}{PhR_k}}=\sqrt{\frac{290}{20}}=3.81.$$

The order size for the first replenishment at time zero is the quantity that will last 3.81 periods, or $8+12+15+0.81(20)=51$ units.

EXAMPLE A-2

From the information given in Example A-1, what is the size of the second replenishment?

The first replenishment lasts until 3.81 periods, which becomes $T=0$ for the second replenishment. For

$$T=0.19, \quad R_T=20, \quad T^2R_T=(0.19)^2 20<290,$$
$$T=1.19, \quad R_T=70, \quad T^2R_T=(1.19)^2 70<290,$$
$$T=2.19, \quad R_T=170, \quad T^2R_T=(2.19)^2 170>290.$$

The T-value must be between 1.19 and 2.19 periods:

$$T=\sqrt{\frac{2C}{PhR_k}}=\sqrt{\frac{290}{170}}=1.31.$$

The order size for the second replenishment is the demand from time 3.81 to 5.12 (3.81+1.31), or $0.19(20)+70+0.12(170)=94$ units.

Silver-Meal Heuristic II

The heuristic developed in the last section (Silver-Meal Heuristic I) allowed replenishments to be at any point in time. This is not valid if all the stock needed during a period must be on hand at the beginning of the period. In this section, an algorithm will be outlined for replenishments to occur at the beginning of a period. It will be assumed that the demand rate can be different for each period, but the rate is constant during a given period.

An order will be placed at time zero, and the length of time (measured in periods) that the replenishment will last is T. The order size can be

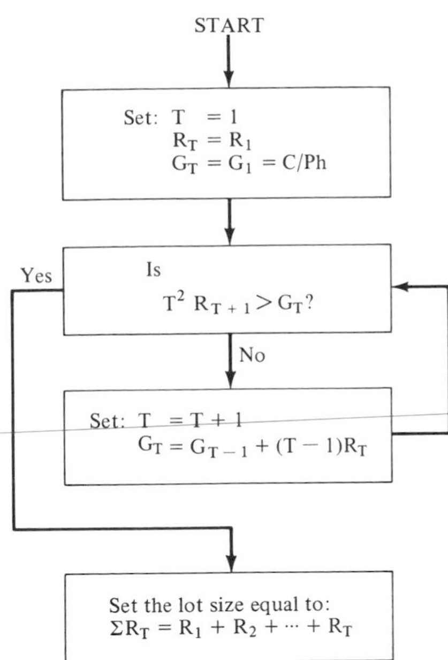
START
Set: T = 1
RT = R1
GT = G1 = C/Ph
Is
T2 RT+1 > GT?
Yes
No
Set: T = T + 1
GT = GT−1 + (T − 1)RT
Set the lot size equal to:
ΣRT = R1 + R2 + ··· + RT

Figure A-2. Silver-Meal Heuristic II.

determined by combining the demands that occur during the length of time T. Figure A-2 contains a flow diagram of the algorithm, where

T = time duration that current replenishment will last,

C = order cost per order,

h = holding cost fraction per period,

P = unit purchase cost.

A simple example will illustrate the procedure.

EXAMPLE A-3

An item has cost parameters such that $C/Ph = 145$. What should be the order size with Silver-Meal Heuristic II if replenishment is required at time zero and the known demand pattern for the next 6 months is as follows:

Time	0	1	2	3	4	5	6
Period	1	2	3	4	5	6	
Demand	8	12	15	20	70	170	

$$\begin{aligned}
T=1,\quad & R_{T+1}=12,\quad G_T=C/PF=145,\\
& T^2R_{T+1}=(1)12=12<145;\\
T=2,\quad & R_{T+1}=15,\quad G_T=G_{T-1}+(T-1)R_T=145+(1)12=157,\\
& T^2R_{T+1}=4(15)=60<157;\\
T=3,\quad & R_{T+1}=20,\quad G_T=G_{T-1}+(T-1)R_T=157+2(15)=187,\\
& T^2R_{T+1}=9(20)=180<187;\\
T=4,\quad & R_{T+1}=70,\quad G_T=G_{T-1}+(T-1)R_T=187+3(20)=247,\\
& T^2R_{T+1}=16(70)=1120>247.
\end{aligned}$$

Since $T^2R_{T+1}>G_T$ for the first time when $T=4$, the replenishment order quantity is $8+12+15+20=55$ units. Another replenishment order will be required when the first is depleted at the beginning of $T=5$.

The Silver-Meal algorithms are simple heuristics for selecting replenishment quantities under conditions of deterministic time-varying demand. While optimal order quantities are not assumed, the procedure will outperform the EOQ rule and approach the optimality of the Wagner-Whitin algorithm with much less effort.

Part-Period Algorithm

The part-period algorithm can determine order sizes under conditions of known but varying demand rates. While the algorithm does not ensure optimality, it does compare well with optimal techniques. Whereas traditional order size formulas equate holding cost and order cost to determine the order size, this algorithm equates order and holding cost derived part-periods to generated part-periods.

A generated part-period value for an item is the number of parts held in inventory multiplied by the number of time periods over which the parts are held. If one part is held in inventory for one period, it incurs a particular holding cost; if it is held two periods, it incurs twice the holding cost. Two parts held one period incur the same holding cost as one part held two periods and so forth. In calculating the generated part-period value, it is assumed that no holding costs are incurred for items consumed in the period in which they arrive.

To express the order cost and holding cost in part-periods, it is necessary to divide the order cost by the holding cost per part per period. The order cost and holding cost part-periods are referred to as the derived part-period value. The derived part-period value is the number of part-periods it takes to make order cost and holding cost equal. A generated part-period value is

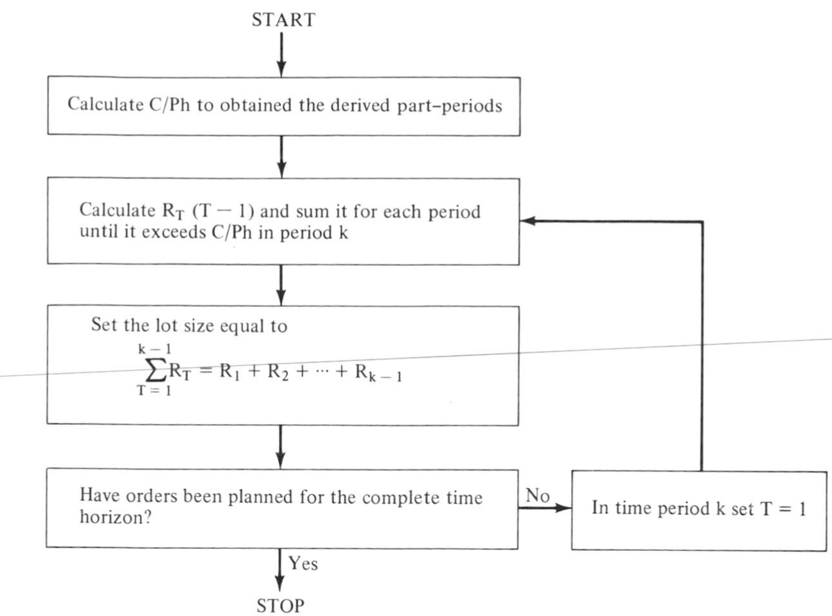
START
Calculate C/Ph to obtained the derived part–periods
Calculate R_T (T − 1) and sum it for each period until it exceeds C/Ph in period k
Set the lot size equal to
$\sum_{T=1}^{k-1} R_T = R_1 + R_2 + \cdots + R_{k-1}$
Have orders been planned for the complete time horizon?
No
In time period k set T = 1
Yes
STOP

Figure A-3. Simplified part-period algorithm.

obtained by accumulating part-periods over the demand time horizons for one or more periods. When the generated part-period value is first greater than the derived part-period value, an order should be placed. The order quantity will be the accumulated demand up to the time period for the next order.

Figure A-3 contains a flow diagram of the logic. The following example will illustrate the procedure.

EXAMPLE A-4

The ordering cost for an item is $25 per order, and the holding cost per unit per period is $.25. Determine the order quantities by the part-period algorithm from the following demand:

Period	1	2	3	4	5	6	7	8	9	Total
Demand	15	20	25	35	30	10	12	16	25	188

$$\text{Derived part-period value} = \frac{25}{0.25} = 100 \text{ part-periods.}$$

Table A-1

Period	1	2	3	4	5	6	7	8	9	Total
Demand	15	20	25	35	30	10	12	16	25	188
Generated part-periods	0	1(20)	2(25)	3(35) 0	1(30)	2(10)	3(12)	4(16) 0	1(25)	
Cumulative part-periods	0	20	70	175	30	50	86	150	25	
Order size	60			87				41		188

Table A-1 develops the part-period strategy assuming a nearly zero lead time. Whenever the cumulative generated part-period value is greater than the derived part-period value of 100, an order is indicated.

The cumulative part-periods exceed 100 in periods 4 and 8. The first order quantity for period 1 is 60 (15+20+25) units. The second order quantity for period 4 is 87 (35+30+10+12) units. The third order quantity for period 8 cannot be determined until further demand data are available, so it is set at the remaining demand of 41 units. The different order sizes indicate the dynamic nature of the algorithm.

Look-ahead and look-backward refinements: When demands do not vary widely between periods, the simplified part-period algorithm outlined in Example A-4 performs very well.[8] However, where the demand variation is large, a refined part-period version of the algorithm can improve performance and overall accuracy. The look-ahead and look-backward features are added to account for wide demand variations. In the refined version, the part-period algorithm goes through the same calculations indicated for the simple (unrefined) version. However, the look-ahead and look-backward tests are applied to the tentative order period to determine if it is faced with large demand in the immediate future or immediate past.

The look-ahead and look-backward features are intended to prevent stock covering peak demands from being carried for extended periods of time, and to avoid orders being keyed to periods with low demands. The adjustments are made only when they improve conditions. The look-ahead test is made first. If it fails, the look-backward test is made. If both tests fail, no

[8]The part-period algorithm without the look-ahead and look-backward refinements is also termed the least total cost (LTC) approach by some authors.

additional action is taken and the orders from the simplified part-period algorithm are implemented.

The look-ahead test looks at the next periods beyond the tentative order period to see if there are any unusual demands coming. The steps are as follows:

1. Determine tentative order period by the simplified part-period algorithm.
2. Look ahead at the demand in the next period:
   a. If the demand in the next period is less than the part-period value in the tentative order period, the tentative order period is accepted.
   b. If the demand in the next period equals or exceeds the part-period value in the tentative order period and that part-period value is less than the derived part-period value, the order period is moved ahead to the next period. Otherwise, the tentative order period is accepted.
   c. The look-ahead test is repeated in successive periods until it fails.

The look-backward test is not invoked if the look-ahead test moves the order to a future period. If the look-ahead test does not move the order ahead, the look-back test is applied as follows:

1. Multiply the demand in the tentative order period by 2.
   a. If demand in the previous period is less, the tentative order period is accepted.
   b. If demand in the previous period is larger, the order period is moved back one period.

Although the look-ahead and look-backward tests are not infallible, they add precision when demand is fluctuating violently.

EXAMPLE A-5

The ordering cost for an item is \$100 per order, and the holding cost per unit per period is \$1.00. Determine the order quantities by the part-period algorithm from the following demand:

Period	1	2	3	4	5	Total
Demand	10	95	10	95	10	220

$$\text{Derived part-period value} = \frac{\$100.00}{\$1.00} = 100 \text{ part-periods.}$$

Table A-2 develops the part-period strategy assuming a near-zero lead time. Apply the look-ahead test to period 3: The demand in the next period 4 is 95 units, and the

Table A-2

Period	1	2	3	4	5	Total
Demand	10	95	10	95	10	220
Generated part-periods	0	1(95)	2(10)			
Cumulative part-periods	0	95	115			
Orders without look-ahead	105		105		10	220
Tentative cumulative costs	100	195	295	390	490	
Orders with look-ahead	115			105		220
Final cumulative costs	100	195	215	315	325	

part-period value in the tentative-order period 3 is 20. Since the demand in period 4 is greater than the part-period value for period 3 (95>20), the order is moved to period 4 and the order quantity for period 1 is increased to 115 units. Since the look-ahead test has not failed, it must be applied to the next period, which is period 5. Since the demand in period 5 is less than the part-period value for period 4 (10<285), the look-ahead test has finally failed. Since the look-ahead test was successful for period 4, the look-backward test need not be applied.

EXAMPLE A-6

The ordering cost for an item is $100 per order, and the holding cost per unit per period is $1.00. Determine the order quantities by the part-period algorithm from the following demand:

Period	1	2	3	4	5	Total
Demand	10	20	40	10	20	100

$$\text{Derived part-periods value} = \frac{100}{1.00} = 100 \text{ part-periods.}$$

Table A-3 develops the part-period strategy assuming a near-zero lead time.

Table A-3

Period	1	2	3	4	5	Total
Demand	10	20	40	10	20	100
Generated part-periods	0	1(20)	2(40)	3(10)	1(20)	
Cumulative part-periods	0	20	100	130	20	
Orders without look-back	70			30		100
Tentative cumulative cost	100	120	200	300	320	
Orders with look-back	30		70			100
Final cumulative cost	100	120	220	230	270	

Applying the look-ahead test to period 4: The demand in the next period 5 is 20 units, and the part-period value in the tentative order period 4 is 30, so the order is not moved ahead.

Applying the look-back test to period 4: Two times the demand in the tentative order period is 20, and it is less than the demand in period 3 of 40, so the order period is moved back to period 3. The order size for period 1 is 30 units (10+20). The order size for period 3 needs additional demand data, so it is set at the remaining demand of 70 units (40+10+20).

Groff's Marginal Cost Algorithm

The part-period algorithm equated total ordering and holding costs in establishing a lot size. Another approach is to equate marginal rather than total costs. Gene Groff developed a marginal cost algorithm that is illustrated in Figure A-4. The demand for a future time period is added to the lot size as long as the marginal cost increase (holding cost for the period) is less than the marginal cost decrease (ordering cost for the period).

The marginal cost decrease (saving) from adding the Tth period's demand to the lot size is the decrease in ordering cost. The marginal cost decrease is the ordering cost if T periods are ordered minus the ordering cost if $T-1$

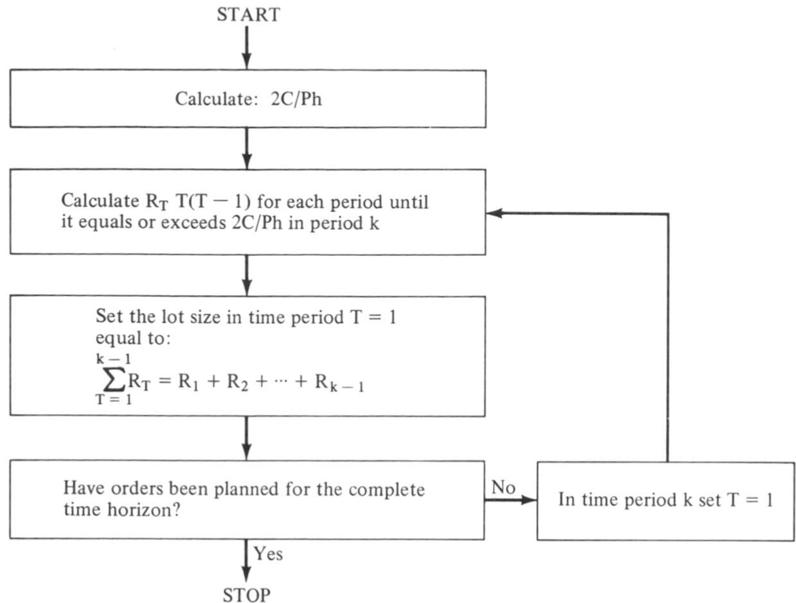
START
Calculate: 2C/Ph
Calculate R_T T(T − 1) for each period until it equals or exceeds 2C/Ph in period k
Set the lot size in time period T = 1 equal to:
k−1
ΣR_T = R_1 + R_2 + ··· + R_k−1
T = 1
Have orders been planned for the complete time horizon?
No
In time period k set T = 1
Yes
STOP

Figure A-4. Groff's marginal cost algorithm.

periods are ordered, or

$$\text{Marginal cost decrease} = \frac{C}{T-1} - \frac{C}{T} = \frac{C}{T(T-1)}.$$

The marginal cost increase from adding the Tth period's demand to the lot size is the increase in holding costs, or

$$\text{Marginal cost increase} = \frac{R_T Ph}{2}$$

The demand for the Tth future period is added if the marginal cost increase is less than the marginal cost decrease. Thus, add the Tth period demand if:

$$\frac{R_T Ph}{2} < \frac{C}{T(T-1)}.$$

By rearranging terms the following expression is obtained:

$$R_T T(T-1) < \frac{2C}{Ph},$$

where

C = ordering cost per order,
P = unit purchase cost,
h = holding cost fraction per period,
T = number of periods in advance of the current period,
R_T = demand in the Tth future period.

The following example will illustrate the use of the algorithm.

EXAMPLE A-7

An item has cost parameters such that $2C/Ph = 400$. For the demand pattern listed below, determine the lot sizes by the marginal cost algorithm.

Period	1	2	3	4	5	6	7	8	9
Demand	80	100	125	100	25	0	100	125	125

Table A-4 develops the lot sizing strategy based on a nearly zero lead time. The lot sizes are 180 units for period 1, 250 units for period 3, and 225 units for period 7. No lot size can be determined for period 9 until more demand data are available.

Table A-4

Period	1	2	3	4	5	6	7	8	9
R_T	80	100	125	100	25	0	100	125	125
$R_T T(T-1)$	0	200	750						
Lot 1	180								
T			1	2	3	4	5		
$R_T T(T-1)$			0	200	150	0	2000		
Lot 2			250						
T							1	2	3
$R_T T(T-1)$							0	250	750
Lot 3							225		

Conclusion

Several optimum-seeking approaches for determining lot sizes when the demand rate is not constant have been outlined. None of the algorithms, with the exception of the Wagner-Whitin, will assure an optimal solution for time-varying demand patterns. The Wagner-Whitin dynamic programming algorithm, which does minimize cost for a deterministic, fixed horizon demand series, is complex and sensitive to changes in planned requirements and planned horizons. Thus, various heuristic procedures have been developed for component lot sizing with MRP. These heuristic approaches are computationally simpler, but they do not ensure optimality. Each starts with the present period (period 1) and scans each successive period until a stopping criterion is met. Then an order is placed to satisfy requirements up to or through the stopping period. The procedure is then repeated for periods beyond the stopping period. Orders for subsequent periods are planned by reapplying the logic. Ordering cost is charged each time an order is placed, and holding cost is usually charged at the beginning of each period for each unit carried forward from the previous period.

For a product with many assembly levels, differing and fluctuating lot sizes at a high level in the product structure may create difficulties in lot sizing at lower levels. None of the approaches considers multi-item or multilevel costs. These costs should be considered in selecting a lot-sizing method. All of the approaches are myopic in the sense that they consider only one item at a time.

9 In-Process Inventory

The primary focus of this text so far has been on finished goods, raw materials, and supplies. Another important category deals with semifinished products known as in-process goods. It represents partially completed final products that are still in the production process. Work has been started on the product but has not been completed. Further processing steps are required before it becomes available. In-process inventory serves to smooth and balance the flow between successive manufacturing operations. Such balance is desirable if high utilization of manpower and equipment is to be maintained.

In-process goods are an inventory category peculiar to organizations that manufacture or produce a physical product. Particularly in organizations that manufacture products to order, in-process goods may represent 50% of the total inventory investment. In-process inventory is the accumulation of direct material, direct labor, and applied manufacturing overhead costs of products in the manufacturing process. The accumulation of these costs *begins* with the transfer of the raw materials to production and *ends* with the movement of completed products into storage or shipping.

In-process inventory provides production economies in terms of capacity utilization. It protects against underutilization of manpower and facilities. Idle workers and facilities represent a loss of productivity. There are opposing costs involved: too little work in process results in underutilization costs, while too much results in excessive inventory costs.

Continuous production processes use sequences of operations that are inseparably tied together. The output rates of the operations are the same, so little in-process inventory is present. This is usually characteristic of assembly lines with balanced operations. The major disadvantage of assembly lines is their inflexibility. If one operation runs out of material or breaks down, the whole line must sit idle until material is supplied or equipment is repaired. *Intermittent production processes* perform a variety of operations in an independent manner. Not all orders require the same number or type of operations. These production processes decouple their operations and have a queue of orders that permit them to function efficiently and independently. The cost of independence is a queue of in-process inventory. In-process inventory control is a minor problem in continuous production processes, but it is a major problem in intermittent production processes.

A job shop is a classical example of an intermittent production process. It produces a wide variety of products with significant product differentiation. Adequate in-process inventory is required to keep work at each work station. As a result of this, process time (time when productive operations are performed) is small in relation to the total time needed to complete an order. An order spends most of its time waiting to be processed. When direct labor and equipment utilization are maximized in a job shop, it incurs other penalties such as:

1. high in-process inventory,
2. long manufacturing cycle time,

3. a complex and costly production control system,
4. high materials movement cost,
5. high floor space requirement for work-in-process storage and movement.

The economies of in-process inventory are primarily derived when the rate of flow of orders between work stations cannot be controlled. When these rates can be controlled at "gateway" work stations or "bottleneck" work stations, the amount of in-process inventory is determined by the control of inputs to these stations. If perfect control is possible, the proper amount is very small (near zero). At "intermediary" work stations where the degree of control is not as certain, the need for in-process inventory is much greater. Many make-to-order firms could benefit from an inventory reduction, but at some point these benefits are outweighed by utilization costs.

In-process inventory is found mainly in manufacturing. It compensates for the irregular rate of flow of work in process. It protects against work stoppages. It generally occurs because of the different output rates of operations. When successive operations do not produce at exactly the same output rate, in-process inventory results. Controlling work in process is largely a matter of moving orders through production as fast as possible. Excess in-process inventory increases the manufacturing cycle time and represents a costly investment.

Some organizations maintain in-process inventory so there is always enough to be worked on in order to maximize labor and machine utilization. This approach clearly tends to inflate inventory. If carried to an extreme, it can be detrimental to scheduling and actually increase product costs because:

1. With more work-in-process, lead times will tend to increase.
2. With longer lead times, the likelihood of priority changes to shop orders increases. If priorities are changed too frequently, setup costs become excessive and output decreases.

If having too much is inefficient and having too little is costly, what is the right amount of inventory? The answer lies in an understanding of the purpose of inventory that is in queue (orders waiting to be worked on). Queue acts as a buffer between the changing rates of various operations in the production process. The object is to make the orders flow as steadily as possible. The steadier the order flow, the less queue is required. If the flow is very uneven, then more orders will be required in the queue.

By reducing in-process inventory, it is possible to also have the additional benefit of a reduced finished goods inventory. Reduced work in process shortens the cycle time required to get a unit through the manufacturing process. With faster cycle time, it may be possible to build to order rather than depend upon finished goods inventory. In any event, smaller safety stocks of finished goods are required with a shorter cycle time. Reduced work in process means reduced cycle time, reduced need for finished goods inventory, better process control, and better use of resources. The overall effect is a reduction in operating costs and operating assets which increases the return on assets (an important measure of productivity).

It is likely that the total cost function of in-process inventory is U-shaped. A small to moderate amount results in exponential savings (from increased plant and manpower utilization). At some point or range, total costs are minimized. Additional increases result in a rapid rise in costs. To go beyond qualitative statements requires quantification of the total cost function. Because of the intricacies of most shop operations, this is very difficult without direct experimentation or simulation analysis. Specification of the underlying cost functions depends on the particular firm's economic environment, shop configuration, and scheduling practices.

LEAD TIME

Lead time can take on many meanings. It may apply to individual items or operations, one at a time or collectively. The total time required to procure all raw materials and purchased components, process them, test them, and package the finished product is the *production cycle time*. The total manufacturing time needed to perform all necessary operations in the plant from the start of the earliest to the completion of the last is the *manufacturing cycle time*. Each of these is the sum of many individual lead times.

The manufacturing lead time is the time elapsed between the release of an order and its completion. It consists of five elements: setup time, process time, move time, wait time, and queue time. The greatest portion of lead time (sometimes up to 90%) usually comes from queue time, which is the time a job spends waiting because another order is being processed.

To reduce in-process inventory levels, under the assumption that material cost and labor cost are adequately controlled, it is necessary to reduce the *manufacturing cycle time*. This is the time a job or order spends in the manufacturing process.[1] If the cycle time is reduced, the in-process inventory investment will be decreased in direct proportion.

As shown in Figure 1, the manufacturing cycle time comprises the following five elements:

1. *Setup time*. The material, machine, or work center is prepared for an operation.
2. *Process time*. The productive operations are performed.
3. *Move time*. Transportation occurs from storage, to storage, or between work centers.
4. *Wait time*. Material is waiting to be moved to its next location.

[1] The cycle time is also referred to as the "flow time" or "manufacturing lead time" by some authors.

Figure 1. Manufacturing cycle time.

5. *Queue time*. Material waits because another order is being processed at a work center.

The process time represents a small fraction of the manufacturing cycle time for most orders. The queue time is usually larger than the combination of all the other time elements. Therefore the major opportunity for reducing the cycle time is to reduce the queue time. Typical reasons for orders being delayed are as follows:

1. waiting for machine or work center availability,
2. waiting to be moved,
3. waiting to be inspected,
4. hot jobs get priority,
5. shortages of tools, materials, or information,
6. machine breakdown,
7. absenteeism.

All of the above reasons for delay are directly or indirectly related to inadequate planning and scheduling. To reduce delay, it is necessary to plan and schedule operations more efficiently.

For a specific order or job, the queue time is also a function of its priority. A high priority order will spend less time in queues and have a shorter manufacturing cycle time. Thus, priorities can dramatically affect an order's manufacturing cycle time in either direction. High priority orders leapfrog all or part of existing queues, which compresses their cycle time, but this tends to expand the cycle time of lower priority orders.

Reduction in investment for in-process inventory is directly proportional to manufacturing cycle time. Queue time, the major constituent of manufacturing cycle time, can best be reduced by eliminating physical backlogs in production. Backlogs can be reduced by better scheduling of operations and planning of the release of work to production. Reduction of the backlog or queue at each work center results in parts waiting less time for their "turn" to be worked, and the final effect is improved turnover of the cash investment in inventory.

Manufacturing lead time should be considered a variable for management to control instead of a constant. Shortening it can improve customer service, reduce inventory costs, and shave product costs. Shorter lead times improve responsiveness to schedule changes thereby softening the effects of forecasting errors and economic cycles. The size of in-process inventory is related to lead times. A reduction of lead times reduces this inventory and may improve schedule performance. Whether it does help schedule performance depends on how much in-process inventory the organization is carrying. If it is excessive, the priorities of orders probably change frequently. This results in excessive setups and teardowns that reduce throughput and raise product costs.

The work through a shop is limited by its capacity. An order should not be released into the shop unless the capacity *and* the material for the job are available. Increasing the input without increasing capacity will increase the manufacturing cycle time. If an organization has a capacity problem, there is a temptation to increase the lead time. This action would only result in larger in-process inventory, which would tend to be counterproductive. The answer is to solve the capacity problem, not lengthen the lead time.

The lead time stretches as the backlog grows. To control the lead time, it is necessary to control the backlog. To control the backlog, release no more work into a facility than it has shown it can turn out. When the output consistently falls short of the input, either an expansion of capacity or a reduction of input is necessary. Managing lead times can provide an enormous competitive edge through lower costs and faster responses.

TIME CYCLE CHARTS

A time cycle chart shows how much time it would take to produce a product starting from scratch with no inventories available. It indicates lead time requirements as well as the minimum planning horizon for the master schedule. If customer delivery is to be made in less than the maximum time on the time cycle chart, inventories must be maintained.

Each material, component, and assembly requires some lead time. Starting with the final product, the time cycle chart works backwards through each manufacturing step, assembly operation, and purchase to map the time relationships. A typical time cycle chart is shown in Figure 2. Product 1 is assembled from subassemblies 2 and 6 and purchased part 21. Subassembly 2 consists of manufactured components 3, 4, and 5, which in turn are made from purchased parts 22, 23, and 24 respectively. Similarly, subassembly 6 consists of manufactured components 7 and 8 and purchased part 27. Manufactured components 7 and 8 are made from purchased parts 25 and 26 respectively. The bottleneck item is purchased part 25, which sets the no inventory lead time at approximately 22 weeks.

Obviously, an organization must have inventories if it is going to offer customer delivery in less than 22 weeks for the product shown in Figure 2. If the organization is going to offer instantaneous customer service, inventory of the finished product must be maintained. If customer service time is not instantaneous, inventory of the finished product should not be maintained,

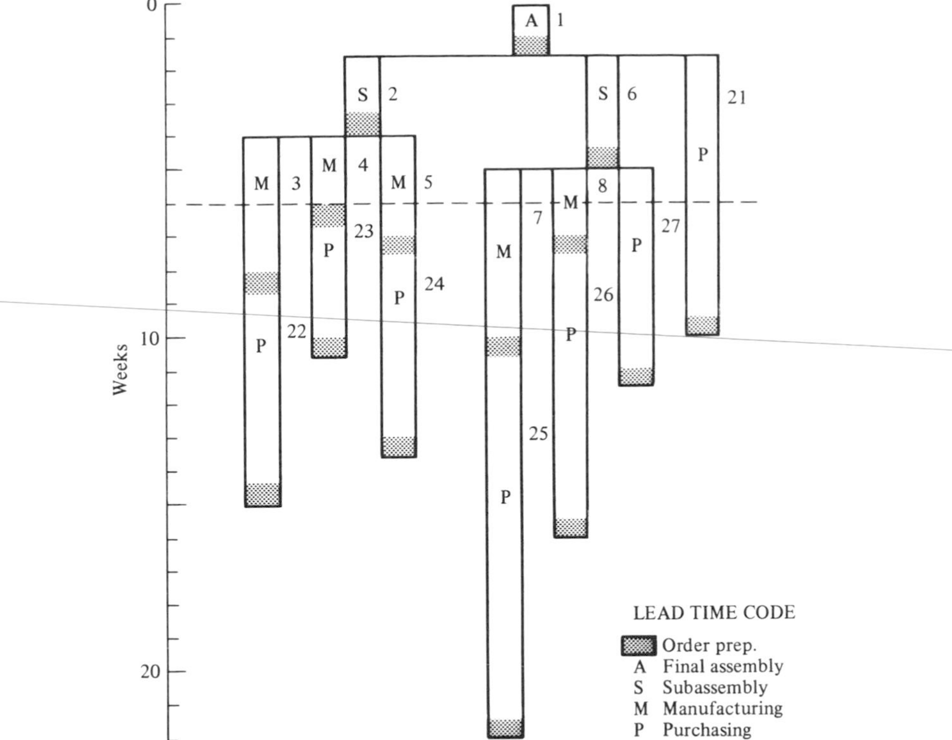

Figure 2. Time cycle chart.

since it frequently includes large production costs which should not be incurred until a firm demand exists.

Suppose a six week lead time is available to all customers who purchase the finished product in Figure 2. Inventories could be maintained at every stage of manufacture and assembly, as well as for each purchased part, but there is an easier way that involves less control and smaller inventories. Stocks are maintained for only a few critical items; others are purchased or manufactured only when there is a definite demand for them. To determine the critical inventory items, a horizontal line is drawn across the time cycle chart at six weeks. The critical items are those items that are crossed by the horizontal line. In Figure 2, the critical items are 3, 4, 5, 7, 8, 21, and 27. The first five critical items are manufactured parts, and the last two are purchased parts. (If there were a ten week sales lead time, there would be a different group of critical items.)

How can the lead time be reduced? And once reduced, how can it be controlled? The best solution is by input/output control. The input to a facility must be equal to or less than the output. Input/output control stabilizes the lead time so in-process inventory can be managed more effectively. The problem many organizations encounter that do not use input/ouput control is that they often release more into the shop than is coming out. This action leads to large queues, which result in large backlogs and consequently long lead times. Many organizations do not realize the importance of controlling input into a facility, but (along with the control of output) it must be done if lead times are to be reduced and controlled. Only by reducing input in reference to output can lead times be reduced. By holding orders in production control until the last possible moment, input/output control spares the shop the ridiculous task of trying to do more work than is possible. It helps keep priorities valid, and only those orders that are really needed are actually worked on.

INPUT/OUTPUT CONTROL

Input/output control regulates (1) the flow of work into a work center by comparing actual input with planned input, and (2) the flow of work from a work center by comparing actual output with planned output. The objective is to highlight deviations before they become acute. Minor divergences are to be expected as work progresses. Delays and disruptions are corrected so the *average input* of new jobs does not differ substantially from the *average output* of completed jobs. If work is released that exceeds the output of completed jobs, backlogs will develop and lead times will increase. If work is released that is less than the output of completed jobs, the backlog will drop and the lead time will be reduced.

It should be noted that the input rate cannot really be "controlled" at any work center except an entry (gateway) work center. Here, work is fed in, and it is possible to increase or decrease the input rate. At subsequent work centers, the input rate is controlled by regulating the output rates at the feeding work centers.

Figure 3 shows an input/output report for a typical job shop work center. The *planned input* of jobs to a work center includes both released ("open") orders that have not arrived yet and unreleased ("planned") orders. The *planned output* is the objective or available capacity for the period, and it equals the planned input plus or minus any desired change in the backlog. The *actual input* is simply the standard hours of work that have arrived. The *actual output* is simply the standard hours of work completed. The *planned backlog* is the previous period's planned backlog plus the planned input minus the planned output. The *actual backlog* is the previous period's actual backlog plus the actual input minus the actual output.

The report in Figure 3 is in abbreviated form: in practice it typically would extend for 12 or more weeks. The planned output rate is 600 hours per week for the first four weeks and thereafter 540 hours per week. The

Work Center 5

Week	12	13	14	15	16	17	18	19	20	21
Planned input	540	540	540	540	540	540	540	540	540	540
Actual input	540	530	500							
Cumulative deviation	0	−10	−50							
Planned output	600	600	600	600	540	540	540	540	540	540
Actual output	610	520	600							
Cumulative deviation	+10	−70	−70							
Planned backlog	180	120	60	0	0	0	0	0	0	0
Actual backlog	170	180	80							

Figure 3. Input/output report. All quantities are in standard hours. There was a released backlog of 240 hours at work center 5 at the beginning of week 12.

planned input rate is 540 hours per week as far as the plan goes. The planned output of 600 for the first four weeks is higher than the planned input of 540. This is intended to reduce the existing backlog by 240 standard hours. The latest week for which data are available is week 14. The report clearly indicates whether or not the backlog is building. It measures capacity in total hours rather than late orders in the work center.

Figure 4 shows an input/output report for another work station. Work center 11 is not an entry point (a starting or gateway work center) for orders, but receives its inputs from the outputs of other work centers. It is a secondary or downstream work center. Against a planned average output rate of 220 standard hours, actual output has fallen short by a cumulative total of 290 standard hours. From reviewing output figures only, a logical

Figure 4. Input/output report. All quantities are in standard hours. There was a released backlog of 60 hours at work center 11 at the beginning of week 21.

Work Center 11

Week	21	22	23	24	25	26	27	28	29	30
Planned input	220	220	220	220	220	220	220	220	220	220
Actual input	110	150	140	130						
Cumulative deviation	−110	−180	−260	−350						
Planned output	220	220	220	220	220	220	220	220	220	220
Actual output	150	140	160	140						
Cumulative deviation	−70	−150	−210	−290						
Planned backlog	60	60	60	60	60	60	60	60	60	60
Actual backlog	20	30	10	0						

conclusion would be that work center 11 needs more capacity. However, input figures reveal the real problem lies in the work centers feeding work center 11. The actual input has fallen short by a cumulative total of 350 hours behind the plan. The work is not arriving at work center 11. To expand capacity would only compound the problem.

Figure 5 shows an input/output report for a different work station. Work center 13 is not an entry point for orders, but receives its inputs from numerous other work centers. Actual inputs have been fairly close to planned inputs, but actual output has consistently fallen short of planned output. The work center suffers from a capacity constraint. Something should be done to improve the capacity problem. The key to using input-output techniques is to establish a planned backlog and a tolerance level, such as ±15%, for each work center. When the backlog tolerance level is exceeded, the work center's capacity should be altered.

Problems in input force the examination of upstream work centers, or in the case of gateway or primary work centers, the examination of the order release system. The gateway work centers are easier to control in terms of input. The input to secondary or intermediate work centers is more difficult to control because input is coming from multiple sources. Problems in output are usually associated with capacity unless they are the direct result of input problems.

As shown in Figure 6, input/output control deals with the throughput (the flow in and the flow out) rather than focusing only on backlogs. Input/output control checks leadtime by developing a planned level of queue at each work center and then regulating the relationship between input and output to each work center to achieve planned queues. Its prime function is capacity control, which results in backlog and lead time control.

Figure 5. Input/output report. All quantities are in standard hours. The released backlog at work center 13 at the beginning of week 5 was 200 hours.

Work Center 13

Week	5	6	7	8	9	10	11	12	13	14
Planned input	100	100	100	100	100	100	100	100	100	100
Actual input	110	105	95	95						
Cumulative deviation	+10	+15	+10	+5						
Planned output	100	100	100	100	100	100	100	100	100	100
Actual output	75	85	75	70						
Cumulative deviation	−25	−40	−65	−95						
Planned backlog	200	200	200	200	200	200	200	200	200	200
Actual backlog	235	255	275	300						

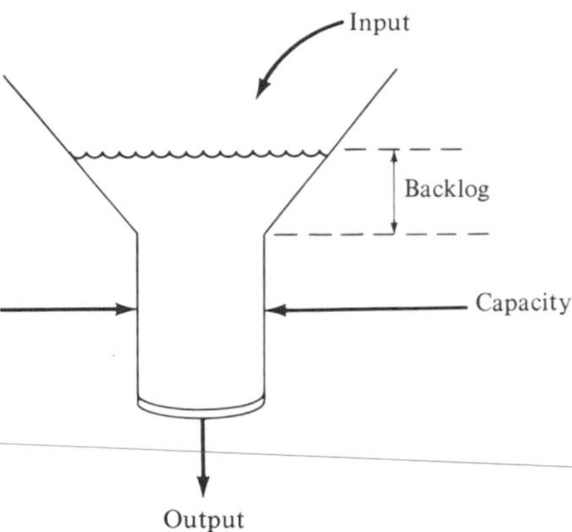

Figure 6. Capacity limitations.
Input must equal or be less than output, or the backlog will increase.

The actions that can reduce the in-process inventory levels for an organization are as follows:

1. Schedule delivery of purchased materials as near as possible to the required first operation start date. Refuse to accept delivery of items that arrive outside defined reasonable limits.
2. Withdraw materials from storerooms as late as possible before their required date. This action keeps material cost from being applied to work in process and keeps material under control until it is needed by production.
3. Balance the input rate of orders with the output rate of completed orders. If the input rate exceeds the output rate, backlogs will increase, as well as the cycle time.
4. Do not release work to production unless personnel, material, tooling, and support services are available in the needed quantities.
5. Schedule work to the shortest possible cycle time that does not result in excessive underutilization of facilities. Do not prerelease orders (the backlog) unless serious underutilization of resources will otherwise occur.
6. Use time increments that are compatible with actual requirements. The use of weeks is not appropriate for routings that actually require a day or two. Too large a time increment can inflate the cycle. It is not uncommon for the time scheduled to be the time taken.

The reaction to large visible backlogs is frequently an attempt to increase capacity in some way. If the backlog consists of early release of orders or jobs for which there is no immediate demand, it is artificial and can only be aggravated by increasing capacity. If schedules are not being met, the bottleneck work centers can be expanded by additional manpower, more shifts, overtime, subcontracting, or more equipment. A consistently high backlog can indicate the need for capacity expansion if it is due to an increase in demand for the product.

CRITICAL RATIO TECHNIQUE

A major function of MRP systems is the establishing and updating of due dates for shop orders. The shop must then determine the sequence in which these orders are to be processed. When several orders simultaneously compete for the services of a given machine, some type of priority rule must be used based on due date information. Numerous priority dispatching rules have been proposed for use in job shops. There are many simulation studies which compare the relative performance of such rules. There is no one best priority rule for all situations. One priority rule that has received a lot of attention is the critical ratio technique.

The critical ratio rule is a dynamic priority rule that facilitates the constant updating of priorities. It is used in conjunction with MRP systems and has broad industrial application. The critical ratio is a measure of the urgency of any order in comparison with the other orders for the same facility. It is based on when the completed order is required and how much time is required to complete it. It is a dimensionless index and is calculated as follows:

$$\text{Critical ratio} = \frac{\text{demand time}}{\text{supply time}} = \frac{\text{time remaining until needed}}{\text{time needed to complete work}}$$
$$= \frac{(\text{date required}) - (\text{today's date})}{\text{days needed to complete the job}}.$$

From the critical ratios, it is possible to determine the orders that are behind schedule, the orders that are ahead of schedule, the orders that are on schedule, the orders that should be processed next, and whether processing rates should be increased. Orders with the lowest critical ratio are processed before orders with higher ratios. If the critical ratio is greater than one, the order is ahead of schedule; if it is equal to one, the order is on schedule; and if it is less than one, the order is behind schedule. The lower the critical ratio, the more critical the order is.

EXAMPLE 1

Sequence the jobs listed in Table 1 by the critical ratio technique. Today is day 43 on the production calendar.

Table 2 lists the jobs in the order in which they should be performed according to their critical ratios. Jobs *C* and *E* are behind schedule and must be speeded up if they are to be completed by the date required; job *B* is on schedule; and jobs *D* and *A* are ahead of schedule.

Table 1

Job	Date required	Process time remaining (days)
A	50	3
B	45	2
C	44	2
D	53	5
E	46	4

Table 2

Job	Critical ratio
C	(44-43)/2=0.50
E	(46-43)/4=0.75
B	(45-43)/2=1.00
D	(53-43)/5=2.00
A	(50-43)/3=2.33

When the critical ratio is used to schedule warehouse operations or determine what items should be shipped on the next delivery truck, the appropriate formula is as follows:

$$\text{Critical ratio} = \frac{\text{days of supply}}{\text{lead time remaining}},$$

$$\text{Days of supply} = \frac{(\text{stock on hand}) - (\text{safety stock})}{\text{average daily demand}}.$$

In practice, all the items being shipped should have their critical ratio calculated and ranked. All items with a critical ratio less than one should be shipped on the next truck. To obtain a full truckload, the next items in order of criticality should be shipped.

CONCLUSION

This chapter addresses the problem of controlling in-process inventory in a job shop. Inventory results when inputs are not matched by outputs. In job shops, control of in-process inventory is difficult, since it involves input and output control of each work center. Since the work center workload is not balanced, queues or backlogs of work are required for efficient utilization of resources. The control of backlogs is the key to efficient operations which directly influence the manufacturing cycle time. Capacity control is achieved by input-output control at each work center, which results in backlog and lead time control.

One of the largest areas of manufacturing concern is the control of queues or backlogs of material waiting to have operations performed. Surveys have shown that in the average job shop actual work only takes from 5 to 25% of the time that an order is in the shop. This indicates that management should pay more attention to the flow of material. This is the work in process (inventory) which is accumulating costs and is using capital badly needed for other purposes. A reduction in queue can translate directly into an immediate increase in bottom line profit.

QUESTIONS

1. What are in-process goods?
2. What costs are associated with in-process inventory?
3. Are there apparent benefits to an organization from in-process inventory?
4. Are in-process inventory levels higher in a continuous or an intermittent production process?
5. Differentiate between a "gateway" and an "intermediary" work station.
6. Name the five elements that make up the manufacturing cycle time.
7. Name the time element that usually represents the largest fraction of the manufacturing cycle time.
8. How does the priority of an order influence its process time? Queue time?
9. What effect does a queue or backlog have on lead time?
10. Of what value are time cycle charts?
11. How does input/output control regulate lead time?
12. If a work center is not obtaining its output goals, what may be the problems?
13. Explain the critical ratio technique.
14. If a job shop wants to reduce its in-process inventory levels, where should it concentrate its initial efforts?
15. What impact does a short manufacturing cycle time have on finished goods inventory?

PROBLEMS

1. Determine critical ratios for the following jobs and sequence them accordingly. This is the 12th day on the production calendar.

Job	Date Required	Process Time Remaining (Days)
A	13	5
B	20	9
C	15	4
D	18	6
E	14	1
F	25	4
G	22	12
H	30	19

2. Use the critical ratio technique to schedule the following warehouse operations:

Job	Days of Supply on Hand	Lead Time Remaining
A	4	5
B	7	5
C	3	5
D	10	5
E	1	5
F	8	5

3. Use the critical ratio technique to determine in which sequence the following items should be shipped for delivery.

Item	Stock on Hand	Safety Stock	Avg. Daily Demand	Lead Time Remaining
A	20	10	5	3
B	18	4	3	4
C	350	50	275	1
D	100	10	20	5
E	72	6	10	7
F	23	18	1	3

4. Complete the input/output report in Figure 4 using the following data, and analyze the results.

Week	21	22	23	24	25	26	27	28	29	30
Actual Input	110	150	140	130	180	170	200	200	190	210
Actual Output	150	140	160	140	150	170	180	210	210	220

5. Complete the input/output control report in Figure 3 using the following data, and analyze the results.

Week	12	13	14	15	16	17	18	19	20	21
Actual Input	540	530	500	520	540	540	560	550	540	530
Actual Output	610	520	600	580	530	520	540	540	530	530

CASE 1: THE SOLUTION

Acacia Company produces a line of solid wood furniture. The production process is such that only about 20% of the process remains after the component parts are produced and ready for assembly. In other words, 80% of the process is making component parts, and 20% is final assembly and finishing. Some of the parts, which require excessive setups and long lead times, are produced in double order quantities. A typical production run for these parts would entail 33% of annual demand or four months' production supply. For this reason in-process inventory is expectedly high. The manufacturing of components incurs large storage space requirements, a costly inventory control system, and long cycle times.

The problem that is perplexing to the company is that all of the component parts of a unit are frequently not ready for final assembly at the scheduled time. Typically, some of the more elaborate components requiring the longest manufacturing lead times arrive late, but this has not been the rule for the basic parts. Mr. Bart was recently employed to apply modern techniques in the solution of this problem. Mr. Bart's original contention was that the firm needed to create an even more complete in-process inventory of component parts ready for final assembly. He also planned an alternative action in the event the increased inventory proposal was rejected; he felt the problem could be resolved equally well by increasing production rates. However, while continuing to research his proposals, he made the following observations:

1. Establishment of an increased parts inventory would be difficult because of lack of available production time. All of the production facilities are fully utilized at present. Often, parts in process are held up to let rush orders continue through.
2. Production of some component parts is not in accord with economic production quantities, either because of insufficient raw materials or because of competition for production capacity.
3. Expansion of the component inventory seems inadvisable because of the likelihood of deterioration. Large expansion also appears risky, since the type of modern furniture produced by Acacia is subject to a higher rate of obsolesence than is typical in the furniture industry.

After considering these points, Mr. Bart wondered if the real problem might be production capacity and not insufficient inventories of components. Consequently, he decided that his second proposal was the better. In order to solve the capacity problem the production rate for components must be increased.

1. Would the proposed increase in component production be a workable solution?
2. Does the structuring of a capacity requirements plan seem integral to Mr. Bart's proposal? Might raw material requirements also be crucial to the firm's capacity?
3. Are there other aspects of Acacia's operation that need analysis, e.g. schedules?

CASE 2: MULTIFACETED

Octagon was founded in 1968 by John Tuxley, who was an established builder and general contractor. He developed the idea of a prefabricated home which could be built cheaply and assembled easily. The home was extremely heavy and awkward to move, so John came up with the idea of a tower crane. He built a prototype which performed excellently and soon found that people were far more interested in his crane than his prefab house. As a result, he started Octagon Manufacturing Company and began to produce tower cranes for industry.

When Octagon first went into production, operations ran smoothly. In more recent years the plant has experienced a rash of bottlenecks, late deliveries, customer cancellations, increased costs, reduced quality, and increased manufacturing cycle times (the usual four weeks increased to seven or eight weeks). The updated load reports continually revealed increased backlogs. What worsened the work load status was the rise in the volume of customer orders and government contracts. Orders had risen by approximately 25% in each of the preceding two years, but firm orders for the first production period of the current year were down for the first time in over ten years.

When operations were progressing methodically, most jobs were dealt with on a first-come, first-served basis. Nowadays orders often accumulate over several weeks. The accumulated orders plus any incoming orders are classified by type and size and then assigned to the work centers. The loading or assignment of tasks to a particular work center is done so as to minimize the number of times the machinery has to be set up. For each machine center (i.e. cutting, welding, casting, etc.), a list is prepared of all orders to be processed in the next two week period. The sequencing of orders at each work center is arranged to reduce setups and to shorten queue time with the saving of setup costs as the number one priority.

Setups have an average cost of $250, so any rush jobs which require additional setups are deemed too costly. The setup priority schedule is rarely altered once it is completed, and tampering with it is protectively disallowed. However, some members of Octagon management think that the tight schedules are the primary cause of delays and bottlenecks. Manufacturing lead times have become excessively long, and they assert this is due to the large accumulations of in-process inventory. It is also their assertion that proper scheduling could reduce in-process inventory by at least 30%. Although limiting setups may have kept production economical from one standpoint, it is causing inefficient compromises of competing goals, e.g. reduction of inventory costs.

This group of adversaries is pushing for a new scheduling system based on a restructuring of goals and priorities. Their position rests with the following assumptions: first, Octagon's situation is faltering due to poor scheduling, and second,

Octagon is failing due to the adoption of misdirected goals. It is their belief that the basic criteria on which job shops compete, specifically cost, delivery, and quality, are not receiving sufficient focus. These adversaries have issued a challenge: "All of the competitive criteria will be improved within a trial phase of a scheduling technique that incorporates unprecedented setups."

As preliminary steps to devising the new schedule, studies are being performed on various aspects of plant activity, and process times are being computed at the work centers. A mean time for each job shop center is to be formulated by averaging a sample of the activities. These estimates will determine capacity. Plant personnel are being questioned as to which operations have proven to cause bottlenecks, and these particular operations will receive isolated study with subsequent closer estimation of time ranges. Job completion dates will be based on forward scheduling, but the actual way to sequence the orders is still under consideration. Lastly, the new scheduling method will reflect the following policies: changing priorities, use of overtime, tracking of progress, and necessary revisions.

1. How is competition affected by the old policies? Could the "challenge" be more effective?
2. Are the dispatching rules acceptable under the old plan? What are some suggestions for the new plan?
3. Since it is practically impossible to develop "the" optimal schedule in a job shop, would the new plan at least be satisfactory?
4. How will in-process inventory be affected by any changes?

CASE 3: THE UNCONTROLLABLE SHOP JUNGLE

Dave Conservative was reviewing the year-end financial statements of Wilson Manufacturing Company, a job shop operation which recently moved into a spacious new facility. Dave noted with alarm the changes that occurred in current assets during the first accounting period following the move. Specifically, he was alarmed by the decline in the cash balance and the growth in inventory.

Dave realized that as the company financial manager, he viewed things differently from John Lathe, who was vice president for production. He recalled John insisting on large stabilization stocks in order to keep production levels high. John scheduled long production runs in centers where frequent production changes had proven expensive. He also realized the disruption of production because of inventory shortages could be more costly than the extra holding costs. Furthermore, the large stocks allowed John to continue the use of flexible scheduling. He felt it important to maintain different input/output rates at work centers so as to maximize the efficiency and productivity of each center. So as a consequence of stabilization stocks, the centers enjoyed independent planning, and the firm as a whole could have flexibility in scheduling different products through the facility.

On Friday morning at the weekly department head meeting, Dave broached the subject of cash and inventory control with John. John proceeded to highlight areas where he saw problems. He said certain costs had definitely increased since the move, but most of these would be remedied in due course. Large cash outlays had gone to compensate the maintenance crew for overtime. The new machinery had many operational problems that were not covered under the purchase warranties.

Another enlarged expense was the rise in materials handling costs. The materials handlers were slow in acquainting themselves with the new facility and its more spacious layout. The materials personnel were still confused on the locations of partially processed goods; more in-process goods were going to temporary storage so the accumulation on the shop floor would be reduced. The storage and retrieval of in-process goods were unfamiliar to the materials handlers.

John also thought that his direct labor costs were up, but he was sure this would also be self-correcting. The employees were having a hard time adjusting their pace to their workload. The employees had always held preconceived notions about the amount of work to be processed through their center by judging the inventory coming in and going out. With the new layout they were having difficulty estimating workloads, and their actual workload was greater than they perceived. For instance, as the firm reduced the input to some centers by leaving more inventory in storage, the workers were slackening their pace to meet the reduced inventory coming to the center. Also contributing to the slower pace was the relative absence of waste and damaged goods which gave the appearance of little in-process inventory.

In defense of other inventory control areas, John was quick to point out that a new purchasing and raw materials inventory control system installed this year had reduced raw material inventory levels. The finished goods inventories were also down. "Look, Dave, marketing is doing a superb job of forecasting demand. To reduce the finished goods any more will only result in excess stockouts, and with the competition we have, we just can't afford that."

Dave, after reviewing the figures on the raw materials and finished goods inventory, had to agree that they were both down. "You're right. The problem is with the in-process inventory. John, I guess you are doing all you can. In-process inventory is just part of the manufacturing process and beyond our control. We can only deal with these labor and maintenance costs that will improve with some training and adjustment. Have a nice weekend, John, I'll see you Monday."

1. Discuss how such diverse things as maintenance, scheduling, and materials handling affect in-process inventory.
2. How do behavioral considerations affect Wilson's cash or inventory problems?
3. Should Dave overlook the inventory problem and concentrate on the cash outlays, or is there some overlap?
4. What recommendations would you make to Dave?

10 Inventory Valuation

FLOW OF COSTS

FIFO

LIFO

Average Cost

Specific Cost

INVENTORY RECORDS

Periodic Count Method

Cycle Count Method

INVENTORY SECURITY

QUESTIONS

PROBLEMS

CASES

Inventory, in an accounting sense, represents value assigned to goods either acquired or produced for subsequent sale or consumption. Inventories are normally valued at cost or some modification of cost, such as the lower of cost or market value. Inventory accounts at a particular point in time are a snapshot view of the total value of inventory items either on hand or in process. As a corollary, the amounts deducted from inventory accounts during any particular period of time are the basic data for determining the cost of goods sold during the period. Obviously, consistent policies and methods of inventory valuation are imperative for the useful measurement of performance between time periods and for the interpretation of one's financial position at any given time.

Inventories pose problems in valuation, control, safeguarding, and cost allocation. They directly affect the income statement and the balance sheet. Inventories are assets consisting of goods owned by an organization for sale or for utilization in the production of goods or services for sale. They usually represent a significant fraction of current assets or even total assets.

Inventory has physical and financial characteristics. The physical characteristics (flow of goods) are factual and objective, whereas financial characteristics (flow of costs) are more subjective. The physical and financial attributes are usually separate, distinct, and independent problem areas for an organization. In this section, emphasis will be placed on the financial characteristics associated with the flow of costs.

The financial significance of inventory is attributable to the need for measuring operating performance or periodic income over a particular time period (month, quarter, or year). The valuation of items consumed during a time period will be used to determine performance or income. Inventory influences performance additionally in that suboptimal inventory policies will reduce income by incurring unnecessary expenses.

Inventory costs and expenses will depend on the accounting procedures adopted. Accounting procedures determine when and how a change in assets owned should be recognized, and when and how assets are transformed into costs and expenses. Facts are not altered, but accounting procedures govern the recognition of events which affect periodic income determination.

The importance of matching costs with revenue for the income statement is generally acknowledged. In periods of rapid price change (inflation), a part of the increase in earnings during the upward cycle is attributable to the rise in prices. During an inflationary period, the goods on hand at the beginning of the period will generally be sold at a higher price than contemplated at the time they were purchased. This increase in revenues will be reflected in the income for the period; however, if inventory is maintained at the same quantity levels, the additional revenues received will have been expended to a substantial extent in purchasing the replacement inventory units. Thus, the increase in income is illusory. It is frequently termed "inventory profits."

The primary basis for inventory accounting is cost. The cost for inventory purposes may be determined under any one of several assumptions as to the flow of costs. Material is ordered, not just once, but on a continuing basis. Therefore, organizations have to plan on the same basis. There is no one prescribed procedure to be used in the determination of inventory costs for accounting purposes. There are a number of standard procedures, together with combinations and variations of each. The major objective in selecting a method is to clearly reflect periodic performance. To determine the dollar amount of inventory at any given point in time, the quantity of inventory items on hand must be known and a value must be assigned to those quantities. The quantity of items on hand is obtained by counting or measuring. The value assigned to individual items is based on one of several accounting methods. The accounting method used is very important, since it can significantly affect the total dollar amount of inventory and the related cost of goods sold.

The inventory methods for accountability can be subdivided into the method of valuation and the inventory flow method. In most cases, the method of valuation is based on the original cost of the item or the lower of cost or market value. There would be no problem if unit costs were constant, but during a period of time, items are frequently purchased or manufactured at different unit costs. This poses a problem, since the items sold must be costed for the income statement (cost of goods sold) and unsold items must be valued for the balance sheet (inventory).

FLOW OF COSTS

The inventory flow method refers to the way items are taken from inventory. The assumed flow for accounting purposes may not be the same as the actual physical flow of goods. The selection of the assumed inventory flow method by the accountant will determine the flow costs. There are various inventory flow assumptions in practice today. Four methods account for more than 90% of current usage. The four methods, listed in order of frequency of use beginning with the most frequent, are:

1. FIFO (first in, first out)
2. LIFO (last in, first out)
3. Average cost
4. Specific cost

The above inventory flow methods are primarily concerned with the flow of costs rather than the flow of physical goods. The selection of a flow method will depend upon several factors, including the type of organization, the projected economy, industry practices, the tax rules, and other regulations. Once a flow method is adopted, it is not easy to change to another method because of income tax requirements and accountants' concerns for consistency in reporting to outsiders.

All of the inventory flow methods are simply schemes to carry costs from the balance sheet to the income statement as expenses. The costs allocated do not have to match the actual physical flow of goods. Goods can be sold by the oldest-first scheme and yet assigned costs according to the last unit produced. The flow of goods does not have to be related in any way to the flow of costs.

FIFO

The most widely used inventory flow method is called FIFO, which stands for "first in, first out." It is assumed that materials are issued from the oldest supply in stock, and units issued are costed at the oldest cost listed on the stock ledger sheets, with materials on hand at all times being the most recent purchases. Under FIFO, the inventory cost is computed on the assumption that goods sold or consumed are those which have been on hand longest and that those remaining in stock represent the latest purchase or production.

FIFO tends to coincide with the actual physical movement of goods through many organizations. It is scrupulously followed for goods that are subject to deterioration and obsolescence. The ending inventory from FIFO closely approximates the actual current value, as the costs assigned to the goods on hand are the most recent. While this technique tends to produce inventory assets at current costs, any advantage derived from a balance sheet presentation can be offset by its impact on the costs of sales for the income statement. When the price of materials and other costs are subject to change, FIFO is not likely to result in matching costs against revenues on a current basis. Thus, cost changes can create income statement distortions from what would be obtained if current costs were applied.

FIFO is fairly simple and compatible with the operations of many organizations. Inventory records are usually kept on a perpetual or a periodic basis. With perpetual systems, all changes to stock (additions, subtractions, or deletions) are recorded for each incoming or outgoing transaction. With periodic systems, only additions to stock are entered, and a physical count of stock is made at specific time intervals to determine the stock status. FIFO is adaptable to either perpetual or periodic inventory systems. The use of FIFO simplifies record keeping requirements, as the actual flow usually coincides with record keeping activities. A few simple examples can best illustrate the FIFO method.

EXAMPLE 1

The periodic inventory record shown in Table 1 is available on an item. A physical count of the items on 1 April reveals an ending inventory of 300 units. What is the value of the ending inventory? What is the cost of goods sold for the period?

Table 1. Periodic Inventory Record (FIFO)

Date	Type of Transaction	Units	Unit Price	Total Cost
1 Jan.	Beginning inventory	200	$1.00	$200
31 Jan.	Purchase	300	1.10	330
28 Feb.	Purchase	400	1.16	464
31 Mar.	Purchase	100	1.26	126
	Total	1000		$1120

Ending Inventory	Units	Unit Price	Total Cost
31 Mar. Purchase	100	$1.26	$126
28 Feb. Purchase	200	1.16	232
Total	300		$358

$$\text{Cost of goods sold} = (\text{total cost}) - (\text{ending inventory})$$

$$= \$1120 - \$358 = \$762.$$

The cost of goods sold with FIFO is $762, and the final inventory is $358 for 300 units.

EXAMPLE 2

From the perpetual inventory record in Table 2 what are the value of the ending inventory and the cost of goods sold?

Table 2. Perpetual Inventory Record (FIFO)

	Received			Issued			Balance		
Date	Units	Unit Cost	Total Cost	Units	Unit Cost	Total Cost	Units	Unit Cost	Total Cost
1 Jan.							200	$1.00	$200
31 Jan.	300	$1.10	$330				200 300	1.00 1.10	200 330
3 Feb.				200 200	$1.00 1.10	$200 220	100	1.10	110
28 Feb.	400	1.16	464				100 400	1.10 1.16	110 464
1 Mar.				100 200	1.10 1.16	110 232	200	1.16	232
31 Mar.	100	1.26	126				200 100	1.16 1.26	232 126

The cost of goods sold for the quarter under the above system is \$762 (\$200 + \$220 + \$110 + \$232), and the final inventory is \$358 (\$232 + \$126) with 300 units.

Note how the perpetual inventory record is more complex and time-consuming than the periodic inventory record. However, FIFO is readily adaptable to either perpetual or periodic systems.

LIFO

LIFO, which stands for "last in, first out" assumes that the most current cost of goods should be charged to the cost of goods sold. Under LIFO, the cost of units remaining in inventory represents the oldest costs available, and the issues are costed at the latest costs available. The stocks sold or consumed in a period are those most recently acquired or produced; the remaining stocks are those earliest acquired or produced. LIFO charges current revenues with amounts approximating current replacement costs.

The underlying purpose of LIFO is to match current revenues against current costs. However, LIFO can result in an unrealistic inventory valuation for balance sheet purposes, which distorts the current ratio and other current asset relationships. It decreases income during periods of rising prices and increases income during periods of falling prices. It is often favored because it results in reducing income taxes during a period of rising prices. Like FIFO, LIFO can be used with either perpetual or periodic inventory systems. A few simple examples illustrate the LIFO method.

EXAMPLE 3

The periodic inventory record shown in Table 3 is available on an item. A physical count of the item on 1 April reveals an ending inventory of 300 units. What is the value of the ending inventory? What is the cost of goods sold for the period?

Table 3. Periodic Inventory Record (LIFO)

Date	Type of Transaction	Units	Unit Price	Total Cost
1 Jan.	Beginning inventory	200	\$1.00	\$200
31 Jan.	Purchase	300	1.10	330
28 Feb.	Purchase	400	1.16	464
31 Mar.	Purchase	100	1.26	126
	Total	1000		\$1120

Cost of goods sold = (total cost) − (ending inventory) = \$1120 − \$310 = \$810.

The cost of goods sold with LIFO is \$810, and the final inventory is \$310 for 300 units. Note that this same item under FIFO in Example 1 had a cost of goods sold of $762 and a final inventory value of $358.

Ending Inventory	Units	Unit Price	Total Cost
1 Jan. Inventory	200	$1.00	$200
31 Jan. Purchase	100	1.10	110
Total	300		$310

EXAMPLE 4

From the perpetual inventory record in Table 4, what are the value of the ending inventory and the cost of goods sold?

Table 4. Perpetual Inventory Record (LIFO)

	Received			Issued			Balance		
Date	Units	Unit Cost	Total Cost	Units	Unit Cost	Total Cost	Units	Unit Cost	Total Cost
1 Jan.							200	$1.00	$200
31 Jan.	300	$1.10	$330				200	1.00	200
							300	1.10	330
3 Feb.				300	$1.10	$330	100	1.00	100
				100	1.00	100			
28 Feb.	400	1.16	464				100	1.00	100
							400	1.16	464
1 Mar.				300	1.16	348	100	1.00	100
							100	1.16	116
31 Mar.	100	1.26	126				100	1.00	100
							100	1.16	116
							100	1.26	126

The cost of goods sold for the quarter under the above system is $778 ($330+$100+$348), and the final inventory is $342 ($100+$116+$126) with 300 units. Note that this same item under FIFO in Example 2 had a cost of goods sold of $762 and a final inventory value of $358. It should also be noted that generally a difference in cost of goods sold and ending inventory will arise between a periodic inventory system and a perpetual inventory system when using the LIFO method, in contrast with the FIFO method.

During inflationary periods, LIFO can mean lower profits, lower income tax, and more cash on hand. Inflation can create a ballooning effect on apparent income if cost of goods sold are costed at their purchase cost which has subsequently increased. Such income ("inventory profits") is unreal because it results from ignoring the need of an organization to replenish inventories at higher prices. LIFO protects against "inventory profits." For organizations with a high rate of inventory turnover, LIFO provides no benefit, since costs already are closely matched to revenues.

Average Cost

In an attempt to provide the elusive perfect combination of a realistic ending inventory and cost of goods sold, the average cost method was developed. This method does not attempt to indicate what unit went out first or last, but rather to determine the average cost for each item during a time period. There are three types of averages that can be used:

1. Simple average
2. Weighted average
3. Moving average

All three averages can be used with a periodic inventory system, but only the moving average is well suited to the perpetual inventory system.

The simple average is determined by dividing the sum of production or purchase unit costs by the number of production runs or orders. The simple average neglects the size of the lot (number of units) and gives the unit production or purchase cost of each lot equal weight, regardless of the variation in the number of units. The weighted average corrects the distortion of the simple average by considering quantity as well as unit cost. The weighted average divides the cost of goods available for sale or use by the total number of units available during the period. The moving average computes an average unit cost after each purchase or addition to stock. It is well suited for computerized inventory operations.

The simple average and weighted average cannot be calculated until the period is over. Thus, they are not well suited to perpetual inventory systems. The moving average is used for perpetual inventory systems. All of the averages are well suited for periodic inventory systems, since in them costs are not allocated until the end of the period.

With the average cost method, the costs of all like items available during the period are averaged to obtain the ending inventory value. During periods of increasing or decreasing costs, the average cost method tends to damp out the extremes. When there is a trend upward or downward, the average cost method responds more gradually than the other inventory flow methods. The average cost method, while simple to apply, reflects all the limitations of any average figure. The unit cost cannot be equated to any tangible figure, and it does not reveal price changes as clearly as may be desired. A few simple examples will illustrate the average cost method.

EXAMPLE 5

The periodic inventory record shown in Table 5 is available on an item. A physical count of the item on 1 April reveals an ending inventory of 300 units. What are the value of the ending inventory and the cost of goods sold using (a) simple average, (b) weighted average, and (c) moving average?

Table 5. Periodic Inventory Record

Date	Type of Transaction	Units	Unit Price	Total Cost
1 Jan.	Beginning inventory	200	$1.00	$200
31 Jan.	Purchase	300	1.10	330
28 Feb.	Purchase	400	1.16	464
31 Mar.	Purchase	100	1.26	126
	Total	1000		$1120

(a) *Simple average*:

$$\text{Simple average} = \frac{1.00+1.10+1.16+1.26}{4} = \$1.13 \text{ unit cost,}$$

$$\text{Ending inventory value} = (\text{ending inventory})(\text{unit cost}) = 300(1.13) = \$339,$$

$$\text{Cost of goods sold} = (\text{units issued})(\text{unit cost}) = 700(1.13) = \$791.$$

(b) *Weighted average*:

$$\text{Weighted average} = \frac{\sum_{i=1}^{4} P_i Q_i}{N} = \frac{1.00(200)+1.10(300)+1.16(400)+1.26(100)}{1000}$$
$$= \$1.12 \text{ unit cost,}$$

$$\text{Ending inventory value} = (\text{ending inventory})(\text{unit cost}) = 300(1.12) = \$336,$$

$$\text{Cost of goods sold} = (\text{units issued})(\text{unit cost}) = 700(1.12) = \$784.$$

(c) *Moving average*: (See Table 6.) The moving average for each addition to stock is obtained by summing the total cost column and dividing by the number of units. The moving average for the period is the last moving average, which is $1.12.

$$\begin{aligned}\text{Ending inventory value} &= (\text{ending inventory})(\text{unit cost})\\ &= 300(1.12)\\ &= \$336,\\ \text{Cost of goods sold} &= (\text{units issued})(\text{unit cost})\\ &= \$700(1.12)\\ &= \$784.\end{aligned}$$

Note how the weighted average and the moving average are true averages that result in the same costs. The simple average resulted in a slight distortion of costs.

Table 6

Date	Units	Unit Price	Total Cost	Moving Average
1 Jan.	200	$1.00	$200	$1.00
31 Jan.	300	1.10	330	1.06
28 Feb.	400	1.16	464	1.10
31 Mar.	100	1.26	126	1.12

EXAMPLE 6

From the perpetual inventory record in Table 7, what are the ending inventory value and the cost of goods sold for the item?

Table 7. Perpetual Inventory Record (Moving Average)

	Received			Issued			Balance		
Date	Units	Unit Cost	Total Cost	Units	Unit Cost	Total Cost	Units	Unit Cost[a]	Total Cost
1 Jan.							200	$1.00	$200
31 Jan.	300	$1.10	$330				500	1.06	530
3 Feb.				400	$1.06	$424	100	1.06	106
28 Feb.	400	1.16	464				500	1.14	570
1 Mar.				300	1.14	342	200	1.14	228
31 Mar.	100	1.26	126				300	1.18	354

[a] The balance unit cost is the moving average which is obtained by dividing the number of units on balance into the balance total cost.

The cost of goods sold is the sum of the total costs for issues, or $766 ($424 + $342). The value of ending inventory is obtained from the final amount in the balance total cost column: $354 for 300 units.

Specific Cost

Of all the inventory flow assumptions, the specific cost method provides the most realistic valuation of ending inventory and cost of goods sold. The cost of maintaining records under the specific cost method can mount very quickly, so it is best suited for goods of significant value which are few in number. Its application is usually limited to large, expensive items handled in small quantities. The procedure consists of tagging or numbering each item as it is placed into inventory so its cost is readily discernable.

This inventory valuation method is frequently used in job shops for custom-made products, although if a large number of custom orders are in process, its implementation can be extremely expensive and difficult. Of course, the cost flow and the physical flow are identical with this method. It has the added flexibility of being suitable for either perpetual or periodic inventory systems. With a large number of items or operations, costs tend to average out, and the extensive record keeping expense is not warranted by the added accuracy of specific cost valuation.

Evidently, there are many methods of inventory costing or valuation that may be used by organizations. The method chosen should be practical, reliable, and as easy to apply as possible. As long as unit costs remain the same, all the methods are essentially equivalent. When unit costs change dramatically, major differences among the methods occur. If the inventory turnover is very high, the differences among the methods are diminished. There is no standard recommended practice for inventory costing. The best method depends upon the nature and objectives of the organization.

EXAMPLE 7

An organization that produces a single product has the production and sales record given in Table 8. The following data also are relevant:

Operating expenses	$5000/year
Opening inventory	400 units at $2.00/unit
Tax rate	50%
Inventory method	Periodic
Ending inventory	210 units, all made in November

Table 8

	Production			Sales		
Month	Quantity	Unit Cost	Total Cost	Quantity	Unit Price	Total Revenue
Jan.	600	$2.04	$1,224.00	500	$3.00	$1,500
Feb.	570	2.05	1,168.50	610	3.00	1,830
Mar.	550	2.10	1,155.00	650	3.00	1,950
Apr.	610	2.08	1,268.80	590	3.00	1,770
May	580	2.15	1,247.00	600	3.20	1,920
June	490	2.17	1,063.30	400	3.20	1,280
July	450	2.25	1,012.50	470	3.20	1,504
Aug.	480	2.30	1,104.00	540	3.20	1,728
Sept.	540	2.50	1,350.00	570	3.50	1,995
Oct.	610	2.57	1,567.70	650	3.50	2,275
Nov.	600	2.59	1,554.00	670	3.50	2,345
Dec.	580	2.60	1,508.00	600	3.50	2,100
Total	6660	$27.40	$15,222.80	6850		$22,197

Table 9

Method:	LIFO	FIFO	Average Cost: Simple	Average Cost: Weighted	Specific Cost
Sales	$22,197	$22,197	$22,197	$22,197	$22,197
Beginning inventory	800	800	800	800	800
Production	15,223	15,223	15,223	15,223	15,223
Goods available for sale	16,023	16,023	16,023	16,023	16,023
Less: ending inventory	546 [a]	420 [b]	479 [c]	480 [d]	544 [e]
Cost of goods sold	15,477	15,603	15,544	15,543	15,479
Gross income	6,720	6,594	6,653	6,654	6,718
Less: operating expenses	5,000	5,000	5,000	5,000	5,000
Income before taxes	1,720	1,594	1,653	1,654	1,718
Less: income taxes	860	797	827	827	859
Net income	$ 860	797	$ 826	$ 827	$ 859

[a](Number of units)(last-in cost) = (210)($2.60) = $546.
[b](Number of units)(first-in cost) = (210)($2.00) = $420.
[c](Number of units)(cost) = (210)($27.40/12) = $479.
[d](Number of units)(cost) = (210)($15,223)/6660 = $480.
[e](Number of units)(Nov. cost) = (210)($2.59) = $544.

Determine the net income for the organization under the FIFO, LIFO, average cost (simple and weighted), and specific cost methods.

The results are shown in Table 9.

As can be seen, costs were rising. As was previously stated, during a period of rising costs, the LIFO method will result in a higher cost of goods sold and therefore lower profit and taxes than the FIFO method. It is important to note, however, that just the opposite holds true in a period of falling prices. The amounts used in this example did not result in a significant difference between the simple and weighted average computations, but it is important to note the difference in the method of calculation.

No two methods resulted in exactly the same ending inventory dollar value. If the example were multiplied by 1000, one can appreciate the dollar difference that could result from the use of the various methods. Fluctuations were generally upward in the example. Should any other significant fluctuations take place during the period, the differences could be changed significantly. Thus the manager needs to know what inventory flow method is in use and what its impact on performance will be.

INVENTORY RECORDS

No inventory system will work efficiently unless records are accurate. If the inventory balance is overstated, there is a risk of stockouts. If the inventory balance is understated, there will be excess inventory. All decisions on when or how much to order are based on the inventory balance of individual items. Inaccurate inventory records trigger a chain reaction of problems: lost sales, shortages, missed schedules, low productivity, late delivery, excessive expediting, premium freight costs. These invariably result in ordering more than needed, which creates excess inventory and high obsolescence.

Inventory items should be classified and properly identified so they can be located for verification. Control over inventory includes the methods of storage and handling. Control is necessary to ensure against errors (inaccurate counts), embezzlement, damage, spoilage, and obsolescence. Control is usually accomplished through a series of inventory records and reports that provide information on usage, balances, and receipts. Appropriate control requires a periodic verification of items and records. It is desirable for record verifications and physical counts to be conducted by an independent agency with no interest of its own in the operations.

Some of the basic data required to keep meaningful and useful inventory records are as follows:

1. Item identification and/or classification
2. Item location(s)
3. Unit costs and net prices
4. Interchangeable and/or substitute items
5. Shelf life
6. End item (what it is used on or with)
7. Dates item entered inventory
8. Dates of withdrawal
9. Supply sources
10. Unit balance

Accurate inventory records are an important aspect of financial accounting as well as a cornerstone of inventory control. The foundation of any inventory control system is the information contained in records upon which decisions are made. Without record accuracy the best designed system is destined for major problems if not failure. Thus, inventory accuracy is a fundamental requirement for any inventory system. True record integrity requires a management policy intolerant of errors. Management must establish a climate of accuracy and the necessary tools for its achievement.

Every inventory system must be concerned with inventory record accuracy. An inventory system is doomed to failure unless data integrity can be maintained. It is not uncommon for more attention to be given to the more interesting technical aspects of a system while overlooking the tedious aspects of inventory record accuracy. Whether manual or computerized, record accuracy is critical to operations. Two requirements for accurate inventory records are:

1. A good system for recording all receipts and disbursements

2. A good system for auditing record accuracy that discovers and corrects the causes of errors

The condition of inventory records is influenced by the personnel involved, physical control, and the system. The *personnel involved* are the people who physically receive, issue, and store material as well as the first line of supervision of these people. The stockroom supervisors must accept responsibility for and take pride in maintaining record accuracy. Without their full support, their subordinates cannot be expected to strive fully for record integrity. Operatives must be instructed and trained in stockroom operating procedures so they recognize the importance of accuracy. It is desirable to set accuracy goals, measure accuracy, and post records of performance in comparison with goals.

An important aspect of *physical control* is to limit and control access to the storeroom. Each time a part is added to the stockroom or withdrawn from it, the transaction should be logged in the appropriate record. Unauthorized and undocumented transactions must be stopped or control is virtually impossible. An enclosed and locked storeroom with access only to authorized personnel can do much to control undocumented transactions. It is desirable for all parts to be identified by part number and geographical location in the storeroom. A clean and well-ordered storage area will reduce lost and misplaced items.

An efficient way to utilize space in the stockroom is to use a locator system. The stockroom is divided into sections and subsections with an appropriate numbering scheme. Parts are stored in the same location or in an available section, with the location noted on the receipt card along with the part number. As part issues are required, the warehouseman proceeds to the designed location of the part. A well-devised locator system can contribute much to data integrity.

A physical count of items is necessary to verify the integrity and accuracy of inventory records. Differences between book (record) and physical inventories must be ascertained. Any differences (variances) must be adjusted and the amount of overage or underage properly accounted for. A periodic physical count of inventory can be made for all items, or a cycle count program can be instituted. A physical count of all items usually involves a closing of the facility for a limited time while the quantities of all items are substantiated and the records are updated. The cycle count method involves the continuous counting of inventory throughout the year.

Periodic Count Method

The periodic count method refers to the periodic auditing of the inventory balances on hand to verify and maintain accurate inventory records. The inventory record may be manually posted, machine posted, or maintained by a computer. The periodic count method requires a complete count of all categories of inventory over a short time period. For most organizations, an annual or semiannual verification is adequate. If only one physical inventory is taken in a year, it is usually timed to coincide with the yearly low point in production and inventory levels.

Taking an annual physical inventory is like selecting a marriage partner: the time spent in preparation can pay off handsomely in the final results. A written standard procedure should be prepared that can also serve as a training document. Preparation for the physical inventory should involve the following:

1. *Housekeeping.* The arrangement of material in its proper location so it can be easily inventoried.
2. *Identification.* The proper identification of all items with part number and nomenclature.
3. *Instruction.* Review of inventory-taking forms and procedures with personnel prior to taking inventory.
4. *Training.* Instruction of appropriate personnel in the use of scales, counters, and measurement procedures.
5. *Teams.* The establishment of inventory teams of two or more members and the assignment of responsibility for counting, checking, and recording the inventory levels.

On the day of the count, operations in the storage areas should be terminated. A holding area should be designated to retain all material secured during the period so it is excluded from the count. All internal movements and shipments should be suspended for the duration except for emergencies. If the physical count will require several days, customers should be advised of the shutdown dates.

The tag method of recording inventory levels is universally used. The inventory teams will take the count, fill out the tags, and place them on the materials. The tags are used for both manual and computer systems. When an area has been completed by an inventory team it should be checked to ensure that all items are tagged (spot checked for accuracy), and then the tags are collected. Items in the shipping dock, export holding area, returned goods area, marketing displays, and so forth should also be included in the count.

The inventory records and the physical inventory should be reconciled with the inventory tags. The inventory data from the tags are transferred to inventory summary sheets. An auditing team should check any significant variations and reconcile discrepancies before materials start to move again. Appropriate adjustments should be made to inventory records and to general ledgers so that the record balance agrees with the quantity actually on hand.

The frequency of physical inventory is often determined by the value of the item and the ease of disposing of the item in the open market. Expensive or precious items may be inventoried much more frequently than general inventory items.

Cycle Count Method

Cycle counting is a physical inventory-taking technique performed continuously rather than periodically. It is a basic step toward controlling the accuracy of inventory records and maintaining it at a high level. Major profit improvements can be achieved by effective cycle counting through a reduction in production disruptions, improved customer service, reduced obsolescence, elimination of the annual physical inventory, and less inventory shrinkage. Frequently, the cycle count method is less expensive than the disruptive periodic count method.

This method involves a continuous counting of stock throughout the year. A limited number of items are checked every day, or at some other time interval. Personnel can be assigned to cycle count on a full-time or part-time basis. The stock items to be checked may be selected at random or according to a predetermined plan. The cycle count method does not require a disruptive termination of operations as is required with the periodic count method.

The cycle count method is becoming more widely used by organizations. It permits the use of specialists or regularly assigned stores personnel to conduct the physical count. When regularly assigned stores personnel are utilized, they can perform the cycle count during lulls in their assigned duties; when specialists are used, they are full-time personnel who continually count inventory items. In large organizations specialists are desirable, since they become familiar with items, the locator system, the storage system, and "peculiar" things that can occur.

The cycle count tests the condition of inventory records and provides a measure of record accuracy. Record accuracy can be measured by the percentage of items in error and the relative magnitude of the errors. The significance of the error relates to the relative value of the item. An error of one unit for an expensive item is significant, while an error of plus or minus 2% might be acceptable for low cost items.

The selection of items and the frequency of count should be evaluated carefully for each organization. The general rules to consider are:

1. In any inventory to be controlled, a selected small fraction of items in the inventory will tend to account for a large fraction of the value of the inventory.
2. The more frequent the activity (transactions) of an item, the higher the probability of record errors.

3. Effort, time, and money spent in the control of inventory should be allocated among the items in proportion to their relative importance.

Cycle counting can prioritize concentration on the integrity of inventory items with high annual dollar usage (*ABC* principle). The "*A*" items (highest annual usage items) should be counted most frequently, "*C*" items least frequently. "*A*" items might be counted every one or two months, "*B*" items every three or four months, and "*C*" items every year. Since "*C*" items may represent the bulk of the inventory, but a small percentage of investment, less effort is expended on them. Each organization must establish a cycle count based on its own peculiarities.

Several procedures have been developed to vary the cycle count frequency. Some of the more prevalent systems are as follows:

1. *ABC system.* The stratification of items based on the *ABC* principle with the highest frequency on "*A*" items and the lowest on "*C*" items.
2. *Reorder system.* The counting of items at the time of reorder.
3. *Receiver system.* The counting of items when a replenishment order is received.
4. *Zero balance system.* The counting of items when the balance on hand is zero or negative (backorder).
5. *Transaction system.* The counting of items after a specific number of transactions have transpired.

Of course, various combinations of the above systems can also be used.

With cycle counting only a small portion of the total stock is being investigated at a given time. This reduces the magnitude of the problem substantially. Each day's count can be reconciled without delay. Cycle counts can be established so that all inventory items are counted at least once during a year, or on a statistical sampling basis. With statistical procedures, a random sample of items in a given category is counted, and the results are generalized to the population of items.

The cycle count method is an excellent method for maintaining the accuracy of records. Some of the more apparent advantages are as follows:

1. Operations do not have to be terminated during the cycle count, and the annual physical inventory is eliminated.
2. Errors are discovered quickly, inventory records adjusted throughout the year, and the cause of errors eliminated.
3. Record accuracy improves and a more correct statement of assets results. Inventory counts are not performed under pressure, resulting in more accurate measurements. Year-end inventory write-offs can be eliminated, and a correct statement of assets be obtained throughout the year.

4. Specialists become efficient in obtaining good counts, reconciling differences, and finding solutions to systematic errors.
5. Efforts are concentrated in problem areas.

INVENTORY SECURITY

Security requirements vary widely among organizations and are dependent upon the nature of the material, its value, size, weight, application, utility, and resaleability. Generally, the more valuable an item, the greater the need for security. However, some expensive items require relatively little protection because of their size, weight, and limited utility (large castings, special molds).

Materials can be safeguarded by establishing and enforcing storeroom regulations. A periodic auditing of storeroom operations can reveal existing or potential security problems. The following measures should apply to storeroom operations:

1. Limit access to store areas to authorized personnel.
2. Count, weigh, and measure all materials on receipt.
3. Require authorized orders and requisitions for all material transactions.
4. Store valuable items in locked cabinets or in safes if necessary.
5. Keep storerooms locked and enclosed except during working hours.
6. Periodically spot-check stock on hand against inventory records.
7. Investigate unusual consumption for improper use.
8. Periodically check the authenticity of signatures and authorizations.
9. Provide security bonds for storeroom personnel to protect against losses through negligence or theft.

The effort, time, and money spent on the security of inventory should be allocated among the items in proportion to their relative importance. At no time should the cost of security exceed the benefits that accrue from it.

QUESTIONS

1. What is meant by the term "inventory profits"?

2. What are two components of the accounting inventory method?

3. Name the four most commonly used inventory flow methods.

4. Which method is best suited for goods that are subject to deterioration and obsolescence?

5. What is the primary disadvantage of the FIFO inventory flow method?

6. How does the LIFO inventory flow method protect against "inventory profits"?

7. Name three types of averages that can be used in the average cost inventory flow method. To which types of inventory system does each apply?

8. What are the limitations of the average cost inventory flow method?

9. What situation is suitable for application of the specific cost inventory flow method?

10. Under what conditions are the four inventory flow methods essentially equivalent? Different?

11. Differentiate between the periodic count and cycle count methods of taking a physical inventory.

PROBLEMS

1. A physical count of an item under a periodic inventory system indicated an ending inventory of 200 units. During the time interval, the inventory card revealed the following data:

	Quantity	Unit Cost	Total Cost
Beginning inventory	100	$1.00	$100
lst receipt	200	1.10	220
2nd receipt	250	1.20	300
3rd receipt	100	1.25	125
4th receipt	150	1.30	195
Total	800		$940

If FIFO is used, what is the value of the ending inventory? What is the cost of goods sold for the item?

2. What would be the ending inventory value in Problem 1 if the simple average method were used?

3. What would be the ending inventory value in Problem 1 if the weighted average method were used?

4. What would be the ending inventory value in Problem 1 if the LIFO method were used?

5. The issues and receipts available on an item for the month of June are shown in the table. Develop a perpetual inventory record on the FIFO basis for the month of June. What is the value of the ending inventory? What is the cost of goods sold?

Date	Unit Receipts	Unit Cost	Unit Issues	Unit Balance
1				100[a]
5	200	$1.10		300
8			175	125
13	250	1.20		375
18			275	100
23	100	1.25		200
23			50	150
26			100	50
29	150	1.30		200

[a]At $1.00.

6. From the issues and receipts data in Problem 5, develop a perpetual inventory record on the LIFO basis for the month of June. What is the value of the ending inventory? What is the cost of goods sold?

7. A physical count of an item under a periodic inventory system reveals an ending inventory of 1300 units. During the time interval the inventory card revealed the following transactions:

	Quantity	Unit Cost	Total Cost
Beginning inventory	1000	$8.00	$8000
1st purchase	250	9.00	2250
2nd purchase	300	10.00	3000
3rd purchase	100	13.00	1300
4th purchase	200	14.00	2800

If FIFO is used, what is the value of the ending inventory?

8. What is the ending inventory value in Problem 7 if LIFO is used?

9. What is the ending inventory value in Problem 7 if the simple average method is used? The weighted average method is used? The moving average method is used?

10. The Irwin Manufacturing Corporation maintains a periodic inventory system. A physical count of one of its products indicated an ending inventory of 650 units. During the time interval, the inventory card revealed the following data:

	Quantity	Unit Cost	Total Cost
Beginning inventory	1200	$14.00	$16,800
1st receipt	800	15.50	12,400
2nd receipt	950	15.60	14,820
3rd receipt	900	15.80	14,220
4th receipt	1100	17.00	18,700
Total	4950		$76,940

If the FIFO method is used, what is the value of the ending inventory? What is the costs of goods sold for the product?

11. What would be the ending inventory value in Problem 10 if the LIFO method were used. What would be the cost of goods sold for the product?

12. The issues and receipts available on an item for the month of October are shown in the table. Develop a perpetual inventory record on the FIFO basis for the month of October. What is the value of the ending inventory? What is the cost of goods sold?

Date	Unit Receipts	Unit Cost	Unit Issues	Unit Balance
1				50[a]
2	400	\$2.60		450
8			375	75
9	50	2.80		125
11	175	2.85		300
20			255	45
25	75	2.95		120
31			50	70

[a]At \$2.50.

13. From the issues and receipts data in Problem 12, develop a perpetual inventory record on the LIFO basis for the month of October. What is the value of the ending inventory? What is the cost of goods sold?

CASE 1: LOOSE SECURITY AND EMPLOYEE THEFT

The Westside Automotive Company repairs automobiles and sells related parts and equipment. The owner, Bill Westside, recently read an article in a newspaper about employee theft. He decided to conduct a study to see if Westside had a theft problem. Bill was shocked when he discovered a substantial amount of money was being lost due to theft. He immediately began a program to tighten control.

Part of the new control procedure was to spot check employees' vehicles as they left work for the day. When the contents of one mechanic's pickup truck were examined, ten boxes of spark plugs, ten sets of points, three distributor caps, and two sets of new spark plug wires were discovered. Further investigation revealed that Bob Gavin, the mechanic, was operating a small repair shop in his garage with parts and equipment stolen from Westside.

Because Gavin had been with the company 15 years and was one of the best mechanics in the area, the company decided to handle the matter internally, instead of reporting it to local authorities. Gavin was asked to appear before a group of three people: Bill Westside; John Stephens, a union representative; and Alan Jones, the personnel manager. Gavin's only defense was that everybody took parts and supplies from the company quite frequently. A thorough investigation found this to be correct. The company accountant estimated that about \$6000 in supplies and equipment had been stolen within the last 12 months.

After considering all the factors and implications of the situation, the personnel manager recommended that Gavin be fired. This, he claimed, would set an example for the other employees. John Stephens argued against firing Gavin. He contended that, through lax control procedures, Westside actually encouraged theft. He also argued that since theft was so widespread, it would be unfair to single out Bob Gavin. Bill Westside was very concerned about losing his best mechanic.

1. What action would you recommend against Gavin? Why?
2. Could the situation have been prevented? How?
3. Is this type of theft common in organizations?
4. What security precautions would you implement for the company?

CASE 2: A NEW NEIGHBOR

Harold Hosiner is the director of material for Conforma Foams Inc., a producer of styrofoam forms used in floral and holiday decorations. Harold's neighbor is Gerry Burns, a junior executive with a local accounting and auditing organization. Gerry recently moved to the area, so, to get acquainted, Harold invited him to his next backyard cookout.

At the cookout Harold and Gerry began to talk shop. Gerry was enthusiastic about his last two assignments, auditing a small plumbing distributor and a producer of eyeglass frames. Gerry's most interesting comments concerned inventory valuations:

"From what I have seen in the past few weeks, I see no reason why all businesses don't switch to LIFO. The profits realized by our clients more than pay for our services. With the economy the way it is today, we are recommending LIFO across the board."

Since Conforma was not using LIFO, Harold had some questions, but the hamburgers had to be turned and Gerry began to mingle with other guests.

The next morning Harold sat in his office pondering the conversation of last evening. He knew Gerry's firm had a good reputation, and he thought Gerry was an intelligent young man. Could a switch in inventory valuation policy improve Conforma's profit picture? Was Gerry's experience applicable to Conforma? Harold began to analyze these questions when he received a call from the director of finance. This would be an excellent opportunity to begin discussions on the feasibility of moving to LIFO.

1. Do you agree with Gerry Burns's comments on LIFO?
2. What advice would you offer to Harold Hosiner?

CASE 3: EVAPORATION OR SHRINKAGE

E. G. Truck Rental is a large national truck leasing and rental company. Although located primarily in the northeastern United States, it has districts in every state except Alaska and Hawaii. For the last ten years E. G. has maintained an edge over its competition by providing better service to its customers. One key aspect of this better service is always being able to supply its long-term lease customers with fuel. E. G. guarantees lease customers that none of their vehicles will sit idle during any fuel shortage.

Prior to a major fuel crisis E. G. purchased all its diesel and gasoline fuel from one major supplier. Fuel was delivered in drops of either 6500 or 8500 gallons. Deliveries were made on a regular basis (usually three times per week), and underground fuel tanks were checked daily. Dipstick readings were recorded and compared weekly against inventory records kept by the office personnel. Pricing of the fuel inventory was also done by office personnel and was a fairly routine task when the price of diesel and gasoline fuel was stable.

When the fuel shortage hit its peak, E. G.'s major fuel supplier refused to fulfill its commitment and supply all the fuel needed. In an attempt to keep its promise to its long-term lease customers, E. G. purchased fuel from several national and local suppliers. Deliveries were made at all hours of the day and night, including weekends. Although dipstick readings of E. G.'s underground fuel tanks were still taken daily, it became very difficult to match the inventory records maintained by the office personnel to the actual gallons of fuel received. Also, some small local suppliers actually pumped fewer gallons of fuel into the underground tank than they billed for.

Due to the fuel shortage the price of diesel and gasoline fuel began to fluctuate by as much as twenty cents per gallon. Many suppliers sent duplicate billings to E. G.'s home office in New Jersey requesting payment, even though they had already billed the location to which the fuel was delivered. In a six month period, approximately 15,000 gallons of fuel were unaccounted for or stolen.

1. How could the fuel shrinkage have been prevented?
2. During times of rising prices what inventory flow method is desirable?
3. Will the shrinkage influence the dollar value of inventory?

CASE 4: HOLDING GAINS

Sara O'Keefe is becoming furious about the understatement of inventory prices on her company's balance sheet. The balance sheet presentation of Vladimar China Company is becoming meaningless under the company adopted LIFO inventory-costing method. Initially, Sara agreed that her accountant's arguments to adopt LIFO had appeal—the influencing of net income and the aftereffect on income tax expense. However, hindsight is causing some disagreement with the decision. The fundamental reason for acceptance of the method is being deemphasized as Sara begins to stress LIFO's inability to reflect current prices on the balance sheet.

Vladimar comprises a growth firm that produces and sells fine quality china and glassware in the United States and an export firm that sells 25% of the tableware production to northern European countries. The inventory accounts are growing yearly due to steady expansion and company policies to maintain considerable safety stock levels of raw materials. Coincidental with the total dollar value increase in inventory is an enlarging undervaluation of the current asset. Sara is blaming unexpectedly fast inflation. At various stages of growth Vladimar has encountered cost problems.

Secondary to the strictly inflationary effects on the inventory accounts is the effect of the stock of obsolete items in the finished goods inventory. Vladimar is carrying large stocks of goods from discontinued lines. These goods are withdrawn to fill replacement orders, but their existence and relative market value makes the inventory portion of the balance sheet even more suspect.

A further complication is the distrust between management and stockholders. The major shareholders are unanimously of the opinion that management is manipulating net income so as to decrease distributable earnings. Part of this conspiracy, they feel, is due to finagling the cost of goods sold. They also are suspicious of the net decrease in income from foreign sales and openly dispute with management that it is attributable to devaluation of the dollar.

Since these problems have arisen, Sara is contemplating a change of technique for valuing inventory. For financial purposes, Sara recognizes that the Internal Revenue Code accepts the LIFO method almost without qualification. Sara's conversations with IRS agents have unfolded that the agency would not allow an inventory method based on replacement costs for reporting purposes but would allow this method for internal use. Sara knows her company would have to undergo federal red tape to make an inventory valuation change, and in practice it could only be done once.

Even with this information, Sara is asking her accountant to check the ramifications of reversing the LIFO inventory valuation decision. Sara wants to adopt a generally accepted accounting practice that is more conservative. She feels if the company would switch to FIFO, the balance sheet would reflect current prices, but there would be a poorer job of matching current costs with revenues on the income statement. Because she wants both a realistic current asset account and a theoretically close match between costs and revenues, she suggests the firm might look either to an average cost method or a specific cost method. In her investigation, Sara does not want to neglect implementation problems.

1. Do the stockholders have cause for complaint concerning dividend payouts?
2. Given Vladimar's present economic environment, would the inventory costing methods give dramatically different financial pictures? Given a large increase in sales, how would this change the financial picture?
3. What are the pros and cons of switching to alternative valuation methods?
4. What qualitative factors could impinge upon the choice?

CASE 5: PICKARD MOTOR COMPANY

The Louisville Assembly Plant of the Pickard Motor Company is the site of the "Launch Program" for the newly engineered S-cars. The Louisville plant has been chosen to build the newest line of energy efficient compacts because of superior quality control records and a location central to suppliers and support facilities. Louisville is producing the S-car line three months prior to scheduled production in two other plants and is responsible for finalizing engineering and production aspects of the most massive engineering change the motor company has experienced in ten years.

In executing the Launch Program, one of the most complicated tasks is stocking the new parts inventory. Ordering and delivery of parts for the S-line are naturally more complex than in ordinary model year changes. Inventory building has engaged the staff for almost two months and is now at its height. So far the most annoying problem has been expediting of parts orders, and the most costly has been payment of premium freight costs for company and privately chartered aircraft to deliver critical and substitution parts. Because of the fury in the Parts Control and Traffic Departments, morale is low, and tension is building.

Similar to the agitation in the inventory offices is the frenzy at the receiving docks. New parts are being delivered by truck, railcar, and aircraft. Extra personnel have been hired and borrowed from other assembly sites to ease the hurried receival and check-in of parts. Even with the additional personnel, the work pace seems to be the quickest in five years. The beleaguered receivers are starting to show signs of inability to cope with the burgeoning workload. They are complaining about the demanding task of deciphering bills of lading and packing slips. Because there is no universal standard for packing slips, the receivers are confused periodically on part numbers, indicated quantities, and other printed notation. In this turmoil, they are disregarding mandatory routines for receival of goods, and in keeping with the nonstandardization of incoming documents, are themselves using dissimilar markings and exception symbols.

From the receiving station the packing slips are inputted by punched cards to the computerized MRP system. The keypunchers assume the roles of major transcribers of the inventory data. Due to the current confusion over the receiving documents, they admittedly are dubious about record accuracy. Given this situation, they have come to rely on the Engineering Specifications and Inventory Audit Department to detect and correct inventory errors.

Spec and Audit has the critical job of ultimate verification of inventory data. Each day they receive and audit computerized inventory error lists that are output from a programmed system designed to detect inventory input discrepancies, e.g., duplicate inputs, quantities varying from invoiced quantities, etc. They have every record at their disposal, but in this situation, they must rely on the packing slips that are forwarded from the keypunchers. At the time of error recognition and subsequent verification, an authorized audit person may input the necessary information and/or back out erroneous input that was previously entered. Any audit person has the capability of entering information into the system. Thus far, the entire department has held the confidence of upper management because of past performance in overseeing enormous amounts of inventory data.

In an attempt to gain more control over an inordinately large influx of materials, the audit staff has temporarily changed the cycle count procedure. Because they suspect a high error rate, the number of full-time cycle counters has been increased. The incoming parts are counted more frequently, albeit not more thoroughly. The new cycle counters are working under the auspices of the more qualified counters, which has resulted in greater supervision but less physical counting by expert personnel. In addition, there is some rechecking of questionable counts, not to affix blame, but to identify gross errors and to evaluate personnel.

The most grandiose part of the Launch is the presence and participation of the engineers from the home office. The large, imported staff of 200 is remaking, redesigning, and substituting parts almost daily. The inventory personnel have full-time jobs accounting for the part substitutions and the paperwork associated with both the permanent and temporary changes. The greatest havoc is keeping track of part numbering and inputting the revised information into the computer so that the system can function properly.

Amid all the commotion, production has just begun and already is plagued with shortages, poor productivity, and rescheduling. The production supervisor wants to issue a general statement to vindicate himself. He wants it known from the beginning that he is not responsible for a "cripple" rate of 1 out of 3 cars produced. He intends to shift the blame to two culprits—the inadequate inventory system and the new hires in the Launch.

1. What inventory problems are resulting from the Launch?
2. What could be causing the production problems?
3. What improvements could be made?

11 Simulation

Simulation is a rapidly growing management science technique. It is a systematic trial-and-error method for solving complex problems. Simulation makes available an experimental laboratory for the manager by permitting him to test various alternatives without risking or committing organizational resources. The effects of numerous alternative policies can be ascertained without tampering with the actual system. This form of system experimentation can reduce the risk of upsetting the existing structure with changes that would not be beneficial. Simulation gives the manager an opportunity to test and evaluate proposals without running the risk of actually installing new approaches and absorbing the costs associated with the changes. With simulation, "trial and error" need not become "trial and catastrophe."

When problems involve risk or uncertainty, an analytical solution may be difficult or impossible to obtain. Simulation is useful in situations where analytical solutions are not appropriate because the models are either too complex or too costly. A mathematical model using the analytical approach can become incredibly complex because of numerous interacting variables. Simulation offers an alternative for complex problems not suitable for rigorous analytical analysis.

A simulation model does not produce an optimum solution. The manager selects the alternatives to evaluate by simulation, but he is not sure that he has included the best alternative. The simulation indicates possible solutions based only on the input of alternatives selected by the manager; it does not indicate which alternatives to evaluate. Simulation models usually develop heuristic rather than analytical solutions to a problem, but they can deal with very complex situations that defy solution by analytical methods.

No analytical solution can be extricated from its premises and assumptions. Simulation can investigate the effect of a relaxation of assumptions. Also, when no analytical solution is possible, simulation becomes important as a last resort. While simulation does not promise optimal solutions, it does tend in that direction. The ability of simulation to handle dependent variable interactions renders it a very powerful tool of systems analysis.

Simulation is used to reproduce a typical series of events (usually in mathematical form) which could have occurred in practice. If enough events are simulated and mean values determined, it can be assumed that they represent what would probably have happened in practice if the real situation existed.

Initial transient phenomena such as oscillations, rapid growth, and sudden decay are not unusual in simulation (or in reality). If system stability is desired, a sufficient startup period should be allowed for stability to develop. In real life such transient phenomena are commonplace occurrences. Whereas analytical methods are usually based on steady state conditions, simulation need not be limited by these assumptions.

The use of simulation techniques would not be very feasible if it were not for the availability of computing equipment. While the design of many simulation models is not very complicated and does not involve a large amount of advanced mathematics, a large number of variables and equations is not uncommon. Thousands of simple manipulations and computations are usually required for each simulation, and the arithmetic operations are usually too numerous for hand computation. With the aid of the computer, simulation has become an important tool to the manager because it allows the manipulation of many variables and constants associated with a problem in an artificial environment.

SIMULATION CATEGORIES

Simulation models can be classified into two basic types—deterministic and probabilistic. Deterministic models have properties that can be stated explicitly, and expected values of variables are inputs. It is common for management simulation games to be deterministic. The classical approach to dynamic systems is deterministic, and it uses equations as the modeling framework. The classical approach is deterministic because it does not include probability distributions, the variables must be continuous, and the relationships among variables must be stable over time. Probabilistic models have key variables defined by probability distributions and not expected values. The variables need not be continuous, and relationships can vary with time. Business situations in the real world are usually probabilistic.

EXAMPLE 1

A supply attendant at a tool crib distributes hand tools to mechanics. It takes him exactly 3 minutes to serve each mechanic. Simulate 15 minutes (10:00 to 10:15) of toolroom operation if the mechanics arrive at 10:00, 10:01, 10:04, 10:10, and 10:15. At any given time, indicate the idle time of the attendant, the waiting time of the mechanic, and the number of mechanics in the queue.

Table 1 develops the relevant information. The attendent is idle $\frac{3}{15}$ or 20% of the time.

Table 1

Arrival Time of Mechanics	Service Begins at	Service Ends at	Idle Time of Attendant	Waiting Time of Mechanics	No. of Mechanics in Queue
10:00	10:00	10:03	0	0	0
10:01	10:03	10:06	0	2	1
10:04	10:06	10:09	1	2	1
10:10	10:10	10:13	2	0	0
10:15	10:15	10:18	0	0	0
			3	4	

MONTE CARLO SIMULATION

Monte Carlo simulation involves determining the probability distributions of the variables under study and the sampling from the distributions by using random numbers to obtain data. It is a probabilistic type of simulation that approximates the solution to a problem by sampling from a random process. A series of random numbers is used to describe the movement of each random variable over time. The random numbers allow an artificial but realistic sequence of events to occur. Monte Carlo simulation permits the manager to determine how varied policies or organizational conditions will be modified by the behavior of random or transient influences. A general approach to solving problems by Monte Carlo simulation is contained in Figure 1.

Figure 1. Monte Carlo simulation.

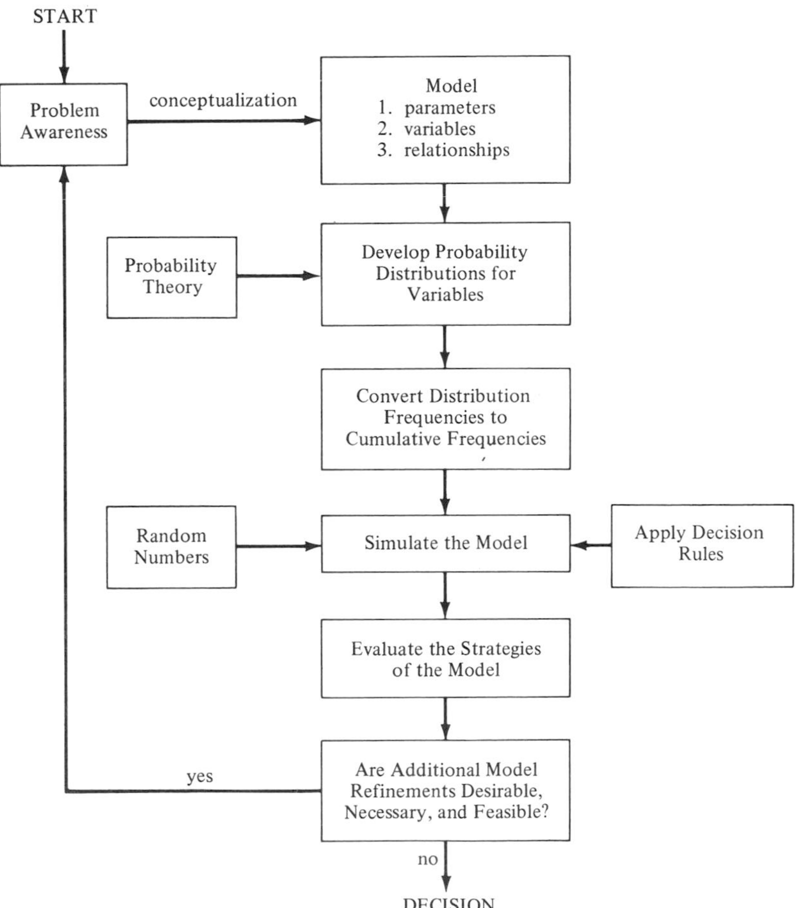

Monte Carlo simulation establishes a stochastic model of a real situation and then performs sampling experiments on the model. This technique generates a vast number of data that might otherwise take a very long time period to obtain. Following the generation of data, analytical computations can be made and then a problem solution derived.

The major steps in Monte Carlo simulation are as follows:

1. Establish the probability distributions for the variables of the problem. The distributions must be known, but the specific mathematical formulation is not necessary.
2. Convert the distributions to cumulative probability distributions. This assures that only one variable value will be associated with a given random number.
3. Sample with random numbers from the cumulative probability distributions to determine specific variable values to use in each replication of the simulation. The easy way to sample is to use numbers from a table of random numbers. In computer simulation it is easier to generate random numbers than to use a table. The random numbers are inserted in the cumulative probability distributions to obtain specific variable values for each replication. The sequence of assigned random numbers will approximate the pattern of variation expected to be encountered in real life.
4. Simulate the operation under analysis for the necessary number of replications. The approximate number of replications is determined in the same manner as the appropriate size of a statistical sample. The ordinary statistical tests of significance can be used. With computerized simulation the size of the sample can be increased without difficulty, and it is economical to run large samples with very small sampling errors.

Everything depends on the choice of frequency distributions, and unless there is some assurance they have been picked well, the entire simulation can be worthless. Distributions can be obtained from historical records or experimentation, or established *a priori* on a quasisubjective basis. Random numbers are numbers of equal long-run frequency. They have a complete lack of sequential predictability, and each number has an equal opportunity to be selected. The randomness of tabulated numbers can be validated by a chi-squared test. The stream of random numbers can be obtained from a published table or created by the computer. In the latter case the computed numbers are termed "pseudorandom numbers." Table 16 at the end of this chapter is a typical random number table.

Monte Carlo simulation has many practical uses, such as waiting line problems where standard distributions for arrival rates and service rates are inadequate, layout problems of multiphase assembly lines, inventory problems determining reorder points and order quantities, equipment replacement problems, and so forth.

EXAMPLE 2

The probability distribution of pogo stick assembly times is given in Table 2. Determine the average assembly time by simulating the performance time for ten replications with the following random numbers: 04, 95, 45, 21, 44, 57, 03, 98, 98, and 10.

Convert the frequency distribution to a cumulative frequency distribution, as in Table 3. The simulated assembly time can be obtained by referring each random

Table 2

Time (Minutes)	Frequency
5	20
6	30
7	20
8	10
9	10
10	10
	100

Table 3

Time	Frequency	Cumulative Frequency	Random Numbers
5	20	20	01–20
6	30	50	21–50
7	20	70	51–70
8	10	80	71–80
9	10	90	81–90
10	10	100	91–00
	100		

Table 4

Replication	Simulated Assembly Time (Minutes)
1	5
2	10
3	6
4	6
5	6
6	7
7	5
8	10
9	10
10	5
	70

number to the cumulative frequency distribution. Random numbers in the range 01–20 give a performance time of 5, 21–50 give 6, 51–70 give 7, 71–80 give 8, 81–90 give 9, and 91–00 give 10 minutes. Thus we have Table 4. The average assembly time is 70/10=7 minutes.

PERPETUAL INVENTORY SIMULATION PROBLEM

You are assigned the task of minimizing inventory costs for a specific item under variable demand (in units per week) and variable lead time (in weeks from order to delivery). You are supplied with the historical demand and lead time data in Table 5. You are further informed of the following costs associated with inventory activity:

$10.00 = order placing cost,

$ 5.00 = holding cost per unit per week,

$20.00 = stockout cost per week of occurrence (it is assumed that a stockout cost is encountered only once in a given week).

Your task is to determine the order quantity and the reorder point (when the balance at the end of the week falls at or below this quantity point, you reorder units) that will minimize the inventory cost.

This problem can be handled by simulation with little difficulty. We will observe 56 possible simulations that could be run. Each cell in the matrix of Table 6 would contain the results of a simulation, and the cell with the smallest cost would indicate the reorder point and quantity. For simplicity, we will show the computations for only a single cell, C_{38}, for 25 replications.

Converting the frequency distributions to cumulative frequency distributions, Table 7 is obtained.

Table 5

Quantity Demand (Units/Week)	Frequency (No. of Weeks)	Lead Time[a] (Weeks)	Relative Frequency
0	2	1	60
1	4	2	30
2	14	3	9
3	20	4	1
4	8		100
5	1		
6	1		
	50		

[a]From order to delivery.

Table 6

Reorder Point	Order Quantity: 1	2	3	4	5	6	7	8
0	C_{01}	C_{02}	C_{03}	C_{04}	C_{05}	C_{06}	C_{07}	C_{08}
1	C_{11}	C_{12}	C_{13}	C_{14}	C_{15}	C_{16}	C_{17}	C_{18}
2	C_{21}	C_{22}	C_{23}	C_{24}	C_{25}	C_{26}	C_{27}	C_{28}
3	C_{31}	C_{32}	C_{33}	C_{34}	C_{35}	C_{36}	C_{37}	C_{38}
4	C_{41}	C_{42}	C_{43}	C_{44}	C_{45}	C_{46}	C_{47}	C_{48}
5	C_{51}	C_{52}	C_{53}	C_{54}	C_{55}	C_{56}	C_{57}	C_{58}
6	C_{61}	C_{62}	C_{63}	C_{64}	C_{65}	C_{66}	C_{67}	C_{68}

In Table 8 we now run through 25 replications of order quantity 8 and reorder point 3. We obtain

$$\text{Average cost} = \frac{(\text{holding cost}) + (\text{order cost}) + (\text{stockout cost})}{N}$$

$$= \frac{545 + 70 + 60}{25} = \frac{675}{25} = \$27.00,$$

$$\text{Average cost} = \$27.00/\text{week}.$$

The simulation gives the cost which would be placed in cell C_{38} in the matrix if 25 replications were considered suitable. To determine the most desirable cell in the matrix, all cells must be simulated in a like manner. The simulation example has built into it the following assumptions:

1. Holding costs are determined from the number of units in stock at the end of each week.

Table 7

Quantity Demanded	Relative Frequency	Cumulative Frequency	Random Numbers
0	4	4	01–04
1	8	12	05–12
2	28	40	13–40
3	40	80	41–80
4	16	96	81–96
5	2	98	97–98
6	2	100	99–00
Lead Time	**Relative Frequency**	**Cumulative Frequency**	**Random Numbers**
1	60	60	01–60
2	30	90	61–90
3	9	99	91–99
4	1	100	00

Table 8

	Random Numbers		Simulated Activity				Simulated Cost		
Simulated Week	Demand	Delivery	Demand	Order Time	Units Received	Unit Balance	Hold Cost	Order Cost	Stockout Cost
0						8			
1	19	20	2			6	30		
2	3	19	0			6	30		
3	80	14	3	1		3	15	10	
4	15	34	2		8	9	45		
5	61	10	3			6	30		
6	74	2	3	1		3	15	10	
7	19	39	2		8	9	45		
8	5	49	1			8	40		
9	32	98	2			6	30		
10	24	21	2			4	20		
11	62	55	3	1		1	5	10	
12	19	78	2		8	7	35		
13	93	40	4	1		3	15	10	
14	44	99	3		8	8	40		
15	26	55	2			6	30		
16	21	82	2			4	20		
17	78	66	3	2		1	5	10	
18	40	37	2			0	0		20
19	84	7	4		8	4	20		
20	55	97	3	3		1	5	10	
21	98	80	5			0			20
22	91	9	4			0			20
23	87	53	4		8	4	20		
24	38	36	2	1		2	10	10	
25	39	63	2		8	8	40		
Total							545	70	60

2. If the demand for the item exceeds the balance on hand, the consumer will accept the number of items which are available even though he desires a larger quantity.
3. If the demand for an item is not satisfied in the given week, it is lost and not recoverable in the following weeks.
4. The stockout cost is a maximum of $20 per week regardless of the number of units of demand which are unfulfilled. (It may be feasible in some cases to include the stockout cost on a per unit basis.)
5. All orders for additional units are received at the beginning of the work week.
6. If the unit balance plus the number of units on order (but not received) exceeds the reorder point, no new order will be initiated for additional units. If the unit balance plus the number of units on order (but not received) is less than the reorder point, a new order will be initiated for additional units.

The simulation example begins with an initial unit balance of 8 units. A demand value for the first period is obtained from the random number by referring to the demand cumulative frequency distribution. The synthetic demand value is subtracted from the unit balance of 8 units from the previous period, which results in an end-of-period unit balance. At the end of each period (replication), the stock position (stock on hand plus stock on order) is compared with the reorder point. If the reorder point has been reached or exceeded, a lead time value is obtained from the random number by referring to the lead time cumulative frequency distribution, and an order is placed. If the reorder point has not been reached or exceeded, no order action is taken. Since one period (replication) has expired, 1 is added to the number of periods and 1 is subtracted from all outstanding lead time values. With the start of a new period, any orders scheduled for delivery are added to the unit balance from the previous period, and the process continues for the specified number of replications, which is 25. Appropriate inventory costs are entered at the end of each simulated time period. The average cost for the simulated cell is obtained by adding all the inventory costs and dividing by the number of replications or simulated time periods.

The preceding simulation of a single cell in the matrix indicated the vast number of simple computations associated with a simulation. While the computations are simple, their quantity dictates the use of a computer. It is an easy matter for a computer to run thousands of replications on each cell in a matrix and indicate a most desirable alternative.

EXAMPLE 3

If stockout costs are $20 per unit per week in the inventory evaluation of cell C_{38}, what would be the average cost per week for the 25 replications? (All other aspects of the problem are unchanged.)

Table 9

Simulated Week	Units Short	Stockout Cost
18	1	20
21	4	80
22	4	80
		180

The order and holding costs are unchanged, and the only difference will be in the stockout cost for weeks 18, 21, and 22 when stockouts occurred (Table 9). Thus

$$\text{Average cost} = \frac{(\text{holding cost}) + (\text{order cost}) + (\text{stockout cost})}{N}$$

$$= \frac{545 + 70 + 180}{25} = \$31.80/\text{week}.$$

PERIODIC INVENTORY SIMULATION PROBLEM

You are assigned the task of minimizing costs for the specific item identified in the previous section (perpetual inventory simulation problem) with a periodic inventory system. The maximum number of units that can be stored at any given time is 50, due to space limitations. Your task is to determine the reorder cycle and the maximum inventory level that will minimize cost. The matrix of possibilities is given in Table 10.

To determine the best policy, each cell would be simulated, and the cell with the lowest cost would be selected as the best strategy. For simplicity, we will show the computation for a single cell using the distributions and cost data from the previous section. A reorder cycle of 5 weeks and a maximum inventory of 30 units will be evaluated, which correspond to cell C_{530}. The simulation will start at time 0 with 25 units on hand. At each review period an order will be placed for 30 units less the number of units in

Table 10

Reorder Cycle (Weeks)	Maximum Inventory (Units):	50	45	40	35	30	25	20
1		C_{150}	C_{145}	C_{140}	C_{135}	C_{130}	C_{125}	C_{120}
2		C_{250}	C_{245}	C_{240}	C_{235}	C_{230}	C_{225}	C_{220}
3		C_{350}	C_{345}	C_{340}	C_{335}	C_{330}	C_{325}	C_{320}
4		C_{450}	C_{445}	C_{440}	C_{435}	C_{430}	C_{425}	C_{420}
5		C_{550}	C_{545}	C_{540}	C_{535}	C_{530}	C_{525}	C_{520}

Table 11

Simulated Week	Random Nos.		Simulated Activity					Simulated Cost		
	Demand	Delivery	Demand	Order Size	Order Time	Units Recd.	Unit Bal.	Holding Cost	Order Cost	Stockout Cost
0							25			
1	19	20	2				23	115		
2	3	19	0				23	115		
3	80	14	3				20	100		
4	15	34	2				18	90		
5	61	10	3	12	1		15	75	10	
6	74	2	3			12	24	120		
7	19	39	2				22	110		
8	5	49	1				21	105		
9	32	98	2				19	95		
10	24	21	2	11	1		17	85	10	
11	62	55	3			11	25	125		
12	19	78	2				23	115		
13	93	40	4				19	95		
14	44	99	3				16	80		
15	26	55	2	14	1		14	70	10	
16	21	82	2			14	26	130		
17	78	66	3				23	115		
18	40	37	2				21	105		
19	84	7	4				17	85		
20	55	97	3	13	3		14	70	10	
21	98	80	5				9	45		
22	91	9	4				5	25		
23	87	53	4			13	14	70		
24	38	36	2				12	60		
25	39	63	2	18	2		10	50	10	
Total								2250	50	0

stock and on order. Table 11 contains 25 replications of cell C_{530}. We have

$$\text{Average cost} = \frac{(\text{holding cost}) + (\text{order cost}) + (\text{stockout cost})}{N}$$

$$= \frac{2250 + 50 + 0}{25} = \$92/\text{week}.$$

To actually determine the best periodic inventory policy, it is necessary to evaluate each cell in the matrix. The 25 replications above would not be sufficient. Several hundred replications of each cell in the matrix would ensure a reliable estimate. With the use of a computer, it is a simple matter to determine a desirable periodic inventory policy by such a simulation.

Throughout the use of Monte Carlo simulation, the solution procedures for establishing a perpetual and periodic inventory system have been outlined for a single product. The technique was illustrated for a very simple problem. Although not illustrated, many other factors could have been introduced and varied, such as quantity discounts, price changes, expediting costs, strikes, material shortages, pilferage, and partial backordering. Additional factors are comparatively easy to include in a simulation, although they are forbiddingly complex in analytical form.[1]

SIMULATION OF JOINT PROBABILITY DISTRIBUTIONS

The interdependence of demand and lead time can be approximated for independent distributions by using Monte Carlo simulation. When demand and lead time are variables in an inventory problem, it is necessary to develop their combined probability so order quantities and reorder points can be set. The resultant joint probability distribution will define the demand during the lead time period.

Although demand and lead time variables can be combined numerically, it involves the algebra of multinomial equations for summing all the possible combinations of variables. With Monte Carlo, the joint behavior of the distribution is simulated by random numbers. The numerical method is exact, but the Monte Carlo method is quicker and sufficiently accurate for practical purposes.

The Monte Carlo method consists of selecting values of lead time and demand on a random basis. Although the procedure requires a large number of replications to establish the joint distribution, it can be extremely useful when standard distributions do not apply. A simple example can best illustrate the procedure.

[1]See Arnold Reisman, *Industrial Inventory Control*, New York: Gordon and Breach Science Publishers, 1972, Chapter 6, for multi-item simulation analysis of inventory.

EXAMPLE 4

Using Monte Carlo simulation, establish the joint probability of lead time demand for 20 replications using random numbers from Table 16 (start with the last two digits from column 1 in Table 16). The independent demand and lead time distributions are shown in Table 12.

Table 12

Daily Demand D (Units)	Probability $P(D)$	Lead Time L (Days)	Probability $P(L)$
0	0.40	1	0.25
1	0.30	2	0.50
2	0.20	3	0.25
3	0.10		1.00
	1.00		

The Monte Carlo process consists of selecting a random number for each lead time period. Additional random numbers will be used to generate demand during the lead time. The lead time demand will consist of the summation of the individual demands during the lead time. The independent distributions are modified to accept random numbers in the manner shown in Table 13.

Table 13

Daily Demand D	Probability	Cumulative Probability	Random Numbers
0	0.40	0.40	01–40
1	0.30	0.70	41–70
2	0.20	0.90	71–90
3	0.10	1.00	91–00
Lead Time L	**Probability**	**Cumulative Probability**	**Random Numbers**
1	0.25	0.25	01–25
2	0.50	0.75	26–75
3	0.25	1.00	76–00

Table 14 contains the 20-replication simulation. From it, the joint probability distribution in Table 15 is obtained.

The above example was for only 20 replications. In practice, to establish a joint probability distribution of lead time demand would require several hundred replications to assure a reliable estimate. See Appendix D to

Table 14

Simulated Lead Time	Random Numbers		Simulated Activity		
	Lead Time	Demand	Lead Time	Daily Demand	Lead Time Demand
1	63	58	2	1	
		66		1	2
2	35	09	2	0	
		72		2	2
3	92	70	3	1	
		14		0	
		27		0	1
4	77	44	3	1	
		80		2	
		21		0	3
5	23	58	1	1	1
6	6	56	1	1	1
7	28	13	2	0	
		91		3	3
8	30	94	2	3	
		7		0	3
9	37	44	2	1	
		20		0	1
10	42	42	2	1	
		99		3	4
11	5	16	1	0	0
12	8	93	1	3	3
13	51	30	2	0	
		34		0	0
14	28	56	2	1	
		85		2	3
15	96	14	3	0	
		92		3	
		57		1	4
16	9	81	1	2	2
17	45	85	2	2	
		1		0	2
18	68	78	2	2	
		32		0	2
19	74	75	2	2	
		91		3	5
20	99	27	3	0	
		3		0	2
		83		2	

Table 15

Lead Time Demand M	Frequency	Probability $P(M)$
0	2	0.10
1	4	0.20
2	6	0.30
3	5	0.25
4	2	0.10
5	1	0.05
6	0	0.00
7	0	0.00
8	0	0.00
9	0	0.00
	20	1.00

Chapter 4 for the numerical method of establishing the joint distribution for the above problem.

LENGTH OF SIMULATION RUN

A simulation run is the same as a statistical sample of a process under study or a process being simulated. The information gained from a simulation is dependent on the length of the simulation run, just as that from statistical sampling depends on the size of the sample taken. The usual method for estimating the length of a simulation run (number of replications) is to perform a few short trial runs using different random numbers to obtain the mean and standard deviation of the variable being measured. By assuming that the measured variable is normally distributed, the length of the simulation run can be determined for a given accuracy and a statistical confidence level. The following formula can be used to determine the desired length of the simulation run:[2]

$$N=\frac{Z^2ms^2}{K^2}=\text{desired length of simulation run,}$$

where

Z=standard normal deviation for a specified confidence level,

m=sample length of simulation run,

s=standard deviation of sample runs,

K=desired accuracy of simulated variable.

[2]For a further explanation of the formulation, see C. D. Lewis, *Scientific Inventory Control*, New York: American Elsevier, 1970, pp. 170–171.

Table 16. Random Numbers

.6663	.0696	.6964	.6935	.3077	.6821	.8774	.1951	.9228	.9856
.8558	.8714	.9132	.3207	.6221	.8776	.9366	.5563	.6306	.2010
.8666	.5692	.0397	.7806	.3527	.5242	.3519	.8278	.9806	.9540
.4535	.3457	.0319	.6396	.0550	.8496	.8441	.2896	.5307	.2865
.7709	.0209	.1590	.1558	.7418	.6382	.7624	.8286	.4225	.7145
.7472	.0681	.9746	.4704	.5439	.7495	.4156	.4548	.4468	.7801
.5792	.0245	.8544	.2190	.6749	.6243	.9089	.5974	.4484	.8669
.5370	.4385	.9413	.4132	.8888	.9775	.8511	.6520	.1789	.0816
.4914	.1801	.9257	.3701	.3520	.0823	.5915	.5341	.2583	.0113
.6227	.8568	.1319	.0681	.8898	.9335	.3506	.4813	.5271	.5912
.7077	.0878	.1730	.0093	.9731	.6123	.6100	.0389	.0522	.7478
.8044	.7232	.7466	.0349	.3467	.0174	.1140	.5425	.2912	.7088
.4280	.3474	.3963	.5364	.7381	.8144	.7645	.5116	.0300	.6762
.8821	.4375	.9853	.9138	.0596	.6294	.3415	.4358	.2713	.8343
.8523	.5591	.3956	.3516	.8472	.2884	.8550	.3524	.3919	.3967
.6558	.3999	.0480	.3046	.8285	.1693	.2330	.7610	.2674	.3679
.1806	.3227	.9710	.8548	.5003	.6345	.6815	.9612	.3378	.5091
.9256	.0103	.1347	.8074	.4534	.0373	.9885	.1182	.0795	.7094
.6128	.2383	.9223	.4459	.8974	.4525	.0441	.7379	.0677	.6135
.4913	.6686	.4453	.0223	.7344	.6333	.8080	.1075	.5077	.2590
.3491	.9060	.0496	.5251	.2385	.3425	.7426	.0827	.7816	.3100
.1530	.7750	.1800	.5491	.4713	.3572	.8914	.3287	.3518	.4199
.5894	.9256	.1529	.4922	.7235	.9046	.5771	.3954	.6794	.1984
.7107	.7293	.5387	.9880	.4642	.6092	.4389	.3820	.4119	.5821
.5337	.8973	.0322	.7474	.5526	.7386	.3476	.0762	.9613	.8789
.9644	.9317	.7214	.9388	.5131	.7891	.6504	.8672	.4880	.1557
.3820	.4209	.4876	.6906	.9257	.4447	.8541	.5250	.8272	.9513
.7142	.7821	.9281	.0016	.4180	.2971	.7259	.3844	.3801	.5372
.3342	.0695	.3189	.7217	.0428	.6227	.8967	.1417	.4771	.0137
.7599	.6804	.3587	.7765	.9790	.5331	.8654	.5337	.8883	.1268
.5905	.5242	.3262	.2409	.1039	.8727	.2752	.3265	.1110	.6722
.9016	.0268	.2134	.8633	.9959	.8970	.2688	.9149	.8124	.3244
.3508	.3038	.3095	.6480	.3089	.7948	.7897	.4792	.9238	.5206
.9393	.2211	.6921	.8622	.2688	.7890	.1363	.1282	.9525	.5299
.8151	.0355	.0688	.3432	.8580	.9888	.2402	.0000	.1307	.1611
.6730	.6635	.9948	.3730	.5977	.6089	.6678	.7734	.1086	.1435
.1834	.3191	.4042	.7264	.9511	.0549	.4267	.2888	.9166	.1935
.9028	.7539	.3215	.9958	.7826	.7569	.0633	.4506	.0807	.5650
.6556	.7547	.1155	.1975	.7882	.5929	.1493	.7455	.4865	.2179
.4285	.8922	.8721	.3307	.6236	.6329	.5228	.7599	.6689	.1966

assignment of evaluating a reorder cycle of 2 weeks and a maximum inventory level of 15 units. Simulate 10 replications using the same random numbers used in Problem 4. (Assume there are 15 units on hand at time 0.)

6. An organization's demand for one of its products is as follows:

Demand per Month (Units)	Probability of Demand
2200	.09
2300	.38
2400	.31
2500	.22

The lead time for the item is very short, and orders are placed at the end of the month for the next month's demand. All stockouts are lost sales, with no backorders. Management is considering the use of a fixed order size each month equal to the expected demand per month. To test this alternative, the following random numbers are to be used: 16, 3, 82, 97, 13, 45, 56, 73, 90, 61, 33, and 20. Simulate the proposed ordering rule from the random numbers and determine the following:

a. Number of orders per year
b. Number of months per year in which a stockout will occur; percentage of months
c. Average shortage in units per month
d. Percentage of total demand satisfied; unsatisfied.

7. A firm owns three copiers which cost $25 per day whether they are used or not. Each additional copier required can be rented for $30 per day. Actual use figures are as follows:

No. of copiers used	0	1	2	3	4	5
No. of days	7	12	25	30	18	8

Using the random numbers below, simulate eighteen days of copying to determine the daily copier cost.

13, 97, 63, 90, 36, 02, 57, 72, 97, 35, 15, 68, 29, 53, 77, 07, 64, 18.

8. In determining the total inventory cost for a periodic inventory system, a series of simulation runs of 13 years were performed which yielded an average cost of $60 with a standard deviation of $8. What is the minimum number of replications needed to yield an average cost of $60, accurate to ±$3 with a confidence level of 95%?

9. What is the minimum number of replications needed in Problem 8 for a confidence level of 99%?

EXAMPLE 5

A series of simulation runs of ten years' duration to determine the average inventory for a perpetual inventory system gives a mean value of 120 units with a standard deviation of 40 units. What would be the minimum length of simulation runs (replications) to specify an average inventory level of 120 units with an accuracy of ±5 units and a confidence level of 95%?

$$Z=1.64 \quad \text{for the 95\% confidence level,}$$

$$N=\frac{Z^2 ms^2}{K^2}=\frac{(1.64)^2 10(40)^2}{(5)^2}=1722 \text{ years.}$$

At least 1722 replications would be required.

CONCLUSION

Simulation serves the dual purposes of system analysis and the improvement of system design. Simulation serves system analysis by generating information on how a system operates and the significance of particular variables and their interrelationships in a system. For system design, it provides insights into potential improvement areas. Simulation can indicate which variables are more important in generating a desirable output.

Simulation can be used to help solve simple, narrowly defined problems or complex multivariable problems. In almost all cases a computer is desirable. The essence of simulation does not lie in its structure, for it lacks structure. The structure for a simulation problem must be defined by its user. For this reason, the development of a simulation model requires a basic understanding of the system under study and a degree of conceptual creativity so the model structure can be designed.

QUESTIONS

1. What is simulation? What are its advantages?
2. Describe two types of simulation models. What are the characteristics of the variables in them?
3. What is involved in Monte Carlo simulation?
4. What are the major steps in Monte Carlo simulation?
5. How are frequency distributions selected for use in Monte Carlo simulation?
6. What are some practical uses for Monte Carlo simulation?

7. How can variable demand and variable lead time be approximated for independent distributions by using Monte Carlo simulation?

8. On what does the accuracy of information gained from a simulation depend?

9. What two purposes are served by simulation?

10. What capabilities are required for development of a simulation model?

PROBLEMS

1. A small construction company owns two backhoes that cost $50.00 a day whether they are used or not. Each additional backhoe required can be rented for $50.00 per day. Actual use figures are listed below:

No. of Backhoes Used	No. of Days
0	13
1	22
2	38
3	16
4	11
	100

Using the random numbers below, simulate 15 days of construction to determine the daily backhoe cost.

56, 10, 40, 65, 45, 01, 69, 16, 13, 12, 78, 88, 62, 43, 67.

2. A manager of a new warehouse operation must determine the number of workers to hire. The daily workload varies from 40 to 70 man-hours as indicated in the table. Pertinent data are as follows:

Hours	Probability	Cumulative Probability
40	0.05	0.05
45	0.13	0.18
50	0.21	0.39
55	0.27	0.66
60	0.17	0.83
65	0.11	0.94
70	0.06	1.00
	1.00	

Regular pay	$4.00/hour
Overtime pay	$6.00/hour
Max. allowed overtime	4 hours per man
Temporary help	$40.00/day per man

If the backlog is over 20 hours, two temporary men are hired by the day unt the backlog goes back below 20 hours. Assuming that all of the regula employees volunteer for all overtime, test work forces of 4, 5, and 6 men over period of 15 days to determine the minimum cost level. Use the rando numbers given below in your computations.

4 men: 77, 44, 80, 21, 23, 58, 06, 56, 28, 13, 91, 30, 94, 07, 37.
5 men: 30, 66, 63, 53, 56, 80, 10, 47, 23, 53, 96, 00, 29, 87, 22.
6 men: 31, 67, 84, 96, 72, 85, 03, 34, 74, 44, 85, 13, 35, 42, 26.

3. In determining the total inventory cost for a periodic inventory system, sample of ten simulation replications was performed which yielded an avera cost of $85 with a standard deviation of $10. What is the minimum number replications to yield an average cost of $85, accurate to ±$2, with a confiden level of 99%?

4. A particular product with a perpetual inventory system has an order quant of 8 units and a reorder point of 3 units. Past records indicate the demand a lead time data given in the table. We also have

Quantity Demand (Units/Week)	Frequency (Weeks)	Lead Time[a] (Weeks)	Frequenc (Weeks)
0	3	1	46
1	6	2	41
2	8	3	11
3	22	4	2
4	7		100
5	4		
	50		

[a]From order to delivery.

Order placing cost	$10.00
Holding cost	$10.00/week per unit
Stockout cost	$20.00/week.

You have been assigned the task of determining the average inventory cos the order quantity and the reorder point were changed to 6 and 4 respectiv With an initial balance of 6 units at time 0, simulate 10 replications with following random numbers:

Demand: 10, 24, 38, 25, 07, 86, 66, 07, 65, 89.
Delivery: 22, 44, 06, 99, 11, 35, 35, 50, 79, 46.

5. The company in Problem 4 is considering shifting to a periodic invent system. The possible reorder cycles range from 1 to 5 weeks, and the possi maximum inventory levels range from 15 to 50 units. You have been given

EXAMPLE 5

A series of simulation runs of ten years' duration to determine the average inventory for a perpetual inventory system gives a mean value of 120 units with a standard deviation of 40 units. What would be the minimum length of simulation runs (replications) to specify an average inventory level of 120 units with an accuracy of ± 5 units and a confidence level of 95%?

$$Z = 1.64 \quad \text{for the 95\% confidence level,}$$

$$N = \frac{Z^2 ms^2}{K^2} = \frac{(1.64)^2 10(40)^2}{(5)^2} = 1722 \text{ years.}$$

At least 1722 replications would be required.

CONCLUSION

Simulation serves the dual purposes of system analysis and the improvement of system design. Simulation serves system analysis by generating information on how a system operates and the significance of particular variables and their interrelationships in a system. For system design, it provides insights into potential improvement areas. Simulation can indicate which variables are more important in generating a desirable output.

Simulation can be used to help solve simple, narrowly defined problems or complex multivariable problems. In almost all cases a computer is desirable. The essence of simulation does not lie in its structure, for it lacks structure. The structure for a simulation problem must be defined by its user. For this reason, the development of a simulation model requires a basic understanding of the system under study and a degree of conceptual creativity so the model structure can be designed.

QUESTIONS

1. What is simulation? What are its advantages?
2. Describe two types of simulation models. What are the characteristics of the variables in them?
3. What is involved in Monte Carlo simulation?
4. What are the major steps in Monte Carlo simulation?
5. How are frequency distributions selected for use in Monte Carlo simulation?
6. What are some practical uses for Monte Carlo simulation?

7. How can variable demand and variable lead time be approximated for independent distributions by using Monte Carlo simulation?

8. On what does the accuracy of information gained from a simulation depend?

9. What two purposes are served by simulation?

10. What capabilities are required for development of a simulation model?

PROBLEMS

1. A small construction company owns two backhoes that cost \$50.00 a day whether they are used or not. Each additional backhoe required can be rented for \$50.00 per day. Actual use figures are listed below:

No. of Backhoes Used	No. of Days
0	13
1	22
2	38
3	16
4	11
	100

Using the random numbers below, simulate 15 days of construction to determine the daily backhoe cost.

56, 10, 40, 65, 45, 01, 69, 16, 13, 12, 78, 88, 62, 43, 67.

2. A manager of a new warehouse operation must determine the number of workers to hire. The daily workload varies from 40 to 70 man-hours as indicated in the table. Pertinent data are as follows:

Hours	Probability	Cumulative Probability
40	0.05	0.05
45	0.13	0.18
50	0.21	0.39
55	0.27	0.66
60	0.17	0.83
65	0.11	0.94
70	0.06	1.00
	1.00	

Regular pay	\$4.00/hour
Overtime pay	\$6.00/hour
Max. allowed overtime	4 hours per man
Temporary help	\$40.00/day per man

If the backlog is over 20 hours, two temporary men are hired by the day until the backlog goes back below 20 hours. Assuming that all of the regular employees volunteer for all overtime, test work forces of 4, 5, and 6 men over a period of 15 days to determine the minimum cost level. Use the random numbers given below in your computations.

4 men: 77, 44, 80, 21, 23, 58, 06, 56, 28, 13, 91, 30, 94, 07, 37.
5 men: 30, 66, 63, 53, 56, 80, 10, 47, 23, 53, 96, 00, 29, 87, 22.
6 men: 31, 67, 84, 96, 72, 85, 03, 34, 74, 44, 85, 13, 35, 42, 26.

3. In determining the total inventory cost for a periodic inventory system, a sample of ten simulation replications was performed which yielded an average cost of \$85 with a standard deviation of \$10. What is the minimum number of replications to yield an average cost of \$85, accurate to ±\$2, with a confidence level of 99%?

4. A particular product with a perpetual inventory system has an order quantity of 8 units and a reorder point of 3 units. Past records indicate the demand and lead time data given in the table. We also have

Quantity Demand (Units/Week)	Frequency (Weeks)	Lead Time[a] (Weeks)	Frequency (Weeks)
0	3	1	46
1	6	2	41
2	8	3	11
3	22	4	2
4	7		100
5	4		
	50		

[a] From order to delivery.

Order placing cost	\$10.00
Holding cost	\$10.00/week per unit
Stockout cost	\$20.00/week.

You have been assigned the task of determining the average inventory cost if the order quantity and the reorder point were changed to 6 and 4 respectively. With an initial balance of 6 units at time 0, simulate 10 replications with the following random numbers:

Demand: 10, 24, 38, 25, 07, 86, 66, 07, 65, 89.
Delivery: 22, 44, 06, 99, 11, 35, 35, 50, 79, 46.

5. The company in Problem 4 is considering shifting to a periodic inventory system. The possible reorder cycles range from 1 to 5 weeks, and the possible maximum inventory levels range from 15 to 50 units. You have been given the

assignment of evaluating a reorder cycle of 2 weeks and a maximum inventory level of 15 units. Simulate 10 replications using the same random numbers used in Problem 4. (Assume there are 15 units on hand at time 0.)

6. An organization's demand for one of its products is as follows:

Demand per Month (Units)	Probability of Demand
2200	.09
2300	.38
2400	.31
2500	.22

The lead time for the item is very short, and orders are placed at the end of the month for the next month's demand. All stockouts are lost sales, with no backorders. Management is considering the use of a fixed order size each month equal to the expected demand per month. To test this alternative, the following random numbers are to be used: 16, 3, 82, 97, 13, 45, 56, 73, 90, 61, 33, and 20. Simulate the proposed ordering rule from the random numbers and determine the following:

a. Number of orders per year
b. Number of months per year in which a stockout will occur; percentage of months
c. Average shortage in units per month
d. Percentage of total demand satisfied; unsatisfied.

7. A firm owns three copiers which cost $25 per day whether they are used or not. Each additional copier required can be rented for $30 per day. Actual use figures are as follows:

No. of copiers used	0	1	2	3	4	5
No. of days	7	12	25	30	18	8

Using the random numbers below, simulate eighteen days of copying to determine the daily copier cost.

13, 97, 63, 90, 36, 02, 57, 72, 97, 35, 15, 68, 29, 53, 77, 07, 64, 18.

8. In determining the total inventory cost for a periodic inventory system, a series of simulation runs of 13 years were performed which yielded an average cost of $60 with a standard deviation of $8. What is the minimum number of replications needed to yield an average cost of $60, accurate to ±$3 with a confidence level of 95%?

9. What is the minimum number of replications needed in Problem 8 for a confidence level of 99%?

10. If it is possible to run 1000 years of replications in Problem 8, how accurately can the average be estimated with 95% confidence?

11. The retail manager of a large department store decided to analyze costs associated with his major product. Researching sales files from the last four years, he compiled the following data:

Quantity Demanded	Number of Weeks
4	2
5	8
6	10
7	12
8	18
9	24
10	24
11	20
12	18
13	22
14	18
15	14
16	8
17	2
18	4
19	4

The carrying costs of inventory are estimated to be $10 per unit, while the cost of placing an order is $5. The manager estimates that 50% of the customers will purchase elsewhere if the store is out of stock. Each unit contributes $80 to profit. An order is placed the first day of every week, and it takes four weeks for delivery. If the beginning inventory is 4, simulate the cost of order quantities of 10 and 11 units with the following random numbers: 234, 753, 709, 792, 582, 231, 768, 091, 365, 248, 472, 176.

CASE 1: DEMAND DEPENDENCE

Konacolor Corporation and Laminado Company located in the same industrial park several years ago because of the conveniences of the park and the inducements offered by the park developer. The move was fortunate for the two companies, since it began a cooperative undertaking that resulted in a joint venture. What started as a bulk shipping arrangement between the firms led to a full-fledged production agreement. Konacolor, a producer of electrical equipment and television components, was ripe for a television production line of its own; Laminado, a company skilled in special order cabinetry, had some capital to invest. The enterprise that ensued allowed Konacolor to open a TV production line with Laminado capital and afforded Laminado the opportunity to supply the cabinets for the two sizes of portable sets that composed Konacolor's line.

The startup costs of the venture were less than Laminado anticipated. The unused capital was expended on a sophisticated computer system for Laminado. The capacity of the system was in excess of needs, so Laminado worked a deal with Konacolor to share computer time. Interestingly enough, Konacolor came to depend on the system more than Laminado. Since it got on the system, Konacolor has implemented an MRP system for all four present styles of TV sets.

The problem that bothered both companies, Laminado as the supplier and Konacolor as the production unit, was the erratic demand for the TV sets. On balance, sales for the six year period had been good to excellent, but the undulations in the demand for the primary items translated into various problems for the dependent items. Because there are several levels of dependence at Konacolor, the market factor dependence of the primary item rippled from final assembly, to subassembly, and to manufacturing of components. Demand for some production periods had been grossly overestimated. As soon as this situation revealed itself, Konacolor made changes. The master schedule was promptly revised, and the MRP system regenerated. This change, combined with what appeared to be inflated requirements schedules, gave the company a large buffer of production parts so that during certain intervals the inventory of dependent items was uncharacteristically high.

A computer analyst for Laminado reckoned with the problem and pinpointed the culprit as the forecasting technique abetted by the lot sizing policy. She felt the inputs were faulty; a master production schedule which based independent demand on an exponentially weighted moving average with a smoothing constant of 0.4 was inadequate for the seasonally popular portables. She also recommended a computer simulation of the multistage environment to determine lot sizing policies for end items. The analyst asserted that once the misapplication of the forecasting technique was corrected, and the company switched from the present EOQ system to an experimentally determined lot sizing policy, all would be well.

The simulation was approved, and in came the results. However, the culmination of the simulation did not imply a clear-cut solution to the problem. The test pitted EOQ against EOI and the part-period method, given the final assembly schedule set in relation to end item demand. The outcome of the run showed EOQ as a slight favorite over the part-period but with no clear dominance in total number of stockouts for final products, total number of setups, or the average dollar value of inventory. While it was a photo finish for EOQ and the part-period, both clearly surpassed EOI.

The analyst was unhappy that the simulation did not resolve the lot sizing policy question and was sure this was due to her assumptions. She ran the simulation under the following conditions: requirements covered normal usage during supply lead time with no buffer stock, no lot splitting was allowed, and Konacolor was loaded under capacity. In reality, Konacolor had operated with projected overloads and with frequent lot splitting.

1. Given the decision rules, is the simulation of any value?
2. Are the usually high levels of dependent items understandable?
3. Should Konacolor accept the fate of being at the mercy of erratic demand, or can it counteract the situation?
4. What lot size policy could be expected to perform best under periods of variable demand? How do the alternative methods fail to recognize much of the information given in the requirements schedule?

CASE 2: WHEELER DEALER

During his ten years as manager of a seaside resort hotel, Sid Smee had seen the small town become one of the boom towns that lie between New York City and Cape Cod. The village previously had catered to the older "urbanites" from the eastern metropolitan districts, but a younger, more energetic crowd had begun to monopolize the resort community, seeking satisfaction, escape, and thrills during short breaks from the city.

Sid had known for some time that the tempo and composition of the stodgy town were changing, and the urbane guests would soon be a thing of the past. Being a very progressive person, Sid felt he should invest in a business that would serve the new breed of visitors. He realized that the pleasures the newcomers were seeking included the town's scenic views. Therefore, he decided to open a moped shop and rent motorbikes that could be driven along the narrow shoreline paths and over the backroads which lead to the elevated coastline.

This was a business about which Sid knew very little. He had read some brochure sketches on similar types of shops located in southern regions, but he needed to gain information on their operating details. In order to gather information on this particular service industry, Sid decided to take a short holiday and use the time for a fact-finding mission to a southern rental shop featured in one of the travel brochures. This shop, he thought, would be the perfect business to duplicate.

Sid visited the South Carolina rental firm and learned that the business had become successful under the management of a retired motor pool sergeant. The retired veteran was an ardent believer in military fashioned organizations and operations research. He was well schooled in vehicular matters, and his knowledge in the fields of maintenance and security was abundant. However, Sid did not find much immediate application of these types of information. Instead, he was searching for ways to ascertain the level of investment required to open his business as well as an approximation of the number of mopeds needed to operate his 5–6 month a year rental service. On this matter, the sergeant was of little use. Specifically, the sergeant's firm operated practically year round, his acquisition of goods appeared unorthodox, and his operating costs seemed to be lower than normal.

The sergeant's son and operations expert, however, had done some quantitative investigations on equipment usage. He had provided statistical data that had been used to plan personnel, workloads, and equipment acquisition and replacement. The son had done two simulation studies that were interesting to Sid from a numerical standpoint, but when articulated by the young developer, did not indicate any transferability to Sid's organizational design.

The first of the studies, conducted two years ago, was a simulation of two eight-hour day rental operations. The study was used to indicate the idle time of the shop attendant who checked out the mopeds, the waiting time of the customers, and the number of customers in the queue. He used a service time of 5 minutes, which was fairly close to the actual time it would take to prepare rental forms and collect deposits. At the conclusion of the simulated days, he calculated attendant idle times at 8% and 37%. The study, executed twice, once for a typically busy day and once for a slower day, was used to determine manpower needs for the two seasons.

The second and more recent study was more complex and of greater value to the firm. Although it was a simplification of their real conditions, it was being used to structure their business decisions. Initially, the son prepared probability distributions using historical rental records which are given below:

1 Hour Rentals		2 Hour Rentals	
Number of People	Probability	Number of People	Probability
1	.04	1	.03
2	.13	2	.16
3	.16	3	.09
4	.10	4	.14
5	.06	5	.04
6	.03	6	.02

The probability distributions were used in conjunction with the following frequency table obtained by taking observations over a 4-day summertime period:

Minutes between Arrivals	Frequency
0–2	6
3–5	13
6–8	17
9–11	24
12–14	21
15–17	14
18–20	5

Using this information he ran a 30-day simulation. He chose random numbers for arrivals and for the type of customer rental. The simulation revealed the percent of usage of the mopeds, the number of stockouts, the percentage of demand satisfied, and the total amount of rental time.

Sid saw no relevance to his situation. In addition, he felt there were obvious shortcomings in the information provided; e.g., there were:

no calculations to determine moped requirements,
no provisions for costs in the model, and
no resource constraints (whereas Sid could obtain licenses for a maximum of 50 mopeds under a city ordinance).

Furthermore, he had not received information on lease versus purchase acquisitions, nor any ways to compensate for the off season.

1. Was the fact-finding mission of any use to Sid? Could there be transfer possibilities to his operation?
2. What simulations would you recommend he try? How could they be structured to his rental service?
3. Would simulation alone be the key to his inventory planning, particularly for investment decisions?

CASE 3: COMBINING PROBABILITIES

Adolph Nolting has been assigned the task of developing an ordering system for inventory item R2D3, which has a variable demand and lead time. He has been given historical demand and lead time data, contained in two independent probability distributions as follows:

Demand		Lead Time	
Units/Day	Probability	Days	Probability
0	.05	2	.27
1	.18	3	.45
2	.23	4	.18
3	.27	5	.10
4	.16		
5	.09		
6	.02		

He has been informed further of the following costs associated with inventory activity: ordering cost=$15.00/order; holding cost per day=$1.00/unit; and stockout cost per day of occurrence=$5.00/unit.

Adolph has considered two techniques to determine his ordering strategy. The first alternative is to form joint probability distributions using the enumeration approach. This method of combining probabilities would define demand during lead time, and consequently could be used to meet his objective of setting the reorder point at its lowest expected cost.

On the other hand, Adolph is considering the use of simulation techniques, and as yet is undecided between his two options, the perpetual or the periodic inventory simulation. To date, the firm has used a perpetual system for R2D3, but Adolph is ready to experiment with both types. What is confusing to Adolph is the structuring of the simulations. He is fully aware that Monte Carlo simulation involves determining the probability distribution of the variables under study and the sampling from the distribution by using random numbers to obtain data. He is uncertain, however, how to perform the simulation and generate the requisite data. More specifically, Adolph does not have definitive decision rules or a predetermined number of replications.

For methodology determination Adolph has chosen the following selection criteria: optimality, suitability, facility, and accommodation to introduction of other factors, e.g. real life occurrences.

1. Which technique should he use (simulation or joint probabilities)?
2. In using the different techniques, will he arrive at similar policies?
3. What benefit would lie in running both perpetual and periodic inventory system simulations?

MATHEMATICAL ABBREVIATIONS AND SYMBOLS USED IN CHAPTER 11

D	Daily demand in units
K	Desired accuracy of simulated variable
L	Lead time in days
M	Lead time demand in units
m	Sample length of simulation run
N	Number of replications or length of simulation run
$P(D)$	Probability of a demand of D units
$P(L)$	Probability of a lead time of L days
$P(M)$	Probability of a lead time demand of M units
s	Standard deviation of sample runs
Z	Standard normal deviate

12 Inventory Control Systems

A good control system provides for self-control and only requires attention on an exception basis. The starting point in developing a control system is an analysis of the objectives of the intended systems. This procedure discloses the critical activities in the operation where control can be most effective. Inventory control systems have advanced beyond the rudimentary concepts of control. They are well established and developed, but still experience the usual control problems.

Control systems delineated in this chapter are concerned with aggregate inventory control. The emphasis is on control procedures for the totality of inventory. An organization may have one or more control systems for managing its inventory. Since there are usually thousands of distinct items in inventory, it is imperative that the control mechanism satisfy the service objectives of the institution at the lowest possible cost. The selection of the control system (or systems) is a top management responsibility. The type of inventory control system selected will have an impact on almost all other organizational activities.

An inventory control system is a coordinated set of rules for routinely answering the questions of when to order and how much to order. The system should indicate how routine and nonroutine situations are to be treated via predetermined rules and procedures. An effective system will accomplish the following:

1. ensure that sufficient goods and materials are available,
2. identify excess and fast- and slow-moving items,
3. provide accurate, concise, and timely reports to management,
4. expend the least amount of cost in accomplishing the first three tasks.

A comprehensive inventory system involves much more than quantitative inventory models. All aspects of the system must be considered, and not just the inventory model. There are six vital areas to be considered:

1. The development of demand forecasts and the treatment of forecast errors
2. The selection of inventory models (EOQ, EOI, EPQ, MRP, or SOQ)
3. The measurement of inventory costs (order, holding, stockout)
4. The methods used to record and account for items
5. The methods for receipt, handling, storage, and issue of items
6. The information procedures used to report exceptions

The use of sophisticated mathematical techniques *per se* does not necessarily result in an effective system. Precise, highly mathematical techniques are of little use unless the information to feed into the models is available at acceptable cost. Systems that select approximate, reasonable inventory levels with low data processing costs are often preferable. In many cases, the lack of accurate and timely data nullifies the advantages of complex control systems. It should be remembered that a breakdown in any one of the above six vital areas (not just the inventory model) can undermine the efficiency of the entire system.

TYPES OF CONTROL SYSTEMS

It is difficult to classify the various inventory control systems in an orderly fashion. Nevertheless, it is possible to distinguish among the systems most frequently used. Common types of inventory systems are the perpetual, two-bin, periodic, optional replenishment, and material requirements planning systems. The perpetual, two-bin, periodic, and optional replenishment systems usually apply to end items, while the material requirements planning system applies to materials and components used to produce an end item.

The perpetual and two-bin systems have a fixed order quantity and a variable review period; the periodic and optional replenishment systems have a fixed review period and a variable order quantity; and the material requirements planning system is geared to planned production requirements (the order quantity is variable and the review period can be fixed or variable). The two-bin system is a special type of perpetual system, while the optional replenishment system is a special type of periodic system.

The perpetual and two-bin systems are referred to as fixed order size systems (quantity-based). The periodic and optional replenishment systems are referred to as fixed order interval systems (time-based). The material requirements planning system is termed a derived order quantity system (production-based). Quantity-based systems are checked continually with each demand to determine if an order should be placed (thus the name "perpetual"). With time-based systems, a count of stock is made on designated review dates (thus the name "periodic"). Production-based systems order stock only to preplanned manufacturing schedules.

There are two major variables in an inventory system. They are the order quantity and the frequency of ordering. If one of the variables is held constant, the other tends to fluctuate. The perpetual inventory system holds the order size constant and lets the frequency of ordering fluctuate according to demand requirements. The periodic inventory system holds the frequency of ordering constant by establishing a fixed order period and lets the order size fluctuate according to demand requirements. In the optional replenishment system, the review period is held constant and the order size is variable, but no orders are placed until the stock level is less than or equal to a reorder point.

Perpetual Inventory System

A perpetual system keeps records of the amount in storage, and it replenishes when the stock drops to a certain level. This system is based on the concepts of economic order quantity (EOQ) and reorder point. Under this system the reorder point and order quantity are fixed, the review period and demand rate are variable, and the lead time can be fixed or variable. Figure 1 describes the behavior of the perpetual inventory system for a single item. The average inventory is the safety stock plus one-half the order quantity (average inventory $= S + Q/2$).

With the perpetual system, each time a unit (or units) is issued from stock the withdrawal is logged and the stock position is compared with the reorder point. If the stock position is at or lower than the reorder point, an order is prepared for a fixed number of units. If the stock position is higher than the reorder point, no action is taken. Thus, with the perpetual system there is constant or perpetual accountability on all items.

The perpetual system is completely defined by knowing the order size and the minimal stock level which signals the placing of an order. The major disadvantage of the perpetual system is that it requires perpetual auditing of the inventory in stock. Since an order can occur at any time, this prevents the economies which result from the amalgamation of several items from one supplier into one order. These potential amalgamation savings can be of considerable magnitude.

Fixed order size systems require a continuing review or observation of inventory levels. The object is to know as quickly as possible when the reorder point is reached. The review may consist of analyzing perpetual inventory records (manual or computerized) as they are posted, or visually noticing the physical stock when it reaches the reorder point (the two-bin

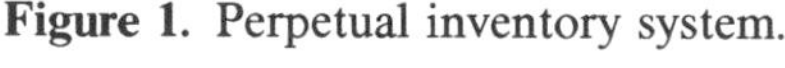

Figure 1. Perpetual inventory system.

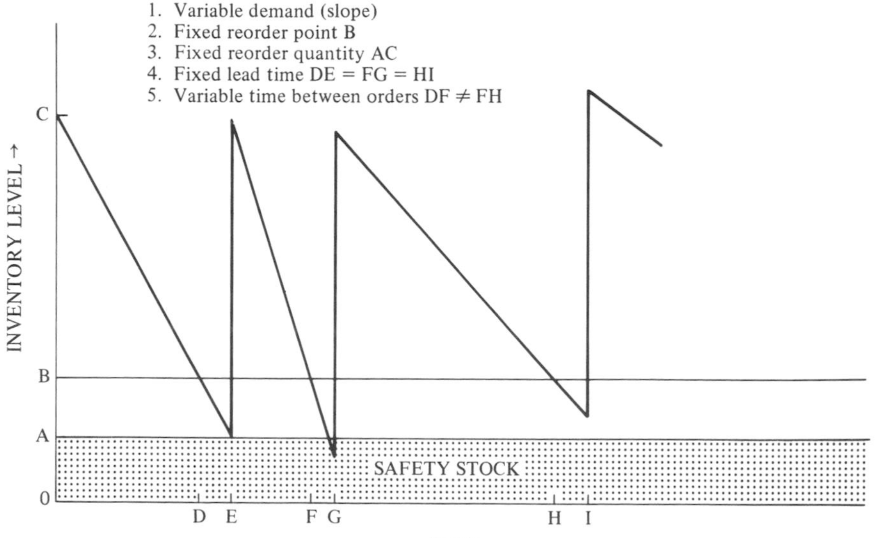

system is based on physical identification without the additional records). The fixed order size system with perpetual inventory records is excellent for high cost items needing close control.

The advantages of a perpetual system are as follows:

1. An efficient, meaningful order size
2. Safety stock needed only for the lead time period
3. Relative insensitivity to forecast and parameter changes
4. Less attention for slow-moving items

A perpetual system can have the following weaknesses:

1. If managers do not take the time to study inventory levels of individual items, order quantities tend to be established by clerks.
2. Reorder points, order quantities, and safety stocks may not be restudied or changed for years.
3. Delays in posting transactions can render the system useless for control.
4. Clerical errors or mistakes in posting transactions can make the system impotent.
5. Numerous independent orders can result in high transportation and freight costs.
6. Large combined orders, which can frequently result in supplier discounts based on dollar value, must be foregone.

The cost of operating a perpetual record system may far exceed the advantages to be gained from it. The cost of record keeping as well as the clerical staff's ability are important considerations in the selection of a system. It is advantageous to use systems which are not quite optimal when the cost of attaining the optimum is prohibitive.

Perpetual control means there is continuous control over the physical units of inventory. Inventory records are kept up to date, an entry being made each time an item is issued or is received from a supplier. Daily records are recorded manually or on punch cards, or are processed by a computer for disk or tape storage. The perpetual system requires (1) an inventory clerk, (2) daily records, (3) material issue and receiving slips, and (4) a guarded or locked storeroom. The two-bin system functions without the daily records, and therefore is a simplified version of the perpetual system.

Two-Bin Inventory System

The distinguishing feature of the two-bin system is the absence of a perpetual inventory record. The two-bin system is a fixed order size system, and it has several advantages. The most important advantage is the reduction in paperwork. Records are not maintained for each transaction. The reorder point is determined by visual observation. When the stock in one bin is depleted, an order is initiated, and demands are then filled from the second bin.

The system can even be used with only one bin. An order can be triggered when the inventory level reaches a physical mark such as a painted line or a given volume level (for gasoline or other liquids). The reorder point quantity can also be placed in a bag or container, so that when the stock is drawn down to the sealed quantity an order is placed.

The two-bin system is best suited for items of low value, fairly consistent usage, and short lead time, such as office supplies, nuts, bolts, and so forth.

Periodic Inventory System

In a periodic inventory system the number of items in storage is reviewed at a fixed time interval. A count must be taken of the goods on hand at the start of each period.[1] In the perpetual system an actual count is not required, since the inventory records contain receipts, issues, and balances on hand. With the periodic system the quantity to be ordered is not fixed, and the decision maker changes the quantity ordered to reflect changes in the demand rate. Under this system, the review period is fixed; the order quantity, the demand rate, and the reorder point are variable; and the lead time can be fixed or variable. Figure 2 describes the behavior of the periodic inventory system for a single item. A maximum inventory level E is established for each item. The order quantity is the maximum inventory level minus the inventory position on the review date.

With the periodic system, the number of units remaining is not reviewed each time a unit (or units) is issued from stock. The periodic system usually accounts for the number of units in stock on the review date by an actual count. The size of the replenishment order is variable and depends on the number of units in stock. The order quantity varies from period to period and depends upon demand.

In the perpetual (continuous review) system, a replenishment order is initiated as soon as the inventory level drops to the reorder point. In the periodic (discrete review) system, the inventory position is checked only at specified time intervals. The perpetual system treats inventory items continuously and independently. The periodic system treats them discretely and dependently. Frequently it is worthwhile to treat items in a dependent manner and order them in joint groups. The advantages of joint orders are as follows:

1. A reduction in ordering cost may be possible because items are processed under a single order.

[1] The count may be from an information system relying on a perpetual inventory record, or from an inspection. New point-of-sale registers and business machines maintain inventory records as well as registering sales. The new machines serve multiple functions and are part of management information systems.

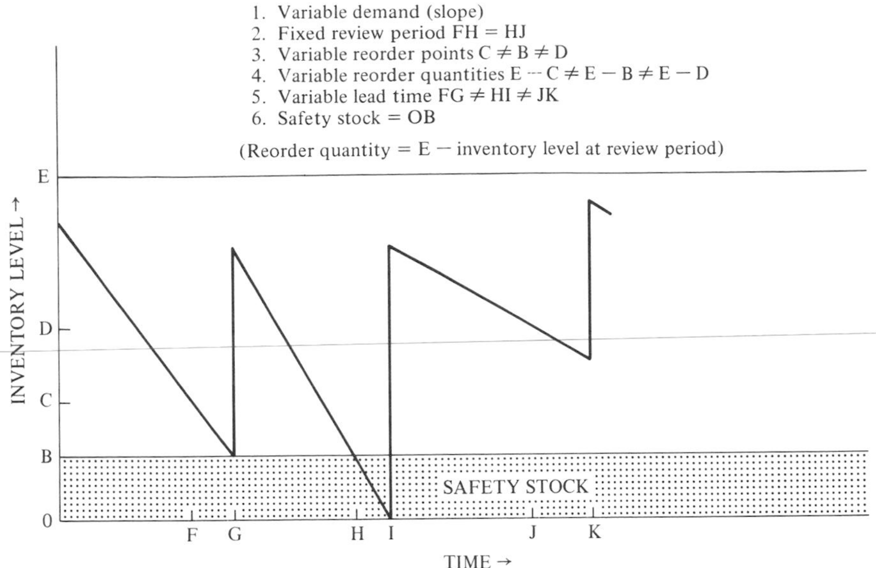

Figure 2. Periodic inventory system.

2. Suppliers may offer discounts for purchases exceeding a given dollar volume. The lumping of several items into a single order can make the discount attainable.
3. Shipping costs may be significantly decreased if an order is of a convenient size, such as a boxcar. The simultaneous ordering of several items can result in convenient sizes.

The presumption in the periodic system is that some sort of physical count is made at the time of review. In many instances records of transactions (sales slips) are available, but the accuracy of the information system may require an actual count for verification (lost or stolen items are not apparent from transaction records). Automatic data processing equipment can provide perpetual inventory records, such that order decisions can be made on a prescribed basis without the need for an actual physical count of items. Some accommodation must be made in these systems for the return of sale items, errors in transaction accounting, lost items, and stock shrinkage.

The periodic system is completely defined by the order period and the maximum inventory levels. In the perpetual system the safety stock represented protection against demand fluctuations during the lead time period.[2]

[2] It can be shown that the average inventory will be lower if orders are placed when needed rather than only at set times. However, the cost of operating the continuous record system may far exceed the advantages to be gained from it.

With a fixed order period, the periodic system requires safety stock for protection against demand fluctuations during both the review period and the lead time. This means that the periodic system will require a larger safety stock for a given item than the perpetual system. This additional safety stock results in the optimal perpetual system being less expensive than the optimal periodic system, though this may be offset by the economies of single supplier item amalgamation. The periodic system is well suited for inventory control when the supply sources are few or the source is a central warehouse.

Optional Replenishment Inventory System

The optional replenishment inventory system, which is also referred to as a min-max system, is a hybrid of the perpetual and periodic systems. Stock levels are reviewed at regular intervals, but orders are not placed until the inventory position has fallen to a predetermined reorder point. Figure 3 describes the behavior of the optional replenishment system for a single item. The maximum inventory level is established for each item. If the inventory position is above the reorder point on the review date, no order is placed. If the inventory position is at or below the reorder point on the review date, an order is placed. The order quantity is the maximum inventory level minus the inventory level at the review period.

The optional replenishment system is commonly referred to in the literature as the (s, S) system, where s is the reorder point (B in our notation)

Figure 3. Optional replenishment inventory system.

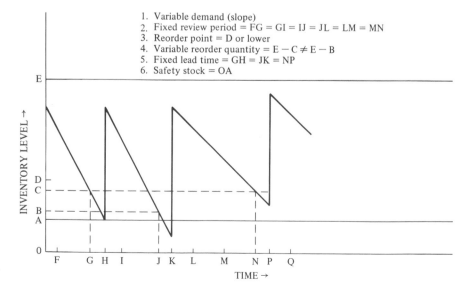

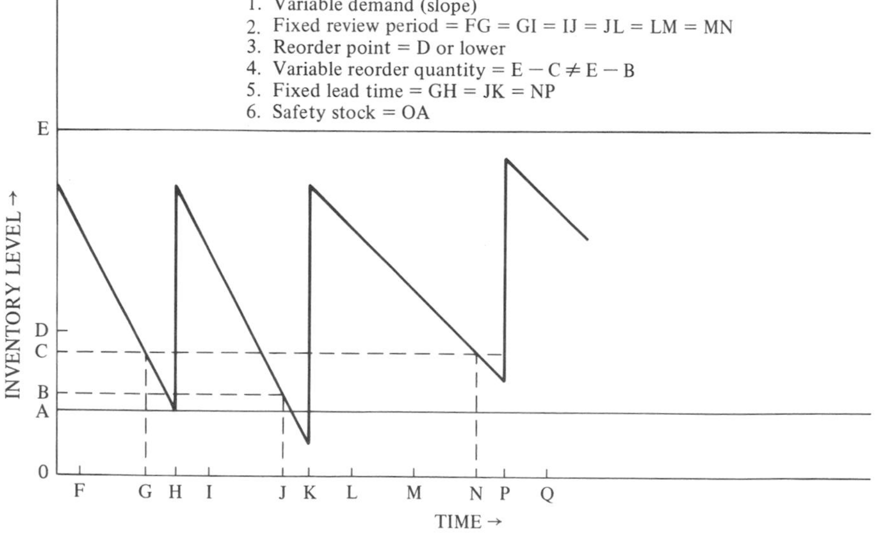

and S is the maximum inventory level (E in our notation). The system is defined by three parameters:

1. The length of the review period T
2. The maximum inventory level E
3. The reorder point B

Note that the perpetual and periodic systems are both defined by only two parameters, while the optional replenishment system requires three parameters.

The system permits orders to be placed in efficient quantities, and it reduces costs resulting from the frequent placement of small orders. Fewer but larger orders are placed than in the periodic system, so order costs are lower. When the review period is so long that an order is triggered at almost every review, the optional replenishment system is indistinguishable from the periodic inventory system.

The optional replenishment system can require substantial safety stocks. If the inventory level at the time of review is slightly above the reorder point, coverage is required for two order intervals plus the lead time. The review period length is established by procedures appropriate to periodic systems. The reorder point will consist of safety stock and the expected demand over the lead time and the review period. The safety stock is determined by analyzing the demand variation occurring for the period covered by the lead time and the review period.

Material Requirements Planning Inventory System

The material requirements planning (MRP) inventory system is used extensively with planned production. For items that are materials or components used by end items, stock levels are derived from the requirements dictated by the end item. The material requirements planning system is a derived order quantity system.

This system (also referred to in the literature as a requirements planning system) functions by working backward from the scheduled completion dates of end products or major assemblies to determine the dates and quantities of the various component parts and materials that are to be ordered. The system works well when (1) a specific demand for an end product is known in advance and (2) the demand for an item is tied in a predictable fashion to the demand for other items.

Overview of Inventory Systems

Some features of the common types of systems are displayed in Table 1. All the inventory systems have advantages and disadvantages as well as different areas of application. The perpetual system is well suited to high-cost

Table 1. Inventory System Features

Factor	Inventory Systems:	Perpetual[a]	Two-Bin[a]	Periodic[b]	Optional Replenishment[c]	Material Requirements Planning[d]
Order quantity		Fixed	Fixed	Variable	Variable	Variable
Reorder point		Fixed	Fixed	Variable	Fixed	Variable
Review period		Variable	Variable	Fixed	Fixed	Fixed/variable
Demand rate		Fixed/variable	Fixed/variable	Fixed/variable	Fixed/variable	Fixed
Lead time		Fixed/variable	Fixed/variable	Fixed/variable	Fixed/variable	Fixed/variable
Safety stock		Medium	Medium	Large	Very large	Small/none

[a] Perpetual and two-bin systems (Q, B): Review inventory status with each transaction. If inventory $I \leq B$, order Q_0. If inventory $I > B$, do not order.

[b] Periodic system (E, T): Review inventory status at intervals of T. Order $E - I$ on each occasion.

[c] Optional replenishment system (E, T, B): Review inventory status at intervals of T. If inventory $I \leq B$, order $E - I$. If inventory $I > B$, do not order.

[d] Material requirements planning (MRP) system: Order items to meet production schedules.

items where constant review is desirable. The two-bin system has application where constant review is not necessary because of low activity and/or low unit cost. The two-bin system defers action until a reasonable size order can be placed, but it can result in relatively high freight costs.

The periodic system finds applications where (1) there are many small issues of items from inventory, so that posting records for each issue is impractical, as in retail stores, supermarkets, automobile parts supply houses, and similar establishments; (2) purchase orders are placed for many different items from one source or a central warehouse; (3) transportation and ordering costs can be reduced significantly by combining orders. The cost of maintaining the periodic system may be higher because of larger safety stock and the review cost.

The optional replenishment system has the advantages of the close control associated with the perpetual system and of the reduction of item orders associated with the periodic system. The optional replenishment system requires the largest safety stock, and the material requirements planning system requires the smallest safety stock. When demand exhibits an upward trend, the perpetual is more desirable than the periodic system. With an upward trend the perpetual system orders more frequently and the safety stock must be increased, but in the periodic system the orders get larger and larger and more safety stock is required. The best choice depends on details.

Although the periodic system involves higher holding costs, the perpetual system tends to involve higher clerical processing costs due to its close control over every transaction (inflow and outflow). The perpetual system with fixed order sizes will be more appropriate if:

1. The number of transactions is low compared to annual demand.
2. Paperwork transaction costs are low compared to ordering costs.
3. The unit cost of the item is high.
4. The stockout cost is high.
5. Demand fluctuations are great and difficult to predict.
6. Holding costs are high.

If the above conditions are reversed, the periodic system will be preferred.

The periodic system has been used extensively in the past. It is probably the most widely used system because of its applicability at the retail level. With the advent of the computer and other less costly business machines, perpetual posting of inventory is becoming more prevalent. At the retail level, the cash register is being replaced by a device that electronically adjusts inventory levels at the point of the cash or credit transaction. These developments permit the manager to determine inventory levels and investment almost instantaneously. They also make available a substantial amount of information (previously unavailable or too costly to obtain) upon which to control inventory levels and to make decisions.

SELECTIVE INVENTORY CONTROL

Materials management involves thousands or even millions of individual transactions each year. To do their job effectively, materials managers must avoid the distraction of unimportant details and concentrate on significant matters. Inventory control procedures should isolate those items that require precise control from those that do not. Selective inventory control can indicate where the manager should concentrate his efforts.

It is usually uneconomical to apply detailed inventory control analysis to all items carried in an inventory. Frequently, a small percentage of inventory items account for most of the total inventory value. It is usually economical to purchase a large supply of low cost items and maintain little control over them. Conversely, small quantities of expensive items are purchased and tight control is exercised over them. It is frequently advantageous to divide inventories into three classes according to dollar usage (the product of annual usage and the unit purchase cost or production cost). The approach is called *ABC* analysis. The *A* class is high value items whose dollar volume typically accounts for 75–80% of the value of the total inventory, while representing only 15–20% of the inventory items. The *B* class is lesser value items whose dollar volume accounts for 10–15% of the value of the inventory, while representing 20–25% of the inventory items. The *C* class is low value items whose dollar volume accounts for 5–10% of the inventory value but 60–65% of the inventory items. Figure 4 shows a

Figure 4. Typical *ABC* inventory analysis.
Key: A=high value items; B=medium value items; C=low value items.

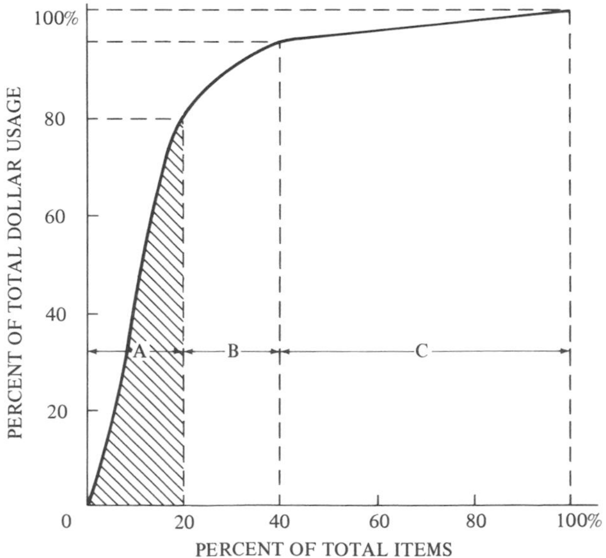

typical *ABC* inventory classification. The breakdown into *A*, *B*, and *C* items is an arbitrary classification, and further groups or divisions may be established.

The inventory value for each item is obtained by multiplying the annual demand by the unit cost. The annual demand is used to avoid any distortions from seasonal usage. The entire inventory is listed in descending order from the largest value to the smallest. The items are then designated by the *ABC* classification system.

The same degree of control is not justified for all items. The class *A* items require the greatest attention and the class *C* items the least attention. Class *C* items need no special calculations, since they represent a low inventory investment. The order quantity might be a one year supply with a periodic review once a year. Class *B* items could have EOQs developed, with a semiannual review of the variables. Class *A* items could have EOQs developed, with a review of the variables each time an order is placed. The major concern of an *ABC* classification is to direct attention to those inventory items that represent the largest annual expenditures. If inventory levels can be reduced for class *A* items, a significant reduction in inventory investment will result.

The purpose of classifying items into groups is to establish appropriate levels of control over each item. The *ABC* analysis is useful for any type of system (perpetual, periodic, optional replenishment, and so forth). With the periodic system, the *ABC* analysis can be subdivided so high usage items receive a short review and low usage items receive a much longer review. On a periodic basis, *A* items might be ordered weekly, *B* items might be ordered biweekly, and *C* items might be ordered quarterly or semiannually. Note that the unit cost of an item is not related to the classification. An *A* item may have a high dollar volume through a combination of either low cost and high usage or high cost and low usage. Likewise, *C* items may have a low dollar volume because of low demand or low cost.

The *ABC* classification tells which items should receive the greatest control, on the basis of dollar usage or sales volume. The classification indicates nothing about the profitability or criticality of the items. Frequently the absence of a *C* item can seriously disrupt production. It can then be forced into the *A* or *B* classification even though its dollar usage alone does not warrant its inclusion. Management judgment must be exercised in the control of critical items.

Class *A* items deserve close control. Because each item may represent a significant amount of inventory value, the perpetual system is often used, since it provides the closest individual control. Class *B* items are usually of less value than *A* items, and the optional replenishment system is frequently employed. It is usually more economical to combine orders for several items. Class *C* items may have a loose policy with 6-month to 1-year purchase quantities. A two-bin inventory system can be effectively used on these items, since it requires very little paperwork. The service levels for

Table 2. Comparison of *ABC* Classifications

Item	Degree of Control	Type of Records	Lot Sizes	Frequency of Review	Size of Safety Stocks
A	Tight	Accurate & Complete	Low	Continuous	Small
B	Moderate	Good	Medium	Occasional	Moderate
C	Loose	Simple	Large	Infrequent	Large

class *C* items can be set very high because of their limited investment. Class *A* and *B* items usually have a lower service level determined by an economic cost analysis. A comparison of the *ABC* classifications is contained in Table 2.

The advantage of an *ABC* analysis lies in a relaxing rather than in a tightening of inventory control (separating the "vital few" from the "trivial many"). The relaxation of control comes from less emphasis put on *C* items, which represent the bulk of the inventory items. The *ABC* analysis gives a measure of inventory importance to each item.

The *A*, *B*, and *C* classes are artificially produced strata. Organizations may choose to group their inventory into more than three classifications, but the principle is the same. High value items receive the most attention and low value items the least. Each organization should tailor its inventory system to its own peculiarities.

EXAMPLE 1

A small firm inventories only ten items, but decides to set up an *ABC* inventory system with 20% *A* items, 30% *B* items, and 50% *C* items. The company records provide the information shown in Table 3.

Table 3

Item	Annual Usage	Cost	Annual Dollar Usage	Rank
G-1	40,000	$.07	2,800	5
G-2	195,000	.11	21,450	1
G-3	4,000	.10	400	9
M-1	100,000	.05	5,000	3
M-2	2,000	.14	280	10
M-3	240,000	.07	16,800	2
M-4	16,000	.08	1,280	6
P-1	80,000	.06	4,800	4
P-2	10,000	.07	700	7
P-3	5,000	.09	450	8
			$53,960	

By rearranging this information, Tables 4 and 5 can be developed.

Table 4

Item	Annual Dollar Usage	Cumulative Dollar Usage	Cumulative Percentage	Class
G-2	$21,450	$21,450	39.8	*A*
M-3	16,800	38,250	70.9	*A*
M-1	5,000	43,250	80.2	*B*
P-1	4,800	48,050	89.0	*B*
G-1	2,800	50,850	94.2	*B*
M-4	1,280	52,130	96.6	*C*
P-2	700	52,830	97.9	*C*
P-3	450	53,280	98.7	*C*
G-3	400	53,680	99.5	*C*
M-2	280	53,960	100.0	*C*

Table 5

Class	Dollars per Group	Percentage of Items	Percentage of Dollar Usage
A=G-2, M-3	$38,250	20	70.9
B=M-1, P-1, G-1	12,600	30	23.4
C=all others	3,110	50	5.7

Before items can be classified into arbitrary categories, other factors than financial ones must be evaluated. Additional considerations can drastically change an item's classification as well as its control procedure. Some important factors might be:

1. Difficult procurement problem (long and erratic lead time)
2. Likelihood of theft
3. Difficult forecasting problem (large changes in demand)
4. Short shelf life (due to deterioration and obsolescence)
5. Too large a storage space requirement (very bulky)
6. The item's operational criticality

The *ABC* system does not apply to dependent demand items controlled under an MRP system. Its primary application is to end items, which are characterized by demand independent of other end items. Dependent demand items tend to be of equal operational importance for the continuation of production. Even the lowest cost item can totally disrupt dependent organizational activities. Therefore, operational criticality overrides the item's financial influence.

INVENTORY SYSTEM DEVELOPMENT

The development and implementation of an inventory control system to meet the needs of a specific organization is a customizing operation. Since inventory management is not an island unto itself, the system must serve the goals of the organization and the service objectives of other departments. It is usually easier to develop an inventory system for a new company. If a revised system is planned for an existing company, the period of change can be traumatic. When a new system is introduced, operational procedures must be revised, forms and reporting techniques changed, and employee work patterns modified, leaving operating efficiency usually diminished.

The decision to implement or subsequently redesign an inventory system rests with top management. However, the ultimate fate of an inventory control system usually lies in the hands of operations personnel lower down. To avoid resistance to change and implementation difficulties, the affected departments should be included in the design of the inventory system. Their inclusion usually results in a better system with fewer behavioral problems when it is installed. Departments which help create the inventory system tend to nurture it during the implementation phase and correct unanticipated design flaws. Without employee support, any inventory system is subject to demise or at least a turbulent future.

Should the system be manual or computerized? Just as with any prospective investment, a cost-benefit analysis should be conducted. The decision will be influenced by many factors, the most important probably being the volume of work to be handled. Minicomputers and similar business machines are making electronic control a viable alternative for more and more organizations. Since electronic systems are providing additional benefits (accounting, control, and administration) beyond stock control, it is no surprise that they are popular.

A popular retail and wholesale device is called a point-of-sale terminal. The two types of point-of-sale terminals are the keyboard and optical scanner. The optical scanner automatically inserts information in a terminal by reading magnetic strips on specially designed tapes when the product is passed over a sensing device. The keyboard is similar to a cash register, but it maintains records of inventory status with each sale or withdrawal.

The use of computers in materials management is growing rapidly. Manual methods (in many cases) have reached their limit. The computer can perform and develop forecasts, reorder points, order quantities, order intervals, product explosions, record maintenance, customer billing, inventory status, and supplier payments. Manual systems with clerical control are viable for small organizations with fewer material needs.

When initiating an inventory system, the following hints can be helpful:

1. Inventory will invariably increase very quickly. Items whose order quantity is increased will be ordered at once, and the stock will

increase. Items whose order quantity is decreased will take time until their level is worked off.

2. Forecasting should be based on a daily or weekly level, since lead times are frequently shorter than a month. Monthly forecasting data can conceal patterns of demand occurring during the month and complicate lead time estimates of shorter duration.
3. Try the system on a limited number of items initially to solve any unforeseen problems before it is totally implemented.
4. Run the initial pilot study manually on a small number of items, so personnel can understand it thoroughly. If the final system will be computer-based, the initial pilot can be studied manually as well as on an automated basis.
5. Before the total system is to be implemented, verify that all personnel involved understand it and are committed to its success.

While there are many approaches to designing an inventory system, this section will cover a single approach that can provide a general framework. The generalized procedure is outlined in Figure 5.

A necessary precondition for developing the inventory system is forecasts of all end items produced or used by the organization. Item forecasts are developed from forecasting models such as were covered in a previous chapter. After item forecasts are obtained, an *ABC* analysis of the inventory will indicate what system or systems would be preferable. If a perpetual or two-bin inventory system is indicated, the EOQ and EPQ models can be employed. If conglomerate orders are necessary, the EOI model can be utilized for the periodic or optional replenishment inventory system. If items fall into the single order category, the SOQ model can be incorporated. If items are needed to support scheduled production operations, the MRP model can be applied.

From the various models and an understanding of the peculiarities of the organization, inventory decision rules can be established for all items. When inventory decision rules indicate items should be ordered, purchase requisitions are transmitted for the appropriate supplier. For external suppliers, purchase requisitions are transmitted to the purchasing department, which then contracts for the items. With internal suppliers, production requisitions are transmitted to the production control department, which then schedules the production of items.

When ordered items are received from the suppliers, they are quality-accepted and put into inventory. Needless to say, all of the transactions involve the generation of paper for accountability and control. Inventory systems are best maintained from a central control location that can indicate the status of any item. These records become the data base for forecasting models. Because of the quantity of items and the proliferation of paperwork, inventory systems are often candidates for computer control.

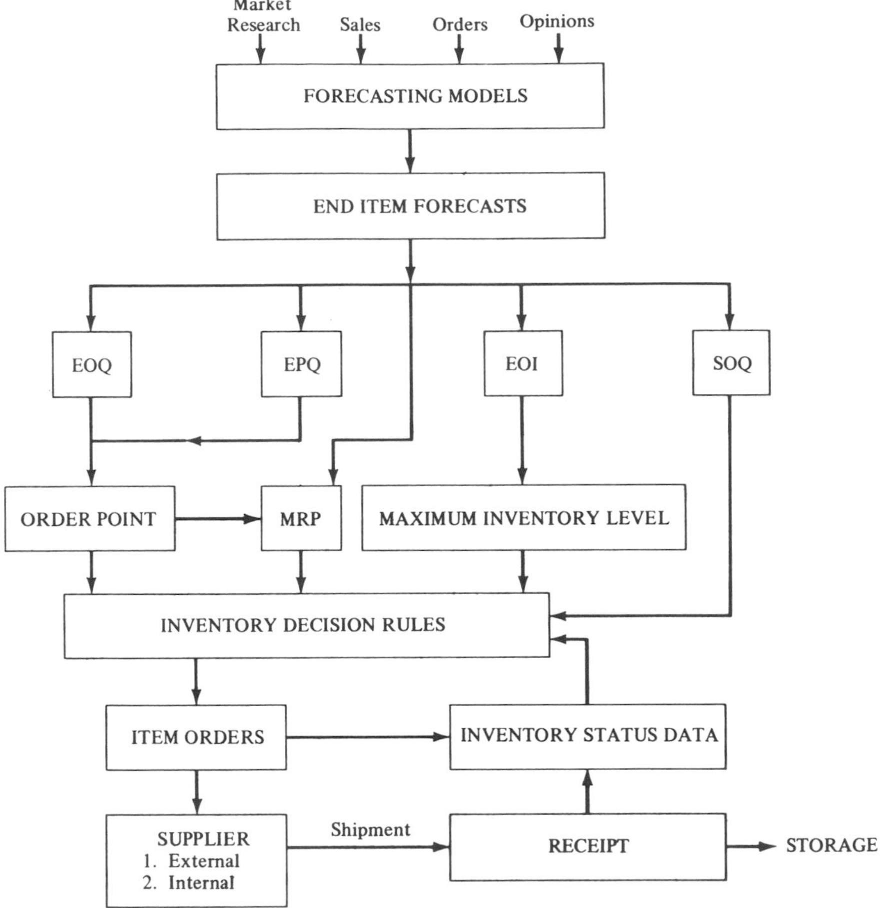

Figure 5. An inventory control system.
Key: EOQ = economic order quantity; EPQ = economic production quantity; EOI = economic order interval; SOQ = single order quantity; MRP = material requirements planning.

The ultimate success of an inventory system is in the transformation of inventory theory into workable detailed procedures. The design of forms and procedures can be more important than precise quantitative accuracy. Any inventory system requires the collection and processing of vast quantities of data.

The foundations of any inventory control system are input data and control records, which must be current and accurate. Inventory control is based on the accuracy of records of inflows and outflows. Poor records and data can destroy a perfectly designed control system. Inadequate records result in operating personnel finding informal methods (usually to the subversion of the formal procedures) for satisfying inventory needs (hoarding, stockpiling, overordering, early ordering, and so forth). Accurate and up-to-date records permit an inventory system to function efficiently and effectively.

Modern analytical techniques have taken much, but not all, of the guesswork out of inventory management. No longer need stock levels be determined solely by habit, hunch, or accident. Formulas are available to establish order quantities and order intervals, while statistical probability theory can be applied to safety stock determination. Intelligent and informed management judgment has not been replaced, however, but only supplemented. Both qualitative and quantitative evaluations, involving considerable study, collaboration, and teamwork, are usually required before intelligent decisions can be made and effective systems implemented.

The design of inventory systems must include sufficient flexibility to permit growth, expansion, and internal change without upsetting the operational system. The system must be able to cope with the exceptional item or event. The inventory system should be capable of being integrated into the other organizational systems with little difficulty.

EXCESS MATERIALS

Of all the problems facing the materials manager, three tend to be particularly troublesome:

1. Disposition of scrap, surplus, and obsolete materials
2. Slow-moving materials
3. Ever-increasing storage space requirements

Scrap is material that cannot be used in its present condition. It might be reworked to be usable, or discarded if no salvage value is evident. *Surplus material* is good material for which there is no use or the available quantity is excessive. *Obsolete materials* are those for which a need no longer exists because of design changes, model changes, style changes, or technological developments.

If management discards or salvages scrap, surplus, or obsolete material, the inventory turnover will increase, but profit for the period will be reduced. The decision to retain or salvage can be based on a cost-benefit ratio. Organizations usually have a simple rule for determining the disposition of material. If the following ratio is greater than one, the material should be retained in inventory; otherwise it should be considered for salvage:

$$\frac{p(M)P}{FV},$$

where

$p(M)$ = probability of sale or use within a year,

P = cost or market value of the material,

F = annual inventory holding cost fraction,

V = salvage value.

Surplus material for which there is no exhibited demand should be searched out and disposed of. Usually some arbitrary rule is applied, such as material that has not been active for a period of one year is classified as surplus. All surplus items should be sold at their best price or discarded. Surplus inventory can result in excessive costs due to their perpetual holding costs. Any losses on surplus inventory are charged off against income, and income taxes are reduced.

Some of the possible disposal routes are as follows:

1. Circulation within organization
2. Return to supplier
3. Direct sale to another firm
4. Sale to a dealer or broker
5. Sale to employees

Obsolescence can be classified as either technical or shelf life. *Technical obsolescence* results from design changes that supersede the previous design. It may be planned as in the garment and automotive industries, or unplanned as in radical design changes to rectify quality or functional problems. *Shelf life obsolescence* results after the usable shelf life is expended. It may be planned as in the dairy and pharmaceutical industries, or unplanned but necessitated by deterioration due to unusual temperature or environmental conditions. Obsolete materials should be disposed of periodically or they will reduce the return on investment and misuse storage space.

Mistakes are inevitable. Items are procured for needs that do not materialize, requirements are overestimated, plans change, and excessive stock tends to mount. Regardless of how efficiently an inventory is managed, surplus materials will accumulate.

For a multitude of reasons, there may be excess stock levels even for usable items in inventory. Even when there is a future demand for items, the level may exceed what should be available. The accrued holding costs for these excess quantities for extended periods of time can be a burden to an organization. It may be economically advantageous to sell or salvage a fraction of such stock levels. The benefit from such a transaction is the savings of holding cost plus the revenue generated from the salvage sale. To determine if excess stock is available, it is necessary to calculate the economic number of time periods of supply. Any stock held beyond the economic number of time periods should be sold. The economic number of time periods of supply is obtained as follows:

$$\begin{pmatrix}\text{accrued excess}\\ \text{holding cost}\end{pmatrix} + \begin{pmatrix}\text{revenue from}\\ \text{salvage}\end{pmatrix} = \begin{matrix}\text{purchase cost}\\ \text{of excess,}\end{matrix}$$

$$NPI_sF + P_sI_s = PI_s,$$

$$N = \frac{P - P_s}{PF},$$

where

N = economic number of time periods of supply in years,

I_s = excess inventory in units,

P = cost or market value per unit of material,

P_s = salvage value per unit,

F = annual inventory holding cost fraction.

The above formulation assumes that transaction costs from the salvage sale are zero, and the replenishment lead time is shorter than the economic number of time periods of supply. Additionally, the economic number of time periods of supply should not be less than the equivalent time supply of the economic order quantity.

EXAMPLE 2

An item with 200 units in inventory and a cost of \$10 per unit has an annual demand of 25 units. The salvage value per unit is \$5, and the inventory holding cost fraction is 0.25. Should any of the inventory be sold as excess stock?

The stock represents 8 years of supply ($200/25 = 8$). The economic number of time periods of supply is as follows:

$$N = \frac{P - P_s}{PF} = \frac{10 - 5}{10(0.25)} = 2 \text{ years.}$$

Since only a 2-year supply is needed and an 8-year supply is available, there are 6 years of excessive supply, or 150 units, to be salvaged, with a resultant inventory level of 50 items.

INVENTORY SYSTEM IMPROVEMENT

Each purchase or production situation must be preceded by a decision making process. The number of items involved can range from scores to millions, and the number of transactions is far in excess of the number of items. The decision making process may be simple or complex, programmed or nonprogrammed, intuitive or mathematical, hasty or deliberate. In this process, there are many ways an inventory manager can reduce costs. Some of the more apparent methods are as follows:

1. *Reduce lead times.* By selecting local suppliers (close to the organization's geographical location), substantial reductions in cost can be achieved. Local supply can reduce lead times, which lowers the reorder point and safety stock. Frequently, it is worth paying a higher unit cost for local supply, since inventory can be maintained at a lower level. Local supply can eliminate purchase order preparation, since one can phone in orders.

2. *Inform suppliers of expected annual demand.* If suppliers are aware of annual needs, they can plan their production to have sufficient inventory available to meet the expected demand. This action can reduce lead time and permit the supplier to better plan and schedule production operations.

3. *Contract with suppliers for minimum annual purchases.* Contract to purchase a fixed annual quantity from suppliers, with payment to coincide with the receipt of materials. Quantity discounts can be obtained in this manner, while materials are ordered and received in economic quantities. This approach can also be a hedge against future price increases.

4. *Offer customers a discount on preordered items.* If customers order items before they need them, inventory reductions can be achieved by specially ordering items. However, if customers receive a discount on items ordered before the items are needed, the price reduction can frequently offset the increase in holding costs associated with higher inventory levels.

5. *Maintain multiple suppliers.* Multiple suppliers can increase costs by reducing bulk purchases. However, multiple suppliers provide an alternate source if one supplier fails to deliver the goods. Multiple suppliers also permit a per unit cost comparison which helps to maintain a competitive price structure. With supplier competition, unit costs tend to be lower. It is not uncommon in production systems for reliability of supply to be more important than minor price differences.

6. *Buy on consignment.* Arrange with suppliers to pay for their items as they are sold or used. This action will transfer a large portion of the holding costs to the supplier.

7. *Consider transportation costs.* Failing to consider transportation costs and the most economical mode of transportation can increase the unit cost considerably.

8. *Order economical quantities.* Overbuying in relation to needs results in excessive holding costs.
9. *Control access to storage areas.* Protect against losses from theft, spoilage, unauthorized withdrawals by employees, and the ravages of the elements.
10. *Obtain better forecasts.* More reliable and precise forecasts can substantially reduce safety stocks.
11. *Standardize stock items.* Inventories can be reduced by a reduction in the quantities of each item or by a reduction in the number of different items used in stock. Inventory investment can be lowered by carrying one standard item instead of five different items that are used for essentially the same purpose.
12. *Dispose of inactive stock.* On a regular basis all stock should be reviewed to identify obsolete, poor quality, surplus, and slow-moving items. Disposal alternatives include return to the vendor, scrapping, reworking, salvage, and reduced-price sale.

Frequently the quickest, most effective way to reduce inventory is better priority/planning and control of operations. A poorly devised operating capacity system may appear efficient with the aid of excessive inventory. Improved planning and scheduling of operations can reduce the investment in inventory.

Organizationally, the inventory control function is usually assigned to the purchasing or the production control department. Purchasing feeds the inventory reservoir, while production control draws from it. Because department managers tend to neglect the significance of costs outside their own departments, the materials management concept has developed. The materials manager consolidates purchasing, inventory control, and production control into a single operating unit. The materials management concept grew out of the frustration of many companies not being able to control inventory effectively. It is not uncommon for departments to continually find fault with each other, when the true culprit is an inadequate organizational structure.

The number of items in inventory has been growing because of the increasingly technical nature of the items, a demand for greater variety by customers, and requirements for better service. The number of dollars invested in inventory is growing at a faster rate than the number of items. Computerization may hold the key to the solution of these problems. The computer aspect of materials management has been intentionally downplayed so as not to divert the reader from the essential subject matter. The computer's contribution lies in its power to execute a multitude of straightforward procedures in a very short time. It is an important tool of materials management but is not fundamental.

Decisions to add new products, purchase foreign components, and add distribution points can have a dramatic effect on inventory investment. Likewise, uncontrolled product proliferation, errors in transaction documentation, and outdated bills of material create serious problems. Computer routines and analytical techniques do not obviate the need for good management.

AGGREGATE INVENTORY MEASUREMENT

Aggregate inventory measurement relates to the overall level of inventory and the techniques for its measurement. Since aggregate inventory management plans and controls for the totality of inventory, it in essence "looks at the forest and not each tree." Four common ways to measure aggregate inventory are as follows:

1. Aggregate inventory value
2. Ratio of aggregate inventory value to annual sales
3. Days of supply
4. Inventory turnover

An organization may use one or more of the above for aggregate inventory measurement.

Aggregate inventory value is simply the total value of inventory at cost. Many organizations set dollar limits or budgets on the amount which can be invested in each general class of materials. They are usually applied to broad classes and not to individual items. The dollar limits indicate the upper investment limit which aggregate inventory value should not exceed. Aggregate inventory value is very simple and easy to use, but it neglects the dynamic nature of inventory and its other financial interactions.

The *inventory to sales ratio* is the aggregate inventory at cost divided by annual sales. This ratio recognizes the dynamic relation between inventory and sales, but it can vary substantially due to cost and/or selling price changes. If profit margins change, the ratio can become distorted for comparison purposes.

The *days of supply* is the total value of inventory at cost divided by the sales per day at cost. The time supply of inventory is dynamic in nature, but it can become confounded if the cost of sales is not maintained and controlled.

Inventory turnover refers to the cycle of using and replacing materials. It is the ratio of the average inventory at cost to the annual sales at cost. It indicates the number of "turnovers" of the investment in inventory for a given time period (usually a year). If an organization sells $600,000 worth of products a year and has an average inventory valued at $300,000, it has two turnovers per year. If the organization could generate the same sales with an average inventory worth $150,000, it would have four turnovers per year.

High turnover reduces the inventory investment and also saves holding costs. But it can be harmful if it means low inventories which result in being out of stock more often. A high inventory turnover at the cost of customer service and manufacturing expense is of dubious value. Inventory turnover recognizes the dynamic nature of inventory, but like most ratios it can easily become distorted.

Aggregate inventory measurement techniques usually reduce inventory items to a common financial denominator of dollars. The techniques measure results in absolute terms or ratios. The desirable range of performance is established historically by industry data, or by management judgment. While measurement in financial terms is desirable, inventory should also be viewed through other dimensions (composition, flexibility, contribution to organizational objectives).

CONCLUSION

It is not uncommon to have different types of inventory systems in use in the same organization at the same time. Management's responsibility is to manage the organization's assets, both human and nonhuman, in the light of preconceived goals and objectives. Inventory tends to have an impact upon all the functional areas. It therefore should not be surprising that inventories are troublesome and controversial. The inventory function is outlined in Figure 6.

Control can be a two-edged sword. Intense overcontrol is just as undesirable and costly as undercontrol. A *carte blanche* attitude towards new sophisticated control systems can be costly. New systems that save hundreds and cost thousands of dollars are unhealthy investments. A control system (or systems) should be installed on the basis of its cost-benefit relationship and not on achieving control as an end in itself.

The design of aggregate materials management systems can be approached from different angles. It is common for emphasis to be put on specific control models rather than on the relevant systems. A broad based aggregate program should include at least the following elements:

1. Determination or delineation of organizational goals
2. Assessment of the significance of materials management to organizational goals
3. Determination of aggregate material needs
4. Design of appropriate material control models
5. Design of forecasting models
6. Measurement and collection of model parameter inputs
7. Model testing and implementation
8. Variable reporting and model redesign
9. Operationalization of the materials management system

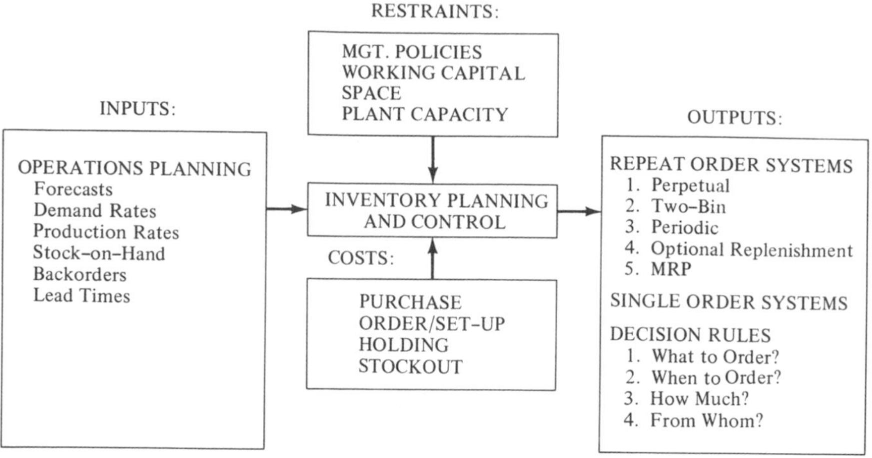

Figure 6. The inventory function.

The decision to institute a materials management system can be just as important as the choice of the particular models for the system. Too frequently an organization is adapted to a mathematical model rather than vice versa. The system designers must tread a narrow path between the pitfalls of oversimplification and the morass of overcomplication.

The problems of inventory and materials management are ubiquitous and complex. No simple formula takes into account all the variables encountered in real situations. The value of good approximations in permitting a practical and understandable solution to a problem is often far greater than any loss caused by a lack of accuracy or precision. Aggregate inventory analysis is not a precise science.

QUESTIONS

1. What is an inventory control system?

2. What should an effective inventory control system accomplish? What typical areas should be considered in developing a comprehensive inventory control system?

3. What are the two major variables in establishing an inventory control system?

4. Name five of the most frequently used types of inventory control systems.

5. What are the advantages of the perpetual inventory control system?

6. What is the major advantage of the two-bin inventory control system when compared with the perpetual inventory control system?

7. For what types of items are the perpetual and two-bin inventory control systems best suited?

8. What two values completely define the periodic inventory control system?

9. Compare the safety stock requirements of the periodic inventory control system with those of the perpetual inventory control system.

10. What are the advantages of the optional replenishment inventory control system?

11. What is derived demand?

12. What considerations can drastically affect an item's classification as well as its control procedure in an *ABC* inventory analysis?

13. What are the differences between scrap, obsolete, and surplus materials?

14. How can inventory costs be reduced by offering customers a discount on preordered items?

15. How can inventory costs be reduced by maintaining multiple suppliers?

PROBLEMS

1. Given the group of inventory items in the table below, develop an *ABC* inventory system where the *A* items constitute 80% of the total dollar value, the *B* items 15%, and the *C* items 5%.

Item	Unit Cost	Annual Unit Demand
1	.15	2,600
2	.05	6,500
3	.10	22,000
4	.22	75,000
5	.08	110,000
6	.16	175,000
7	.03	8,500
8	.12	2,500
9	.18	42,000
10	.05	2,000

2. An item has a market value of $20 and can be salvaged for $3. The holding cost fraction is 0.18, and the annual demand is 50 units. Currently, 275 units are in stock. Should the firm sell off any of this item's inventory?

3. An item is purchased for $.50 and salvaged for $.15. The holding cost fraction is 0.30, there are 1800 units in stock, and the annual demand is 1000 units. How much inventory should be sold off as excess inventory?

4. Item 1248 has a warehouse shelf life of 2 years, and 1700 units are in stock. They were purchased for $4 each, and the holding cost fraction is 0.25. The annual demand is 600 units, and the salvage value is $1.50. How much excess stock should be sold?

CASE 1: MATERIAL SHORTAGES AND DELAYED PRODUCTION

Zoom Equipment, Inc. produces a full line of earth moving equipment including tractors, dirtmovers, and shovels. It manufactures almost all component parts for the machines with a few exceptions. Sam Irwin, the new production manager, realized quickly that a major problem existed in the production department. A shortage of parts on the assembly lines was costing Zoom thousands of dollars.

Sam's first step in attempting to alleviate the problem was to investigate the company's make or buy decision procedures. He started his investigation in the accounting department. After some searching he realized he'd have to get actual out-of-pocket costs from the manufacturing department itself. There he was told the actual costs of parts varied considerably from one run to another for several reasons, the main one being that when it came time to assemble a piece of equipment there was seldom a sufficient quantity of all parts needed. The result was usually a schedule-upsetting rush order through the machine shop to make needed parts.

Sam decided to track down the reasons for the parts shortages on the assembly lines. He spent the next several days talking to the workers and supervisors. Sam learned that the marketing department forecasted sales of all equipment and parts about nine months in advance. The production control supervisor then prepared a list of all parts required and added a manufacturing spoilage allowance to the quantities needed. This allowance was as follows:

a. Large items, 1%
b. Costly or intricate parts, 2%
c. Other parts, 3%

The quantities of parts in inventory were compared with this list. If requirements exceeded inventory, a purchase order or manufacturing order was placed to bring inventory up to the required level.

Sam got the impression that the shortage problem had gone unnoticed for some time, because the cost accounting department actually budgeted for excess labor costs resulting from shortages on the assembly lines. After completing his investigation Sam made a list of reasons for the shortages:

a. Inadequate spoilage allowances
b. Errors in annual physical inventory count
c. Incorrect count of parts put into production
d. Poor machine loading
e. Insufficient raw materials purchased
f. Foremen performing clerical tasks

1. Are any of Sam's reasons for shortages on the assembly line valid?
2. How would you correct for the shortages?
3. What type of inventory control system should be adopted by Zoom?

CASE 2: CONTROL AND OPERATING METHODS

Automobile dealerships have a large and continuing need for supplies and materials in their function of selling and servicing automobiles. Facilities usually include buildings spread over several acres of land. Below are listed the departments that have special needs for supplies.

a. *Office*: office supplies and special forms.
b. *New car predelivery service*: cleanup material and lubricants.
c. *Used car reconditioning*: cleanup material and lubricants.
d. *Body shop*: paint and material, including thinner, sandpaper, files, tape, etc.
e. *Mechanical shop*: supplies and material.

At Tidewater Motors, salesmen from various suppliers make regular calls, check inventory levels, and recommend purchases. Normally the dealership parts manager acts as purchasing agent. However, salesmen go directly to the foreman of the different departments, since in most cases the supplies are stored at the department location. In this case, the foreman is the real purchasing authority who instructs the parts manager to issue the necessary purchase orders.

The advantages of the existing system are that the salesmen can solve any problems with their products, salesmen can check inventory levels, and little of the parts manager's time is required. Disadvantages of the system are that the salesmen try to sell the foreman and workers on their products as being best (this often creates problems when brands are changed), the salesmen tend to oversell actual needs, and price increases frequently go unnoticed.

Recently, Dick Terry took over as owner of the Tidewater Motors dealership. Upon reviewing his investment in inventory, he concluded that his inventory turnover was too low. He decided to investigate new control and operating procedures that might reduce his inventory investment.

1. Should all material and supplies be kept in one central location instead of being stored in close proximity to where they are used?
2. Should the parts manager make all decisions concerning the purchase of supplies?
3. Should salesmen be able to deal directly with foremen and workers, or should they deal only with the parts manager?

CASE 3: POOR RECEPTION

Warwick Electronic Services (WES) is a service company that services home entertainment equipment. It services all types of home entertainment equipment, but 70% of the revenue is derived from television set repairs.

WES is an authorized Zenith service center, which must stock a complete line of spare parts for Zenith TV sets. The spare parts are purchased from Zenith in a kit and then exchanged for new and rebuilt parts as they are used. If the parts exchange is the result of warranty service, they are replaced at no charge. The Zenith repairs account for 30% of total revenue. Another 40% of revenue is derived from servicing television sets manufactured by other companies, but there are no service agreements with them. The remaining revenue comes from stereo and miscellaneous equipment repairs.

The commonly used parts are stocked by a local distributor (parts house), which is three miles from the repair shop. The slower moving items have to be ordered through the distributor with a lead time of two weeks. The service records show that $60,000 was spent on parts last year. The annual inventory holding cost is 20% and the inventory level averages $40,000. The consumption of parts is directly related to the gross revenue, and the revenue is forecasted to increase at a rate of 10% during the next three years.

The present inventory system is unorganized and inefficient. As parts are needed, a few extra (like items) parts are ordered and stored until they are needed. This practice has led to a large accumulation of obsolete parts. The manager wants to formalize the inventory system and is ready to implement a new system.

1. What inventory system options are available to WES?
2. What inventory system or systems would you recommend? Why?
3. Does the dollar size of the inventory investment influence the type of system?

CASE 4: DEFENSIVE PURCHASING

The Propulsion Division of Tinker Air Force Base is a government operated facility for reworking military aircraft engines. The division supports five families of engines plus component parts. The disassembled engines flow through a series of continuous and intermittent process shops by means of an automated conveyor system with selected inventory control and feed points. The actual route and replacement work of an individual part entering the overhaul process is dependent on its condition as determined by nondestructive inspection techniques.

The purchasing function to support the rework facility is encumbered with several obstacles. The quantities of required parts have wide variability. Not only do work loads tend to be sporadic (partly a budgetary decision), but the types of rework necessary to repair or rebuild the incoming engines are also subject to extreme variation. Furthermore, purchasing, as a legislated procurement procedure, is done by contract with the recipients promising least cost delivery of federally specified parts. Many suppliers are becoming reluctant to submit bids. Other peculiarities are also increasing supplier reluctance, e.g. fear of short-term agreements after expensive setups, tight governmental guidelines, costs that restrict profit potential, and worse yet, the recent wave of favoritism. Therefore, as either a cause or an effect, an extension of the already successful inhouse production of replacement parts is expected.

Tinker has an excellent staff of six civil service purchasing agents, skilled in public purchasing and experienced in make-or-buy decisions. The total budget for the purchasing department is $425,000 annually, with 50% allocated to staff salaries. The agents typically process 12,500 purchase orders per year, amounting to a total annual expenditure of $60 million. A work measurement study conducted in the purchasing department disclosed that preparation and follow-up on orders is required at the 90% performance level for rework operations.

There are other costs of particular importance to the purchasing department. Materials and expediting expenses are $12 per order for phone calls, forms, etc.

Obsolesence costs are approximated at 3% of total inventory value, and costs for insurance, deterioration, and warehouse space are roughly 6%. Presently, the annual expense to operate the stores for inventory storage is budgeted at $125,000, the interest rate the military is assumed to pay on borrowed capital is 10%, and the required return on investment used for performance evaluation is set at 15%. These costs are used as in private enterprise to determine operating and inventory policies. The purchasing department calculates EOQs for purchased replacement parts and orders.

These costs are expected to change as the nation confronts an economic crisis. The administration and congressional bodies are formulating a comprehensive revitalization program. A significant part of the program is massive Federal restraint. Tinker is not certain how this will affect operations directly, but cutbacks in personnel and operating budgets seem imminent. With drastic cutbacks, the purchasing department feels it will have to cope in the short run by cutting some variable costs.

However, there is another administrative program that appears to be receiving popular support—increased defense spending. Provided this program receives approval, activity at Tinker could increase measureably. The not so invisible hand of the government could change rework orders substantially.

With operations so tightly predicated on government policies, the purchasing department cannot predict future circumstances. If cutbacks are severe, are changes in ordering strategies necessary or are changes in inventory systems preferred, e.g. EOQ to two-bin? If defense spending is a priority item, are EOQ's changed proportionately and are fixed costs likely to increase? If either or both situations occur, how is inventory management affected? These and more unanswered questions abound.

1. What ordering costs and holding costs are relevant prior to a revitalization program?
2. How might purchasing and inventory management change with stringent budgetary controls? With military proliferation?
3. What operating practices might come into play with the new program? Could another inventory control system be better in the deployment of the revitalization plan?
4. What effect could the federal programs have on suppliers and on in-house production?

CASE 5: SECOND-HAND GOODS

The Pickard Motor Company is imperiled by the contemporary problems that have nearly destroyed much of the American automobile industry. With the critical domestic economic situation, sales are falling dramatically, and ability to compete with foreign auto makers is seriously hampered. Proof of their financial jeopardy comes with the announcement of the latest quarterly earnings; Pickard is declaring the largest losses in corporate history. Witnessing the rapid decline of corporate solvency, Pickard is undertaking a recovery program whereby drastic changes are being instituted in product offerings. Pickard is converting a large portion of passenger car production to energy efficient cars. To do so, Pickard is paying enormous retooling and inventory replacement costs with capital borrowed at record high interest rates.

The Louisville Assembly Plant of Pickard Motors (Case 5, Chapter 10) is nearing the production "launch" of the newly engineered S-cars, Pickard's first energy efficient compacts. Since the Louisville plant is the site for finalizing engineering and production changes, the model year changeover to introduce the new line to production precedes operations at the other assembly plants by three months. Current model year production ends company-wide in four months, and all aspects of capital and procedural modification at Louisville must occur within that time.

Currently, Louisville has over $2.6 million worth of parts that are technologically acceptable for the present production year. Calculations show that these parts will carry over well beyond the final four weeks of scheduled production. Unfortunately, most of these parts are obsolete for the S-line, which is the only line to remain in production at the Louisville site. The number of obsolete parts becomes inordinately high after subtraction of the few "carryover" parts. The only possibilities of parts that could carry over to next year's line are certain sizes of tires and sparkplugs, a few incidental nuts and bolts, some standard paint colors, and other parts with dollar values that exclude even their mention.

Pickard headquarters is greatly disturbed about the dollar value of excess materials and is demanding prompt disposition of all surplus parts. The Louisville staff also recognizes the need for immediate disposition in order for the plant to attain operational status for the S-car "Launch Program." Louisville is more interested in getting the parts "off the books" than in the losses that will be suffered through quick disposition. The corporate headquarters, on the other hand, is taking an opposing view; headquarters is stressing reasonable cash recovery from the disposition of the goods.

Customarily, Pickard's initial disposition step would be return of the excess parts to the supplier and assumption of a small loss on the transaction. The present difficulty with this disposition route is time consumption and the predatory attitude the suppliers have taken in the current automobile producer dilemma. Pickard feels there has been systematic and conspired erosion of supplier repurchase prices, and therefore would rather choose an alternative route.

In the past, Pickard has also sold excess materials to employees. Recently, the company has considered forbidding this practice, because it has been used discriminately and has become a perquisite of top management. Furthermore, many of those who have participated in employee surplus sales have used the materials to start side-line businesses rather than for personal repairs or avocations.

Jim Jones, Louisville's scrap materials manager, seems to have been left with the bulk of the disposition task and has been instructed to get rid of as much dollar value of inventory as possible. As his first sources of solutions, he has been phoning friends in scrap materials businesses in automobile related fields. However, most of his hopes lie internally with great expectations of his counterpart at the San Jose Assembly Plant; he is sure he can ride to laurels on the proven disposition paths of the San Jose expert.

Ironically, San Jose, Louisville's sister plant, is found to seldom face excesses but chronically experience shortages. So, with little assistance from surplus materials personnel with understandably good track records and given headquarters's apprehensions concerning customary routes, Jim may have to push to pursue the old disposition means or quickly find new ones.

1. What disposition options are available?
2. Given their orientation, what would Louisville and the corporate headquarters most likely want done?
3. Should Louisville sacrifice sell and take the tax writeoff?
4. Could an *ABC* approach be applicable to Jim Jones's task?

MATHEMATICAL ABBREVIATIONS AND SYMBOLS USED IN CHAPTER 12

B	Reorder point in units
E	Maximum inventory level in units
EOI	Economic order interval
EOQ	Economic order quantity
EPQ	Economic production quantity
F	Annual inventory holding cost fraction
I	Stock position (units on hand plus units on order minus backorders)
I_s	Excess inventory in units
MRP	Material requirements planning
N	Economic number of time periods of supply in years
P	Cost or market value of material
P_s	Salvage value per unit
$p(M)$	Probability of sale or use within a year
Q	Order quantity in units
S	Safety stock in units
SOQ	Single order quantities
T	Order interval in years
V	Salvage value of material

Bibliography

Alfandary-Alexander, Mark. *An Inquiry into Some Models Of Inventory Systems*, Pittsburgh, PA: University of Pittsburgh Press, 1962.

Aljian, George W., ed. *Purchasing Handbook*, New York: McGraw-Hill, 1973.

American Management Association. *Company Approaches to Production Problems: Inventory, Warehousing, Traffic*, New York: American Management Association, 1955.

———. *Key Consideration to Inventory Management*, New York: American Management Association, 1953.

American Production and Inventory Control Society. *Management of Lot-Size Inventories*, Washington, DC: APICS, 1963.

———. *Material Requirements Planning by Computer*, Washington, DC: APICS, 1971.

Ammer, D. S. *Materials Management and Purchasing*, Homewood, IL: Richard D. Irwin, 1980.

Arrow, K. J., et al. *Studies in the Mathematical Theory of Inventory and Production*, Stanford, CA: Stanford University Press, 1958.

Baily, P. J. *Design of Stock Control Systems and Records*, London: Gower Press, 1970.

Baily, Peter, and David Farmer. *Managing Materials in Industry*, London: Gower Press, 1972.

Ballot, Robert P. *Materials Management*, New York: American Management Association, 1971.

Ballou, Ronald H. *Business Logistics Management*, Englewood Cliffs, NJ: Prentice-Hall, 1973.

Barrett, D. A. *Automatic Inventory Control Techniques*, London: Business Books Limited, 1972.

Bierman, Harold, et al. *Quantitative Analysis for Business Decisions*, Homewood, IL: Richard D. Irwin, 1969.

Blanchard, B. S. *Logistics Engineering and Management*, Englewood Cliffs, NJ: Prentice-Hall, 1974.

Bowersox, Donald J. *Logistical Management*, New York: Macmillan Publishing Company, 1974.

Bowman, Edward H., and Robert B. Fetter. *Analysis for Production and Operations Management*, Homewood, IL: Richard D. Irwin, 1967.

Box, G. E. P., and G. M. Jenkins. *Time Series Analysis: Forecasting and Control*, San Francisco: Holden-Day, 1970.

Briggs, Andrew J. *Warehouse Operations Planning and Management*, New York: John Wiley and Sons, 1960.

Brown, R. G. *Materials Management Systems*, New York: John Wiley and Sons, 1977.

———. *Decision Rules for Inventory Management*, New York: Holt, Rinehart and Winston, 1967.

———. *Smoothing, Forecasting, and Prediction of Discrete Time Series*, Englewood Cliffs, NJ: Prentice-Hall, 1963.

———. *Statistical Forecasting for Inventory Control*, New York: McGraw-Hill, 1959.

Buchan, Joseph, and Ernest Koenigsberg. *Scientific Inventory Management*, Englewood Cliffs, NJ: Prentice-Hall, 1963.

Buffa, E. S., and J. G. Miller. *Production-Inventory Systems: Planning and Control*, Homewood, IL: Richard D. Irwin, 1979.

Carroll, Phil. *Practical Production and Inventory Control*, New York: McGraw-Hill, 1966.

D'Anna, John P. *Inventory and Profit: The Balance of Power in Buying and Selling*, New York: American Management Association, 1966.

Davis, Grant M., and Stephen W. Brown. *Logistics Management*, Lexington, MA: Lexington Books, 1974.

Dudick, T. S., and R. Cornell. *Inventory Control for the Financial Executive*, New York: John Wiley and Sons, 1979.

England, Wilbur B. *The Purchasing System*, Homewood, IL: Richard D. Irwin, 1967.

England, Wilbur B., and Michiel R. Leenders. *Purchasing and Materials Management*, Homewood, IL: Richard D. Irwin, 6th edition, 1975.

Enrick, Norbert Lloyd. *Inventory Management*, San Francisco, CA: Chandler Publishing Company, 1968.

Fabrycky, W. J., and Jerry Banks. *Procurement and Inventory Systems: Theory and Analysis*, New York: Reinhold Publishing Corp., 1967.

Fetter, Robert B., and Winston C. Dalleck. *Decision Models for Inventory Management*, Homewood, IL: Richard D. Irwin, 1961.

Forrester, Jay W. *Industrial Dynamics*, Boston: M.I.T. Press, 1961.

Fourre, James P. *Applying Inventory Control Techniques*, New York: American Management Association, 1969.

Fuchs, J. H. *Computerized Inventory Control Systems*, Englewood Cliffs, NJ: Prentice-Hall, 1978.

Greene, James H. *Production and Inventory Control Handbook*, New York: McGraw-Hill, 1970.

———. *Production and Inventory Control*, Homewood, IL: Richard D. Irwin, 2nd edition, 1974.

Gross, Harry. *Make or Buy*, Englewood Cliffs, NJ: Prentice-Hall, 1966.

Hadley, G., and T. M. Whitin. *Analysis of Inventory Systems*, Englewood Cliffs, NJ: Prentice-Hall, 1963.

Hanssmann, Fred. *Operations Research in Production and Inventory Control*, New York: John Wiley and Sons, 1962.

Hedrich, Floyd D. *Purchasing Management in the Smaller Company*, New York: American Management Association, 1971.

Heinritz, Stuart F., and Paul V. Farrell. *Purchasing: Principles and Applications*, 5th edition, Englewood Cliffs, NJ: Prentice-Hall, 1971.

Heskett, James L., et al. *Business Logistics*, New York: The Ronald Press, 2nd edition, 1973.

Hobbs, John A. *Control Over Inventory and Production*, New York: McGraw-Hill, 1973.

Hoffman, Raymond A., and Henry Gunders. *Inventories: Control, Costing and Effect upon Income and Taxes*, New York: Ronald Press, 2nd edition, 1970.

Holt, Charles C., et al. *Planning Production, Inventories, and Work Force*, Englewood Cliffs, NJ: Prentice-Hall, 1960.

——— et al. *Operations Research in Production and Inventory Control*, New York: John Wiley and Sons, 1962.

Jenkins, Creed H. *Modern Warehouse Management*, New York: McGraw-Hill, 1968.

Johnson, Lynwood A., and Douglas C. Montgomery. *Operations Research in Production Planning, Scheduling, and Inventory Control*, New York: John Wiley and Sons, 1974.

Killeen, Louis M. *Techniques of Inventory Management*, New York: American Management Association, 1969.

Lee, Jr., Lamar, and Donald W. Dobler. *Purchasing and Materials Management*, New York: McGraw-Hill, 2nd edition, 1971.

Leenders, M. R., et al. *Purchasing and Materials Management*, Homewood, IL: Richard D. Irwin, 1980.

Lewis, C. D. *Scientific Inventory Control*, New York: American Elsevier, 1970.

Lipman, Burton E. *How to Control and Reduce Inventory*, Englewood Cliffs, NJ: Prentice-Hall, 1973.

Love, S. F. *Inventory Control*, New York: McGraw-Hill, 1979.

Magee, John F. *Physical Distribution Systems*, New York: McGraw-Hill, 1967.

——— and David M. Boodman. *Production Planning and Inventory Control*, New York: McGraw-Hill, 1967.

Mathews, Lawrence M. *Control of Materials*, London: Industrial and Commercial Techniques, Ltd., 1971.

McGarrah, Robert E. *Production and Logistics Management*, New York: John Wiley and Sons, 1963.

McMillan, Claude, and Richard F. Gonzalez. *Systems Analysis: A Computer Approach to Decisions Models*, Homewood, IL: Richard D. Irwin, 2nd edition, 1968.

Mills, Edward S. *Price, Output, and Inventory Policy*, New York: John Wiley and Sons, 1962.

Mize, Joe H., et al. *Operations Planning and Control*, Englewood Cliffs, NJ: Prentice-Hall, 1971.

Montgomery, D. J., and L. A. Johnson. *Forecasting and Time Series Analysis*, New York: McGraw-Hill, 1976.

Morse, Philip M. *Queues, Inventories, and Maintenance*, New York: John Wiley and Sons, 1958.

Mossman, Frank H., and Newton Morton. *Logistics of Distribution Systems*, Boston: Allyn and Bacon, Inc., 1965.

Mudge, Arthur E. *Value Engineering: A Systematic Approach*, New York: McGraw-Hill, 1971.

Naddor, Eliezer. *Inventory Systems*, New York: John Wiley and Sons, 1966.

National Association of Accountants. *Techniques in Inventory Management*, Research Report No. 40, New York: NAA, 1964.

Nelson, C. R. *Applied Time Series for Managerial Forecasting*, San Francisco: Holden-Day, 1973.

New, Colin. *Requirements Planning*, New York: John Wiley and Sons, 1973.

Niland, Powell. *Production Planning, Scheduling, and Inventory Control*, London: Macmillan, 1970.

Orlicky, Joseph. *Material Requirements Planning*, New York: McGraw-Hill, 1975.

———. *The Successful Computer System*, New York: McGraw-Hill, 1969.

Oxenfeldt, Alfred R. *Make or Buy: Factors Affecting Decisions*, New York: McGraw-Hill, 1965.

Peckham, Herbert H. *Effective Materials Management*, Englewood Cliffs, NJ: Prentice-Hall, 1972.

Peterson, R., and E. A. Silver. *Decision Systems for Inventory Management and Production Planning*, New York: John Wiley and Sons, 1979.

Plossl, G. W., and W. E. Welch. *The Role of Top Management in the Control of Inventory*, Reston, VA: Reston Publishing, 1979.

Plossl, G. W. *Manufacturing Control*, Reston, VA: Reston Publishing, 1973.

——— and O. W. Wight. *Production and Inventory Control*, Englewood Cliffs, NJ: Prentice-Hall, 1967.

Prabhu, N. *Queues and Inventories*, New York: John Wiley and Sons, 1965.

Prichard, James W., and Robert H. Eagle. *Modern Inventory Management*, New York: John Wiley and Sons, 1965.

Putnam, Arnold Q., et al. *Unified Operations Management*, New York: McGraw-Hill, 1963.

Raymond, Fairfield E. *Quantity and Economy in Manufacturing*, New York: McGraw-Hill, 1931.

Reisman, Arnold, et al. *Industrial Inventory Control*, New York: Gordon and Breach Science Publishers, 1972.

Sampson, Roy J., and Martin T. Farris. *Domestic Transportation: Practice, Theory, and Policy*, Boston: Houghton Mifflin Co., 1971.

Scarf, Herbert E., et al. *Multistage Inventory Models and Techniques*, Stanford, CA: Stanford University Press, 1963.

Sims, E. Ralph. *Planning and Managing Materials Flow*, Boston: Industrial Education Institute, 1968.

Smykay, Edward W. *Physical Distribution Management*, New York: Macmillan Publishing Co., Inc., 3rd edition, 1973.

Starr, Martin K., and David W. Miller. *Inventory Control: Theory and Practice*, Englewood Cliffs, NJ: Prentice-Hall, 1962.

Stelzer, W. R. *Materials Management*, Englewood Cliffs, NJ: Prentice-Hall, 1970.

Stockton, R. Stansbury. *Basic Inventory Systems: Concepts and Analysis*, Boston: Allyn and Bacon, 1965.

Sussams, J. E. *Industrial Logistics*, Boston: Cahners Books, 1972.

Taff, Charles A. *Management of Physical Distribution and Transportation*, Homewood, IL: Richard D. Irwin, 5th edition, 1972.

Tersine, R. J. *Production/Operations Management: Concepts, Structure, and Analysis*, New York: North-Holland, 1980.

Tersine, R. J. et al. *Problems and Models in Operations Management*, Columbus, OH: Grid Publishing, 1980.

———. *Modern Materials Management*, New York: North-Holland, 1977.

Thomas, Adin B. *Inventory Control in Production and Manufacturing*, Boston: Cahners Publishing Company, 1970.

Tyler, Elias S. *Material Handling*, New York: McGraw-Hill, 1970.

Van DeMark, R. L. *Inventory Control Techniques*, Dallas, TX: Van DeMark, Inc., 2nd edition, 1972.

———. *Managing Material Control*, Dallas, TX: Van DeMark, Inc., 1970.

———. *Production Control Techniques*, Dallas, TX: Van DeMark, Inc., 1970.

———. *New Ideas in Materials Management*, Dallas, TX: Van DeMark Inc., 1963.

Van Hees, R. N., and W. Monhemius. *Production and Inventory Control: Theory and Practice*, New York: Harper and Row Publishers, Inc., 1972.

Wagner, Harvey M. *Statistical Management of Inventory Systems*, New York: John Wiley and Sons, 1962.

———. *Principles of Operations Research*, Englewood Cliffs, NJ: Prentice-Hall, 1969.

Warman, J. *Warehouse Management*, London: William Heinemann, Ltd., 1971.

Welch, W. E. *Tested Scientific Inventory Control*, Greenwich, CT: Management Publishing Company, 1956.

Westing, J. E., et al. *Purchasing Management: Materials in Motion*, New York: John Wiley and Sons, 3rd edition, 1969.

Whitin, T. M. *Theory of Inventory Management*, Princeton, NJ: Princeton University Press, 1957.

Wight, Oliver W. *Production and Inventory Management in the Computer Age*, Boston: Cahners Publishing Company, 1974.

Willets, Walter E. *Fundamentals of Purchasing*, New York: Appleton-Century-Crofts, 1969.

Zimmerman, Hans-Jurgen, and Michael G. Sovereign. *Quantitative Models in Production Management*, Englewood Cliffs, NJ: Prentice-Hall, 1974.

Index

J

K

L

M

N

O

P

Q

R

S